java™

SOFTWARE STRUCTURES

for AP Computer Science AB

java™

SOFTWARE STRUCTURES

for AP Computer Science AB*

JOHN LEWIS
Villanova University

JOSEPH CHASE
Radford University

LEIGH ANN SUDOL
Fox Lane High School

PEARSON
Addison
Wesley

Boston   San Francisco   New York
London   Toronto   Sydney   Tokyo   Singapore   Madrid
Mexico City   Munich   Paris   Cape Town   Hong Kong   Montreal

*AP is a registered trademark of The College Board, which was not involved
in the production of, and does not endorse, this product.

Senior Acquisitions Editor	Michael Hirsch
Editorial Assistant	Maria Campo
Marketing Manager	Michelle Brown
Project Management	Edalin Michael, Argosy Publishing
Copyeditor	William McManus
Proofreader	Kim Cofer
Indexer	Larry Sweazy
Composition and Art	Argosy Publishing
Cover and Interior Designer	Joyce Cosentino Wells
Cover Photo	© 2004 Masterfile
Senior Prepress Supervisor	Caroline Fell
Senior Manufacturing Buyer	Hugh Crawford

Access the latest information about Addison-Wesley titles from our World Wide Web site: http://www.aw-bc.com/computing

Many of the designations used by manufacturers and sellers to distinguish their products are claimed as trademarks. Where those designations appear in this book, and Addison-Wesley was aware of a trademark claim, the designations have been printed in initial caps or all caps.

The programs and applications presented in this book have been included for their instructional value. They have been tested with care, but are not guaranteed for any particular purpose. The publisher does not offer any warranties or representations, nor does it accept any liabilities with respect to the programs or applications.

Cataloging-in-Publication Data on file at the Library of Congress

ISBN 0-321-33161-3
2 3 4 5 6 7 8 9 10-VH-07 06

To Sharon, Justin, Kayla, and Nathan Lewis
who give me cause to sing,
even though they'd prefer I not.
–J. L.

To my parents who taught me to fly,
my wife who flies with me providing both support and direction,
and our families that provide us a friendly place to roost.
–J. C.

To my students, who inspire me.
–L. A. S.

Preface

Welcome to *Java Software Structures for AP* Computer Science AB*. Specifically designed for beginning programmers who are ready to take the next step and study data structures, this Advanced Placement* book matches the AP* computer science topic outline and Java subset set forth by the College Board.

What's in this AP Book

This book has been specifically designed to meet the needs of today's AP* students. Let's hit the highlights:

- > This book is designed specifically for the AB exam.
- > We have created supplemental materials for each chapter that align with the current case study.
- > The AP* Java subset is used so that students get comfortable with language features that will be tested on the exam.
- > The discussions and examples fully embrace Java 2 Version 1.4.
- > We use hundreds of fully implemented example programs, so students can experiment.
- > The self-review questions, exercises, and programming projects have been designed to adhere to AP* student learning styles, and are similar to those on the exam.
- > A robust supplemental package is available for students and teachers, and is outlined in the Supplements section of this preface.
- > Many successful features that are also incorporated in the widely used Lewis/Loftus/Cocking: *Java Software Solutions for AP* Computer Science* are used in this book.

The Principles of This Text

This text is based around the following ideas, which we believe make for a sound introductory text.

Consistent Presentation

When exploring a particular type of collection, we carefully address each of the following issues in order.

1. Concept: We discuss the collection conceptually, establishing the services it provides (its interface).

2. Use: We explore examples that illustrate how the particular nature of the collection, no matter how it's implemented, can be useful when solving problems.

3. Implementation: We explore various implementation options for the collection.

4. Analysis: We compare and contrast the implementations.

The Java Collections API is included in the discussion as appropriate. If there is support for a particular collection type in the API, we discuss it and its implementation. Thus we embrace the API, but are not completely tied to it. And we do not hesitate to point out its shortcomings.

The analysis is kept at a high level. We establish the concept of Big-Oh notation in Chapter 1 and use it throughout the book, but the analysis is more intuitive than mathematical.

Sound Program Design

Throughout the book sound software engineering practices are a high priority. Our design of collection implementations and the programs that use them follow consistent and appropriate standards. Of primary importance is the separation of a collection's interface from its implementation. The services that a collection provides are always formally defined in a Java interface. The interface name is used as the type designation whenever it is needed to reinforce the collection as an abstraction. In addition to practicing solid design principles, we stress them in the discussion throughout the text. We try to teach both by example and by continual reinforcement.

Clean Organization

The contents have been carefully organized to minimize distractions and reinforce the overall purpose of the book. The organization supports the book in its role as a pedagogical exploration of data structures and algorithms for AP* computer science.

The material in the book is presented primarily in the context of the data structures being studied. The first two chapters review of basic software engineering, analysis, and object oriented programming concepts. Chapters 3 through 5 introduce some data structures as well as possible implementations for those structures. Chapters 6 and 7 begin a look at algorithms, specifically recursive thinking and searching and sorting. Chapter 8 through 10 look at stacks, queues, and lists, abstract data types that can be implemented in a variety of ways. Chapter 11 introduces the concept of trees.

Appendix A contains a discussion of fundamental principles of Java programming: control structures, loops, variable declarations, and so on. The student may use this as a reference or as an introductory chapter to brush up on these concepts.

Appendix B lists many of the commonly used classes in the Java class library. Having this information on hand makes it easier for students to develop their programs.

Chapter Breakdown

Chapter 1 (Software Engineering) discusses various aspects of software quality and provides an overview of software development issues. It is designed to establish the appropriate mindset before the details of data structure and algorithm design are introduced. It also provides a reference for anyone needing a review of fundamental object-oriented concepts and how they are accomplished in Java. Included are the concepts of abstraction, classes, encapsulation, inheritance, and polymorphism, as well as many related Java language constructs such as interfaces.

Chapter 2 (Object Orientation) discusses fundamental object-oriented concepts and how those concepts are accomplished using Java. It can be used as a review or serve as a Java-specific tutorial for students who may have been introduced to object-oriented concepts in another language.

Chapter 3 (Collections) establishes the concept of a collection, stressing the need to separate the interface from the implementation. As an example, it introduces a set collection and discusses an array-based implementation.

Chapter 4 (Linked Structures) discusses the use of references to create linked data structures. It explores the basic issues of linked list management, and defines an alternative implementation of a set collection (introduced in Chapter 2) using an underlying linked data structure.

Chapter 5 (Maps) introduces the concept of a Map data structure where objects are stored according to key value. Basic map operations as well as an array implementation of a map are discussed.

Chapter 6 (Recursion) is a general introduction to recursion and how recursive solutions can be elegant. It explores the implementation details of recursion and discusses the basic idea of analyzing recursive algorithms. It also provides students with an understanding of recursive tracing.

Chapter 7 (Searching and Sorting) discusses the linear and binary search algorithms, as well as the algorithms for several sorts: selection sort, insertion sort, bubble sort, quick sort, and merge sort. Programming issues related to searching and sorting, such as using the Comparable interface as the basis of comparing objects, are stressed in this chapter. Searching and sorting that are based in particular data structures are covered in the appropriate chapter later in the book.

Chapter 8 (Stacks) begins the series of chapters that investigates particular collections. We begin with stacks, which is a fairly intuitive collection, both conceptually and from an implementation perspective. This chapter examines array-based and linked implementation approaches and then compares them.

Chapter 9 (Queues) explores the concept and implementation of a first-in, first-out queue, and a priority queue. Radix sort is discussed as an example of using queues effectively. The implementation options covered include an underlying linked list as well as both fixed and circular arrays.

Chapter 10 (Lists) covers three types of lists: ordered, unordered, and indexed. These types are compared and contrasted, and the operations that they share and those that are unique to each type are discussed. Inheritance is used appropriately in the design of the various types of lists, which are implemented using both array and linked representations.

Chapter 11 (Trees) provides an overview of trees establishing key terminology and concepts. It discusses various implementation approaches.

Chapter 12 (Binary Search Trees) takes a more in depth look at the specifics of a binary search tree. It defines the classic binary search tree and examines a linked implementation of a BST as well. Included is a discussion of how the balance of the tree nodes is key to its performance.

Appendix A (Review of Basic Concepts) contains a review of introductory Java programming concepts.

Appendix B (The Java Class Library AP* Subset) is a reference for AP* subset classes.

Supplements

Students are welcome to visit www.aw.com/cssupport for the following resources:

> Source code for program listings from the text.

> A case study, modeled after the current AB exam case study, that parallels the textbook chapter-by-chapter, including additional programming assignments and examples.

The following supplements are available online to qualified teachers only. To obtain access visit suppscentral.aw.com and select "U.S. High School Adopters click here" and register as requested. You will receive Email access information after we have contacted your school to verify that you are a teacher.

> Lesson plans, with week-by-week pacing guide.

> Test bank, in a powerful test generating software with a wealth of multiple choice type questions modeled after the questions found on the AP* exam

> PowerPoint slides for presentation of the book content
> Case study resource guide, tied to the current College Board case study, including test questions and solutions to the case study projects

Acknowledgements

First and most importantly we want to thank our students, for whom this book is written and without whom it never could have been. Your feedback helps us become better teachers and writers. Please continue to keep us on our toes.

John and Joe would like to thank Leigh Ann for all her energy and hard work. She had the vision to see the benefits that this book could provide to students and teachers of AP* computer science, and really made it happen. Leigh Ann is a fabulous high school teacher, a longtime AP* exam reader, and a leader in AP* computer science education. Above all, she's a really great person. This book wouldn't be in your hands right now if not for her.

Leigh Ann would like to thank Chris Nevison and Barbara Wells for putting her on the path to working with AP* computer science on a larger spectrum. She would also like to thank the CS teachers from across the country and around the world that have listened to her, inspired her, and offered insight into the teaching of computer science, not just the act of programming. Much thanks goes to Rich Sgroi, truly a mentor of a department chairperson, who has shaped her teaching more than he realizes, and the math department at Fox Lane HS who put up with the odd questions, pacing, and ongoing drama.

We would like to thank all of the reviewers, listed below, who took the time to share their insight on the content and presentation of the material in this book. Your input was invaluable.

Mary P. Boelk, Marquette University
Robert Burton, Brigham Young University
Jack Davis, Radford University
Bob Holloway, University of Wisconsin–Madison
Nisar Hundewale, Georgia State University
Chung Lee, California State Polytechnic University
Mark J. Llewellyn, University of Central Florida
Ronald Marsh, University of North Dakota
Eli C. Minkoff, Bates College; University of Maine–Augusta
Ned Okie, Radford University
Salam Salloum, California State Polytechnic University–Pomona
Don Slater, Carnegie Mellon University
Ashish Soni, University of Southern California

The folks at Addison-Wesley have gone to great lengths to support and develop this book along with us. Senior Acquisitions Editor Michael Hirsch has always been there to help. Michelle Brown and Jake Zavracky work tirelessly to make sure that teachers understand the goals and benefits of the book. Patty Mahtani and Joyce Wells lead the production and design of the book. They are supported with amazing skill by Daniel Rausch and Edalin Michael at Argosy Publishing. Thank you all very much.

Contents

Software Engineering

1

CHAPTER OBJECTIVES

- > Discuss the goals of software development

- > Identify software quality

- > Examine the development life cycle

- > Explore the Unified Modeling Language (UML)

- > Examine error handling

- > Introduce algorithm analysis

We begin our exploration of software development with a discussion of software engineering.

Instead of just writing programs, we should try to engineer our software. We want to develop high-quality software systems that will stand the tests of users as well as the test of time. Understanding software engineering will help us toward this goal. This chapter discusses software engineering issues and the vocabulary we need to explore data structures and software design.

1.1   **SOFTWARE DEVELOPMENT**

Imagine you are nearing a bridge over a large river. As you approach, you see a sign saying that the bridge was designed and built by local construction workers and that engineers were not involved in the project. Would you drive across the bridge? Would it make a difference if the sign told you that the bridge was designed by engineers and built by construction workers?

The word "engineer" here means a person who has been educated in engineering, such as electrical engineering, mechanical engineering, and chemical engineering. *Software engineering* is the study of the techniques and theory of high-quality software.

When the term "software engineering" was first coined in the 1970s, it was a goal set out by leaders in the industry who realized that much of the software being created was of poor quality. They wanted developers to move away from the idea of just writing programs and toward engineering software. "Software engineer" is more than just a title—it is a completely different attitude.

As software developers we share a common history, we follow common theory, and we must understand current methods and practices in order to work together.

We want to satisfy the *client,* the person or organization who pays for the software, as well as the final *users* of the system. Clients and users may be the same people, depending on the situation.

The goals of software engineering are the same as those for other engineering disciplines:

> Solve the right problem

> Deliver a solution on time and within budget

> Deliver a high-quality solution

Key Concept

The first step in software development is to understand the problem and develop a set of requirements.

It may sound strange that we need to be worried about solving the wrong problem, but that issue causes trouble for almost every project. Too often a software developer will deliver a product only to find out that it is not exactly what the client wanted. Therefore, one of the first steps in any software development process is to make sure we understand the problem we want to solve. To do so, we must develop a list of the requirements for the software.

To get a list of requirements we will need to interview clients, look at existing processes, and analyze existing software, if any. The requirements must include not only the functions, such as letting a user log on to a system with a username and password, but also the limits of those functions and how they are developed, such as what characters can be used in a password. By understanding the problem, we can develop a solution that solves the right problem.

Professionalism and Ethics

As professionals, if we agree to deliver a system by a certain date for a particular price, then we are obligated to deliver on time and within budget. Obviously, a business cannot survive long if it continually disappoints its clients. But this issue goes beyond that practical aspect. Part of an engineering discipline is being able to make plans, schedules, and budgets that work. Failing to deliver on time and within budget may hurt not only the company and the client but the reputation of our profession as well.

True software engineers have a code of ethics, which includes the concept of competence. If we do not think the project requirements are workable, we must say so up front.

> **Key Concept**
>
> A software engineer must try to deliver on time and within budget.

To create the highest quality software possible, we must first realize that quality means different things to different people. We explore software quality in the next section.

1.2 SOFTWARE QUALITY

What is high-quality software? There are many quality characteristics to consider. Figure 1.1 lists several of them.

Quality Characteristic	Description
Correctness	How closely the final software matches the requirements.
Reliability	How often or how badly the software fails.
Robustness	How gracefully errors are handled.
Usability	How easily users can learn and execute tasks within the software.
Maintainability	How easily changes can be made to the software.
Reusability	How easily pieces of the software can be reused in the development of other software systems.
Portability	How easily pieces of the software can be reused in multiple computer environments.
Efficiency	How well the software does its job without wasting resources.

FIGURE 1.1 Software quality

Correctness

The idea of *correctness* goes back to our original goal to develop the right solution. At each step of the way, we want to keep an eye on the requirements list. Almost everything else is meaningless if the software doesn't solve the right problem.

Correctness also means that the solution produces the correct results. This means more than just adding and subtracting accurately. Software should also display graphics and user interfaces in a well-organized and visually pleasing way. It should produce text (including error messages) that is carefully worded and spelled correctly.

Reliability

If you have ever tried to get your bank balance on line and couldn't, or lost a homework assignment because your computer crashed, you are already familiar with the idea of *reliability*. A software *failure* is unacceptable behavior that happens within permissible operating conditions. We can measure reliability, such as the mean time between failures. Reliability also includes the fact that some failures are more critical than others. Above all, software should do no harm in the event of a failure.

Sometimes reliability is an issue of life and death. In the early 1980s, a piece of medical equipment called the Therac 25 was designed to deliver a dose of radiation according to the settings made by a technician on a special keyboard. An error existed in the software that controlled the device such that, when the technician made a very specific adjustment to the values on the keyboard, the internal settings of the device were changed drastically and a lethal dose of radiation was issued. The error occurred so infrequently that several people died before the source of the problem was found.

In other cases, reliability can affect hundreds, even millions, of people. One day in November, 1998, the entire AT&T network in the eastern United States failed. The problem was eventually traced back to a software error. That one failure cost millions of dollars.

Robustness

Reliability has to do with how *robust* a system is. A robust system handles problems gracefully. For example, if an input field is designed to handle numbers, what happens when the user types in letters? The program could just terminate. However, a more robust solution would be for the system to give the user an error message and wait for the correct input.

One rule in software development is "never trust the user." That is, never assume the user will always interact with your system in normal ways.

Developing a thoroughly robust system may or may not be worth the development cost. In some cases, it may be perfectly okay for a program to quit if very strange conditions occur. On the other hand, if adding such protections is not expensive, including them is good development practice. Furthermore, clear system requirements should carefully spell out the situations in which robust error handling is required.

Usability

A software system must also be truly *usable*. If a system is too difficult to use, it doesn't matter what good points it has. Within computer science there is a field of study called Human-Computer Interaction (HCI), which focuses on the analysis and design of user interfaces. The interaction between the user and system must be well designed, including help options, error messages, layout, use of color, error prevention, and error recovery.

Maintainability

Software developers must *maintain* their software. That is, they fix errors and improve system functionality. A well-maintained software system may be useful for many years after its original development. The software engineers that do maintenance are often not the people who originally developed it. To help them, a software system should be well structured, well written, and well documented in order to maximize its maintainability.

Large software systems are rarely written by a single person or even a small group of developers. Instead, large teams, often working in different locations, develop systems. For this reason, communication among developers is critical.

> **Key Concept**
>
> Software systems must be carefully designed, written, and documented to support the work of developers, maintainers, and users.

Reusability

Suppose that you are a contractor building an office tower. You could design and build each door in the building from scratch, but this would be a lot of work, not to mention expensive. Or you could use ready-made doors in the building. You would save time and money because you can rely on a design that has been used many times before. You know it has been tested and you know its capabilities. However, this does not mean that there might not be a few doors in the building that you will need to custom engineer and custom build to fit a specific need.

When developing a software system, we often use ready-made software components if they fit our needs. Why reinvent the wheel? Ready-made components can range from entire subsystems to individual classes and methods. They may come from part of another system developed earlier or from libraries created just for this purpose. Some ready-made software is called Commercial Off-The-Shelf (COTS) product. This software is often reliable because it has usually been tested in other systems.

Using ready-made software can cut down on the amount of work you have to do, but reuse comes at a price. You must take the time to find the right components. You may have the change the component to fit your new system. So it is helpful if the component is truly *reusable*. That is, software should be written and documented so that it can be easily fitted into new systems, and easily changed to suit new requirements.

Another form of reuse is the *software pattern,* a set of common processing steps. Software patterns let you capitalize on the expertise of generations of developers working on similar problems. Components designed with attention to these patterns are generally more reusable. Recently, software engineers have tried to identify and categorize software development patterns. This approach is viewed as promising by many developers because it is rooted in the concept of software reuse.

Portability

Software that is easily *portable* can be moved from one computing environment to another with little or no effort. Software developed using one operating system and central processing unit (CPU) may not run well or at all in another environment. One obvious problem is a program that has been compiled into one CPU's machine language. Since each type of CPU has its own machine language, moving it to another machine would require another translated version. Differences in the translations may cause the "same" program on two types of machines to behave differently.

The Java programming language addresses this issue by compiling into *bytecode,* which is a low-level language that is not the machine language for any particular CPU. Bytecode runs on a *Java Virtual Machine* (JVM), which is software that executes the bytecode. Therefore, at least theoretically, any system that has a JVM can execute any Java program.

Efficiency

> **Key Concept**
>
> Software must make efficient use of resources such as CPU time and memory.

The last software quality characteristic listed in Figure 1.1 is efficiency. Software systems should make *efficient* use of their resources, such as CPU time and main memory. User demands on computers and their software have risen steadily ever since computers were first created. Software must always make the best use of its resources in order to meet those demands. The efficiency of algorithms is discussed in more detail later in this chapter and throughout the book.

Quality Issues

To some extent, quality is in the eye of the beholder. That is, some quality characteristics are more important to certain people than to others. We must consider the needs of the *stakeholders*—the people affected one way or another by the project. For example, the end user wants reliability, usability, and efficiency, but may not care about maintainability or reusability. The client wants to make sure the user is satisfied, but is also worried about the cost. The developers and maintainers, on the other hand, may worry more about maintainability and reusability than cost.

> **Key Concept**
>
> Quality characteristics must be prioritized, and then maximized to the extent possible.

Some quality characteristics compete with each other. For example, to make a program more efficient, we may choose to use an algorithm that is hard to understand and hard to maintain. These types of trade-offs mean we must have clear priorities and (back where we started) system requirements. If we decide that we must use the more complex algorithm for efficiency, we can also document the code especially well to help future maintenance.

1.3 DEVELOPMENT LIFE CYCLE MODELS

To engineer a product, including a software system, we must develop a plan using the best techniques known to us, and execute that plan with care. The *development life cycle* defines a process we can use to do just that. This process defines how developers communicate and provides an outline for the history and future of the project.

Many software development life cycle models have been defined over the years, but every life cycle model addresses the basics: analysis, design, implementation, and evaluation.

> **Key Concept**
>
> A development life cycle model defines a process to be followed during development.

The *analysis* process helps us define the problem through

> Interviews and negotiation with the client

> Modeling the problem structure and data flow

> Observation of client activities

> Analysis of existing solutions and systems

The *design* process helps us define the solution or solutions to the problem. In the design process, we identify objects, attributes, operations, relationships between objects within the system, and the user interface. We may sometimes design more than one solution to a problem and compare them.

The *implementation* process involves turning the design into a working system by reusing existing code, writing new code, or both.

The implementation process also includes testing and debugging—finding and getting rid of faults in the system. It is important to understand that we can't test everything about a new system. For example, imagine a simple program that asks the user to enter a 20-character string. Assuming a 256-character set, there are 256^{20} possible strings that the user could enter. Therefore, it is important to develop tests that will test as many strings as possible, but it might be *im*possible to test them all! Tests usually test both the way a system works and the way it is built, or structured. Using black-box testing, we test a range of inputs without knowing the internal structure of the system. The we check that the output is correct. In white-box testing, we test the system with a range of inputs designed to check the known structure of the system.

> **Key Concept**
>
> Because exhaustive testing of most systems is not possible, we must develop test plans that work well. Key Concept sysems that are well designed and implemented are much easier to maintain.

The *evaluation* process involves checking that the new system meets the requirements we listed before we began. Note that evaluation is not simply testing and debugging. It is quite possible to build a system that has no bugs yet is completely wrong because it does not do what the client and users needed it to do.

After a system is developed, it must be maintained. The *maintenance* process involves ongoing changes of the system to meet new requirements. This is often time-consuming and expensive. The better the earlier stages of the development process are done, the easier maintenance will be. Systems that are well thought out, well designed, and well written are also much easier and cheaper to maintain.

The Waterfall Model

One of the earliest formal software development life cycle models is called the *waterfall model,* shown in Figure 1.2. Other engineering disciplines have long used a waterfall process like this. The name of the waterfall model comes from the way one phase flows into the next. That is, the information from one phase is used to guide the next.

The waterfall process begins with an analysis phase, which focuses on identifying the problem. During analysis, requirements are gathered and written down in a requirements document. The requirements document becomes the basis for

> **Key Concept**
>
> The waterfall model is a set of milestones and deliverables.

the design phase, in which solutions to the problem are explored until one solution is chosen. That solution is fully documented in a design document. The design document becomes the basis for the implementation phase in which code is written and/or fitted together. The implemented system is next tested, in the evaluation phase. Finally, evaluation yields to maintenance.

The waterfall model has several advantages. First, the model lays out a clear set of milestones and deliverables. *Milestones* are points in time that mark the end of some activity. *Deliverables* are products, or pieces of products, that are delivered to the client.

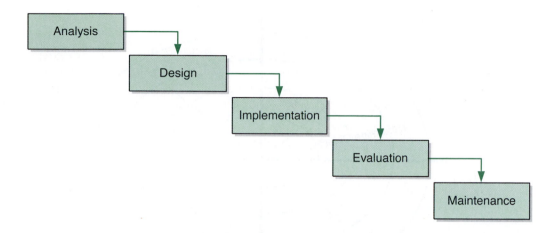

FIGURE 1.2 The waterfall software development model

Second, from a management perspective, the waterfall model is said to have high visibility. *Visibility* means that managers and clients can easily see what has been completed and what is yet to be done.

Third, since the waterfall model is a traditional engineering model used in the development of hardware, if there is hardware being developed as part of the system, then the hardware and software can be developed using the same life cycle.

While the waterfall model has been very successful in some ways, one major disadvantage is how late in the process evaluation is done. In the waterfall method, an entire system could be written before any testing was done.

The Spiral Model

The *spiral model* was developed by Barry Boehm in the mid-1980s. This model is shown in Figure 1.3. The spiral model was designed to reduce the two most serious risks in the software development process: building the wrong system and building the system wrong.

> **Key Concept**
>
> The spiral model may reduce the risks in software development.

This model follows a spiral that keeps refining the requirements for the system being developed, because software requirements are hard to define, and our understanding of them may change as we create the system. This model allows us to use a series of ever-larger prototypes and high-level designs.

Each cycle in the spiral is a phase of the process. Therefore each phase goes through the four main arcs of the spiral. At first, the objectives of the phase are determined and the alternatives considered. Then the risks for following this approach are assessed and minimized. For example, what is the risk that the new database system we are planning to use will not process enough transactions per second to meet our requirements? Prototypes are often developed. Then the objectives of this phase are developed and evaluated. Finally, plans are made for the next phase.

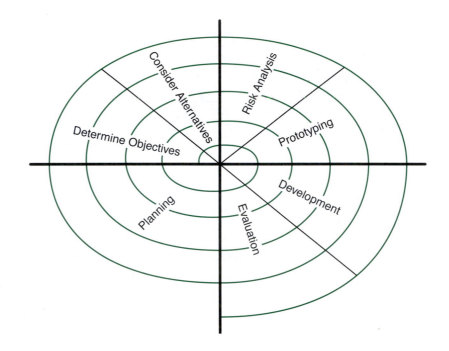

FIGURE 1.3 The spiral model of software development

The spiral model is much more flexible than the waterfall model. Each phase can be tailored to address issues that have come up in earlier phases. The spiral model is simply more realistic than the waterfall model.

The Evolutionary Development Model

Another development model created to address the unique nature of software is the *evolutionary development* model, shown in Figure 1.4. Like the spiral model,

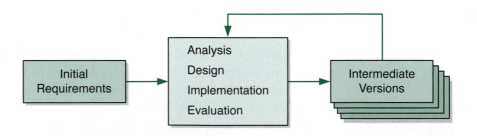

FIGURE 1.4 The evolutionary development model

the evolutionary development model also uses the concept of iterative refinement. However, unlike the spiral model, this model keeps refining the requirements, the design, and the software product, not just the requirements and the high-level design.

The evolutionary development model has proven to be very effective for the development of relatively small systems and for systems that will not require evolution and maintenance. Systems developed using this process are not usually as well structured as systems developed using the other methods and therefore are harder to maintain or change.

1.4   THE UNIFIED MODELING LANGUAGE (UML)

Software engineering deals with the analysis, synthesis, and communication of ideas in the development of software systems. In order to facilitate the methods and practices necessary to accomplish these goals, software engineers have developed various notations to capture and communicate information. While there are a great number of notations available, a few have become popular and one in particular has become a de facto standard in the industry.

The *Unified Modeling Language* (UML) was developed in the mid-1990s. It is actually a combination of three design notations, each popular in its own right. We use UML throughout this book to illustrate program designs, and this section describes UML diagrams. Keep in mind that UML is language-independent. It uses generic terms and has features that are not relevant to Java. We focus on the parts of UML that are appropriate for this book.

> **Key Concept**
>
> The Unified Modeling Language (UML) provides a notation with which we can capture and illustrate program designs.

A UML *class diagram* describes the classes in the system, the static relationships among them, the attributes and operations associated with a class, and the limits on the connections among objects. The terms "attribute" and "operation" are generic object-oriented terms. An *attribute* is any class-level data, including variables, constants, and specific values stored by the program. An *operation* is pretty much the same as a method, which is an action, calculation, or task performed by the object.

In UML, a class is shown by a rectangle that is usually divided into three sections containing the class name, its attributes, and its operations. Figure 1.5 shows a class named `LibraryItem`. There are two attributes associated with the class: `title` and `callNumber`. There are also two operations associated with the class: `checkout` and `return`.

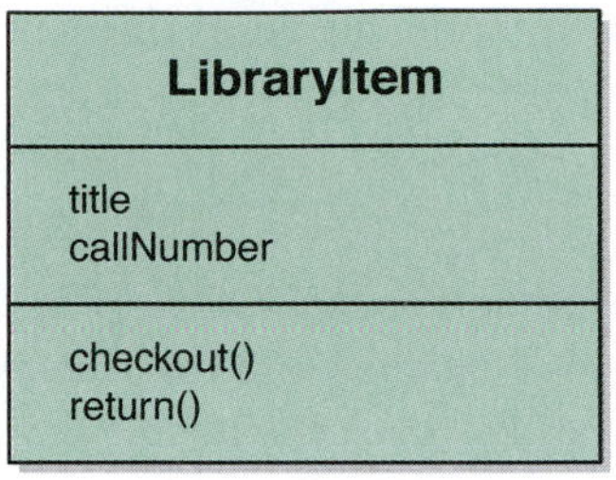

FIGURE 1.5 `LibraryItem` class diagram

We don't have to inclue the attributes and operations in a class rectangle. We may represent a class by a single rectangle containing only the class name. We can include the attributes and/or operations whenever they are important in the diagram. If we include attributes or operations, we show both sections (not necessarily filled) to make it clear which is which.

There are many more pieces of information we can include in the UML class notation. Words bracketed using << and >> are called *stereotypes*. The `<<abstract>>` stereotype or the `<<interface>>` stereotype could be added above the name to show that it represents an abstract class or an interface. The visibility of a class is assumed to be public, though we can show that a class is nonpublic by including the word *private* in curly braces: `{private}`.

Attributes listed in a class can give additional information. The full syntax for showing an attribute is

   visibility name : *type* = *default-value*

The visibility may be spelled out as `public`, `protected`, or `private`, or you may use the symbols + to represent public visibility, # for protected visibility, or – for private visibility. For example, we might have listed the title of a `LibraryItem` as

   `- title : String`

to show that the attribute `title` is a private variable of type `String`. A default value is not used in this case. Also, we can add the stereotype `<<final>>` to indicate that an attribute is a constant.

The full syntax for an operation is

   visibility name (*parameter-list*) : *return-type* { *property-string* }

Like the syntax for attributes, all of the items other than the name are optional. The visibility modifiers are the same as they are for attributes. The *parameter-list* can include the name and type of each parameter, separated by a colon. The *return-type* is the type of the value returned from the operation.

UML Relationships

There are several kinds of relationships among classes that UML diagrams can represent. Usually they are shown as lines or arrows connecting one class to another. Different types of lines and arrowheads have different meanings in UML. These relationships will be discussed as we explore each topic.

> **Key Concept**
>
> Many kinds of relationships can be represented in a UML class diagram.

1.5 ERROR HANDLING

Many very important software engineering decisions must be made in the development of a system. As an illustration, let's take a closer look at how errors are handled in a system. As discussed in Section 1.2, a robust program is one that handles errors gracefully. Therefore, the way a program is designed to handle these situations is basic to the software engineering process.

In Java, a program might throw an error or an exception, depending on the situation. An *error* is almost always an unrecoverable situation and results in termination of the program. An *exception* is an exceptional situation. That is, an exception is a situation that does not usually happen. An exceptional situation does not necessarily mean that the program should terminate. An exception can be caught and handled using a `try-catch` statement.

> **Key Concept**
>
> A Java error is an unrecoverable problem, whereas a Java exception is an unusual situation that may or may not be recoverable.

In Java an exception is an object that can be created and used when it is needed. We can design and throw our own exceptions under whatever conditions we choose. Exceptions we design are no different, really, than the exceptions that are predefined in the Java class libraries and thrown by the runtime environment or other Java API classes.

How exceptions are handled is one of the most important decisions we make when designing a software system. There are many questions to consider. What custom exception classes should be defined? When should those classes be instantiated and thrown? How and when should they be caught and handled?

As we explore the larger world of software development, especially when it involves the management of large amounts of data, we must carefully consider these questions. Perhaps the most important step is to decide how and when exceptions are used.

When a method is called that causes an error, the program could respond in any of the following ways:

> Return a value that represents the error rather than a valid return value.

> Throw an exception that the user must handle or ignore.

> If possible, handle the situation inside the method so that the calling object never needs to worry about it.

At one time, most programs just returned an error value. This meant finding a return value that could be used to indicate the error and checking for that value in the calling object. The second option is more versatile and isn't a function of the return value at all. The last option is the best, but might not always be possible. That is, the called method may not have enough information to handle the situation, or it may be best left to the calling object to decide.

Error handling is a function of many factors. We examine these factors as they come up in the book.

1.6 ANALYSIS OF ALGORITHMS

Another quality characteristic discussed in Section 1.2 is the efficient use of resources. One of the most important resources is CPU time. The efficiency of an algorithm we use for a task can determine how fast a program executes. Although we can look at how much memory an algorithm uses, CPU time is usually the more interesting issue.

The *analysis of algorithms* is a basic computer science topic. It involves several techniques and concepts. This section introduces algorithm analysis and lays the groundwork for using analysis techniques.

Let's start with an everyday example: washing dishes by hand. If washing a dish takes 30 seconds and drying a dish takes another 30 seconds, then it would take n minutes to wash and dry n dishes:

Time (n dishes) = n * (30 seconds wash time + 30 seconds dry time)

= 60n seconds

On the other hand, suppose we were careless while washing the dishes and splashed too much water around. Suppose each time we washed a dish, we had to dry not only that dish but also all of the dishes we had washed before that one. It would still take 30 seconds to wash each dish, but now it would take 30 seconds to dry the last dish (once), 2 * 30 or 60 seconds to dry the second-to-last dish (twice), 3 * 30 or 90 seconds to dry the third-to-last dish (three times), and so on:

Time (n dishes) = n * (30 seconds wash time) + (the sum of the time to wash all the other dishes)

$$= 30n + 30n(n+1)/2$$

$$= 15n^2 + 45n \text{ seconds}$$

If we had 30 dishes to wash, the first approach would take 30 minutes, and the second (careless) approach would take 247.5 minutes. The more dishes we wash the larger the difference between the two processes becomes.

Growth Functions and Big O() Notation

For every algorithm we want to analyze, we need to define the size of the problem. For our dishwashing example, the size of the problem is the number of dishes to be washed and dried. We also must determine the value that represents efficient use of time or space. For time considerations, we often pick an important part of the process that we'd like to minimize, such as the number of times a dish has to be washed and dried. The amount of time spent at the task is directly related to how many times we have to do that task. The algorithm's efficiency can be defined in terms of the problem size and the processing step.

Consider an algorithm that sorts a list of numbers into increasing order. One way to show the size of the problem would be to count the number of values to be sorted. The step we are trying to improve is the number of comparisons we have to make for the algorithm to put the values in order. The more comparisons we make, the more CPU time is used.

A *growth function* shows the relationship between the size of the problem (n) and the value we hope to improve. This function represents the amount of time or space the algorithm requires.

> **Key Concept**
>
> A growth function shows time or space utilization relative to the problem size.

The growth function for our second dishwashing algorithm is

$$t(n) = 15n^2 + 45n$$

However, we don't need to know the exact growth function for an algorithm. Instead, we are mainly interested in the general nature of the function as n (the size of the problem) increases. This characteristic is based on the *dominant term* of the expression—the term that increases most quickly as n increases. As n gets very large, the value of the dishwashing growth function approaches n^2 because the n^2 term grows much faster than the n term. The constants and the secondary term matter less and less as n increases.

This simplification is called the *order* of the algorithm. Our dishwashing algorithm is said to have order n^2 time complexity, written $O(n^2)$. This is called Big O() or Big-Oh notation. A growth function that executes in constant time regardless of the size of the problem is said to have $O(1)$. Figure 1.6 shows several growth functions and their Big-Oh notation.

Because the order of the function is the key factor, the other terms and constants are often not even mentioned. All algorithms within a given order are considered generally equally efficient. For example, all sorting algorithms of $O(n^2)$ are considered to be equally efficient in general.

Growth Function	Order
`t(n)=17`	`O(1)`
`t(n)=20n − 4`	`O(n)`
`t(n)=12n log n + 100n`	`O(n log n)`
`t(n)=3n`^{2}` + 5n − 2`	`O(n`^{2}`)`
`t(n)=2`^{n}` + 18n`^{2}` + 3n`	`O(2`^{n}`)`

FIGURE 1.6 Some growth functions and their Big-Oh notation

Comparing Growth Functions

We might think that because processors have become faster and memory cheaper, algorithm analysis would no longer be necessary. Nothing could be farther from the truth. Processor speed and memory cannot make up for the differences in efficiency of algorithms.

> **Key Concept**
>
> If the algorithm is inefficient, a faster processor will not help.

Aho, Hopcroft, and Ullman (1974) developed another way of looking at it. The table in Figure 1.7 compares four algorithms with different time complexities and the effects of speeding up the processor by a factor of 10. Algorithm A_1, with a time complexity of n, is indeed improved by a factor of 10. However, algorithm A_2, with a time complexity of n^2, is only improved by a factor of 3.16. In the same way, algorithm A_3 is only improved by a factor of 2.15. For algorithms with *exponential complexity,* in which the size variable is in the exponent of the complexity term, the situation is far worse. In the grand scheme of things, if an algorithm is inefficient, speeding up the processor will not help.

Figure 1.8 graphs different growth functions. Note that, when n is small, there is little difference between the algorithms. If you can guarantee a very small problem size (5 or less), it doesn't really matter which algorithm you use. However, as n gets larger, the differences between the growth functions become obvious.

Algorithm	Time Complexity	Max Problem Size Before Speed-Up	Max Problem Size After Speed-Up
A_1	n	s_1	$10s_1$
A_2	n^2	s_2	$3.16s_2$
A_3	n^3	s_3	$2.15s_3$
A_4	n^4	s_4	$s_4 + 3.3$

FIGURE 1.7 Increase in problem size with a 10-fold increase in processor speed

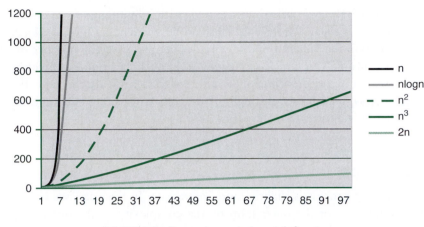

FIGURE 1.8 Comparing typical growth functions

Analyzing Loop Execution

To determine the order of an algorithm, we often have to decide how often a particular statement or set of statements gets executed. Therefore, we often have to decide how many times the body of a loop is executed. To do that, first we look at the order of the body of the loop. Then we multiply that by the number of times the loop will execute relative to n. Keep in mind that n is the problem size.

> **Key Concept**
>
> Analyzing algorithm complexity often means analyzing the execution of loops.

Assuming that the body of a loop is $O(1)$, then a loop such as this

```
for (int count = 0; count < n; count++)
{
    /* some sequence of O(1) steps */
}
```

would have $O(n)$ time complexity. This is because the body of the loop has $O(1)$ complexity but is executed n times by the loop structure. In general, when a loop structure steps through n items and the body of the loop is $O(1)$, then the loop is $O(n)$. Even when the loop is designed to skip some elements, as long as the order of skipped elements is linear, the loop is still $O(n)$. For example, if the loop in our example skipped every other number, the growth function of the loop would be n/2, but since constants don't affect the asymptotic complexity, the order is still $O(n)$.

Let's look at another example. If the progression of the loop is logarithmic such as the following

```
count = 1
while (count < n)
{
    count *= 2;
    /* some sequence of O(1) steps */
}
```

then the loop is O(log n). When we use a logarithm in an algorithm complexity, we almost always mean log base 2. This can be written as $O(\log_2 n)$. Each time through the loop the value of count is multiplied by 2, so the number of times the loop is executed is $\log_2 n$. An easy way to judge logarithmic complexity is in how the loop (or algorithm) control variable progresses toward the value that will stop the process. If each time through the process reduces the remaining distance by half, then it is a logarithmic process.

Nested Loops

The nested loop process is slightly more interesting. In this case, we must multiply the complexity of the outer loop by the complexity of the inner loop. For example, the following nested loops

```
for (int count = 0; count < n; count++)
{
    for (int count2 = 0; count2 < n; count2++)
    {
        /* some sequence of O(1) steps */
    }
}
```

> **Key Concept**
>
> The analysis of nested loops must include the inner and outer loops.

would have complexity $O(n^2)$. Both the inner and outer loops have complexity $O(n)$, which, when multiplied together, results in $O(n^2)$.

What is the complexity of the following nested loop?

```
for (int count = 0; count < n; count++)
{
    for (int count2 = count; count2 < n; count2++)
    {
        /* some sequence of O(1) steps */
    }
}
```

In this case, the inner loop index is initialized to the current value of the index for the outer loop. The outer loop executes n times. The inner loop executes n times the first time, n − 1 times the second time, and so on. However, remember that we are only interested in the dominant term, not in constants or any lesser terms. If the progression is linear, it doesn't matter whether some elements are skipped, the order is still O(n). Thus the resulting complexity for this code is $O(n^2)$.

1.7   SOFTWARE ENGINEERING AND DATA STRUCTURES

Why spend so much time talking about software engineering in a text about data structures and their algorithms? Well, as you begin to develop more complex programs, you'll need a more mature outlook on the process. As we discussed at the beginning of this chapter, the goal should be to engineer software, not just write code. The data structures we study in this book lay the foundation for designing complex, carefully designed software.

For each data structure that we study, we first need to know why, how, and when it should be used. From this analysis, we will be able to design an interface to the data structure that can stand alone. We will also design solutions that provide the required functionality. We will document these designs using UML class diagrams and examine multiple solutions for each data structure. We will examine our solutions for the proper use of exception handling and analyze their use of resources, especially CPU time and memory space.

> **Key Concept**
>
> Data structure design requires solid software engineering practices.

The topics of data structure design and software engineering are intertwined. Throughout this text, as we discuss data structures, we will also practice good software engineering.

Summary of Key Concepts

> The first step in software development is to analyze the problem and make a thorough and accurate list of requirements.

> A software engineer must try to deliver on time and within budget.

> Reliable software seldom fails and, when it does, it keeps the effects of that failure to a minimum.

> Software systems must be carefully designed, written, and documented to support the work of developers, maintainers, and users.

> Software must make efficient use of resources such as CPU time and memory.

> Quality characteristics must be prioritized and then maximized.

> A development life cycle model lays out a process to be followed during development.

> Because we can't test everything, we must develop test plans that are effective.

> Systems that are well designed and implemented are much easier to maintain.

> The waterfall model has a specific set of milestones and deliverables.

> The spiral model is designed to reduce the risks in software development.

> We can use the Unified Modeling Language (UML) to capture and illustrate program designs.

> Many kinds of relationships can be shown in a UML class diagram.

> A Java error is an unrecoverable problem; a Java exception is an unusual situation that may or may not be recoverable.

> The way in which exceptions are generated and handled is an important design decision.

> Algorithm analysis is a basic computer science topic.

> A growth function shows the use of time or space relative to the problem size.

> If the algorithm is inefficient, a faster processor will not help.

> Analyzing algorithm complexity often means analyzing loops.

> The analysis of nested loops must take into account the inner and outer loops.

> Data structure design requires solid software engineering practices.

Self-Review Questions

1.1 What is the difference between software engineering and programming?

1.2 Name several software quality characteristics.

1.3 How are all development life cycle models included?

1.4 What is the main problem with the waterfall software development model?

1.5 What is the difference between a milestone and a deliverable?

1.6 What do the spiral and evolutionary development models have in common?

1.7 What does a UML class diagram represent?

1.8 What are the types of relationships represented in a class diagram?

1.9 What is an exception?

1.10 What is the difference between the growth function of an algorithm and the order of that algorithm?

1.11 Why does speeding up the CPU not necessarily speed up the process?

Exercises

1.1 Compare and contrast software engineering with other engineering disciplines.

1.2 Give a specific example of each software quality characteristic listed in Figure 1.1.

1.3 Explain the difference between debugging and evaluation.

1.4 Compare and contrast the waterfall, spiral, and evolutionary models of software development.

1.5 What is visibility and why is it important in the software development process?

1.6 Create a UML class diagram for the organization of your high school, where the the school is made up of departments, which are made up of classes, which contain teachers and students.

1.7 What is the order of the following growth functions?

    a. $10n^2 + 100n + 1000$

    b. $10n^3 - 7$

    c. $2^n + 100n^3$

    d. $n^2 \log n$

1.8   Arrange the growth functions of the previous exercise in order of efficiency for n = 10 and again for n = 1,000,000.

1.9   What is the growth function and order of the following code fragment?

```
for (int count=0; count < n; count++)
{
    for (int count2=0; count2 < n; count2=count2*2)
    {
        /* some sequence of O(1) steps */
    }
}
```

Answers to Self-Review Questions

1.1   Software engineering is concerned with the larger goals of system design and development, not just the writing of code. Programmers become software engineers when they begin to understand the development of high-quality software and begin to use the appropriate practices.

1.2   Software quality characteristics include correctness, reliability, robustness, usability, maintainability, reusability, portability, and efficiency.

1.3   In one way or another, all software development models include requirements analysis, design, implementation, evaluation, and maintenance.

1.4   The waterfall model was developed for traditional engineering fields dealing with a product with more completely specified requirements. Iterative processes work better for software development simply because of the intangible nature of software.

1.5   Milestones mark the end of a process activity. Deliverables are some product delivered to the client.

1.6   The spiral and evolutionary development models are iterative, easily allowing the developer to revisit previous activities.

1.7   A class diagram describes the types of objects or classes in the system, the static relationships among them, the attributes and operations of a class, and the constraints on the connections among objects.

1.8   Relationships shown in a UML class diagram include subtypes or extensions, associations, aggregates, and the implementation of interfaces.

1.9   An exception is an unusual situation in a program. Some exceptions are serious problems that are unrecoverable. Others are processing that can be handled under program control.

1.10   The growth function of an algorithm represents the exact relationship between the problem size and the time complexity of the solution. The order of the algorithm is the asymptotic time complexity.
As the size of the problem grows, the complexity of the algorithm
approaches the asymptotic complexity.

1.11   Linear speed up only happens if the algorithm has a linear order,
$O(n)$. As the the algorithm gets more complicated (and less linear),
faster processors have less impact.

References

Aho, A. V., J. E. Hopcroft, and J. D. Ullman. *The Design and Analysis of Computer Algorithms*. Reading, Mass.: Addison-Wesley, 1974.

Boehm, B. "A Spiral Model for Software Development and Enhancement." *Computer* 21, no. 5 (May 1988): 61–72.

Sommerville, I. *Software Engineering*. 6th Ed. Harlow, England: Addison-Wesley, 2001.

Object-Oriented Concepts in Java 2

CHAPTER OBJECTIVES

> Review the concepts behind object-oriented programming

> Review how these concepts work in a Java program

This chapter looks at Java as an object-oriented programming language. Students who've seen this material before can use this chapter to fill in any holes in their knowledge. Students who learned object-oriented concepts using a different language can see how those concepts are accomplished in Java.

2.1   AN OVERVIEW OF OBJECT-ORIENTATION

Java is an object-oriented language. An *object* is a basic part of a Java program. In addition to objects, a Java program also manages primitive data. *Primitive data* includes common values such as numbers and characters. An object usually represents something more complicated, such as a bank account. An object often contains primitive values. For example, an object that represents a bank account might contain the account balance, which is stored as primitive data.

> **Key Concept**
>
> An object is defined by a class.

An object is defined by a *class*, which can be thought of as the data type of the object. The operations that can be performed on the object are defined by the methods in the class.

Once a class has been defined, many objects can be created from that class. For example, we could define a class to represent a bank account. We can then create objects that represent individual bank accounts. Each bank account object would keep track of its own balance. This is an example of *encapsulation*, meaning that each object protects and manages its own information. The methods defined in the bank account class would let us perform operations on individual bank account objects. For instance, we might withdraw money from a particular account. We can think of these operations as services that the object performs. Invoking a method on an object is sometimes called sending a *message* to the object, asking that the service be performed.

> **Key Concept**
>
> Classes can be created from other classes using inheritance.

Classes can be created from other classes using *inheritance*. Inheritance is a kind of software *reuse*, where one class can be used as the blueprint for several new classes, called *derived classes*. Derived classes can then be used as the blueprint for even more classes. This creates a hierarchy of classes, where characteristics defined in one class are inherited by its children, which in turn pass them on to their children, and so on. For example, we might create a family of classes for types of bank accounts. Common characteristics are defined in high-level classes, and specific differences are defined in derived classes.

Classes, objects, encapsulation, and inheritance are the main ideas of object-oriented software. They are shown in Figure 2.1.

2.2   USING OBJECTS

The following `println` statement shows how an object is used:

```
System.out.println ("Whatever you are, be a good one.");
```

The `System.out` object represents an output device, usually the monitor screen. The object's name is `out` and it is stored in the `System` class.

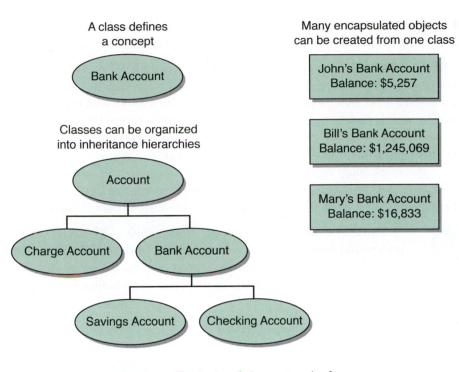

FIGURE 2.1 The basics of object-oriented software

The println method is a service that the System.out object can do for us. Whenever we ask, the object will print a string of characters to the screen. We send the println message to the System.out object to ask that some text be printed.

Abstraction

An object is an *abstraction,* meaning that the details of how it works don't matter to the user. We don't really need to know how the println method prints characters to the screen, as long as we can count on it to do its job. Of course, sometimes it is helpful to understand how println works, but we don't have to know that in order to *use* the object.

Sometimes it is important to hide or ignore certain details. A human being can manage around seven (plus or minus two) pieces of information in short-term memory. Beyond that, we start to lose track of some of the pieces. However, if we group pieces of information together, then those pieces can be managed as one "chunk" in our minds. We don't don't need to know all of the details in the chunk as long as we know how to manage the chunk. Therefore, we can deal with a lot of information by organizing it into chunks. An object organizes information and lets us hide the details inside. An object is a wonderful abstraction.

We use abstractions every day. Think about a car for a moment. You don't need to know how an engine works in order to drive a car. You just need to know how to turn it on, how to put it in gear, how to make it move with the pedals and steering wheel, and how to stop it. These operations define the way a person interacts with the car. They hide the details of what is happening inside the car that allow it to function. When you're driving a car, you're not usually thinking about the spark plugs igniting the gasoline that drives the piston that turns the crankshaft that turns the axle that turns the wheels. If we had to worry about all of these details, we'd never be able to operate something as complicated as a car.

> **Key Concept**
>
> An abstraction hides details. A good abstraction hides the right details at the right time so that we can manage complexity.

Years ago, all cars had manual transmissions. The driver had to understand how and when to change gears with the stick shift. Then automatic transmissions were developed, and the driver no longer had to worry about shifting gears. Those details were hidden by raising the *level of abstraction.*

Of course, someone has to deal with the details. The car manufacturer has to know the details in order to design and build the car in the first place. A car mechanic must have the expertise and tools to fix a car when it breaks.

The level of abstraction must be appropriate for each situation. Some people like to drive a manual transmission car. A race car driver, for instance, needs to control the shifting manually to get the best performance.

Likewise, someone has to create the code for the objects we use. Later in this chapter we explore how to define objects by creating classes. For now, we can create and use objects from classes that have been defined for us already. Abstraction makes that possible.

Creating Objects

A Java variable can hold either a primitive value or a *reference to an object*. Like variables that hold primitive types, a variable that serves as an object reference must be declared. A class is used to define an object, and the class name can be thought of as the type of an object. The declarations of object references are like the declarations of primitive variables.

The following declaration creates a reference to a `String` object:

```
String name;
```

That declaration is like the declaration of an integer: The type is followed by the variable name we want to use. However, no `String` object actually exists yet. To create an object, we use the `new` operator:

```
name = new String ("James Gosling");
```

Creating an object using the new operator is called *instantiation*. An object is said to be an *instance* of a class. After the new operator creates the object, a *constructor* is called to help set it up initially. A constructor has the same name as the class and is like a method. In this example, the parameter to the constructor is a string literal that specifies the characters that the String object will hold.

We can declare the object reference variable and create the object all in one step by initializing the variable in the declaration, just as we do with primitive types:

```
String name = new String ("James Gosling");
```

After an object has been instantiated, we use the *dot operator* to get its methods. The dot operator appears after the object reference, followed by the method being invoked. For example, to get the length method in the String class, we use the dot operator like this:

```
count = name.length();
```

An object reference variable (such as name) stores the address where the object is stored in memory. However, we don't usually care about the actual address value. We just want to access the object, wherever it is.

Even though they are not primitive types, strings are so basic and are used so much that Java puts string literals in double quotation marks. This is a shortcut notation. Whenever a string literal appears, a String object is created. Therefore, the following declaration is valid:

```
String name = "James Gosling";
```

That is, for String objects, we don't need to use the new operator or call the constructor. In most cases, this simpler string syntax is used.

2.3   CLASS LIBRARIES AND PACKAGES

A *class library* is a set of classes that support the development of programs. A compiler often comes with a class library. You can also buy class libraries from software companies. The classes in a class library are valuable to a programmer because of the special functions they offer. In fact, programmers often become dependent on the methods in a class library and begin to think of them as part of the language. But, technically, they are not in the language definition.

The String class, for instance, is not a part of the Java language. It is part of the Java *standard class library* that can be found in any Java development environment. The classes in the standard library were created by employees at Sun Microsystems, the company that created the Java language.

The class library is made up of clusters of classes, which are sometimes called Java APIs. API stands for *application programmer interface*. For example, the Java Database API set of classes helps us write programs that interact with a database. Another example of an API is the Java Swing API, which is a set of classes used in a graphical user interface. Sometimes the entire standard library is called the Java API.

The classes of the Java standard class library are also grouped into *packages,* which, like the APIs, let us group related classes by one name. Each class is part of a package. The `String` class and the `System` class, for example, are both part of the `java.lang` package.

The package organization is more basic and language-based than the API names. Though package and API names are sometimes the same or similar, the groups of classes that make up an API might cross packages. We refer to classes in terms of their package organization in this text.

Appendix B serves as a general reference for many of the classes in the Java class library.

The `import` Declaration

The classes of the package `java.lang` are available whenever we want to write a program. To use classes from any other package, however, we must either *fully qualify* the reference or use an `import` *declaration*.

If you wanted to use a class from a class library in a program, you could use its fully qualified name, including the package name, every time it is referenced. For example, every time you want to refer to the `Random` class that is defined in the `java.util` package, you can write `java.util.Random`. However, writing the whole thing each time gets tiring, so Java gives us the `import` declaration to make it easier.

The `import` declaration identifies the packages and classes that will be used in a program, so that we don't have to write the fully qualified name with each reference. Here is an example of an `import` declaration:

```
import java.util.Random;
```

This declaration tells us that the `Random` class of the `java.util` package may be used in the program. Once this `import` declaration is made, all we need to do is use the simple name `Random` when referring to that class in the program.

Another form of the `import` declaration uses an asterisk (*) to indicate that any class inside the package might be used in the program. Thus, the declaration

```
import java.util.*;
```

lets us reference all classes in the `java.util` package without mentioning the package by name. If only one class of a particular package will be used in a program, it is usually better to name the class in the `import` declaration. However, if two or more classes will be used, the * is fine. Once a class is imported, it is as if its code has been brought into the program with it. The code is not actually moved, but that is the effect.

The classes of the `java.lang` package are automatically imported because they are like basic extensions to the language. Therefore, any class in the `java.lang` package, such as `String`, can be used without an `import` declaration. It is as if all programs automatically contain the following declaration:

```
import java.lang.*;
```

2.4   OBJECT STATE AND BEHAVIOR

Think about objects in the world around you. How would you describe them? Let's use a ball as an example. A ball has characteristics such as its size, color, and bounce. Formally, we say the properties that describe an object, called *attributes*, define the object's *state of being*. We also describe a ball by what it does, such as the fact that it can be thrown, bounced, or rolled. These activities define the object's *behavior*.

All objects have a state and a set of behaviors. We can see these characteristics in software objects as well. The values of an object's variables describe the object's state, and the methods that can be invoked using the object define the object's behaviors.

> **Key Concept**
>
> Each object has a state and a set of behaviors. The values of an object's variables define its state. The methods to which an object responds define its behaviors.

Consider a computer game that uses a ball. The ball could be represented as an object. It could have variables to store its size and location, and methods that draw it on the screen and calculate how it moves when thrown, bounced, or rolled. The variables and methods defined in the ball object establish the state and behavior that are relevant to the ball's use in the computerized ball game.

Each object has its own state. Each ball object has a particular location, for instance, which typically is different from the location of all other balls. Behaviors, though, tend to apply to all objects of a particular type. For instance, in general, any ball can be thrown, bounced, or rolled. The act of rolling a ball is generally the same for all balls.

The state of an object and its behaviors work together. How high a ball bounces depends on its elasticity. The action is the same, but the result depends on that object's state. An object's behavior often modifies its state. For example, when a ball is rolled, its location changes.

Any object can be described in terms of its state and behavior. Let's look at another example. In software that is used at a university, a student could be represented as an object. The collection of all such objects represents the student body. Each student has a state. That is, each student would contain the variables that store information about a particular student, such as name, address, major, courses taken, grades, and grade point average. A student object also has behaviors. For example, the class of the student object may contain a method to add a new course.

Although software objects often represent tangible items, they don't have to. For example, an error message can be an object, with its state being the text of the message, and behaviors including the process of issuing (perhaps printing) the error. A common mistake made by new programmers to the world of object-orientation is to limit the possibilities to tangible entities.

2.5   CLASSES

An object is defined by a class. A class is the model, pattern, or blueprint from which an object is created. Consider the blueprint created by an architect when designing a house. The blueprint defines the important characteristics of the house: walls, windows, doors, electrical outlets, and so forth. Once the blueprint is created, several houses can be built using it.

In one sense, the houses built from the blueprint are different. They are on different lots, have different addresses, are different colors, and different people live in them. Yet, in many ways they are the "same" house. The layout of the rooms and other crucial characteristics are the same in each. To create a different house, we would need a different blueprint.

> **Key Concept**
>
> A class is a blueprint for an object; it has no memory space for data. Each object has its own data space and its own state.

A class is a blueprint of an object. But a class is not an object any more than a blueprint is a house. In general, there is no space to store data values in a class. To allocate space to store data values, we have to instantiate one or more objects from the class (the exception to this rule is discussed in Section 2.10 of this chapter). Each object is an instance of a class. Each object has space for its own data, which is why each object can have its own state.

A class contains the declarations of the data that will be stored in each instantiated object, and the declarations of the methods that can be invoked using an object. These are called the *members* of the class. See Figure 2.2.

Consider the following class, called `Coin`. It represents a coin that can be flipped and that at any point in time shows a face of either heads or tails.

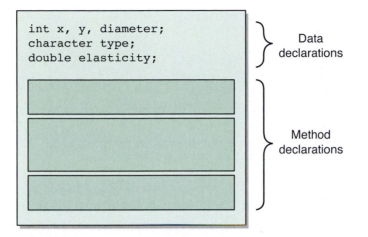

FIGURE 2.2   The members of a class: data and method declarations

Listing 2.1

```java
//************************************************************
//   Coin.java        Authors: Lewis/Loftus
//
//   Represents a coin with two sides that can be flipped.
//************************************************************

import java.util.Random;

public class Coin
{
   private final int HEADS = 0;
   private final int TAILS = 1;

   private int face;

   //-----------------------------------------------------------
   //  Sets up the coin by flipping it initially.
   //-----------------------------------------------------------
   public Coin ()
   {
      flip();
   }


   //-----------------------------------------------------------
   //  Flips the coin by randomly choosing a face value.
   //-----------------------------------------------------------
```

Listing 2.1   continued

```java
public void flip ()
{
    face = (int) (Math.random() * 2);
}

//------------------------------------------------------------
//  Returns true if the current face of the coin is heads.
//------------------------------------------------------------
public boolean isHeads ()
{
    return (face == HEADS);
}

//------------------------------------------------------------
//  Returns the current face of the coin as a string.
//------------------------------------------------------------
public String toString()
{
    String faceName;

    if (face == HEADS)
        faceName = "Heads";
    else
        faceName = "Tails";

    return faceName;
}
}
```

In the Coin class, we have two integer constants, HEADS and TAILS, and one integer variable, face. The rest of the Coin class is the Coin constructor and three regular methods: flip, isHeads, and toString.

Constructors are special methods that have the same name as the class. The Coin constructor gets called when the new operator is used to create a new instance of the Coin class. The rest of the methods in the Coin class define the various services provided by Coin objects.

A class we define can be used in multiple programs. This is the same as using the String class in whatever program we need it. When we design a class, we should always look to the future to try to give the class behaviors that may be useful in other programs, not just for the program we're writing now.

Instance Data

Note that in the `Coin` class, the constants `HEADS` and `TAILS` and the variable `face` are declared inside the class, but not inside any method. Where a variable is declared defines its *scope*. The scope is the area within a program in which that variable can be referenced. Because they are declared at the class level, not within a method, these variables and constants can be referenced in any method of the class.

> **Key Concept**
>
> The scope of a variable, which determines where it can be referenced, depends on where it is declared.

Attributes declared at the class level are also called *instance data,* because memory space for the data is reserved for each instance of the class that is created. Each `Coin` object, for example, has its own `face` variable with its own data space. Therefore, at any point in time two `Coin` objects can have their own states: one can be showing heads and the other can be showing tails, perhaps.

Java automatically initializes any variables declared at the class level. For example, all variables of numeric types such as `int` and `double` are initialized to zero. However, it is good practice to initialize variables yourself (usually in a constructor) so that anyone reading the code will clearly understand the intent.

2.6   ENCAPSULATION

We can think about an object in two ways, depending on what we are trying to do. First, when we are designing and implementing an object, we need to think about how an object works. That is, we have to design the class, we have to define the variables that will be held in the object, and we have to define the methods that make the object useful.

However, when we are designing a solution to a larger problem, we have to think about how the objects in the program interact. We have to think about what an object does, not about how it does it. As we discussed earlier, an object provides a level of abstraction that lets us focus on the larger picture when we need to.

An object should be *self-governing,* which means that the variables contained in an object should be changed only within the object. Only the methods within an object should have access to the variables in that object. We should make it difficult, if not impossible, for code outside of a class to "reach in" and change the value of a variable that is declared inside the class.

The object-oriented term for this is *encapsulation*. An object should be encapsulated from the rest of the system. It should be able to work with other parts of a program only through the methods that define what that object does. These methods define the *interface* between that object and the program that uses it.

> **Key Concept**
>
> Objects should be encapsulated. The rest of a program should be able to work with an object only through a well-defined interface.

The code that uses an object, sometimes called the *client* of an object, should not be allowed to get to variables directly. The client should interact with the object's methods, which in turn interact on behalf of the client with the data encapsulated within the object.

Visibility Modifiers

In Java, we use *modifiers* to encapsulate an object. A modifier is a Java reserved word that is used to spell out the characteristics of a programming language construct. For example, the `final` modifier is used to declare a constant. Java has several modifiers that can be used in different ways. Some modifiers can be used together, and some cannot.

Some Java modifiers are called *visibility modifiers* because they control access to the members of a class. The reserved words `public` and `private` are visibility modifiers that can be applied to the variables and methods of a class. If a member of a class has *public visibility,* then it can be directly referenced from outside of the object. If a member of a class has *private visibility,* it can be used anywhere inside the class definition but cannot be referenced from outside the class. A third visibility modifier, `protected`, has to do with inheritance and is discussed in Section 2.12.

> **Key Concept**
>
> Instance variables should be declared with private visibility to promote encapsulation.

Public variables violate encapsulation. They allow code outside the class to reach in and access or change the data. That's why instance data should be defined with private visibility. Data that is declared as private can be accessed only by the methods of the class. That makes the objects created from that class self-governing.

Which kind of visibility we give to a method depends on the purpose of that method. Methods that provide services to the client of the class must be declared with public visibility, so that they can be invoked by the client. These methods are sometimes called *service methods*. A private method cannot be invoked from outside the class. The only purpose of a private method is to help the other methods of the class do their job. Therefore they are sometimes called *support methods*.

The table in Figure 2.3 sums up the effects of public and private visibility on both variables and methods.

Note that a client can still access or modify `private` data by invoking service methods that change the data. A class must provide service methods for legitimate client operations. The code of those methods must be carefully designed to allow only appropriate access and changes.

It is usually okay to give constants public visibility because they were declared using the `final` modifier, so they can't be changed. Keep in mind that encapsulation means that data values should not be able to be *changed* directly by another

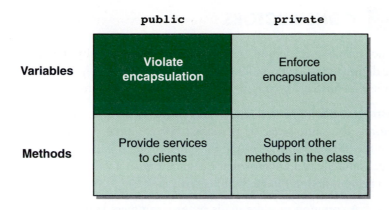

	public	**private**
Variables	Violate encapsulation	Enforce encapsulation
Methods	Provide services to clients	Support other methods in the class

FIGURE 2.3 The effects of public and private visibility

part of the code. Because constants, by definition, cannot be changed, encapsulation isn't an issue.

UML diagrams show the visibility of a class member. A member with public visibility is preceded by a plus sign (+), and a member with private visibility is preceded by a minus sign (–).

Local Data

As we said earlier, the scope of a variable or constant is the part of a program in which a reference to that variable can be made. A variable can be declared inside a method, making it *local data* as opposed to instance data. Recall that instance data is declared in a class but not inside any particular method. Local data is limited to the method in which it is declared. Any reference to local data of one method in any other method would cause an error message. A local variable simply does not exist outside of its method. Instance data, declared at the class level, has a scope of the entire class. Any method of the class can refer to it.

> **Key Concept**
>
> A variable declared in a method is local to that method and cannot be used outside of it.

Because local data and instance data have different levels of scope, a local variable can have the same name as an instance variable declared at the class level. Referring to that name in the method will reference the local version of the variable. However, calling local and instance data by the same name might confuse anyone reading the code, so it should be avoided.

The formal parameter names in a method header serve as local data for that method. They don't exist until the method is called, and cease to exist when the method is exited.

2.7 CONSTRUCTORS

A constructor is like a method that is invoked when an object is instantiated. When we define a class, we usually define a constructor to help us set up the class. We often use a constructor to initialize the variables associated with each object.

A constructor differs from a regular method in two ways. First, the name of a constructor is the same name as the class. For example, the name of the constructor in the `Coin` class is `Coin`, and the name of the constructor in the `Account` class is `Account`. Second, a constructor cannot return a value and does not have a return type specified in the method header.

> **Key Concept**
>
> A constructor cannot have any return type, even `void`.

A common mistake made by programmers is to put a `void` return type on a constructor. As far as the compiler is concerned, putting any return type on a constructor, even `void`, turns it into a regular method that happens to have the same name as the class. If the method has the same name as the class, it cannot be invoked as a constructor. This leads to error messages that are sometimes hard to understand.

A constructor is used to initialize the newly instantiated object. We don't have to define a constructor for every class. Each class has a *default constructor* that takes no parameters and is used if we don't provide our own. This default constructor generally has no effect on the newly created object.

2.8 METHOD OVERLOADING

When a method is invoked, control transfers to the code that defines the method. After the method has been executed, control returns to the place in the code where the method was invoked and processing continues.

Often all we need is the method name to identify a method. But in Java, as in other object-oriented languages, you can use the same method name with different parameter lists for multiple methods. This technique is called *method overloading*. Method overloading is useful when you need to perform similar methods on different types of data.

> **Key Concept**
>
> You can tell the versions of an overloaded method apart by their signatures: the number, type, or order of their parameters.

The compiler must still be able to match each invocation to a method. If the name for two methods is the same, the compiler will need more information. In Java, a method name can be used for many methods as long as the number of parameters, the types of those parameters, or the order of the types of parameters is different for each one. A method's name along with the number, type, and order of its parameters is called the method's *signature*. The compiler uses the complete method signature to *bind* a method invocation to the appropriate definition.

The compiler must be able to look at a method invocation, including the parameter list, to decide which method is being invoked. If you try to give two method names with the same signature, the compiler will issue an error message and will not create an executable program.

The return type of a method is not part of the method signature. That is, two overloaded methods cannot differ only by their return type. The reason is that the value returned by a method can be ignored by the invocation. The compiler would not be able to tell which version of an overloaded method is being referenced.

The `println` method is an example of a method that is overloaded several times, each accepting a single type. Here are some of its various signatures:

> `println (String s)`

> `println (int i)`

> `println (double d)`

> `println (char c)`

> `println (boolean b)`

The following two lines of code actually invoke different methods that have the same name:

```
System.out.println ("The total is: ");
System.out.println (count);
```

The first line invokes the `println` that accepts a string, and the second line invokes the version of `println` that accepts an integer. We often use a `println` statement that prints several types, such as

```
System.out.println ("The total is: " + count);
```

In this case, the plus sign is the string concatenation operator. First, the value in the variable `count` is changed to a string, then the two strings are concatenated into one longer string, and the definition of `println` that accepts a single string is invoked.

Constructors are good candidates for overloading. By providing multiple versions of a constructor, we provide several ways to set up an object.

2.9   REFERENCES REVISITED

In earlier examples, we've declared *object reference variables* through which we access particular objects. Let's look at this relationship in more detail.

An object reference variable and an object are two separate things. Remember that declaring the reference variable and creating the object are separate steps. We often declare the reference variable and create an object on the same line, but we don't have to do that. In fact, in many cases, we won't want to.

The reference variable holds the address of an object even though we never see it. When we use the dot operator to invoke an object's method, we are actually using the address in the reference variable to locate the object, look up the method, and invoke it.

Null Reference

A reference variable that does not point to an object is called a *null reference*. When a reference variable is first declared as an instance variable, it is a null reference. If we try to follow a null reference, we'll get a `NullPointerException`, because there is no object to reference. For example, consider the following situation:

```java
class NameIsNull
{
    String name; // not initialized, therefore null

    void printName()
    {
        System.out.println (name.length()); // causes an exception
    }
}
```

The declaration of the instance variable `name` says it is a reference to a `String` object, but doesn't create a `String` object. The variable `name`, therefore, contains a null reference. When the method tries to invoke the `length` method of the object to which `name` refers, an exception is thrown because there is no object to execute the method.

This can happen only in the case of instance variables. Suppose, for instance, the following two lines of code were in a method:

```java
String name;
System.out.println (name.length());
```

In this case, the variable `name` is local to whatever method it is declared in. The compiler would complain that we were using the `name` variable before it had been initialized. In the case of instance variables, however, the compiler doesn't know whether a variable had been initialized or not. That's why to follow a null reference is dangerous.

The identifier `null` is a reserved word in Java and represents a null reference. We can set a reference to `null` to ensure that it doesn't point to any object. We can also use it to check whether a particular reference currently points to an object. For example, we could have used the following code in the `printName` method to keep us from following a null reference:

```
if (name == null)
    System.out.println ("Invalid Name");
else
    System.out.println (name.length());
```

The this Reference

Another special reference for Java objects is called the this reference. The word this is a reserved word in Java. It allows an object to refer to itself. As we have discussed, a method is always invoked through a particular object or class. Inside that method, the this reference can be used to refer to the currently executing object.

> **Key Concept**
>
> The this reference always refers to the currently executing object.

For example, in the ChessPiece class there could be a method called move, which could contain the following line:

```
if (this.position == piece2.position)
    result = false;
```

In this situation, the this reference shows which position is being referenced. The this reference refers to the object through which the method was invoked. So when the following line is used to invoke the method, the this reference refers to bishop1:

```
bishop1.move();
```

But when another object is used to invoke the method, the this reference refers to it. Therefore, when the following invocation is used, the this reference in the move method refers to bishop2:

```
bishop2.move();
```

The this reference can also be used to tell the parameters of a constructor from their instance variables with the same names. For example, the constructor of a class called Account could be defined as follows:

```
public Account (String owner, long account, double initial)
{
    name = owner;
    acctNumber = account;
    balance = initial;
}
```

In this constructor, we deliberately came up with different names for the parameters so we can tell them apart from the instance variables name, acctNumber, and balance. But we didn't have to do this. We could have written the constructor using the this reference:

```
public Account (String name, long acctNumber, double balance)
{
    this.name = name;
```

```
        this.acctNumber = acctNumber;
        this.balance = balance;
    }
```

In this version of the constructor, the `this` reference specifically refers to the instance variables of the object. The variables on the right-hand side of the assignment statements refer to the formal parameters. This approach eliminates the need to come up with different yet equivalent names. This situation sometimes happens in other methods, but comes up more often in constructors.

Aliases

Because an object reference variable stores an address, we must be careful when we're managing objects. In particular, the semantics of an assignment statement for objects must be carefully understood. First, let's review primitive type assignments. Consider the following declarations of primitive data:

```
    int num1 = 5;
    int num2 = 12;
```

In the following assignment statement, a copy of the value that is stored in `num1` is stored in `num2`:

```
    num2 = num1;
```

The original value in `num2`, 12, is overwritten by the value 5. The variables `num1` and `num2` still refer to different locations in memory, and both of those locations now contain the value 5.

Now look at these object declarations:

```
    ChessPiece bishop1 = new ChessPiece();
    ChessPiece bishop2 = new ChessPiece();
```

Here `bishop1` and `bishop2` refer to two different `ChessPiece` objects. The following assignment statement copies the value in `bishop1` into `bishop2`:

```
    bishop2 = bishop1;
```

When an assignment like this is made, the address stored in `bishop1` is copied into `bishop2`. At first the two references referred to different objects. After the assignment, `bishop1` and `bishop2` contain the same address, so they refer to the same object.

> **Key Concept**
>
> Several references can refer to the same object. These references are aliases of each other.

The `bishop1` and `bishop2` references are now *aliases* of each other, because they are two names that refer to the same object. All references to the object that was originally referenced by `bishop2` are now gone; that object cannot be used again in the program.

This means that when we use one reference to change the state of the object, it is also changed for the other reference, because there is really only one object. If you change the state of `bishop1`, for instance, you change the state of `bishop2`, because they both refer to the same object. Unless you are careful, aliases can cause real headaches.

Another important aspect of references is the way they affect how we decide if two objects are equal. The `==` operator that we use for primitive data can be used with object references, but it returns true only if the two references are aliases of each other. It does not "look inside" the objects to see if they contain the same data. That is, the following expression is true only if `bishop1` and `bishop2` refer to the same object:

> **Key Concept**
>
> The `==` operator compares object references for equality, returning true if the references are aliases of each other.

```
bishop1 == bishop2
```

A method called `equals` is defined for all objects, but unless we replace it with a specific definition when we write a class, it has the same semantics as the `==` operator. That is, the `equals` method returns a `boolean` value that will be true if the two objects being compared are aliases of each other. The `equals` method is invoked through one object, and takes the other one as a parameter. The expression

```
bishop1.equals(bishop2)
```

returns true if `bishop1` and `bishop2` refer to the same object. However, we could define the `equals` method in the `ChessPiece` class any way we like. That is, we could define the `equals` method to return true under whatever conditions we want to mean that one `ChessPiece` is equal to another.

> **Key Concept**
>
> The `equals` method can be defined to determine equality between objects in any way we consider appropriate.

The `equals` method has been given a definition in the `String` class. When comparing two `String` objects, the `equals` method returns true only if both strings contain the same characters. A common mistake is to use the `==` operator to compare strings, which compares the *references* for equality, when most of the time we want to compare the *characters* in the strings for equality. The `equals` method is discussed in more detail in Section 2.14.

Garbage Collection

All interaction with an object occurs through a reference variable, so we can use an object only if we have a reference to it. When all references to an object are lost (perhaps by reassignment), the program can no longer use the object. At this point the object is called *garbage*.

> **Key Concept**
>
> If an object has no references to it, a program cannot use it. Java automatically reclaims the memory occupied by objects the program cannot use.

Java performs *automatic garbage collection*. Occasionally, the Java run time executes a method that "collects" all of the objects marked for garbage collection and returns their memory space to the system for future use.

If you want to, you can define a method called `finalize` in the object's class. The `finalize` method takes no parameters and has a `void` return type. It will be executed after the object is marked for garbage collection and before it is actually destroyed. The `finalize` method is not used very often because the garbage collector does most normal cleanup. However, it is useful for activities that the garbage collector does not address, such as closing files.

Passing Objects as Parameters

Another important issue comes up when we want to pass an object to a method. Java passes all parameters to a method *by value*. That is, the value of the actual parameter (in the invocation) is copied into the formal parameter in the method header. Basically, parameter passing is like an assignment statement, assigning to the formal parameter a copy of the value stored in the actual parameter.

We need to think about this when we are making changes to a formal parameter inside a method. The formal parameter is a separate copy of the value that is passed in, so any changes we make to it have no effect on the actual parameter. After control returns to the calling method, the actual parameter will have the same value as it did before the method was called.

However, when an object is passed to a method, we are actually passing a reference to that object. The value that gets copied is the address of the object. Therefore, the formal parameter and the actual parameter become aliases of each other. If we change the state of the object through the formal parameter reference inside the method, we are changing the object referenced by the actual parameter, because they refer to the same object. On the other hand, if we change the formal parameter reference (to make it point to a new object, for instance), we have not changed the fact that the actual parameter still refers to the original object.

> **Key Concept**
>
> When an object is passed to a method, the actual and formal parameters become aliases of each other.

2.10   THE `static` MODIFIER

We've seen how visibility modifiers let us decide the encapsulation characteristics of variables and methods in a class. Java has several other modifiers that determine other characteristics. For example, the `static` modifier associates a variable or method with its class rather than with an object of the class.

Static Variables

So far, we've seen two categories of variables: local variables that are declared inside a method, and instance variables that are declared in a class but not inside a method. The term *instance variable* is used because an instance variable is accessed through a particular instance (an object) of a class. In general, each object has memory space for each variable, so that each object can have a value for that variable.

Another kind of variable, called a *static variable* or *class variable,* is shared by all instances of a class. There is only one copy of a static variable for all objects of a class. So if we change the value of a static variable in one object, it changes for all of the others. The reserved word `static` is used as a modifier to declare a static variable:

```
private static int count = 0;
```

Memory space for a static variable is established when the class that contains it is referenced for the first time in a program. A local variable declared within a method cannot be static.

Constants are often declared using the `static` modifier. Because the value of constants cannot be changed, there might as well be only one copy of the value.

> **Key Concept**
>
> A static variable is shared by all instances of a class.

Static Methods

A *static method* (also called a *class method*) can be invoked through the class name (all of the methods of the `Math` class are static methods, for example). You don't have to instantiate an object of the class to invoke a static method. For example, the `sqrt` method is called through the `Math` class as follows:

```
System.out.println ("Square root of 27: " + Math.sqrt(27));
```

We make a method static by using the `static` modifier in the method declaration. As we've seen, the `main` method of a Java program must be declared with the `static` modifier; this is so that `main` can be executed by the interpreter without instantiating an object from the class that contains `main`.

> **Key Concept**
>
> A method is made static by using the `static` modifier in the method declaration.

Because static methods do not belong to a particular object, they cannot reference instance variables, which exist only in an instance of a class. The compiler will issue an error if a static method attempts to use a nonstatic variable. A static method can, however, reference static variables, because static variables do not belong to specific objects. Therefore, the `main` method can access only static or local variables.

The methods in the `Math` class do basic math using values passed as parameters. There is no object state, so there is reason to create an object.

2.11   WRAPPER CLASSES

In some object-oriented programming languages, everything is represented using classes and the objects that are instantiated from classes. In Java there are primitive types (such as int, double, char, and boolean) in addition to classes and objects.

Having two categories of data to manage (primitive values and object references) can be a challenge. For example, we might create an object that holds many types of other objects. But sometimes we may want the collection to hold simple integer values. In these cases we need to "wrap" a primitive type into a class so that it can be treated as an object.

A *wrapper class* is a particular primitive type. For instance, the Integer class has a simple integer value. An object created from the Integer class stores a single int value. The constructors of the wrapper classes accept the primitive value. For example,

```
Integer ageObj = new Integer(45);
```

> **Key Concept**
>
> A wrapper class has a primitive value so that it can be treated as an object.

Once this declaration and instantiation are performed, ageObj represents the integer 45 as an object. It can be used wherever an object is called for in a program.

For each primitive type in Java there is a corresponding wrapper class in the Java class library. All wrapper classes are defined in the java.lang package. There is even a wrapper class for the type void. However, unlike the other wrapper classes, the Void class cannot be instantiated. It simply represents the concept of a void reference.

The wrapper classes also provide various methods related to the management of the associated primitive type. For example, the Integer class contains methods that return the int value stored in the object, and that convert the stored value to other primitive types. Details of all wrapper classes can be found in Appendix B.

Wrapper classes also contain static methods that can be invoked independent of any instantiated object. For example, the Integer class contains a static method called parseInt to convert an integer that is stored in a String to its corresponding int value. If the String object str holds the string "987", then the following line of code converts and stores the integer value 987 into the int variable num:

```
num = Integer.parseInt(str);
```

The Java wrapper classes often contain static constants that are helpful. For example, the Integer class contains two constants, MIN_VALUE and MAX_VALUE, which hold the smallest and largest int values. The other wrapper classes contain similar constants for their types.

2.12 **INHERITANCE**

A class establishes the characteristics and behaviors of an object, but it does not set aside memory space for variables (unless those variables are declared as static). Classes are the blueprint, and objects are the houses.

Many houses can be created from the same blueprint. They are really just the same house in different places with different people living in them. But suppose you want a house that is like a friend's house, but with a small bathroom off the kitchen, and an enclosed porch instead of a garage. You want to start with the same basic blueprint but change it to suit your needs and desires. Many housing developments are created this way. The houses in the development have the same basic layout, but they can have unique features.

It's likely that the housing developer hired a master architect to create a single basic blueprint for all houses in the development, then a series of variations to appeal to different buyers. Creating the series of blueprints was simple because they were all based on the master blueprint, while the variations give them unique characteristics that may be very important to the prospective owners.

Creating a new blueprint from a master blueprint is like the object-oriented concept of *inheritance,* which lets a software designer define a new class in terms of an existing one. It is a powerful software development technique and a defining characteristic of object-oriented programming.

Derived Classes

Inheritance is the process in which a new class is created from an existing one. The new class automatically contains some or all of the variables and methods in the original class. Then, the programmer can add new variables and methods to the new class or change the inherited ones.

> **Key Concept**
>
> Inheritance is the process of creating a new class from an existing one.

In general, new classes can be created by inheritance faster, easier, and more cheaply than by writing them from scratch. At the heart of inheritance is the idea of *software reuse*. Using already existing software to create new software means the design, implementation, and testing of the existing software doesn't go to waste.

> **Key Concept**
>
> One purpose of inheritance is to reuse existing software.

Remember that the word *class* comes from the idea of classifying groups of objects that have similar characteristics. Classification often uses levels of classes that have things in common. For example, all mammals share certain characteristics: they are warm-blooded, have hair, and bear live offspring. Now consider a subset of mammals, such as horses. All horses are mammals, and have all of the characteristics of mammals. But they also have unique features that make them different from other mammals.

If we put this idea in software terms, a class called `Mammal` would have certain variables and methods that describe mammals. A `Horse` class could be derived from the `Mammal` class, automatically inheriting the variables and methods contained in `Mammal`. The `Horse` class can refer to the inherited variables and methods as if they had been declared locally in that class. New variables and methods can then be added to the derived class that describe how a horse is different from other mammals.

The original class that is used to derive a new one is called the *parent class, superclass,* or *base class.* The new class is called a *child class,* or *subclass.* Java uses the reserved word `extends` to show that a new class is being created from an existing class.

This process establishes a special relationship between two classes called an *is-a relationship.* This type of relationship means that the derived class should be a more specific version of the original. For example, a horse is a mammal. Not all mammals are horses, but all horses are mammals.

Let's look at an example. The following class can be used to define a book:

```java
class Book
{
   protected int numPages;

   protected void pages()
   {
      System.out.println ("Number of pages: " + numPages);
   }
}
```

To derive a child class that is based on the `Book` class, we use the reserved word `extends` in the header of the child class. For example, a `Dictionary` class can be derived from `Book` as follows:

```java
class Dictionary extends Book
{
   private int numDefs;

   public void info()
   {
      System.out.println ("Number of definitions: " + numDefs);
      System.out.println ("Definitions per page: "
                            + numDefs/numPages);
   }
}
```

By saying that the `Dictionary` class extends the `Book` class, the `Dictionary` class automatically inherits the `numPages` variable and the `pages` method. Note that the `info` method uses the `numPages` variable.

Inheritance is a one-way street. The `Book` class cannot use new variables or methods that are declared only in the `Dictionary` class. For instance, if we created an object from the `Book` class, we could not use it to invoke the `info` method. This restriction makes sense because a child class is a more specific version of the parent. A dictionary has pages, because all books have pages; but although a dictionary has definitions, not all books do.

Inheritance relationships are represented in UML class diagrams by an arrow with an open arrowhead pointing from the child class to the parent class.

The protected Modifier

Not all variables and methods are inherited this way. The visibility modifiers used to declare the members of a class determine which ones are inherited and which are not. The child class inherits variables and methods that are declared public and does not inherit those that are declared private.

However, if we declare a variable with public visibility so that a derived class can inherit it, we violate the principle of encapsulation. To get around this, Java provides a third visibility modifier: `protected`. When a variable or method is declared with protected visibility, a derived class will inherit it, keeping some of its encapsulation properties. The encapsulation with protected visibility is not as tight as it would be if the variable or method were declared private, but it is better than if it were declared public. A variable or method declared with protected visibility can be accessed by any class in the same package.

> **Key Concept**
>
> Visibility modifiers determine which variables and methods are inherited. Protected visibility provides the best possible encapsulation that permits inheritance.

Each inherited variable or method keeps its original visibility modifier. For example, if a method is public in the parent, it is public in the child.

Constructors are not inherited in a derived class, even though they have public visibility. Constructors are special methods that are used to set up an object, so it wouldn't make sense for a class called `Dictionary` to have a constructor called `Book`.

The super Reference

The reserved word `super` can be used in a class to refer to its parent class. Using the `super` reference, we can access a parent's members, even if they aren't inherited. Like the `this` reference, what the word `super` refers to depends on the class in which it is used. However, unlike the this reference, which refers to a particular instance of a class, super is a general reference to the members of the parent class.

One use of the super reference is to invoke a parent's constructor. If the following invocation is performed at the beginning of a constructor, the parent's constructor is invoked, passing any appropriate parameters:

```
super (x, y, z);
```

A child's constructor is responsible for calling its parent's constructor. Generally, the first line of a constructor should use the super reference call to a constructor of the parent class. If no such call exists, Java will automatically make a call to super() at the beginning of the constructor. This rule ensures that a parent class initializes its variables before the child class constructor begins to execute. Using the super reference to invoke a parent's constructor can be done in only the child's constructor, and if included it must be the first line of the constructor.

The super reference can also be used to reference other variables and methods defined in the parent's class.

Overriding Methods

Sometimes you may want most but not all of the methods from a parent class. You may need one method that is slightly different, for example. So your child class would define a method with the same name and signature as a method in the parent. We say that the child's version *overrides* the parent's version. Overriding occurs often in inheritance.

The object that is used to invoke a method determines which version of the method is actually executed. If it is an object of the parent type, the parent's version of the method is invoked. If it is an object of the child type, the child's version is invoked. This flexibility allows two objects that are related by inheritance to use the same naming conventions for methods that accomplish the same general task in different ways.

A method can be defined with the final modifier. A child class cannot override a final method. This technique is used to ensure that a derived class uses a particular definition for a method.

Method overriding is an important idea in inheritance. These issues are explored in later sections of this chapter.

Shadowing Variables

It is possible for a child class to declare a variable with the same name as one that is inherited from the parent. This technique is called *shadowing variables*. Shadowing is like overriding, but it can cause confusion.

Because an inherited variable is already available to the child class, there is usually no good reason to declare it again. Someone reading code with a shadowed variable will find two different declarations that seem to apply to a variable used in the child class and could get confused. Declaring a particular variable name over again could change its type, though that is not usually necessary. In general, shadowing variables should be avoided.

2.13 CLASS HIERARCHIES

A child class can be the parent of its own child class. What's more, many classes can be created from a single parent. When this happens, inheritance relationships develop into *class hierarchies*. The UML class diagram in Figure 2.4 shows a class hierarchy in the inheritance relationship between classes `Mammal` and `Horse`.

> **Key Concept**
>
> The child of one class can be the parent of one or more other classes, creating a class hierarchy.

There is no limit to the number of children a class can have, or to the number of levels to which a class hierarchy can extend. Two children of the same parent are called *siblings*. Although siblings share the characteristics passed on by their common parent, they are not related by inheritance, because one is not used to create the other.

In class hierarchies, common features should be kept as high in the hierarchy as possible. That way, the only characteristics established in a child class are those that make the class different from its parent and siblings. Keeping common features high on the hierarchy makes maintenance easier, because when changes are made to the parent, they are

> **Key Concept**
>
> Common features should be located as high in a class hierarchy as possible.

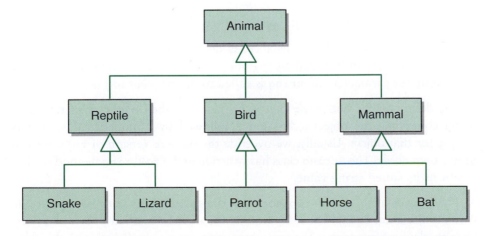

FIGURE 2.4 A UML class diagram showing a class hierarchy

automatically made in the children as well. Always remember to keep the is-a relationship when building class hierarchies.

A parent passes along a trait to a child class, and that child class passes it along to its children, and so on. An inherited feature might have started in the parent or several levels higher.

There is no single best hierarchy organization for all situations. The decisions you make when designing a class hierarchy will limit and affect the design decisions you can make later so you must make them carefully.

The Object Class

In Java, all classes ultimately come from the `Object` class. If a class definition doesn't use the `extends` clause to create itself from another class, then that class is automatically created from the `Object` class. Therefore, the following two class definitions are equal:

```
class Thing
{
    // whatever
}
```

and

```
class Thing extends Object
{
    // whatever
}
```

> **Key Concept**
>
> All Java classes are created, directly or indirectly, from the `Object` class.

Because all classes are created from `Object`, any public method of `Object` can be invoked through any object created in any Java program. The `Object` class is defined in the `java.lang` package of the standard class library.

The `toString` method, for instance, is defined in the `Object` class, so the `toString` method can be called on any object. When a `println` method is called with an object parameter, `toString` is called to decide what to print.

The definition for `toString` that is provided by the `Object` class returns a string containing the object's class name followed by a numeric value that is unique for that object. Usually, we override the `Object` version of `toString` to fit our own needs. The `String` class has overridden the `toString` method so that it returns its stored string value.

The `equals` method of the `Object` class is also useful. Its purpose is to decide if two objects are equal. The definition of the `equals` method provided by the `Object` class returns true if the two object references actually refer to the same object (that is, if they are aliases). Classes often override the inherited definition of the `equals` method and use a definition that works better in that case. For instance, the `String` class overrides `equals` so that it returns true only if both strings contain the same characters in the same order.

> **Key Concept**
>
> The `toString` and `equals` methods are defined in the `Object` class and therefore are inherited by every class in every Java program.

Abstract Classes

An *abstract class* represents a general idea in a class hierarchy. An abstract class cannot be instantiated and usually contains one or more abstract methods, which have no definition. In this way, an abstract class is like an interface. Unlike interfaces, however, an abstract class can contain methods that are not abstract, and it can contain data declarations other than constants.

We declare a class as abstract by including the `abstract` modifier in the class header. Any class that contains one or more abstract methods must be declared as abstract. In abstract classes (unlike interfaces), the `abstract` modifier must be applied to each abstract method. A class declared as abstract does not have to contain abstract methods.

Abstract classes act as placeholders in a class hierarchy. An abstract class represents something that cannot be fully defined. Instead, an abstract class may contain a partial description that is inherited by all of its children, where the class can be better defined.

> **Key Concept**
>
> An abstract class cannot be instantiated. It represents an idea on which other classes can build their definitions.

Consider the class hierarchy shown in Figure 2.5. The `Vehicle` class at the top of the hierarchy may be too general for a particular application. Therefore, we may choose to implement it as an abstract class. Concepts that apply to all vehicles can be represented in the `Vehicle` class and are inherited by its descendants. That way, each of its descendants doesn't have to define the same concept over again, and perhaps inconsistently.

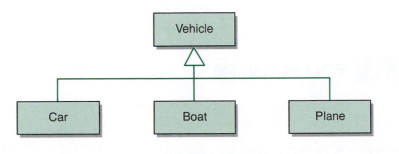

FIGURE 2.5 A vehicle class hierarchy

For example, we may say that all vehicles have a particular speed. Therefore, we declare a `speed` variable in the `Vehicle` class, and all specific vehicles below it in the hierarchy automatically have a `speed` variable. Any change we make to the representation of the speed of a vehicle is automatically reflected in all children classes. Or we may declare an abstract method called `fuelConsumption`, whose purpose is to calculate how quickly fuel is being used by a particular vehicle. The details of the `fuelConsumption` method must be defined differently by each type of vehicle, but all vehicles consume fuel and so the `Vehicle` class provides a consistent way to compute that value.

Some concepts don't apply to all vehicles, so we wouldn't put those concepts at the `Vehicle` level. For instance, we wouldn't include a variable called `numberOfWheels` in the `Vehicle` class, because not all vehicles have wheels (boats, for example). The child classes can add the wheels concept at their own level in the hierarchy.

An abstract class can be defined anywhere in a hierarchy. Usually they are located at the upper levels of a class hierarchy. However, you can create an abstract class from a nonabstract parent.

Key Concept

A class created from an abstract parent must override all of its parent's abstract methods, or the child class will also be abstract.

Usually, a child of an abstract class will define the abstract method inherited from its parent. This is just a case of overriding a method—giving a different definition than the one the parent provides. If a child of an abstract class does not give a definition for every abstract method that it inherits from its parent, then the child class is also abstract.

Notice that an abstract method cannot be modified as `final` or `static`. Because a final method cannot be overridden in subclasses, an abstract final method would have no way of being given a definition in subclasses. A static method can be invoked using the class name without declaring an object of the class. Because abstract methods have no implementation, an abstract static method would make no sense.

Choosing which classes and methods to make abstract is an important part of the design process. Such choices should be made only after careful consideration. By using abstract classes wisely, we can create flexible, extensible software designs.

2.14   POLYMORPHISM

Usually, the type of a reference variable matches the class of the object it refers to exactly. That is, if we declare a reference as

```
ChessPiece bishop;
```

bishop refers to an object created by instantiating the ChessPiece class. However, the relationship between a reference variable and the object it refers to is more flexible than that.

The term *polymorphism* can be defined as "having many forms." A *polymorphic reference* is a reference variable that can refer to different types of objects at different points in time. The specific method invoked through a polymorphic reference can change from one invocation to the next.

> **Key Concept**
>
> A polymorphic reference can refer to different types of objects over time.

Consider the following line of code:

```
obj.doIt();
```

If the reference obj is polymorphic, it can refer to different types of objects at different times. If that line of code is in a loop or in a method that is called more than once, that line of code might call a different version of the doIt method each time it is invoked.

At some point, the commitment is made to execute certain code to carry out a method invocation. This commitment is called *binding* a method invocation to a method definition. In most situations, binding a method invocation to a method definition happens at compile time. For polymorphic references, however, the decision cannot be made until run time. This is called *late binding* or *dynamic binding*. It is less efficient than binding at compile time because the decision has to be made during the execution of the program. We accept this because a polymorphic reference gives us so much flexibility.

There are two ways to create a polymorphic reference in Java: using inheritance and using interfaces. The following sections describe the inheritance approach.

References and Class Hierarchies

In Java, a reference that refers to an object of a particular class can also refer to an object of any class related to it by inheritance. For example, if the class Mammal is used to create the class Dog, then a Mammal reference can be used to refer to an object of class Dog, as shown here:

> **Key Concept**
>
> A reference variable can refer to any object created from any class related to it by inheritance.

```
Mammal pet;
Dog lassie = new Dog();
pet = lassie;  // a valid assignment
```

The reverse operation, assigning the Mammal object to a Dog reference, is also valid, but requires an explicit cast, where the type of object is stated in the code. Assigning a reference in this direction is generally less useful and more likely to cause problems, because although a dog *is-a* mammal, the reverse is not necessarily true.

This relationship works anywhere in a class hierarchy. If the `Mammal` class came from a class called `Animal`, then we could do this:

```
Animal creature = new Dog();
```

Of course, an `Object` reference can be used to refer to any object, because ultimately all classes are descendants of the `Object` class. An `ArrayList`, for example, uses polymorphism in that it is designed to hold `Object` references. That's why an `ArrayList` can be used to store any kind of object. In fact, a particular `ArrayList` can be used to hold several different types of objects at one time, because they are all `Object` objects.

Polymorphism via Inheritance

Let's go back to the reference variable `creature`, as defined in the previous section. The variable `creature` can be polymorphic, because it can refer to an `Animal` object, a `Mammal` object, or a `Dog` object. Suppose that all three of these classes have a method called `move` that are implemented in different ways (because the child class overrode the definition it inherited). The following invocation calls the `move` method, but which version of the method it calls is determined at run time:

```
creature.move();
```

> **Key Concept**
>
> A polymorphic reference uses the type of the object, not the type of the reference, to determine which version of a method to invoke.

When this line is executed, if `creature` currently refers to an `Animal` object, the `move` method of the `Animal` class is invoked. Likewise, if `creature` currently refers to a `Mammal` or `Dog` object, the `Mammal` or `Dog` version of `move` is invoked.

Of course, because `Animal` and `Mammal` are general concepts, they may be defined as abstract classes. However, they could still have polymorphic references. Suppose the `move` method in the `Mammal` class is abstract, and is given unique definitions in the `Cat`, `Dog`, and `Whale` classes. A `Mammal` reference variable can be used to refer to any objects created from any of the `Cat`, `Dog`, and `Whale` classes, and can be used to execute the `move` method on any of them.

Let's consider another situation. The class hierarchy shown in Figure 2.6 contains classes that represent types of employees that might work at a company: volunteers, executives, hourly workers, and so on.

Polymorphism could be used to pay employees in different ways. One list of employees (of whatever type) could be paid using a single loop that invokes each employee's pay method. But the pay method that is invoked each time will depend on the type of employee that is executing the pay method during that iteration of the loop.

This is a classic example of polymorphism—letting different types of objects handle one operation in different ways.

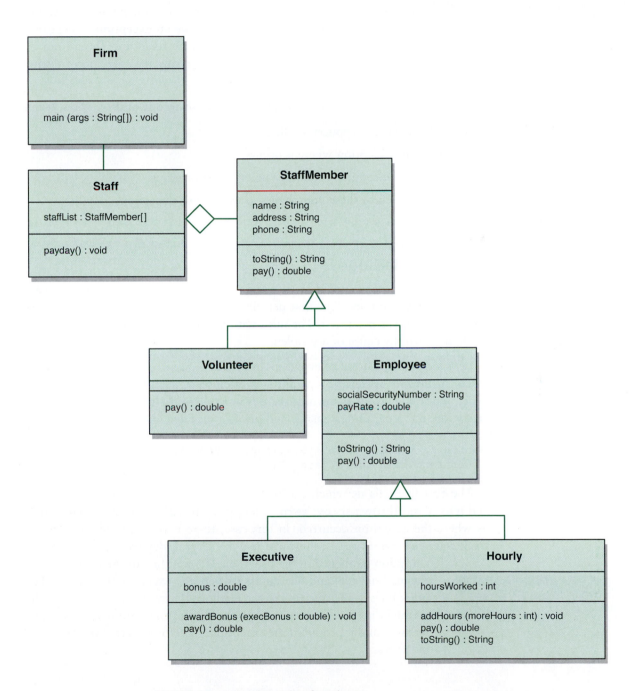

FIGURE 2.6 A class hierarchy of employees

2.15 EXCEPTIONS

Problems that come up in a Java program may cause exceptions or errors. An *exception* is an object that defines an unusual situation. An exception is thrown by a program or the run-time environment, and can be caught and handled. An *error* is like an exception, except that an error generally represents a situation that can't be fixed and should not be caught. Java has a set of predefined exceptions and errors that may occur during the execution of a program.

A program can be designed to process an exception in one of three ways. It can

> Not handle the exception at all.

> Handle the exception where it occurs.

> Handle the exception at another point in the program.

We explore each of these approaches in the following sections.

Exception Messages

If an exception is not handled at all by the program, the program will terminate (stop) and produce a message that describes what the exception is and where in the program it was produced. The information in the message is often helpful in tracking down the cause of a problem.

Let's look at the output of an exception. An `ArithmeticException` is thrown when an invalid arithmetic operation is attempted, such as dividing by zero. When that exception is thrown, if there is no code in the program to handle the exception, the program terminates and prints a message like this:

```
Exception in thread "main" java.lang.ArithmeticException: / by zero
        at Zero.main (Zero.java:17)
```

The first line tells us which exception was thrown (`ArithmeticException`) and why it was thrown (`/ by zero`). The rest is the *call stack trace,* which tells us where the exception occurred. In this case, there is only one line in the call stack trace (`at Zero.main`), but there may be several, depending on where the exception happened in the program. The first line of the trace gives us the method, file, and line number where the exception happened. The other lines in the trace tell us the methods that were called to get to the method that produced the exception. In this program, there is only one method, and it produced the exception; therefore, there is only one line in the trace.

We can also get the call stack trace information by calling methods of the exception object that is being thrown. The method `getMessage` returns a string explaining the reason the exception was thrown. The method `printStackTrace` prints the call stack trace.

The `try` Statement

Let's now examine how we catch and handle an exception when it is thrown. A try *statement* is a `try` block followed by one or more `catch` clauses. The `try` block is a group of statements that may throw an exception. A `catch` clause defines how a particular exception is handled. A `try` block can have several `catch` clauses, each dealing with a particular kind of exception. A `catch` clause is sometimes called an *exception handler*.

Here is the general format of a `try` statement:

```
try
{
    // statements in the try block
}
catch (IOException exception)
{
    // statements that handle the I/O problem
}
catch (NumberFormatException exception)
{
    // statements that handle the number format problem
}
```

When a `try` statement is executed, the statements in the `try` block are executed. If no exception is thrown, processing continues with the statement following the `try` statement (after all of the `catch` clauses). This is the normal flow and should occur most of the time.

> **Key Concept**
>
> Each `catch` clause on a `try` statement handles a particular kind of exception that may be thrown within the `try` block.

If an exception is thrown at any point, however, control immediately goes to the exception handler if there is one. That is, control goes to the first `catch` clause whose exception matches the class of the exception that was thrown. After the statements in the `catch` clause are executed, control goes to the statement after the entire `try` statement.

Exception Propagation

If an exception is not caught and handled where it occurs, control is immediately returned to the method that invoked the method that produced the exception.

We can design our software so that the exception is caught and handled at this level. If it isn't caught there, control returns to the method that called it. This is called *exception propagation*.

Exception propagation continues until the exception is caught and handled, or until it is propagated out of the main method, which stops the program and produces an exception message. To catch an exception at an outer level, we must invoke the method that produced the exception, inside a try block that has a catch clause to handle it.

A programmer must pick the best level at which to catch and handle an exception. Which level that is depends on the situation and the design of the system. Sometimes the right approach will be not to catch an exception at all and let the program crash.

The Exception Class Hierarchy

The classes that define exceptions are related by inheritance, creating the class hierarchy that is shown, in part, in Figure 2.7.

The Throwable class is the parent of both the Error class and the Exception class. Many types of exceptions are derived from the Exception class, and these classes also have many children. Though these classes are defined in the java.lang package, many child classes that define exceptions are part of several other packages. Inheritance relationships can cross package boundaries.

We can define our own exceptions by deriving a new class from Exception or one of its descendants. The class we choose as the parent depends on the situation.

After creating the class that defines the exception, we can create an object of that type as needed. The throw statement is used to throw the exception. For example:

```
throw new MyException();
```

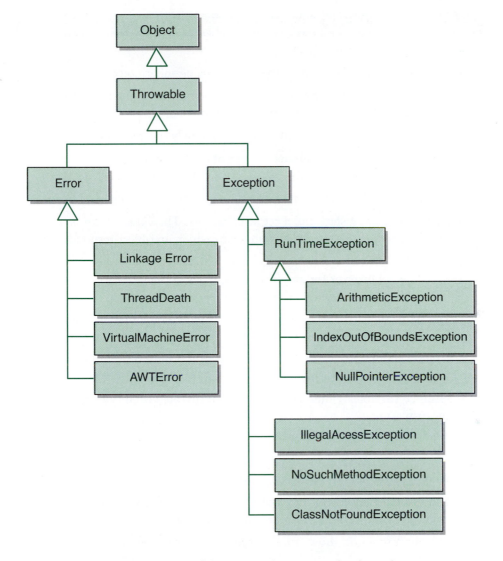

FIGURE 2.7   Part of the Error and Exception class hierarchy

Summary of Key Concepts

> An object is defined by a class.

> Classes can be created from other classes using inheritance.

> An abstraction hides details. A good abstraction hides the right details at the right time so that we can manage complexity.

> The new operator returns a reference to a newly created object.

> The Java standard class library is a set of classes that anyone can use when writing Java programs.

> A package is used to group related classes under one name.

> Each object has a state and a set of behaviors. The values of an object's variables define its state. The methods to which an object responds define its behaviors.

> A class is a blueprint for an object; it reserves no memory space for data. Each object has its own data space, thus its own state.

> The scope of a variable, which determines where it can be referenced, depends on where it is declared.

> Objects should be encapsulated. The rest of a program should interact with an object only through a well-defined interface.

> Instance variables should be declared with private visibility to promote encapsulation.

> A variable declared in a method is local to that method and cannot be used outside of it.

> A constructor cannot have any return type, even `void`.

> You can tell the versions of an overloaded method apart by their signatures: the number, type or order of their parameters.

> A growth function shows time or space utilization relative to the problem size.

> The reserved word `null` represents a reference that does not point to a valid object.

> The `this` reference always refers to the currently executing object.

> Several references can refer to the same object. These references are aliases of each other.

> The `==` operator compares object references for equality, returning true if the references are aliases of each other.

> The `equals` method can be defined to determine equality between objects in any way we consider appropriate.

> When an object is passed to a method, the actual and formal parameters become aliases of each other.

> A static variable is shared among all instances of a class.

> A method is made static by using the `static` modifier in the method declaration.

> A wrapper class has a primitive value so that it can be treated as an object.

> Inheritance is the process of creating a new class from an existing one.

> One purpose of inheritance is to reuse existing software.

> Inherited variables and methods can be used in the derived class as if they had been declared locally.

> Inheritance creates an is-a relationship between parent and child classes.

> Visibility modifiers determine which variables and methods are inherited. Protected visibility provides the best possible encapsulation that permits inheritance.

> A parent's constructor can be invoked using the `super` reference.

> A child class can override (redefine) the parent's definition of an inherited method.

> The child of one class can be the parent of one or more other classes, creating a class hierarchy.

> All java classes are created, directly or indirectly, from the `Object` class.

> The `toString` and `equals` methods are defined in the Object class and therefore are inherited by ever class in every java program.

> An abstract class cannot be instantiated. It represents an idea on which other classes can build their definitions.

> A class created from an abstract parent must override all of its parent's abstract methods, or the child class will also be abstract.

> A polymorphic reference can refer to different types of objects over time.

> A reference variable can refer to any object created from any class related to it by inheritance.

> A polymorphic reference uses the type of the object, not the type of the reference, to determine which version of a method to invoke.

> Errors and exceptions represent unusual or invalid processing.

> The messages printed by a thrown exception indicate the nature of the problem and provide a method call stack trace.

> Each catch clause on a `try` statement handles a particular kind of exception that may be thrown within the try block.

> If an exception is not caught and handled where it occurs, the exception is propagated to the calling method.

> A programmer must carefully consider how exceptions should be handled, if at all, and at what level.

> A new exception is defined by deriving a new class from the `Exception` class or from one of its descendants.

Self Review Questions

2.1   What is an object?

2.2   Why is abstraction important for large computer systems?

2.3   How are object variables in Java stored?

2.4   What is the difference between state and behavior of an object?

2.5   What is encapsulation? What modifiers should be used for state variables and methods in order to provide for the best implementation of encapsulation?

2.6   What is the function of the constructor?

2.7   How does the compiler decide which method to execute when more than one method in the class has the same name?

2.8   What is an alias?

2.9   What is the purpose of static variables?

2.10   What is a wrapper class?

2.11   What is the major benefit of inheritance?

2.12   What is an exception? How are they used in programs?

Exercises

2.1   Computer Operating Systems are programs, consider your current operating system. Name two objects that you could see as part of your operating system. Give at least one property and behavior for each.

2.2   Encapsulation is an important concept in Object Oriented Design. In an instant messaging program each user has certain information stored about them. Describe what information would be kept private to the user class.

2.3   Consider a spreadsheet program. Cells can store all different types of information to be processed. A cell object is being created—what might be an example of an overloaded method in that object?

2.4   The println method of the System object is a static method. Find at least two other static methods belonging to the System object.

2.5   Give an example of when a static method might be used. Do not use the example of a Math or System class.

2.6   Arrange the following items in an inheritance hierarchy: Diver, Swimmer, Runner, Distance runner, Athlete

2.7   From the hierarchy given in exercise 2.6, which of the objects defined could make a call to super for which other object?

2.8   From the hierarchy given in exercise 2.6, give one example of a method that might be overloaded from a parent to a child class.

2.9   Look at the exception hierarchy given on page 61. Choose one exception and give an example (not used in the text) of where it might be thrown.

Programming Projects

2.1   Write a class declaration for a mouse class. Include the class header, at least 3 private variables for the state of the mouse, and 4 methods you feel are appropriate.

2.2   Write a class declaration for a remote class, designed to store information from a TV remote. Include at least 2 state variables, and 3 methods.

2.3   Write a class declaration for a furniture item to be sold at a store. Include at least 3 state variables, a constructor, and 3 methods.

2.4   Write a class declaration for a DVD player. Include overloaded methods for play (CD vs. DVD) as well as state variables, a constructor, and other appropriate methods.

2.5   Consider the task of writing a library class to do specific string operations. The methods should be able to take a string parameter and calculate the following: The number of occurrences of any given letter in the string, remove all of the white space in any given string (any spaces or return characters), and finally a method to create an acronym from a string that may contain multiple words separated by a space. The methods should be defined as class methods.

2.6   Create a SmallInteger object designed to be a wrapper class for integers between -10 and 10 inclusive. The object should have basic functionality and should throw an exception if a number not in the range specified is attempted to be stored.

2.7   Write a series of classes to model a camera, a disposable camera, and a digital camera. Include appropriate inheritance, overriding methods where appropriate.

Answers to Self Review Questions

2.1   An object is a term used to describe a collection of data and methods in a program that represent a specific item in that program.

2.2   Abstraction is important for large computer systems, especially where multiple programmers are working on completing the system. The ability to use an object solely through its interface saves both time and effort in creating complex interacting systems.

2.3   Object variables in Java are stored as references. Each variable contains a reference to another memory location where the actual state of the object is maintained.

2.4   State is the information that is stored by the object, while behavior is the actual actions (methods) that the object can perform.

2.5   Encapsulation is the practice of keeping the data stored by the class separate from users of that class. This allows for extra checks for data integrity. State variables should be kept private while methods can have either public or private visibility depending upon their purpose.

2.6   The constructor serves as a means to provide initialization of state variables. It can be used to set default values, or assign starting values passed as parameters to the object.

2.7   The compiler (and processor) use the parameters by looking at the number of parameters and their types, in order to determine which overloaded method should be executed.

2.8   The term alias refers to multiple variable names that reference the same object. Because all objects in Java are stored as references it is possible to have two references pointing at the same memory location.

2.9   Static variables provide a way for one variable to be consistent throughout all instances of any given class. This could be used for a constant, a counter, or other such variable.

2.10 A wrapper class is a class designed to provide a way to store primitive data as an object.

2.11 Inheritance provides for object reusability as well as sharing of common themes. When we inherit an object we are able to use all of its functionality as well as add some of our own. This flexibility makes it much more likely that a given object can fit into a new program.

2.12 Exceptions are used by Java to recover from an error in a program. They are also used to generate error messages.

Collections 3

> Define collection concepts and terms

> Explore the basic structure of the Java Collections API

> Discuss collection design

> Define a set collection

> Use a set collection to solve a problem

> Examine an array implementation of a set

This chapter explores collections and the data structures used to implement them. It lays the groundwork for the study of collections by carefully defining the issues and goals related to their design. This chapter also introduces a collection called a set and uses it to illustrate the design, implementation, and use of collections.

3.1 INTRODUCTION TO COLLECTIONS

A *collection* is an object that gathers and organizes other objects. It defines how those objects, which are called *elements* of the collection, can be accessed and managed. The user of a collection, usually another class or object in the software system, must interact with the collection only in those defined ways.

Over the past 50 years, several types of collections have been defined. Each type is good for solving particular kinds of problems. Most of this book explores these classic collections.

There are two categories of collections: linear and nonlinear. In a *linear collection* the elements are organized in a straight line. In a *nonlinear collection* the elements are organized in a hierarchy or a network, or any other way *except* a straight line. For that matter, a nonlinear collection may not have any organization at all.

Figure 3.1 shows a linear and a nonlinear collection. It usually doesn't matter if the elements in a linear collection are shown horizontally or vertically.

The organization of the elements in a collection is usually determined by one of two things:

> The order in which they were added to the collection.

> Some other relationship among the elements themselves.

For example, one linear collection may always add new elements to one end of the line, so the order of the elements is the order in which they are added. Another linear collection may be kept in sorted order, such as a list of names kept in alphabetical order. The organization of the elements in a nonlinear collection can be determined in either of these two ways as well.

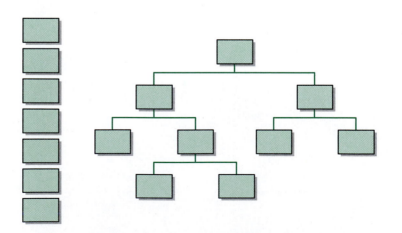

FIGURE 3.1 A linear and a nonlinear collection

Abstraction

An *abstraction* hides or ignores certain details at certain times. It's easier to deal with an abstraction than it is to deal with too many details at one time. In fact, we couldn't get through a day without relying on abstractions. For example, we couldn't possibly drive a car if we had to worry about all the details that make the car work: the spark plugs, the pistons, the transmission, and so on. Instead, we can focus on the *interface* to the car: the steering wheel, the pedals, and a few other controls. These controls are an abstraction, hiding the underlying details and allowing us to control an otherwise very complicated machine.

> **Key Concept**
> A collection is an abstraction where the details of the implementation are hidden.

A collection is an abstraction. A collection defines how the user can manage the objects in the collection, such as adding and removing elements. The user interacts with the collection through an interface, as shown in Figure 3.2. However, the user doesn't see the details of how this is done. A class that implements the collection's interface takes care of that.

Abstraction is an important software engineering concept. In large software systems, it is almost impossible for a person to grasp all of the details of the system at once. Instead, the system is divided into abstract subsystems, which are assigned to different developers or groups of developers to develop the subsystem to meet its specification.

An object is perfect for creating a collection because, if it is designed correctly, the internal workings of an object are *encapsulated* from the rest of the system. In almost all cases, the instance variables defined in a class should be declared with private visibility. Therefore, only the methods of that class can get to and change them. The only interaction a user has with an object should be through its public methods, using the services that that object provides.

> **Key Concept**
> Encapsulation: The internal workings of an object are inaccessible to other objects in the system.

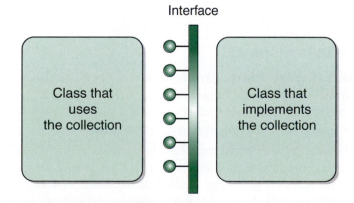

FIGURE 3.2 A well-defined interface separates the interface with the user from the implementation

As we study collections, we will always stress the idea of separating the interface from the implementation. Therefore, for every collection we look at, we should consider the following:

> How does the collection work?

> How do we define the interface to the collection?

> What kinds of problems does the collection help us solve?

> What ways can we implement the collection?

> What are the benefits and costs of each implementation?

Before we continue, we'll need to learn some new terms:

> **Data type.** A *data type* is a group of values and their operations. The primitive data types defined in Java are the primary examples. For example, the integer data type defines a set of numeric values and the operations (addition, subtraction, etc.) that can be used on them.

> **Abstract data type (ADT).** An *abstract data type* (ADT) has values and operations that are not automatically defined in a programming language. The details of an ADT's implementation must be defined and should be hidden from the user. A collection, therefore, is an abstract data type.

> **Data structure.** A *data structure* is made up of of programming constructs used to implement a collection. For example, a collection might be implemented using an array.

Because we want to separate the user interface from the implementation, we may, and often do, end up with a linear data structure, such as an array, being used to implement a nonlinear collection, such as a tree.

Historically, the terms *ADT* and *data structure* have been used in many ways. We carefully define them here to avoid any confusion, and will use them consistently. Throughout this book we will look at several data structures and how they can be used to implement collections.

> **Key Concept**
>
> A data structure is made up of programming constructs used to implement a collection.

The Java Collections API

The Java programming language has a huge library of classes that we can use to develop software. Parts of the library are organized into *application programming interfaces* (APIs). The *Java Collections API* is a set of classes for a few specific types of collections, implemented in different ways.

You might ask why we should learn how to design and implement collections if we can just use the Java Collections API. There are several reasons. First, the Java Collections API only gives you a subset of the collections you may want to use. Second, the Java API classes may not implement the collections the way you want. Third, and perhaps most important, as a software developer you need to have a deep understanding of the issues involved in the design of collections and the data structures used to implement them.

As we explore different collections, we will also look at the corresponding classes of the Java Collections API. In each case, we analyze the implementations that we develop and compare what we have done to the classes in the standard library.

3.2   A SET COLLECTION

Let's look at an example of a collection. A *set* can be defined as a collection that groups elements with no particular ordering. The only restrictions placed upon a set is that no element may exist within the set twice. Once an element is put in a set, there is no guarantee about where that element is in relation to any other element in the set. Imagine that you could pull an element out of the set. You have an equal chance of getting any item that is stored—in other words there is no element defined as the "first" element of the set and likewise there is no "last" element of the set. Figure 3.3 shows a set collection of unorganized elements.

A set is a nonlinear collection. That is, there is essentially no organization to the elements in the collection at all. The elements in a set have no relationship with each other, and there is no significance to the order in which they have been added to the set. The only restriction is that the same element cannot be added twice.

How a collection is defined is important. There is general agreement among software developers about collection types. However, a specific set of operations is not carved in stone. There are many variations possible for any given collection type, although the defined operations should stick to its underlying purpose. The operations we define for a set collection are listed in Figure 3.4.

> **Key Concept**
>
> A set is a nonlinear collection in which there is no organization. No object may be added to the set twice.

Every collection has operations that let us add and remove elements, though they vary in their details. Some operations, such as `isEmpty` and `size`, are common to almost all collections as well. A set collection incorporates an element of randomness, as well as a guarantee of unique items.

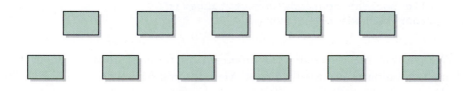

FIGURE 3.3   A set collection

Operation	Description
add	Adds an element to the set.
addAll	Adds the elements of one set to another set.
removeRandom	Removes an element at random from the set.
remove	Removes a particular element from the set.
union	Combines the elements of two sets to create a third.
contains	Determines if a particular element is in the set.
equals	Determines if two sets contain the same elements.
isEmpty	Determines if the set is empty.
size	Determines the number of elements in the set.
iterator	Provides an iterator for the set.
toString	Provides a string representation of the set.

FIGURE 3.4   The operations on a set collection

Interfaces

To make it easy to separate interface operations from the methods that implement them, we can define a Java interface structure for a collection. A Java interface gives us a way to define the set of operations for any collection.

In earlier programs and examples, you may have seen the term *interface* used to mean the public methods through which we can interact with an object. Now we are going to formalize this idea by using a particular language construct in Java.

> **Key Concept**
>
> A Java interface defines a set of abstract methods and is useful in separating the concept of an abstract data type from its implementation.

A *Java interface* is defined as a collection of constants and abstract methods. An abstract method is a method that does not have an implementation. That is, there is no body of code defined for an abstract method. The header of the method, including its parameter list, is simply followed by a semicolon. An interface cannot be instantiated.

A partial definition for our SetADT interface is shown below. It shows two of the methods from Figure 3.4.

```
interface SetADT
{
public void add(Object element);
public boolean contains(Object target);
//Other methods not shown
}
```

We can put the reserved word abstract in front of an abstract method, though in interfaces we usually do not. Methods in interfaces have public visibility by default. We will later implement this interface in order to provide functionality for these methods.

Listing 3.1 defines a Java interface for a set collection in full. We follow the collection name with the abbreviation ADT (for abstract data type). Thus, `SetADT.java` contains the interface for a set collection. It is defined as part of the jss2 package, which contains all of the collection classes and interfaces presented in this book.

Note that in some methods, the return type is given as `SetADT`. This indicates that the method returns a set collection. Because we use the interface name as the return type, the interface doesn't commit the method to the use of any particular class that implements a set. This is important for the definition of the interface, which is deliberately not tied to a particular implementation. This same argument can be made about the methods that accept a set collection as a parameter.

> **Key Concept**
>
> Because we use the interface name as a return type, the interface doesn't commit the method to the use of any particular class that implements a set.

Listing 3.1

```java
//***********************************************************************
//   SetADT.java        Authors: Lewis/Sudol
//
//   Defines the interface to a set collection.
//***********************************************************************

package jss2;

import java.util.Iterator;

public interface SetADT
{
   //  Adds one element to this set
   public void add (Object element);

   //  Removes and returns a random element from this set
   public Object removeRandom ();

   //  Removes and returns the specified element from this set
   public Object remove (Object element);

   //  Returns the union of this set and the parameter
   public BagADT union (SetADT set);

   //  Returns true if this set contains the parameter
   public boolean contains (Object target);

   //  Returns true if this set and the parameter contain exactly
   //  the same elements
   public boolean equals (SetADT bag);
```

Listing 3.1   continued

```
    //  Returns true if this set contains no elements
    public boolean isEmpty();

    //  Returns the number of elements in this set
    public int size();

    //  Returns an iterator for the elements in this set
    public Iterator iterator();

    //  Returns a string representation of this set
    public String toString();
}
```

Each time we introduce an interface, a class, or a system in this text, we will accompany that description with the UML description of that interface, class, or system. This should help you become accustomed to reading UML descriptions and creating them for other classes and systems. Figure 3.5 illustrates the UML description of the SetADT interface. Note that UML provides flexibility in describing the methods associated with a class or interface. In this case we have identified each of the methods as public (+), but we have not listed the parameters for each.

Iterators

An *iterator* is an object that allows the user to get and use each element in a collection in turn (called *iterating over*). Most collections give us one or more ways

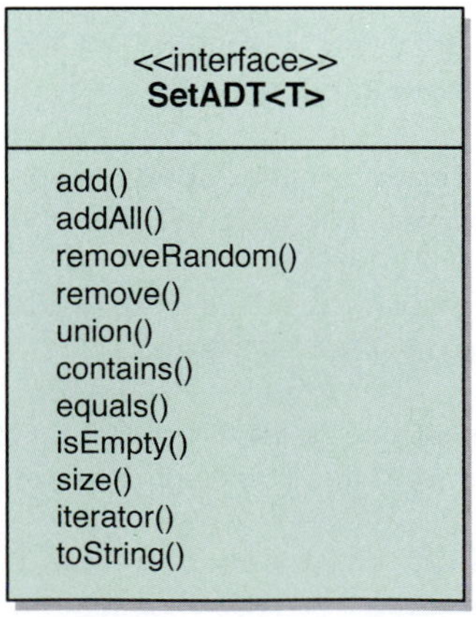

```
          <<interface>>
          SetADT<T>

       add()
       addAll()
       removeRandom()
       remove()
       union()
       contains()
       equals()
       isEmpty()
       size()
       iterator()
       toString()
```

FIGURE 3.5   UML description of the SetADT interface

to iterate over their elements. In the case of the `SetADT` interface, we define a method called `iterator` that returns an `Iterator` object.

The `Iterator` interface is defined in the Java standard class library. The two main abstract methods defined in the `Iterator` interface are

> `hasNext`, which returns true if there are more elements in the iteration

> `next`, which returns the next element in the iteration

The `iterator` method of the `SetADT` interface returns an object that implements this interface. The user can then interact with that object, using the `hasNext` and `next` methods, to get the elements in the set.

Note that it doesn't matter in what order an `Iterator` object delivers the elements from the collection. In a set, there is no particular order to the elements. In other cases, an iterator may follow an order that makes sense for that collection.

Now let's consider what happens if the collection is changed while the iterator is in use. Most of the collections in the Java Collections API are *fail-fast*. This means that they will, or should, throw an exception if the collection is changed while the iterator is in use. However, this cannot be guaranteed. Throughout this book, we will illustrate some of the ways an iterator can be built. These include creating iterators that allow changes made during an iteration to show in the iteration, and iterators that show only a "snapshot," not ongoing changes.

Exceptions

As we discussed in Chapter 1, how exceptions are used is important to the definition of a software system. Exceptions could be thrown in many situations in a collection. Usually it's best to throw exceptions whenever an invalid operation is attempted. For example, in the case of a set, we will throw an exception whenever the user tries to remove an element from an empty set. The user could check the situation beforehand to avoid the exception:

```
if (! theSet.isEmpty())
    element = theSet.removeRandom();
```

Or the user can use a `try-catch` statement to handle the situation when it does occur:

```
try {
    element = theSet.removeRandom()
}
catch (EmptySetException exception)
{
    System.out.println ("No elements available.");
}
```

As we explore implementation techniques for a collection, we will also discuss exceptions.

3.3   USING A SET: BINGO

We can use a bingo game to demonstrate the use of a set collection. In bingo, wooden number balls are drawn from a wire cage at random. Usually there are 75 balls, numbered 1 to 75 with no duplicates. Players each get a card with the letters B, I, N, G, O across the top and a column of numbers underneath each letter. The numbers from 1 to 15 are associated with the letter B, 16 to 30 with the letter I, 31 to 45 with the letter N, 46 to 60 with the letter G, and 61 to 75 with the letter O. The person managing the game (the "caller") draws a number randomly, and then announces the letter and the number. The caller then sets aside that number so that it cannot be used again in that game. All of the players then mark any squares on their card that match the letter and number called. Once any player has five squares in a row marked (vertically, horizontally, or diagonally), he or she yells BINGO! and claims the prize. Figure 3.6 shows a sample bingo card. Because no number is repeated in the game, a set models the situation perfectly.

A set is perfect for helping the caller select numbers randomly. All we need to do is create an object for each of the numbers and place them in a set. Then, each time the caller needs to select a number, we would call the removeRandom method. Listing 3.2 shows the BingoBall class needed to represent each possible selection. The program in Listing 3.3 adds the 75 bingo balls to the set and selects some of them randomly to illustrate the task.

Figure 3.7 shows the relationship between the Bingo and BingoBall classes illustrated in UML.

B	I	N	G	O
9	25	34	48	69
15	19	31	59	74
2	28	FREE	52	62
7	16	41	58	70
4	20	38	47	64

FIGURE 3.6 A bingo card

Listing 3.2

```java
//********************************************************************
//  BingoBall.java        Authors: Lewis/Chase
//
//  Represents a ball used in a BINGO game.
//********************************************************************

public class BingoBall
{
   private char letter;
   private int number;

   //------------------------------------------------------------
   //  Sets up this BINGO ball with the specified number and the
   //  appropriate letter.
   //------------------------------------------------------------
   public BingoBall (int num)
   {
      number = num;

      if (num <= 15)
         letter = 'B';
      else
         if (num <= 30)
            letter = 'I';
         else
            if (num <= 45)
               letter = 'N';
            else
               if (num <= 60)
                  letter = 'G';
               else
                  letter = 'O';
   }

   //------------------------------------------------------------
   //  Returns a string representation of this BINGO ball.
   //------------------------------------------------------------
   public String toString ()
   {
      return (letter + " " + number);
   }
}
```

Listing 3.3

```
//*****************************************************************
//  Bingo.java          Authors: Lewis/Chase
//
//  Demonstrates the use of a set collection.
//*****************************************************************

import jss2.ArraySet;

public class Bingo
{
   //----------------------------------------------------------------
   //  Creates all 75 bingo balls and stores them in a set. Then
   //  pulls several balls from the set at random and prints them.
   //----------------------------------------------------------------
   public static void main (String[] args)
   {
      final int NUM_BALLS = 75, NUM_PULLS = 10;

      ArraySet bingoSet = new ArraySet();
      BingoBall ball;

      for (int num = 1; num <= NUM_BALLS; num++)
      {
         ball = new BingoBall (num);
         bingoSet.add (ball);
      }

      System.out.println ("Size: " + bingoSet.size());
      System.out.println ();

      for (int num = 1; num <= NUM_PULLS; num++)
      {
         ball = (BingoBall) bingoSet.removeRandom();
         System.out.println (ball);
      }
   }
}
```

FIGURE 3.7 UML description of the `Bingo` and `BingoBall` classes

IMPLEMENTING A SET: WITH ARRAYS

So far we've described the basic idea of a set collection and the operations that allow the user to interact with it. In software engineering terms, we would say that we have done the analysis and perhaps the high-level design for a set collection. We've also used a set, without knowing the details, to solve a problem (bingo number selection). Now let's turn our attention to those details.

There are several ways to implement a class that represents a set. In this section we look at an implementation strategy that uses an array to store the objects in the set. In the next chapter we examine a second technique for implementing a set.

As we explore this implementation, we must recall several key characteristics of Java arrays. The elements stored in an array are indexed from 0 to n – 1, where n is the total number of cells in the array. Remember that an array is an object, which is instantiated separately from the objects it holds. And when we talk about an array of objects, we are actually talking about an array of references to objects, as pictured in Figure 3.8.

Keep in mind the separation between the collection and the underlying data structure used to implement it. Our goal is to design an implementation that provides the functionality of every operation defined in the set abstract data type. In this case, as we discussed earlier, we happen to be using an array (a linear data structure) to represent a set (a nonlinear collection). The array is just a convenient way to store the objects. The fact that an array stores objects in a particular order doesn't matter because, in a set collection, there is no defined order among the elements. Therefore, the order in which objects are held in the array won't matter for our solution.

> **Key Concept**
>
> Implementing collection operations should not change the way users interact with the collection.

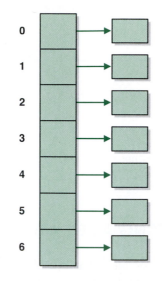

FIGURE 3.8 An array of object references

Managing Capacity

When an array object is created, it is given a number of cells into which elements can be stored. For example, the following instantiation creates an array that can store 500 elements, indexed from 0 to 499:

```
Object[] collection = Object[500];
```

The number of cells in an array is called its *capacity*. This value is stored in the `length` constant of the array. The capacity of an array cannot be changed once the array has been created.

So what will happen when all the cells of the array are being used to store elements? What happens when the collection becomes "full"? We have three options:

> We could implement operations that add an element and if the data structure is full they throw an exception.

> We could implement the `add` operations to return a status indicator that the user can check to see if the `add` operation was successful.

> We could automatically expand the capacity of the underlying data structure whenever necessary so that it would never become full.

In the first two cases, the user must know that the collection could get full and it is up to the user to deal with it. For these solutions we would provide extra operations that allow the user to check to see if the collection is full and to expand the capacity of the array. The advantage is that the user has more control over the capacity.

However, we want to separate the user interface from the implementation. We don't want the user to have to deal with it—or even know about it, really.

So in this book, we implement fixed data structure solutions by automatically expanding the capacity of the underlying data structure. Sometimes we explore other options as programming projects.

The ArraySet Class

In the Java Collections API framework, class names tell us about the underlying data structure and the collection. We follow the same naming rule in this book. Thus, we define a class called `ArraySet` that represents an array-based implementation of a set collection. We present pieces of the `ArraySet` class throughout this section.

> **Key Concept**
>
> In the Java Collections API and throughout this text, class names tell us about the data structure and the collection.

The `ArraySet` class implements the `SetADT` interface we discussed earlier in this chapter. A class *implements* an interface by providing method implementations for each of the abstract methods in the interface. A class that implements an interface uses the reserved word `implements`, followed by the interface name in the class header. To implement a particular interface, a class must provide a definition for all methods in the interface. The compiler will produce errors if any of the methods in the interface are not given a definition in the class.

> **Key Concept**
>
> A class implements an interface, which in turn defines a set of methods used to interact with objects of that class.

The key instance data for the `ArraySet` class includes the array, which holds the contents of the set and the integer variable `count`, which keeps track of the number of elements in the collection. We also define a `Random` object to draw a random element from the set, and a constant to define a default capacity. Another constant, called `NOT_FOUND`, is also created to help with searches. The `ArraySet` instance data is declared as follows:

```
private static Random rand = new Random();

private final int DEFAULT_CAPACITY = 100;
private final int NOT_FOUND = -1;

private int count;
private Object[] contents;
```

Notice that the `Random` object is declared as a static variable and is instantiated in its declaration (rather than in a constructor). Because it is static, the `Random` object is shared among all instances of the `ArraySet` class. This strategy means we don't have to create two sets that have random-number generators that start with the same seed value.

The value of the variable count comes from two related pieces of information. First, the count value is the number of elements currently stored in the set collection. Second, because Java array indexes start at zero, the count value also tells us the next open slot into which a new element can be stored in the array.

Right now, the elements contained in our set are gathered at one end of the array. This makes some operations simpler, though it does mean if we remove an element we will have to "fill in the gaps." Figure 3.9 shows an array used to store the elements of a set.

The following constructor is defined for the ArraySet class to set up an empty set. The value of count is set to zero and the array is instantiated. This constructor uses a default value for the initial capacity of the contents array.

```
//-------------------------------------------------------------------
//  Creates an empty set using the default capacity.
//-------------------------------------------------------------------
public ArraySet()
{
    count = 0;
    contents = new Object[DEFAULT_CAPACITY];
}
```

We can also define a second constructor that accepts a single value for the initial capacity of the contents array. In some situations, the user may know about how many elements will be stored in a set, and can specify that value from the beginning. This overloaded constructor can be defined as follows:

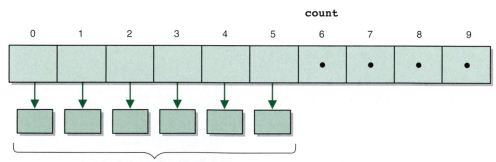

FIGURE 3.9 An array implementation of a set

```
//------------------------------------------------------------
//  Creates an empty set using the specified capacity.
//------------------------------------------------------------
public ArraySet (int initialCapacity)
{
    count = 0;
    contents = new Object[initialCapacity];
}
```

As we design each operation, we must consider any situations that would require special processing. For example, if the collection is empty, an element cannot be removed from it. Likewise, we cannot add an element to a collection that is full.

The size and isEmpty Operations

You can find the operations size and isEmpty in almost any collection. In the ArraySet class, the count variable is the number of elements in the set, so we can use it to help us with size and isEmpty.

The size method simply returns the value of the count variable:

```
//------------------------------------------------------------
//  Returns the number of elements currently in this set.
//------------------------------------------------------------
public int size()
{
    return count;
}
```

The isEmpty method returns true if the value of count is zero:

```
//------------------------------------------------------------
//  Returns true if this set is empty and false otherwise.
//------------------------------------------------------------
public boolean isEmpty()
{
    return (count == 0);
}
```

The `ArraySet` implementation relies on the value of `count` in several situations. Therefore, all operations that change the state of the set collection must carefully make sure the `count` value is up to date.

The add Operation

The purpose of the `add` method is to add an element to the set collection. For our array, that means storing the element in an empty slot in the array. The instance variable `count` tells us which is the next empty space in the array, so we can simply store the new element at that location.

However, the `add` operation must also take into account what happens when the array is full. As we discussed earlier in this chapter, our solution is to automatically expand the capacity of the array.

The following method implements the `add` operation for the `ArraySet` class:

```
//-----------------------------------------------------------------
//  Adds the specified element to the set, expanding the capacity
//  of the set array if necessary. Throws DuplicateElementException
//  if the object already exists in the set.
//-----------------------------------------------------------------
public void add (Object element) throws DuplicateElementException
{
   if (contains(element))
      throw new DuplicateElementException

   if (size() == contents.length)
      expandCapacity();

   contents[count] = element;
   count++;
}
```

The `add` method uses the `size` method to find out how many elements are already in the collection. If this value equals the total number of cells in the array (the value of the `length` constant), then the `expandCapacity` method is called. Whether the capacity is expanded or not, the element is then stored in the array and the number of elements in the set collection is increased by one. That way, after the `add` method finishes, the value of the `count` variable continues to represent both the number of elements in the set and the next open slot in the array.

Instead of calling the `size` method, the `add` method could have looked at the value of the `count` variable to see if the capacity of the array needed to be expanded. The value of `count` is, after all, exactly what the `size` method returns. However, if we have a choice between using a variable or a method, we are better off using the method. If the design is later changed to determine the size of the set in a different way, the `add` method would still work.

The `add` method must also be able to tell whether an item already exists in the set. The `add` method uses the already implemented `contains` method and throws a `DuplicateElement` exception if a duplicate element is found.

The `expandCapacity` method increases the size of the array by creating a second array that is twice the size of the one currently storing the contents of the set. Then it copies all of the current references into the new array and resets the `contents` instance variable to refer to the larger array. The `expandCapacity` method is implemented as follows:

```
//----------------------------------------------------------------
//  Creates a new array to store the contents of the set with
//  twice the capacity of the old one.
//----------------------------------------------------------------
private void expandCapacity()
{
    Object[] larger = new Object[contents.length*2];

    for (int index=0; index < contents.length; index++)
        larger[index] = contents[index];

    contents = larger;
}
```

Note that the `expandCapacity` method is declared with private visibility. It is designed as a support method, not as a service for the user.

Also note that the `expandCapacity` method doubles the size of the `contents` array. It could have tripled the size, or simply added ten more cells, or even just one. The amount of the increase determines how soon we'll have to increase the size again. We don't want to have to call the `expandCapacity` method too often, because it copies the entire contents of the collection from one array to another. We also don't want to have too much unused space in the array. There is some mathematical analysis that could be done to determine the best size increase, but at this point we will simply make reasonable choices.

The addAll Operation

The purpose of the `addAll` method is to add all of the objects from one set into the set collection. For our array, this means that we can use our `iterator` method to step through the contents of one set and our `add` method to add those elements to the current set. One advantage of using the `add` method in this way is that the `add` method already checks capacity and expands the array if necessary, as well as checks for duplicates.

The following method implements the `addAll` operation for the `ArraySet` class:

```
//------------------------------------------------------------------
//  Adds the contents of the parameter to this set.
//------------------------------------------------------------------
public void addAll (SetADT set)
{
   Iterator scan = set.iterator();

   while (scan.hasNext())
      add (scan.next());
}
```

The `removeRandom` Operation

The `removeRandom` operation chooses an element from the collection at random, removes that element from the collection, and returns it to the calling method. This operation relies on the static `Random` object called `rand`, which is defined as instance data.

The only special case for this operation is when we try to remove an element from an empty set. If the set collection is empty, `removeRandom` throws an `EmptySetException`.

The `removeRandom` method of the `ArraySet` class is written as follows:

```
//------------------------------------------------------------------
//  Removes a random element from the set and returns it. Throws
//  an EmptySetException if the set is empty.
//------------------------------------------------------------------
public Object removeRandom() throws EmptySetException
{
   if (isEmpty())
      throw new EmptySetException();

   int choice = rand.nextInt(count);

   Object result = contents[choice];

   contents[choice] = contents[count-1];   // fill the gap
   contents[count-1] = null;
   count--;

   return result;
}
```

The `nextInt` method of the `Random` class picks a pseudorandom value in the range from `0` to `count-1`. This range represents the indices (locations) of all elements currently stored in the array. Once the random element is chosen, it is stored in the local variable called `result`, which is returned to the calling method when this method is complete.

Remember that all elements in our set are stored at one end of the `contents` array. When this method removes one of the elements, we must "fill the gap" in some way. We could use a loop to shift all of the elements down one, but because the elements are stored in no particular order, we can simply take the last element in the list (at index `count-1`) and put it in the cell of the removed element—we don't have to do any looping.

The remove Operation

The `remove` operation removes one element from the set and returns it. This method will throw an `EmptySetException` if the set is empty and a `NoSuchElementException` if the element is not in the set.

With our array, the `remove` operation simply searches the array for the element, removes it, and replaces it with the element stored at `count-1`, or the last element stored in the array. Because the elements of a set are not stored in any particular order, there is no need to shift more than the one element. We then subtract 1 from the count.

```
//-----------------------------------------------------------------
//   Removes one occurrence of the specified element from the set
//   and returns it. Throws an EmptySetException if the set is
//   empty and a NoSuchElementException if the target is not in
//   the set.
//-----------------------------------------------------------------
public Object remove (Object target) throws EmptySetException,
                                    NoSuchElementException
{
    int search = NOT_FOUND;

    if (isEmpty())
        throw new EmptySetException();

    for (int index=0; index < count && search == NOT_FOUND; index++)
        if (contents[index].equals(target))
            search = index;

    if (search == NOT_FOUND)
        throw new NoSuchElementException();
```

```
      Object result = contents[search];

      contents[search] = contents[count-1];
      contents[count-1] = null;
      count--;

      return result;
   }
```

The union Operation

The union operation returns a new set that is the combination, or *union* of this set and the parameter; that is, a new set that contains all of the elements from both sets. Again, we can use our existing operations. We use our constructor to create a new set and then step through our array and use the add method to add each element to the new set. Next we create an iterator for the set passed as a parameter, step through each element of that set, and add each of them to the new set. Since the elements aren't in any particular order, it does not matter which set's contents we add first. Again, we use the add method because it checks for duplicate items.

There are several interesting designs we could choose from here. First, since the method is returning a new set that is the combination of this set and another set, the method could simply be a static method accepting two sets as input. Or we could use the addAll method (i.e., both.addAll(this) followed by both.addAll(set)). However, we have chosen to use a for loop and an iterator to demonstrate an important idea. Because the process occurs "inside" one set, we can use its private instance data and a for loop to traverse the array. However, for the set passed as a parameter, we use an iterator to access its elements.

```
//------------------------------------------------------------------
//  Returns a new set that is the union of this set and the
//  parameter.
//------------------------------------------------------------------
public SetADT union (SetADT set)
{
   ArraySet both = new ArraySet();
```

```
        for (int index = 0; index < count; index++)
            both.add (contents[index]);

        Iterator scan = set.iterator();
        while (scan.hasNext())
            both.add (scan.next());

        return both;
    }
```

The contains Operation

The contains operation returns true if this set contains the element we are looking for. Because we are using an array, this operation is a simple search of an array to locate a particular element.

```
    //-----------------------------------------------------------------
    //  Returns true if this set contains the specified target
    //  element.
    //-----------------------------------------------------------------
    public boolean contains (Object target)
    {
        int search = NOT_FOUND;

        for (int index=0; index < count && search == NOT_FOUND; index++)
            if (contents[index].equals(target))
                search = index;

        return (search != NOT_FOUND);
    }
```

The equals Operation

The equals operation will return true if the current set contains exactly the same elements as the set passed as a parameter. If the two sets are different sizes, then there is no reason to continue the comparison. However, if the two sets are the same size, we create a deep copy of each set. We then use an iterator to step through the elements of the set passed as a parameter and use the contains method to confirm that each of those elements is also in the current set. As we find elements in both sets, we remove them from the copies. If both of the copies are empty at the end of the process, then the sets are equal. Notice that we iterate over the original set passed as a parameter while removing matching elements from the copies. This avoids any problems with changing a set while using the associated iterator.

```
//-----------------------------------------------------------------
//  Returns true if this set contains exactly the same elements
//  as the parameter.
//-----------------------------------------------------------------
public boolean equals (SetADT set)
{
   boolean result = false;
   ArraySet temp1 = new ArraySet();
   ArraySet temp2 = new ArraySet();
   Object obj;

   if (size() == set.size())
   {
      temp1.addAll(this);
      temp2.addAll(set);

      Iterator scan = set.iterator();

      while (scan.hasNext())
      {
         obj = scan.next();
         if (temp1.contains(obj))
         {
            temp1.remove(obj);
            temp2.remove(obj);
         }

      }

      result = (temp1.isEmpty() && temp2.isEmpty());
   }

   return result;
}
```

The iterator Operation

So far we have emphasized reusing code whenever possible. The iterator operation is an excellent example of this idea. We could, for example, create an iterator method just for the array implementation of a set. Instead we have created a general ArrayIterator class that will work with any array-based implementation of any collection. The iterator method for the array implementation of a set creates an instance of the ArrayIterator class. Listing 3.4 shows the ArrayIterator class.

```
//-----------------------------------------------------------------
//   Returns an iterator for the elements currently in this set.
//-----------------------------------------------------------------
public Iterator iterator()
{
    return new ArrayIterator (contents, count);
}
```

The `toString` Operation

The `toString` operation simply returns a string made up of the letter and number of each ball in the set as provided by the `toString` operation of the `BingoBall` class.

```
//-----------------------------------------------------------------
//   Returns a string representation of this set.
//-----------------------------------------------------------------
public String toString()
{
    String result = "";

    for (int index=0; index < count; index++)
        result = result + contents[index].toString() + "\n";

    return result;
}
```

Listing 3.4

```
//****************************************************************
//   ArrayIterator.java        Authors: Lewis/Chase
//
//   Represents an iterator over the elements of an array.
//****************************************************************

package jss2;

import java.util.*;

public class ArrayIterator implements Iterator
```

Listing 3.4   **continued**

```java
{
   private int count;      // the number of elements in the collection
   private int current;    // the current position in the iteration
   private Object[] items;

   //-----------------------------------------------------------------
   //  Sets up this iterator using the specified items.
   //-----------------------------------------------------------------
   public ArrayIterator (Object[] collection, int size)
   {
      items = collection;
      count = size;
      current = 0;
   }

   //-----------------------------------------------------------------
   //  Returns true if this iterator has at least one more element
   //  to deliver in the iteration.
   //-----------------------------------------------------------------
   public boolean hasNext()
   {
      return (current < count);
   }

   //-----------------------------------------------------------------
   //  Returns the next element in the iteration. If there are no
   //  more elements in this iteration, a NoSuchElementException is
   //  thrown.
   //-----------------------------------------------------------------
   public Object next()
   {
      if (! hasNext())
         throw new NoSuchElementException();

      current++;
      return items[current - 1];
   }

   //-----------------------------------------------------------------
   //  The remove operation is not supported in this collection.
   //-----------------------------------------------------------------
   public void remove() throws UnsupportedOperationException
   {
      throw new UnsupportedOperationException();
   }
}
```

UML Description

Now that we have defined our classes, we can draw a UML diagram of the entire hierarchy, as illustrated in Figure 3.10.

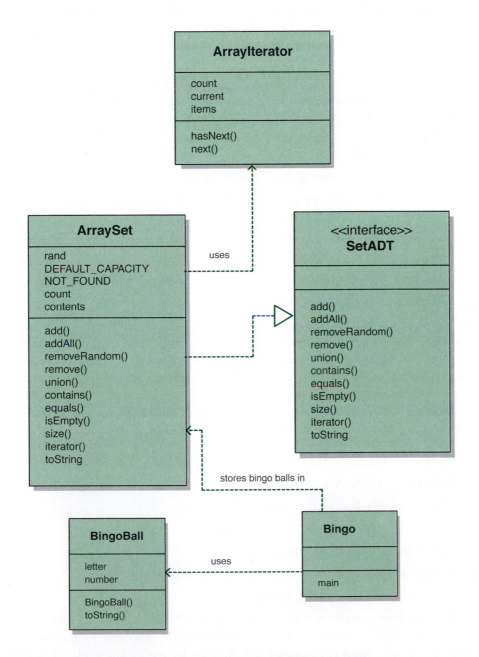

FIGURE 3.10 UML description of the bingo system

3.5   ANALYSIS OF THE ARRAY IMPLEMENTATION OF A SET

The analysis of the space complexity of the array implementation of a set is like the array implementations we will see for other collections. Array implementations are very effecient with each element, only allowing enough space per element for the object reference variable. However, array implementations usually allow space for more elements than are stored in the array. If managed properly, this additional space is not a problem.

The analysis of the time complexity of the operations for the array implementation of a set is simple. Let's look at each operation separately.

Analysis of add

The add operation consists of the following steps:

> Check to make sure the item does not already exist in the collection and throw a DuplicateElementException if it does.
> Check to make sure that the array is not full, expanding capacity if it is.
> Set the pointer in position count of the array to the object being added to the set.
> Increment (increase) the count.

If the array is not full, the check for duplicates is O(n) and the rest of the steps are O(1). Since complexity depends on the largest term, the operation would then be O(n). If the array is full, the expandCapacity method must create a new array, twice as large as the original, and copy all the elements of the set into the new array. This process is also O(n). This happens so seldom that, taken across all instances of add, expanding capacity has almost no effect on analysis. Even if we did consider it, the time needed would still remain O(n).

Analysis of remove

The remove operation consists of the following steps:

> Check to make sure the set is not empty.
> Find the element to be removed.
> Move the last element in the array down to fill the position.
> Decrement (decrease) the count.

The best-case scenario is if the element we want happens to be the first one we check. The worst-case scenario is that the elment is the last one we check, and on average we can expect n/2 comparisons. Because we ignore constants when considering the complexity, the remove operation for the array implementation has time complexity O(n).

Analysis of `removeRandom`

The `removeRandom` operation for the array implementation is like the `remove` method except that we do not have to search for the element to be removed. We simply choose one at random and remove it. Thus the `removeRandom` operation is $O(1)$.

Analysis of `addAll`

The `addAll` operation uses an iterator to step through the contents of a set, adding each element in turn to the set. Because the `add` method is $O(n)$, and the iterator will step through n elements, this operation is also $O(n^2)$.

Analysis of `find` and `contains`

Both the `find` and `contains` methods step through the elements of a set searching for a particular element. Like the discussion of the `remove` method, the best case is 1 comparsion, the worst case is n comparisons, and the expected case is n/2 comparisons. Thus these methods are both $O(n)$.

Analysis of `union`

The `union` operation steps through both the current set and the set passed as a parameter, adding each of their elements, one at a time, to a new set. If the total number of elements between the two sets is n, then this operation is $O(n^2)$. The elements are added one at a time; however, for each add the elements in the set must be searched for duplicates. Another way to look at this is to assume that there are n elements in the current set and m elements in the set passed as a parameter. Then the operation would be $O(mn)$.

Analysis of `equals`

The `equals` method uses three iterators, one each as copies of the sets are made using `addAll` (remember `addAll` has a complexity of $O(n^2)$), and then one to step through checking the contents of the copies. Assuming that each of the sets has roughly n elements, then the time complexity would be roughly $n^2 + 2 * n$ or $O(n^2)$.

3.6   INTERFACES AND POLYMORPHISM

As we've seen, a class name is used to declare the type of an object reference variable. An interface name can be used the same way. An interface reference variable can be used to refer to any object of any class that implements that interface.

Suppose we declare an interface called `Speaker` as follows:

```
public interface Speaker
{
    public void speak();
    public void announce (String str);
}
```

Now we can use the interface name, `Speaker`, to declare an object reference variable:

```
Speaker current;
```

And we can use the reference variable `current` to refer to any object of any class that implements the `Speaker` interface. For example, if we define a class called `Philosopher` that implements the `Speaker` interface, we could assign a `Philosopher` object to a `Speaker` reference:

```
current = new Philosopher();
```

This works because a `Philosopher` is, in fact, a `Speaker`.

This kind of flexibility lets us create polymorphic references. As we saw earlier, using inheritance, we can create a polymorphic reference that can refer to any one of a set of objects that are related to each other by inheritance. We can create similar polymorphic references with inheritance, except that the objects being referenced are related by implementing the same interface.

For example, if we create a class called `Dog` that also implements the `Speaker` interface, it too could be assigned to a `Speaker` reference variable. The same reference, in fact, could refer to a `Philosopher` object, and then later refer to a `Dog` object:

```
Speaker guest;
guest = new Philosopher();
guest.speak();
guest = new Dog();
guest.speak();
```

In this code, the first time the `speak` method is called, it invokes the `speak` method from the `Philosopher` class. The second time it is called, it invokes the `speak` method of the `Dog` class. As with polymorphic references created through inheritance, it is not the type of the reference that determines which method gets invoked, it's the type of the object that the reference points to.

When we are using an interface reference variable, we can invoke only the methods defined in the interface, even if the object it refers to has other methods it can respond to. For example, suppose the `Philosopher` class also defined a public method called `pontificate`. The second line of the following code would cause a compiler error, even though the object can in fact respond to the `pontificate` method:

```
Speaker special = new Philosopher();
special.pontificate();   // generates a compiler error
```

The problem is that the compiler only knows that the object is a `Speaker`, and only that the object can respond to the `speak` and `announce` methods. Because the reference variable `special` could refer to a `Dog` object (which cannot pontificate), the compiler does not allow the reference. If we know ahead of time that an invocation is valid, we can cast the object into the appropriate reference so that the compiler will accept it:

```
((Philosopher) special).pontificate();
```

Like polymorphic references based in inheritance, an interface name can be used as the type of a method parameter. In such situations, any object of any class that implements the interface can be passed into the method. For example, the following method takes a `Speaker` object as a parameter. Now, both a `Dog` object and a `Philosopher` object can be passed into it in separate invocations.

```
public void sayIt (Speaker current)
{
    current.speak();
}
```

Summary of Key Concepts

> A collection is an object that gathers and organizes other objects.

> Elements in a collection are usually organized by the order they were added to the collection or by some relationship among the elements.

> A collection is an abstraction where the details of the implementation are hidden.

> Encapsulation: The internal workings of an object are inaccessible to other objects in the system.

> A data structure is made up of programming constructs used to implement a collection.

> A set is a nonlinear collection in which there is no organization to the elements. No object may be added to the set twice.

> A Java interface defines a set of abstract methods and is useful in separating the concept of an abstract data type from its implementation.

> Because it uses the interface name as a return type, the interface doesn't tie the method to any particular class.

> An iterator is an object that allows the user to find the elements in a collection.

> Implementing the collection operations should not change the way users interact with the collection.

> How we handle exceptional conditions determines whether the collection or the user of the collection controls the behavior.

> In the Java Collections API and throughout this text, class names tell us about the data structure and the collection.

> A class implements an interface, which in turn defines a set of methods used to interact with objects of that class.

> An interface name can be used to declare an object reference variable. An interface reference can refer to any object of any class that implements the interface.

Self-Review Questions

3.1   What is a collection?

3.2   What is a data type?

3.3   What is an abstract data type?

3.4   What is a data structure?

3.5   What is abstraction and what advantage does it provide?

3.6   What is a set?

3.7   Why is a class an excellent representation of an abstract data type?

3.8   What is an iterator and why is it useful for ADTs?

3.9   Why should we develop collections if they are provided in the Java Collections API?

3.10   How should exceptional conditions be handled in ADTs?

3.11   What would the time complexity be for the `size` operation if there were no `count` variable?

3.12   What would the time complexity be for the `add` operation if there were no `count` variable?

Exercises

3.1   Compare and contrast data types, abstract data types, and data structures.

3.2   List the collections in the Java Collections API and mark the ones that are covered in this text.

3.3   Define the concept of abstraction and explain why it is important in software development.

3.4   Define the concept of a set. List additional operations that might be considered for a set.

3.5   List each occurrence of one method in the `ArraySet` class calling on another method from the same class. Why is this good programming practice?

3.6   Write an algorithm for the `add` method that would place each new element in position 0 of the array. What would the time complexity be for this algorithm?

3.7   A bag is a very similar construct to a set except that there are duplicates in a bag. What changes would have to be made to our methods to create an implementation of a bag?

Programming Projects

3.1   Change the `ArraySet` class so that it lets the user control the set's capacity. Get rid of the automatic expansion of the array. Your new class should throw a `FullSetException` when an element is added to a full set. Add a method called `isFull` that returns true if the set is full. And add a method that the user can call to expand the capacity by the number of cells the user chooses.

3.2   An additional operation that might be implemented for a set is `difference`. This operation would take a set as a parameter and subtract the contents of that set from the current set if they exist in the current set. The result would be returned in a new set. Implement this operation. Be careful to consider possible exceptional situations.

3.3   Another operation that might be implemented for a set is `intersection`. This operation would take a set as a parameter and would return a set containing those elements that exist in both sets.

3.4   A bag is a very similar construct to a set except that there are duplicates in a bag. Implement a bag collection by creating both a `BagADT` interface and an `ArrayBag` class. Include the additional operations described in the earlier projects.

3.5   Create a simple application with a button labeled Add that, when pressed, will take a string from a text field and add it to a set, and another button labeled Remove Random that, when pressed, will remove a random element from the set. After processing in either case, the contents of a text area should be set to the set's `toString` method to display the contents of the set.

Answers to Self-Review Questions

3.1   A collection is an object that gathers and organizes other objects.

3.2   A data type is a set of values and operations on those values, defined within a programming language.

3.3   An abstract data type is a data type that is not defined in the programming language and must be defined by the programmer.

3.4   A data structure is the set of objects necessary to implement an abstract data type.

3.5   Abstraction is the idea of hiding the implementation of operations and data storage in order to simplify the use of a collection.

3.6   A set is a collection of elements in no particular order, with no duplicates.

3.7   Classes naturally provide abstraction, because only the methods that provide services to other classes have public visibility.

3.8   An iterator is an object that gives us a way of stepping through way elements of a collection one at a time.

3.9   The Java Collections API provides implementations of many ADTs but not all of them. Developers may want to create their own definitions to customize the behavior of the ADT.

3.10 The question should always be asked, "Is this a condition that should be handled automatically or by the user?" An excellent example of this dilemma is the issue of automatically resizing the array in the array-based implementation of a set.

3.11 Without a `count` variable, the most likely solution would be to traverse the array using a `while` loop, counting as you go, until you get to the first null element of the array. Thus, this operation would be O(n).

3.12 Without a `count` variable, the most likely solution would be to traverse the array using a `while` loop until you get to the first null element of the array. The new element would then be added into this position. Thus, this operation would be O(n).

Linked Structures 4

CHAPTER OBJECTIVES

> Describe the use of references to create linked structures

> Compare linked structures to array-based structures

> Learn how to manage a linked list

> Discuss the need for a separate node object to form linked structures

> Implement a set collection using a linked list

This chapter explores how we can create data structures by using references to create links between objects. Linked structures are basic to software development, especially the design and implementation of collections. Using linked structures has advantages and disadvantages over using arrays.

4.1   REFERENCES AS LINKS

In Chapter 3 we discussed collections and explored one collection in particular: a set. We defined the operations on a set collection and designed an implementation using an array-based data structure. In this chapter we explore a new approach to designing a data structure.

A *linked structure* is a data structure that uses object reference variables to create links between objects. Linked structures are the best alternative to array-based structures. After discussing linked structures, we will define a new implementation of a set collection that uses the structure.

Recall that an object reference variable holds the address of an object, telling us where the object is stored in memory. The following declaration creates a variable called `obj` that is only large enough to hold the numeric address of an object:

```
Object obj;
```

This line of code creates a small chunk of memory which will hold a reference to an object, although right now it holds a null value (see Figure 4.1).

Usually the address that an object reference variable holds is unimportant. So, instead of showing addresses, we usually show a reference variable as a name that "points to" an object, as shown in Figure 4.2. A reference variable, used in this context, is sometimes called a *pointer*.

Consider the situation in which a class defines as instance data a reference to another object of the same class. For example, suppose we have a class named `Person` that contains a person's name, address, and other relevant information. Now suppose that in addition to this data, the `Person` class also contains a reference variable to another `Person` object:

obj

FIGURE 4.1   No caption provided

FIGURE 4.2   An object reference variable pointing to an object, after the `obj` variable has been instantiated to a new object, or assigned to an already existing one

```java
public class Person
{
    private String name;
    private String address;

    private Person next;   // a link to another Person object

    //  whatever else
}
```

Using only this class, we can create a linked structure. One `Person` object contains a link to a second `Person` object. This second object also contains a reference to a `Person`, which contains another, and so on. This type of object is sometimes called *self-referential* because it references itself.

This is the basis of a *linked list*: one object referring to the next, which refers to the next, and so on. A linked list is shown in Figure 4.3. Often the objects in a linked list are called the *nodes* of the list.

We need a special reference variable to indicate the first node in the list, and the list ends in a node whose `next` reference is `null`.

A linked list is only one kind of linked structure. We could also set up a class that has many references to objects, creating a more complex structure, such as the one depicted in Figure 4.4. The way in which the links are managed decides how the structure is organized.

front

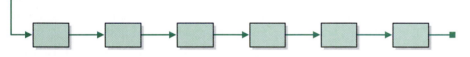

FIGURE 4.3   A linked list

entry

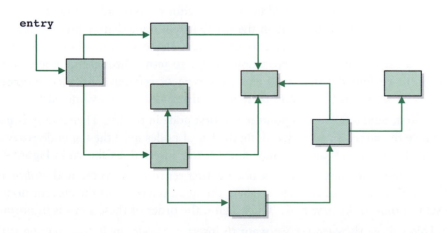

FIGURE 4.4   A complex linked structure

For now, we will focus on linked lists. Many of these techniques apply to more complicated linked structures as well.

An array has a fixed size, but a linked list can be as big as you want, as long as you have enough memory. A linked list is considered to be a *dynamic* structure because its size grows and shrinks to accommodate the number of elements stored. In Java, all objects are created dynamically from an area of memory called the system *heap*, or *free store*.

The next section explores some of the ways we can manage a linked list.

4.2   MANAGING LINKED LISTS

There are a few basic techniques we can use to manage the nodes on a linked list. Nodes are added to a list and they are removed from the list. We must be careful when dealing with the first node in the list so that the reference to the entire list is maintained appropriately.

Inserting Nodes

A node may be inserted into a linked list at any location: at the front of the list, in the middle of the list, or at the end of the list. When we add a node to the front

of the list we must reset the reference to the entire list, as shown in Figure 4.5. First, the `next` reference of the added node is set to point to the current first node in the list. Second, the reference to the front of the list is reset to point to the newly added node.

We would get in trouble if we reversed if these steps. If we reset the `front` reference first, we would lose the only reference to the existing list and it could not be retrieved.

Inserting a node into the middle of a list requires some additional processing. First we have to find the node in the list that will immediately precede the new node being inserted. In an array, we can access elements using subscripts, but in a linked list we must use a separate reference to move through the nodes of the list until we find the one we want. This type of reference is called `current`, because it shows us the current node in the list that is being examined.

At first, `current` is set to point to the first node in the list. Then a loop is used to move the `current` reference along the list of nodes until the the node we want is found. Once it is found, the new node can be inserted, as shown in Figure 4.6.

The `next` reference of the new node is first set to point to the node *following* the one to which `current` refers. Then, the `next` reference of the current node is reset to point to the new node. Once again, the order of these steps is important.

This will work wherever we want to insert the node, including making it the new second node in the list or making it the last node in the list. If the new node

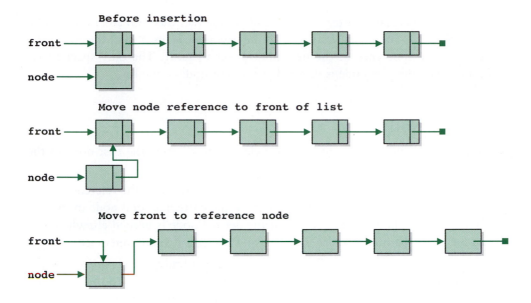

FIGURE 4.5.1 A good insertion

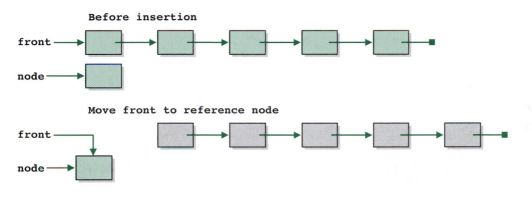

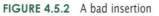

FIGURE 4.5.2 A bad insertion

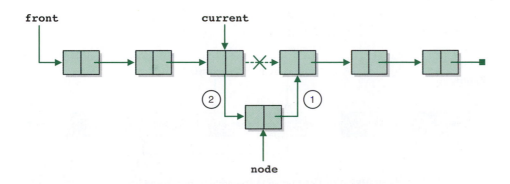

FIGURE 4.6 Inserting a node in the middle of a linked list

is inserted immediately after the first node in the list, then `current` and `front` will still refer to the same (first) node. If the new node is inserted at the end of the list, the `next` reference of the new node is set to `null`. The only special case occurs when the new node is inserted as the first node in the list.

Deleting Nodes

Any node in the list can be deleted, but deleting the first node in the list is a special case.

To delete the first node in a linked list, we reset the reference to the front of the list so that it points to the current second node in the list. This process is shown in Figure 4.7. If the deleted node is needed elsewhere, we can set up a separate reference to it before we reset the `front` reference.

To delete a node from inside the list, we must first find the node *in front of* the node that is to be deleted. For this we need two references: one to find the node to be deleted and another to keep track of the node immediately preceding that one. Thus, they are often called current and previous, as shown in Figure 4.8.

Once the current and previous nodes have been found, the `next` reference of the previous node is reset to point to the node pointed to by the `next` reference of the current node. The deleted node can then be used as needed.

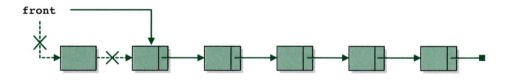

FIGURE 4.7   Deleting the first node in a linked list

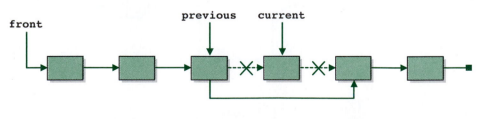

FIGURE 4.8   Deleting an inside node from a linked list

Dummy Nodes

We can work around the special case of inserting or deleting a first node by introducing a *dummy node* at the front of the list. A dummy node doesn't actually represent an element in the list. Using a dummy node means all nodes will be "inside" nodes so we can insert and delete without resetting references. In spite of this, some developers do not like using dummy nodes.

4.3   ELEMENTS WITHOUT LINKS

Before we turn our attention to using a linked list instead of a collection, we need to separate the details of the linked list structure from the elements that the list stores.

Earlier in this chapter we discussed the idea of a `Person` class that contains, among its other data, a link to another `Person` object. The problem is that the self-referential `Person` class must "know" it may become a node in a linked list of `Person` objects. This is impractical, and it violates our goal of separating the implementation details from the parts of the system that use the collection.

> **Key Concept**
>
> Objects that are stored in a collection should not contain any implementation details of the underlying data structure.

The solution is to define a separate node class that links the elements together. A node class is fairly simple, containing only two important references: one to the next node in the linked list and another to the element being stored in the list. This approach is shown in Figure 4.9.

The linked list of nodes can still be managed using the techniques discussed in the previous section. The only new thing is that the elements stored in the list are accessed using a separate reference in the node objects.

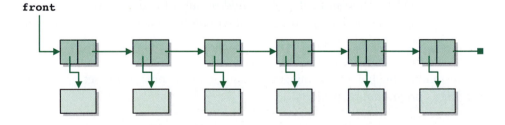

FIGURE 4.9 Using separate node objects to store and link elements

Doubly Linked Lists

Another linked structure is the doubly linked list, shown in Figure 4.10. In a doubly linked list, one reference points to the first node in the list and another points

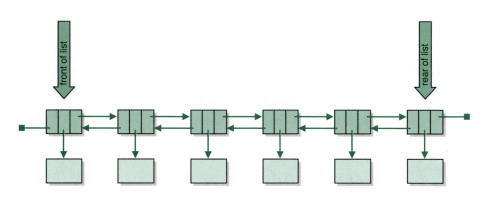

FIGURE 4.10 A doubly linked list

to the last node in the list. Each node in the list stores a reference to the next element and a reference to the previous one. We discuss doubly linked lists in Chapter 10.

4.4 IMPLEMENTING A SET: WITH LINKS

Let's use a linked list to implement a set collection as defined in Chapter 3. Note that we are not changing the way a set works. We are just changing the data structure used to implement it.

> **Key Concept**
>
> Any implementation of a collection can be used to solve a problem as long as it validly implements the appropriate operations.

The purpose of the set, and the solutions it helps us to create, also remain the same. The bingo example from Chapter 3 used the `ArraySet` class, but any valid implementation of a set could be used instead. Once we create the `LinkedSet` class to define an alternative implementation, `LinkedSet` could be substituted into the bingo solution without having to change anything but a class name. That is the beauty of abstraction.

In the following discussion, we discuss the methods that are important to understanding the linked list implementation of a set. Some of the set operations are left as programming projects.

The LinkedSet Class

The `LinkedSet` class implements the `SetADT` interface, just as the `ArraySet` class does. Both provide the operations defined for a set collection.

Because we are using a linked list, we don't have an array for storing the elements of the collection. Instead, we need a single reference to the first node in the list. We will also maintain a count of the number of elements in the list. Finally, we need a `Random` object to support the `removeRandom` operation. The instance data of the `LinkedSet` class is therefore:

```
private static Random rand = new Random();

private int count;  // the current number of elements in the set

private LinearNode contents;
```

The `LinearNode` class serves as the node class, holding a reference to the next `LinearNode` in the list and a reference to the element stored in that node. It also contains methods to set and get these values. The `LinearNode` class is shown in Listing 4.1.

Listing 4.1

```java
//********************************************************************
//  LinearNode.java       Authors: Lewis/Chase
//
//  Represents a node in a linked list.
//********************************************************************

package jss2;

public class LinearNode
{
    private LinearNode next;
    private Object element;

    //-----------------------------------------------------------------
    //  Creates an empty node.
    //-----------------------------------------------------------------
    public LinearNode()
    {
        next = null;
        element = null;
    }

    //-----------------------------------------------------------------
    //  Creates a node storing the specified element.
    //-----------------------------------------------------------------
    public LinearNode (Object elem)
```

Listing 4.1   continued

```
   {
      next = null;
      element = elem;
   }

   //----------------------------------------------------------------
   //  Returns the node that follows this one.
   //----------------------------------------------------------------
   public LinearNode getNext()
   {
      return next;
   }

   //----------------------------------------------------------------
   //  Sets the node that follows this one.
   //----------------------------------------------------------------
   public void setNext (LinearNode node)
   {
      next = node;
   }

   //----------------------------------------------------------------
   //  Returns the element stored in this node.
   //----------------------------------------------------------------
   public Object getElement()
   {
      return element;
   }

   //----------------------------------------------------------------
   //  Sets the element stored in this node.
   //----------------------------------------------------------------
   public void setElement (Object elem)
   {
      element = elem;
   }
}
```

Note that the LinearNode class is not tied to the implementation of a set collection. We can use this class in any linear linked list implementation of a collection. We can also use it for other collections as needed.

Using the LinearNode class and keeping track of how many elements are in the collection creates the implementation strategy shown in Figure 4.11.

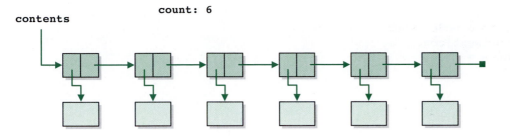

FIGURE 4.11   A linked implementation of a set collection

The constructor of the `LinkedSet` class, shown below, sets the count of elements to zero and the front of the list, represented by the variable `contents`, to `null`. Note that because a linked list does not have to worry about capacity limitations, there is no need to create a second constructor, as we did in the `ArraySet` class.

```
//---------------------------------------------------------------
//   Creates an empty set.
//---------------------------------------------------------------
public LinkedSet()
{
    count = 0;
    contents = null;
}
```

The add Operation

The `add` method incorporates the element passed as a parameter into the collection. Because the elements of a set are not in any order, we can simply add the new element to the front of the list (after checking for duplicates):

```
//---------------------------------------------------------------
//   Adds the specified element to the set.
//   Throws DuplicateElementException
//   if the object already exists in the set.
//---------------------------------------------------------------
public void add (Object element) throws DuplicateElementException
{
    if (contains(element))
        throw new DuplicateElementException
```

```
        LinearNode node = new LinearNode (element);
        node.setNext(contents);
        contents = node;
        count++;
    }
```

After checking to make sure the element is not already in the set, the `add` method creates a new `LinearNode` object, using its constructor to store the element. Then the new node's `next` reference is set to the first node in the list, the reference to the first node is reset to point to the newly created one, and the count is incremented. See Figure 4.5 for an example.

The `removeRandom` Operation

The `removeRandom` method shows how a linked list is sometimes more complicated than an array. In the `ArraySet` class, the `removeRandom` method simply chose an index into the array and returned that element. In this version of `removeRandom`, we must walk down the list, called *traversal*, counting the elements until we get to the one that has been selected for removal:

```
//-----------------------------------------------------------------
//  Removes a random element from the set and returns it. Throws
//  an EmptySetException if the set is empty.
//-----------------------------------------------------------------
public Object removeRandom() throws EmptySetException
{
    LinearNode previous, current;
    Object result = null;

    if (isEmpty())
        throw new EmptySetException();

    int choice = rand.nextInt(count) + 1;

    if (choice == 1)
    {
        result = contents.getElement();
        contents = contents.getNext();
    }
    else
```

```
   {
      previous = contents;
      for (int skip=2; skip < choice; skip++)
         previous = previous.getNext();
      current = previous.getNext();
      result = current.getElement();
      previous.setNext(current.getNext());
   }

   count--;

   return result;
}
```

Like the `ArraySet` version, this method throws an `EmptySetException` if there are no elements in the set. If there is at least one, a random number is chosen in the proper range. If the first element is chosen for removal, that situation is handled separately to maintain the reference to the front of the list. If any other element is chosen, a `for` loop is used to traverse the list and the node is deleted using the technique shown in Figure 4.8.

The remove Operation

The `remove` method works like the `removeRandom` method, except that it is looking for a particular element to remove. If the first element matches the target element, it is removed. Otherwise, `previous` and `current` references are used to traverse the list to the right place.

```
//-----------------------------------------------------------------
//  Removes one occurence of the specified element from the set
//  and returns it. Throws an EmptySetException if the set is
//  empty and a NoSuchElementException if the target is not in
//  the set.
//-----------------------------------------------------------------
public Object remove (Object target) throws EmptySetException,
                                    NoSuchElementException
{
   boolean found = false;
   LinearNode previous, current;
   Object result = null;
```

```
   if (isEmpty())
      throw new EmptySetException();

   if (contents.getElement().equals(target))
   {
      result = contents.getElement();
      contents = contents.getNext();
   }
   else
   {
      previous = contents;
      current = contents.getNext();
      for (int look=0; look < count && !found; look++)
         if (current.getElement().equals(target))
            found = true;
         else
         {
            previous = current;
            current = current.getNext();
         }

      if (!found)
         throw new NoSuchElementException();

      result = current.getElement();
      previous.setNext(current.getNext());
   }

   count--;

   return result;
}
```

What if the target element is not found in the collection? In that case, a
NoSuchElementException is thrown. If the exception is not thrown, the element
found is stored so that it can be returned at the end of the method. The node is
deleted from the list by adjusting the references as shown in Figure 4.8.

The iterator Operation

The iterator method simply returns a new LinkedIterator object:

```
//-------------------------------------------------------------------
//  Returns an iterator for the elements currently in this set.
//-------------------------------------------------------------------
public Iterator iterator()
{
   return new LinkedIterator (contents, count);
}
```

Like the `ArrayIterator` class discussed in Chapter 3, the `LinkedIterator` class is written so it can be used with multiple collections. It stores the contents of the linked list and the count of elements, as shown in Listing 4.2.

Listing 4.2

```
//************************************************************************
//  LinkedIterator.java        Authors: Lewis/Chase
//
//  Represents an iterator for a linked list of linear nodes.
//************************************************************************

package jss2;

import java.util.*;

public class LinkedIterator implements Iterator
{
   private int count;  // the number of elements in the collection
   private LinearNode current;  // the current position

   //-------------------------------------------------------------------
   //  Sets up this iterator using the specified items.
   //-------------------------------------------------------------------
   public LinkedIterator (LinearNode collection, int size)
   {
      current = collection;
      count = size;
   }
```

Listing 4.2 **continued**

```java
//------------------------------------------------------------
//  Returns true if this iterator has at least one more element
//  to deliver in the iteration.
//------------------------------------------------------------
public boolean hasNext()
{
   return (current != null);
}


//------------------------------------------------------------
//  Returns the next element in the iteration. If there are no
//  more elements in this iteration, a NoSuchElementException is
//  thrown.
//------------------------------------------------------------
public Object next()
{
   if (! hasNext())
      throw new NoSuchElementException();

   Object result = current.getElement();
   current = current.getNext();
   return result;
}


//------------------------------------------------------------
//  The remove operation is not supported.
//------------------------------------------------------------
public void remove() throws UnsupportedOperationException
{
   throw new UnsupportedOperationException();
}
}
```

The LinkedIterator constructor sets up a reference that is designed to move across the list of elements when called by the next method. The iteration is done when current becomes null, which is the condition returned by the hasNext method. As in the case of the ArrayIterator from Chapter 3, the remove method is left unsupported. Figure 4.12 shows the UML description for the LinkedSet class.

The remaining methods are like their counterparts in the ArraySet class from Chapter 3.

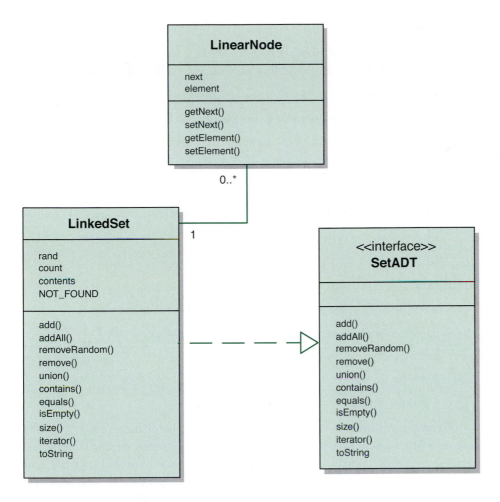

FIGURE 4.12 UML description of the `LinkedSet` class

4.5   LINKED IMPLEMENTATION OF A SET

The linked implementation of a set is very much like the linked implementations for other collections when it comes to memory. Linked implementations are usually dynamic, meaning that they only allocate as much space as they need and that space can grow and shrink as needed. However, linked implementations do come with an additional space requirement for the references associated with each element.

Let's take each operation separately.

Analysis of add

Since the order of elements in a set is unimportant, we can simply add each new element to the front of the list. Adding an elment to a linked set takes five steps:

1. Check to see whether the element already exists in the set.
2. Create a new node pointing to the element to be added.
3. Set the `next` reference of the new node to the front of the list.
4. Set the `front` reference to the new node.
5. Increment the `count`.

Because the call to method `contains` is O(n) and all other steps are O(1) the `add` operation is O(n).

Analysis of remove

The `remove` operation for the linked implementation takes four steps:

1. Check to make sure the set is not empty.
2. Find the element to be removed.
3. Remove it.
4. Decrement the `count`.

All of these steps are also O(1) except for finding the element. Step 2 requires best-case one comparison if the element is the first one we check, worst-case n comparisons if the element is the last one we check, and expected case n/2 comparisons. Because we ignore constants when considering order, the `remove` operation for the array implementation has time complexity O(n).

Analysis of removeRandom

The `removeRandom` operation for the linked implementation is like the `remove` method except that we do not have to search for the element we want to remove. However, we cannot simply choose an index at random and remove that element. Instead, we must choose a random number and then traverse the list to that position. The best case would be index 0 requiring no traversal, the worst case would require traversal of all n nodes, and the expected case is traversal of n/2 nodes. Thus the `removeRandom` operation is O(n).

Summary of Key Concepts

> Object reference variables can be used to create linked structures.

> A linked list is made of objects that each point to the next object in the list.

> A linked list grows as big as needed.

> The order in which references are changed is important to maintaining a linked list.

> Changing, moving, or deleting the first node in a linked list often requires special handling.

> Objects in a collection should not contain any implementation details of the underlying data structure.

> Any data structure can be used to solve a problem as long as all of the methods of the collection are implemented correctly.

> A traversal is any algorithm that processes list items one by one.

Self-Review Questions

4.1   How do object references help us define data structures?

4.2   What's the difference between a linked list and an array? How are they alike?

4.3   When changing a linked list, what specific cases require special processes?

4.4   Why should a linked list node be separate from the element stored on the list?

4.5   What do the `LinkedSet` and `ArraySet` classes have in common?

4.6   What would be the time complexity of the `add` operation if we chose to add at the end of the list instead of the front? How would this change (both adding at the beginning and at the end) if we didn't need to check for duplicates?

4.7   What is the difference between a doubly linked list and a singly linked list?

4.8   How would dummy records affect a doubly linked list implementation?

Exercises

4.1   Explain what will happen if the steps in Figure 4.5 are reversed.

4.2   Explain what will happen if the steps in Figure 4.6 are reversed.

4.3   Draw a UML diagram showing the relationships among the classes in the linked list implementation of a set.

4.4   Write an algorithm for the add method that will add at the end of the list instead of the beginning.

4.5   Change the algorithm from Exercise 4.4 so that it uses a rear reference. How does this affect this and the other operations?

4.6   What would happen to a linked list if there were no count variable?

4.7   Draw an example using a dummy record at the head of the list.

Programming Projects

4.1   Complete the implementation of the LinkedSet class by providing the definitions for the size, isEmpty, addAll, union, contains, equals, and toString methods.

4.2   Change the Bingo program from Chapter 3 so that it uses the LinkedSet class instead of the ArraySet class.

4.3   An additional operation that might be implemented for a set is difference. This operation would take a set as a parameter and subtract the contents of that set from the current set if they exist in the current set. The result would be returned in a new set. Implement this operation. Be careful to consider all possible situations.

4.4   A bag is like a set except that there are duplicates in a bag. Implement a bag collection by creating both a BagADT interface and a LinkedBag class. Include the additional operations described in the earlier projects.

4.5   Create a new version of the LinkedSet class that uses a dummy record at the head of the list.

4.6   Create a simple graphical application that will allow a user to perform add, remove, and removeRandom operations on a set and display the resulting set (using toString) in a text area.

Answers to Self-Review Questions

4.1   An object reference can be used as a link from one object to another. A group of linked objects can form a data structure, such as a linked list, on which a collection can be based.

4.2   A linked list has no space limitations, while an array does. However, arrays provide direct access to elements using indexes, while a linked list must be traversed one element at a time.

4.3 The main special case in linked list processing happens when we're handling the first element in the list. A special reference variable specifies the first element in the list. If that element is deleted, or a new element is added in front of it, we have to move the `front` reference.

4.4 Not every object we want to put in a collection can be designed to fit. Furthermore, the implementation details are supposed to be kept distinct from the user of the collection, including the elements the user chooses to add to the collection.

4.5 Both the `LinkedSet` and `ArraySet` classes implement the `SetADT` interface. This means that they both represent a set collection, providing the operations needed to use a set. Though they each have their own approaches to managing the collection, from the user's point of view they are the same.

4.6 To add at the end of the list, we would have to traverse the list to reach the last element. This traversal would not change the time complexity to be O(n). An alternative would be to modify the solution to add a `rear` reference that always pointed to the last element in the list. This would help the time complexity for `add` but would have consequences if we try to remove the last element. If we did not need to check for duplicates, the `add` method (at the beginning) would be O(1), while the `add` at the rear algorithm would still be O(n).

4.7 A singly linked list has a reference to the first element in the list and then a `next` reference from each node to the following node in the list. A doubly linked list maintains two references: `front` and `rear`. Each node in the doubly linked list stores both a `next` and a `previous` reference.

4.8 It would take two dummy records in a doubly linked list, one at the front and one at the rear, to get rid of the need for dealing with the first and last node in a special way.

Maps  5

CHAPTER OBJECTIVES

> Define a map

> Examine inserting and removing items in a map

> Detail implementing a map with arrays

> Discuss using a hash table to implement a map

> Analyze the put and remove methods

When we store information we need a way to find it again. A special value, unique to each item, is used to make this efficient. Patient files in a doctor's office are stored by patient name, banks use account numbers, and businesses use job numbers. In all of these situations we can use a data structure called a map to locate each item.

5.1   WHAT IS A MAP?

In our discussions of collections, we have made two assumptions about the way elements are stored in a collection:

> Where we store an element has nothing to do with the element itself, as in the case of our set and unordered lists. In order to find any item we must search the entire collection.

> The element is stored based on an index (numeric integer) value that may or may not (often not) be related to any piece of the item itself.

> **Key Concept**
>
> Maps associate each piece of information stored with a key value unique to each item.

> **Key Concept**
>
> Items in a map are stored in no particular order.

In this chapter we explore how an item is stored based on some unique key value. For each element to be stored in a map, a key must be provided that will determine where the element is placed and how it is retrieved.

A map is like an array where the index has a meaning. For example, each account in an array of bank accounts might be stored by its account number.

In the map in Figure 5.1, each item is associated with its key value. It doesn't matter what order we add the items to the map, because the map will store them by their key values.

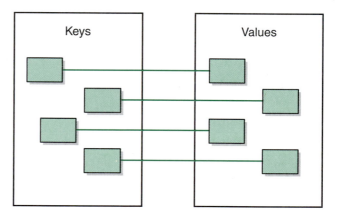

FIGURE 5.1 A conceptual view of a map

5.2   MAP OPERATIONS

There are many ways to implement maps. We will start by looking at a `MapADT` class and identifying properties that are common to all maps.

Insertion into a Map

Adding items to a map is called *associating a value with its key*. Both the value being inserted into the map and the key for that value must be stored in a way that makes it easy or at least possible to find it again.

In Figure 5.2 the new element has been inserted at the end of the map, but this may not always be the case. Where elements are in a map depends on the type of data storage used in the map implementation.

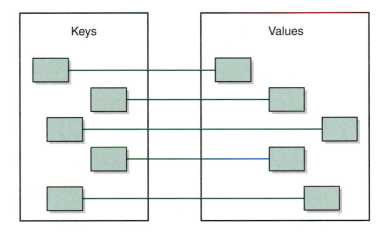

FIGURE 5.2   Map insertion

Because values in a map are stored by a unique key, no two items in the map can have the same key. The usual way of associating a new object with an already existing key is to replace the current object within the map's storage, returning the current object from the `put` method, as shown in Figure 5.3.

> **Key Concept**
>
> When adding a value-key pairing to a map, if the key already exists with a different value, the old value is returned by the add method and replaced with the new value.

Removing Associations

When associations are removed from a map, both the value being stored and the key value are removed. If the data structure is asked for a set of all of the items stored in the map it will not return either the removed value or the key. Figure 5.4 illustrates a map before and after a `remove` operation.

> **Key Concept**
>
> When a value or key is removed from the map, its associated key or value is removed as well.

Before:

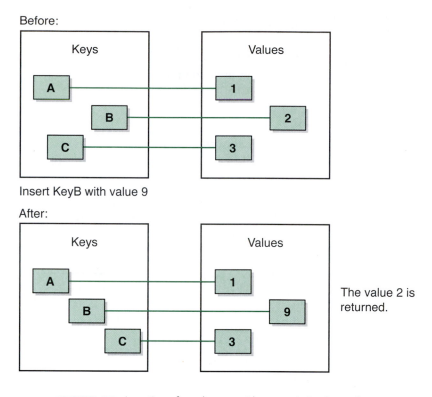

Insert KeyB with value 9

After:

The value 2 is returned.

FIGURE 5.3   Insertion of an element with a preexisting key value

5.3   IMPLEMENTING A MAP WITH ARRAYS

One way to implement a map is to use an array. Consider a class called `ArrayMap`, designed to implement a `MapADT` interface. The `MapADT` interface needs the implementation to have a `clear` method, methods to determine whether a particular element or key exists, a `get` method to retrieve a specific element based on its key, a `boolean` method to determine whether the collection is empty, a method to return a set of all of the keys stored in the map, a way to put new associations into the map, a `remove` method, and a `size` method.

The ArrayMap Class

In order to store all of the keys and values of a map we are going to use a `MapElement` object, which will store the key and value together. The `ArrayMap` class will then have a private-data array of `MapElement` objects.

Before:

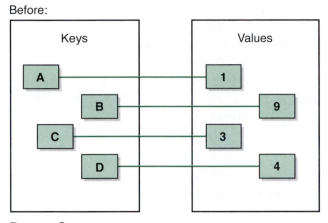

Remove C

After:

The value 3 is returned.

FIGURE 5.4 Removing associations from a map

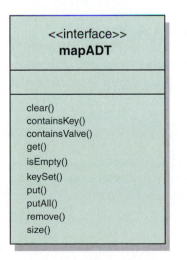

FIGURE 5.5 MapADT interface

Because we want to add and remove elements efficiently we are going to use a count variable to keep track of the number of associations and only resize the array when we need to. The instance data of the `ArrayMap` class is then

```
private int count;
private MapElement contents[];
```

By storing both the key and value in one class we can be sure that we will not mix up associations when we add and remove elements.

Listing 5.1

```
//******************************************************************
// MapElement.java         Author: Leigh Ann Sudol
//
// Stores a single value-key association for a map.
//******************************************************************
public class MapElement
{
    private Object myValue;
    private Object myKey;
    //--------------------------------------------------------------
    // Create a MapElement for the given value-key pair
    // throws IllegalArgumentException if either parameter is null
    //--------------------------------------------------------------
    public MapElement(Object k, Object val) throws
                                         IllegalArgumentException
    {
        if(k == null || val == null)
            throw new IllegalArgumentException();

        myKey = k;
        myValue = val;
    }
    //--------------------------------------------------------------
    // Returns the value stored within this association.
    //--------------------------------------------------------------
    public Object value()
    {
        return myValue;
    }
}
```

Listing 5.1   **continued**

```
//-----------------------------------------------------------
// Returns the key stored within this association.
//-----------------------------------------------------------
public Object key()
{
    return myKey;
}
}
```

Notice that there is no way to change the values stored by the `MapElement` class. This is because maps are not designed to store constantly changing associations. If a new association is added to the map, a new `MapElement` instance will be created for that association.

The constructor of the ArrayMap object, given below, starts the array at a default size (10 in this example) and initializes the `count` variable.

```
//-----------------------------------------------------------
// Creates an empty map.
//-----------------------------------------------------------
public ArrayMap()
{
    contents = new MapElement[10];
    count = 0;
}
```

The `indexOfKey` Operation

Many map operations need us to identify the association between a key and its value. In this program we have written a private helper method to search and return the associated value for a key.

```
//-------------------------------------------------------------
// Searches the map for a specific key.
//-------------------------------------------------------------
private int indexOfKey(Object key)
{
    for(int k=0; k<count; k++)
    {
        if(contents[k].key().equals(key))
                return k;
    }
    return -1;
}
```

The put Operation

The put method needs two parameters: the value to be stored and its key value. Because things don't need to be in order for a map, we can just insert the element at the end of the array. The put method uses the helper method to determine whether the key-value association already exists. The put method is shown below.

```
//-------------------------------------------------------------
// Puts the specified association into the map. Returns the
// previous value for the given key if it already exists.
//-------------------------------------------------------------
public Object put(Object key, Object value)
{
    if(count == contents.length)
        expandCapacity();
    Object temp = null;
    int place = indexOfKey(key);
    if(place != -1)
        temp = contents[place];
    else
        place = count;
    contents[place] = new MapElement(key, value);
    count++;
    return temp;
}
```

The put method checks whether the array is already full. If it is, the put method expands the array so more items can be stored. The put method then looks to see whether the key has an association mapped to it. If it does the put method stores that value. If it doesn't, the `put` method prepares to add the new value to the next open spot in the array. If a value was previously stored for that key, it is returned; otherwise null is returned.

The get Method

The `get` method lets us retrieve an item using its key value. If the key value is not associated with any value in the map, the `get` method returns null.

```
//-----------------------------------------------------------
// Returns the value associated with the provided key.
//-----------------------------------------------------------
public Object get(Object key)
{
    int place = indexOfKey(key);
    if(place == -1)
        return null;
    return contents[place];
}
```

Notice that the `get` method also uses the `indexOfKey` method to find the key in the array.

The keySet Method

One way to traverse a map is to get a set of the keys, iterate over that set, and then retrieve each element from the map based on its individual keys. You may notice that, unlike a set, there is no direct way to iterate over a map. The `keySet` method returns a set of all of the keys stored in the list.

```
//-----------------------------------------------------------
// Returns a set of all of the keys used by this map.
//-----------------------------------------------------------
public SetADT keySet(){
    SetADT myKeys = new LinkedSet();
    for(int i=0; i<count; i++)
        myKeys.add(contents[i].key());
    return myKeys;
}
```

The `keySet` method uses the `SetADT` interface and `LinkedSet` class discussed in Chapter 4.

The `remove` Method

The `remove` method removes the key-value association for the given key. The `remove` method will return the value associated with that key, if one exists, or null if it does not exist.

```
//-------------------------------------------------------------
// Removes the mapping associated with the given key.
//-------------------------------------------------------------
public Object remove(Object key)
{
    int place = indexOfKey(key);
    if(place = -1)
        return null;
    Object temp = contents[place];
    Contents[place] = contents[count-1];
    count--;
    return temp;
}
```

As a part of the `remove` operation, the `contents` array is shifted so that there are no blank spaces. Because the order of the elements does not matter, the last element is simply moved to fill in the empty space. Each of the mappings is then moved up to fill in the space.

The `contains`, `clear`, and `size` methods of this map are left for exercises at the end of the chapter.

5.4   USING A HASH TABLE TO IMPLEMENT A MAP

A more efficient way to implement a map is by using a hash table. A hash table is generally implemented as an array whose indexes are based on an integer hash value preferably unique to each item in the table. In this hash table the order (the location of an item within the collection) is determined by a hashing function based upon the key. Each location in the table is called a *cell* or *bucket*.

Consider a simple example. We create an array that will hold 26 elements. We want to store names in our array, so we create a hashing function that links each name to a position in the array based on

Key Concept

An efficient implementation of a map is using a hash table.

the first letter of the name. For example, the name Ann, first letter A, is mapped to position 0 of the array, and Doug, first letter D, is mapped to position 3. Figure 5.6 shows the array after several names have been added.

In a map array the values and keys are not stored in any particular order, so the time it takes to access a particular element depends on the size of the array. But in a hashing table the time it takes to access an element has nothing to do with the number of elements in the table because the key value takes you straight to the element. That is, we don't have to do comparisons to find a particular key—we simply calculate where the key should be. This means the operations on an element in a hash table are all O(1).

> **Key Concept**
>
> Where elements are stored in a hash table is determined by a hashing function.

However, this only works if each element maps to a unique position in the table. Consider our example from Figure 5.6. What will happen if we try to store the name Ann *and* the name Andrew? When two elements or keys map to the same location in the table, we have a *collision*. But even though collisions can slow things down, many of the objects we use for key values have efficient hash methods that will result in minimal collisions and O(1) access.

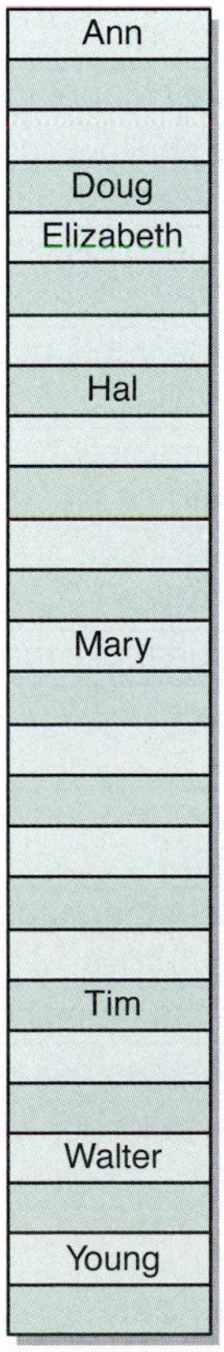

Ann
Doug
Elizabeth
Hal
Mary
Tim
Walter
Young

FIGURE 5.6   A simple hashing example

HashMaps

In this text we use the `HashMap` implementation provided in the Java library classes as part of the java.util package. The `HashMap` class implements the `Map` interface using a hash table.

Table 5.1 shows the operations on the `HashMap` class.

Return Value	Method	Description
	`HashMap()`	Constructs a new, empty map with a default capacity and load factor, which is 0.75.
	`HashMap(int initial Capacity)`	Constructs a new, empty map with the specified initial capacity and default load factor, which is 0.75.
	`HashMap(int initial Capacity, float loadFactor)`	Constructs a new, empty map with the specified initial capacity and the specified load factor.
	`HashMap(Map t)`	Constructs a new map with the same mappings as the given map.
void	`clear()`	Removes all mappings from this map.
Object	`clone()`	Returns a shallow copy of this `HashMap` instance: the keys and values themselves are not cloned.
boolean	`containsKey(Object key)`	Returns true if this map contains a mapping for the specified key.
boolean	`containsValue (Object value)`	Returns true if this map maps one or more keys to the specified value.
set	`entrySet()`	Returns a collection view of the mappings contained in this map.
Object	`get(Object key)`	Returns the value to which this map maps the specified key.
boolean	`isEmpty()`	Returns true if this map contains no key-value mappings.
Set	`keySet()`	Returns a set view of the keys contained in this map.
Object	`put(Object key, Object value)`	Associates the specified value with the specified key in this map.
void	`putAll(Map t)`	Copies all of the mappings from the specified map to this one.
Object	`remove(Object key)`	Removes the mapping for this key from this map if present.
int	`size()`	Returns the number of key-value mappings in this map.
Collection	`values()`	Returns a collection view of the values contained in this map.

TABLE 5.1   Operations on the `HashMap` class

5.5 ANALYSIS OF THE TWO IMPLEMENTATIONS OF A MAP

The two types of maps—array and hash—use space in similar ways. They both store the value and keys for all information contained within the map. But because the hash functionality is provided through a method and not a lookup table, a hashmap does not need additional storage space.

Let's analyze the time complexity of each operation separately.

Analysis of put

Because the order of the elements in the ArrayMap implementation of Map doesn't matter, we can simply add to the end of the array. Therefore placing an element in the map takes the following steps:

1. Check to see whether the key is already in the map.
2. Create a new `MapElement` to be added to the map.
3. Check to see whether the array is full, and if it is, resize it.
4. Insert the new `MapElement` where it belongs.

Checking to see whether the key is already in the map takes O(n), so the array implementation of `put` as a whole has a complexity of O(n).

In the hash implementation, the elements are ordered by a hashing method based on the key value. Therefore the steps are as follows:

1. Check to see whether the key is already in the map.
2. Create a new `MapElement` to be added to the map.
3. Insert the `MapElement` where appropriate based upon the hashing function.

Because getting an element based on its key is O(1), the hash table implementation of put as a whole has a complexity of O(1).

Analysis of remove

Because the order of the elements in an array does not matter, when we remove an element the last element in the array can move to fill in the space left by the previous association pair of key and value. The steps required for this are

1. Determine whether the key given exists in the map.
2. Remove the association (if it exists) from the map.

Determining whether the key exists in the map has a worst-case complexity of O(n), so the time for this operation in an array implementation of a map is, as before, O(n).

A hash implementation of a map would take the same steps, but determining whether the key exists in the map is an O(1) time complexity thanks to the hashing function, so the `remove` method in a hashmap has a complexity of O(1).

Summary of Key Concepts

> Maps associate each piece of information stored with a key value unique to each item.

> Items in a map are stored in no particular order.

> When adding a value-key pairing to a map, if the key already exists with a different value, the old value is returned by the add method and replaced with the new value.

> When a value or key is removed from the map, its associated key or value is removed as well.

> A possible, although inefficient, method of implementing a map is using an array.

> An efficient implementation of a map is using a hash table.

> Where elements are stored in a hash table is determined by a hashing function.

Self-Review Questions

5.1   How is data is stored in a map?

5.2   Why would Social Security numbers be better map associations for data on people than, say, birthdays?

5.3   Why is it important that when values are removed from the map, their key is removed also?

5.4   How many arrays would it take to store key-value associations if the MapElement object were not used?

5.5   Why does storing a count improve the efficiency of a map? Aside from returning the size of the method, what other ways is the count useful?

5.6   What is the benefit of storing the key and its value together in a class used by the map?

5.7   Why is the indexOfKey method of ArrayMap a private method?

5.8   Why is the grouping of keys returned as a set?

5.9   What type of value should a hash code be?

5.10   What part of the hashmap implementation makes it more efficient than an array map?

Exercises

5.1   Using the expression `x.put(myString.substr(0,1), myString)` and given that `x` is a map and `myString` is a string variable, what is the relationship between key and value?

5.2   Describe possible solutions for an imperfect mapping (where keys share multiple values). Reworking the keys to be used is not an option.

5.3   How would the time complexity of `put` and `get` change in an array map if there were no count variable?

5.4   What other data structures can you think of for a map besides an array or a hash table?

5.5   Consider a database to store research information for elementary students studying countries. They need to record the name of the country, population, and name of the current head of state (ruler). Describe how and why this could be implemented as a map.

5.6   Look at the Java API and find another implementation of a map besides array and hash. Describe how it is different.

5.7   Why does a hashmap accept an `object` variable if every item needs a hashing function? What guarantees that the function will exist?

5.8   Use the Java API to find out what other type of collection also has a hash table implementation. (Hint: It's in the same package as the hashmap.)

5.9   Why will the `keyset` method of a map never have a time better than O(n) for any implementation of a map?

Programming Projects

5.1   Implement the `clear` method of `ArrayMap` based on `public void clear()`, shown in this chapter.

5.2   Implement the `containsKey` method of `ArrayMap` based on `public boolean containsKey(Object key)`, shown in this chapter.

5.3   Implement the `keySet` method of `ArrayMap` based on `public SetADT keySet()`, shown in this chapter.

5.4   Consider implementing a map to store information about countries and their capitol cities. Use the name of the country as the key. Write a program that uses your completed `ArrayMap` and stores country names and their capitols. The program should store several countries and then use an iteration over the set of keys in order to print a complete list.

5.5   Create your own implementation of a hashmap. Consider a program to store student records for a high school. The school has at most 500 students. Write a program that uses a student number (from 1 to 500) as a hash-code value in order to store it in an array. The key value for the map should be an integer representation of that student number. Write a `Student` class as well as an `ArrayHashMap` class.

5.6   Repeat problem 5.4 using `java.util.TreeMap` as your data structure. Read the documentation for `TreeMap`. What is the time analysis for retrieval of any value stored in the set with a given key?

5.7   Repeat problem 5.5 using `java.util.HashMap`. What principles of object-oriented design made this easy to implement with your already created design?

5.8   Sometimes it is necessary to store more than one object at a particular key. Consider a mailbox. Items in the mailbox are in no particular order. Implement a `Mail` object that is able to store the name of the sender as well as the receiver of the mail. A map can be used by a post office to track the mail that comes through the system. Each mailbox has a unique key (its postal address). However, each must store multiple pieces of mail. Implement a program that uses a map, with postal addresses for keys, that stores a set of mail currently in the mailbox. Use `java.util.HashMap` for your implementation of a map.

Answers to Self-Review Questions

5.1   Data in a map is stored based on a key value that is unique to each element and can be used to retrieve information.

5.2   For each Social Security number there exists only one person, but many people may share a birthday, which makes for a poor key-value association.

5.3   The common way of traversing a map is to get a set of the keys and then iterate over that set. If the keys are not removed when the values are removed, a traversal of the set of keys will yield null values.

5.4   It would take two arrays—one array to store the values and one array to store the keys. The associations could be kept through parallel arrays with matching indexes.

5.5   Storing a count improves the efficiency of the map because you do not need to traverse the data structure in order to calculate the count whenever you need it. The other operations that rely on the count property (depending on your implementation) could be `put` and `remove`.

5.6   If the key and its value are not stored together, the programmer of the data structure must be careful not to separate the items stored within the map.

5.7   In order to maintain encapsulation, a user of the `ArrayMap` class should not have anything to do with the indexes of the interior array, or should not have any use for the `MapElement` objects it stores.

5.8   Because maps need not be in any particular order, the collection of keys should also be in no particular order.

5.9   Hash codes should be integer (the primitive type) values because they will be used to index values in an array.

5.10   Hashing a key gives you an extreme advantage because no searching is needed for each element.

Recursion 6

CHAPTER OBJECTIVES

> Explain the underlying concepts of recursion

> Examine recursive methods and unravel their processing steps

> Define infinite recursion and discuss ways to avoid it

> Explain when recursion should and should not be used

> Demonstrate the use of recursion to solve problems

Recursion is a powerful programming technique. It is particularly helpful for implementing some data structures and for searching and sorting data. This chapter introduces recursive processing by explaining basic recursion and exploring the use of recursion in programming.

6.1   RECURSIVE THINKING

We know that one method can call another method for help with its task. A method can also call itself. This is called *recursion*.

Before we get into how we use recursion, we need to explore the general idea. In fact, me must learn to *think* recursively if we are to use recursion as a programming technique.

In general, recursion means defining something in terms of itself. For example, consider the following definition of the word *decoration*:

decoration: n. any ornament or adornment used to decorate something

The word *decorate* is used to define the word *decoration*. You may recall your grade-school teacher telling you not to do just this. But sometimes recursion is the right way to express an idea or definition. For example, suppose we want to formally define a list of one or more numbers, separated by commas. Such a list can be defined recursively as either a number or as a number followed by a comma followed by a list. This definition can be expressed as follows:

```
A list is a    number
or a           number   comma   list
```

This recursive definition of a list defines each of the following lists of numbers:

```
24, 88, 40, 37
96, 43
14, 64, 21, 69, 32, 93, 47, 81, 28, 45, 81, 52, 69
70
```

No matter how long (or short) a list is, the recursive definition describes it. A list of one element, such as in the last example, is defined completely by the first (nonrecursive) part of the definition. For any list longer than one element, the recursive part of the definition (the part that refers to itself) is used as many times as needed, until the last element is reached. The last element in the list is always defined by the nonrecursive part of the definition. Figure 6.1 shows how one list of numbers matches the recursive definition of list.

Infinite Recursion

Note that this definition of a list contains one option that is recursive (number comma LIST), and one option that is not (number). The part of the definition that is not recursive is called the *base case*. We must always have a base case—without a base case the recursion would never end. For example, if the definition of a list was simply "a number followed by a comma followed by a list," then no list could ever

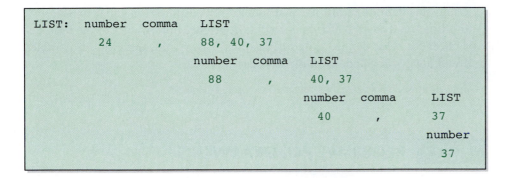

FIGURE 6.1   Tracing the recursive definition of a list

end. This is called *infinite recursion*. It is like an infinite loop, except that the "loop" happens in the definition.

A programmer must be careful to design algorithms so that they avoid infinite recursion. Any recursive definition must have a base case that does not result in a recursive option. The base case of the list definition is a single number that is not followed by anything. In other words, when the last number in the list is reached, the base case option ends the recursion.

Recursion in Math

Let's look at an example of recursion in mathematics. The value referred to as N! (which is pronounced *N factorial*) is defined for any positive integer N as the product of all integers between 1 and N, inclusive. For example, if N is 3,

```
3!  =  3*2*1  =  6
```

and if N is 5,

```
5!  =  5*4*3*2*1  =  120
```

Mathematical formulas are often expressed recursively. The definition of N! can be expressed recursively as

```
1! = 1
N! = N * (N-1)! for N > 1
```

The base case of this definition is 1!, which is defined to be 1. All other values of N! (for N > 1) are defined recursively as N times the value (N–1)!. The recursion is that the factorial function is defined in terms of the factorial function.

Key Concept

Mathematical problems and formulas are often expressed recursively.

Using this definition, 50! is equal to 50 * 49!. And 49! is equal to 49 * 48!. And 48! is equal to 48 * 47!. This process continues until we get to the base case of 1. Because N! is defined only for positive integers, this definition is complete and will always conclude with the base case.

The next section describes recursion in programs.

6.2   RECURSIVE PROGRAMMING

Let's use a simple mathematical operation to demonstrate recursive programming. Consider the process of summing the values between 1 and N, inclusive, where N is any positive integer. The sum of the values from 1 to N can be expressed as N plus the sum of the values from 1 to N–1. That sum can be expressed as the sum of the values from 1 to N–1 *plus* the values from 1 to N–2, and so on, as shown in Figure 6.2.

For example, the sum of the values between 1 and 20 is equal to 20 plus the sum of the values between 1 and 19. Continuing this approach, the sum of the values between 1 and 19 is equal to 19 plus the sum of the values between 1 and 18. This may sound like a strange way to think about this problem, but it is a straightforward example that can be used to demonstrate how recursion is programmed.

> **Key Concept**
>
> Each recursive call to a method creates new local variables and parameters.

In Java (and in many other programming languages) a method can call itself. Each call to the method creates a new environment in which to work. That is, all local variables and parameters are newly defined with their own unique data space every time the method is called. Each parameter is given an initial value based on the new call. Each time a method finishes, processing returns to the method that called it (which may be an earlier invocation of the same method). These rules are the same as those governing any "regular" method invocation.

$$\text{Sum}\,(1, N) = \text{Sum}\,(1, N{-}1) + N = \text{Sum}\,(1, N{-}2) + N + N{-}1$$

$$= \text{Sum}\,(1, N{-}3) + N + N{-}1 + N{-}2$$

$$= N + N{-}1 + N{-}2 \ + \ \ldots \ + \ 2 \ + \ 1$$

FIGURE 6.2   The sum of the numbers 1 through N, defined recursively

What does this look like? Well, for example a recursive solution to the summation problem is defined by the recursive method called sum:

```java
// This method returns the sum of 1 to num
public int sum (int num)
{
    int result;
    if (num == 1)
        result = 1;
    else
        result = num + sum (num-1);
    return result;
}
```

Note that this method includes our recursive definition that the sum of the numbers between 1 and N is equal to N plus the sum of the numbers between 1 and N–1. The sum method is recursive because sum calls itself. The parameter (num in the code, N in the equation) passed to sum is reduced each time sum is called, until it reaches the base case of 1. Recursive methods usually contain an if-else statement, with the base case as one of the branches.

Suppose the main method calls sum, passing it a value of 1, which is stored in the parameter num. Because num is equal to 1, the result of 1 is returned to main and no recursion occurs.

Now let's trace the execution of the sum method when it is passed a value of 2. Now that num does not equal 1, sum is called again with an argument of num-1, or 1. This is a new call to the method sum, with a new parameter num and a new local variable result. Because this num is equal to 1, the result of 1 is returned without any more recursive calls. Control returns to the first version of sum that was invoked. The return value of 1 is added to the initial value of num in that call to sum, which is 2. Therefore, result is assigned the value 3, which is returned to the main method. The method called from main correctly calculates the sum of the integers from 1 to 2, and returns the result of 3.

> **Key Concept**
>
> When we carefully trace recursive processing we can see how it was used to solve a problem.

The base case in the summation example is when N equals 1. At that point no more recursive calls are made. The recursion begins to fold back into the earlier versions of the sum method, returning the correct value each time. Each return value contributes to the computation of the sum at the higher level. Without the base case, recursion would go on forever. Each call to a method needs more memory space, which often results in a runtime error indicating that memory has been exhausted.

Trace the sum function with different values of num until this processing becomes familiar. Figure 6.3 illustrates the recursive calls when main invokes sum to get the sum of the integers from 1 to 4. Each box represents a copy of the method as it is invoked, setting aside space to store the formal parameters and any local variables. Invocations are shown as solid lines, and returns as dotted

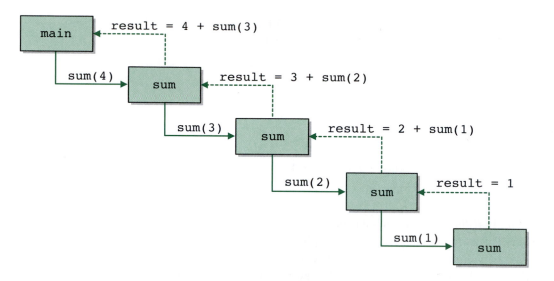

FIGURE 6.3 Recursive calls to the sum method

lines. The return value `result` is shown at each step. The recursive path is followed completely until the base case is reached; then the calls begin to return their result up through the chain.

Recursion vs. Iteration

Of course, there is another way to solve the summation problem. We could also use an iterative, or looping, algorithm.

```
sum = 0;
for (int number = 1; number <= num; number++)
    sum += number;
```

This solution is more straightforward than the recursive version. We used the summation problem to demonstrate recursion because it is easy to understand, not because you would use recursion to solve it normally. Recursion in this case is a more complicated solution than iteration.

A programmer must learn when to use recursion and when not to use it. Which approach is best depends on the problem being solved. All problems can be solved in an iterative manner, but in some cases the iterative version is much more complicated. For some problems, recursion allows us to create short, elegant programs.

Direct vs. Indirect Recursion

Direct recursion is when a method calls itself, such as when sum calls sum. *Indirect recursion* is when a method calls another method, which calls a method, and so on until the original method is called again. For example, if method m1 calls method m2, and m2 calls method m1, we can say that m1 is indirectly recursive. The amount of indirection could be several levels deep, as when m1 invokes m2, which invokes m3, which invokes m4, which invokes m1. Figure 6.4 illustrates indirect recursion. Method calls are shown with solid lines, and returns are shown with dotted lines. The whole path is followed, and then the recursion unravels along the return path.

Indirect recursion requires base cases just as direct recursion does. Indirect recursion can be more difficult to trace because of the calls to different methods—sometimes many methods. Therefore, we have to be very careful when we design or evaluate indirectly recursive methods. First and most important, we must be sure that the indirection is truly necessary and clearly explained in documentation.

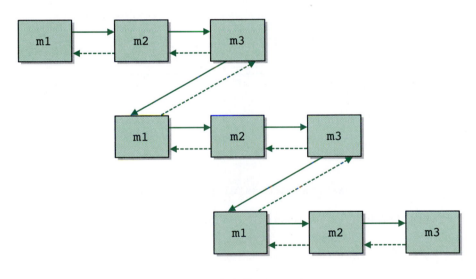

FIGURE 6.4 Indirect recursion

6.3   USING RECURSION

The following sections describe problems that we can solve using recursion. For each one, we look at the role recursion plays in the solution and how a base case is used to end the recursion. As you explore these examples, think about how complicated a nonrecursive solution for each problem would be.

Traversing a Maze

Solving a maze involves a lot of trial and error: first we follow one path, then we hit a dead end and we backtrack, then we try another path, and so on. Recursion can help us with this. The program shown in Listing 6.1 creates a `Maze` object and tries to traverse it.

Listing 6.1

```java
//********************************************************************
//  MazeSearch.java       Authors: Lewis/Chase
//
//  Demonstrates recursion.
//********************************************************************

public class MazeSearch
{
   //-----------------------------------------------------------------
   //  Creates a new maze, prints its original form, attempts to
   //  solve it, and prints out its final form.
   //-----------------------------------------------------------------
   public static void main (String[] args)
   {
      Maze labyrinth = new Maze();

      System.out.println (labyrinth);

      if (labyrinth.traverse (0, 0))
         System.out.println ("The maze was successfully traversed!");
      else
         System.out.println ("There is no possible path.");

      System.out.println (labyrinth);
   }
}
```

Output

```
1110110001111
1011101111001
0000101010100
1110111010111
1010000111001
1011111101111
1000000000000
111111111111
```

Listing 6.1   continued

```
The maze was successfully traversed!

7770110001111
3077707771001
0000707070300
7770777070333
7070000773003
7077777703333
7000000000000
7777777777777
```

The Maze class, shown in Listing 6.2, uses a two-dimensional array of integers to represent the maze. The goal is to move from the top-left corner (the entry point) to the bottom-right corner (the exit point). At first, a 1 indicates a clear path, and a 0 indicates a blocked path. As the maze is solved, these array elements are changed to other values to indicate attempted paths and ultimately a successful path through the maze if one exists. Figure 6.5 shows the UML illustration of this solution.

The only valid moves through the maze are in the directions down, right, up, and left. No diagonal moves are allowed. In this example, the maze is 8 rows by 13 columns, although the code is designed to handle a maze of any size.

Let's think this through recursively. The maze can be solved if it can be traversed successfully from position (0, 0). Therefore, the maze can be solved if it can be traversed successfully from any position next to (0, 0): namely position (1, 0), position (0, 1), position (–1, 0), or position (0, –1). Picking a next step, say (1, 0), we find ourselves in the same situation as before. To solve the maze from the new position, we must successfully traverse it from a position next to our new position. At any point, some of the positions may be invalid, may be blocked, or

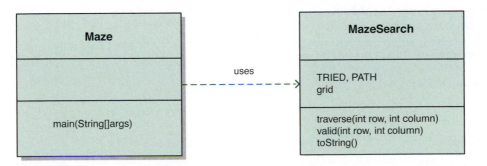

FIGURE 6.5 UML description of the Maze and MazeSearch classes

may represent a possible successful path. We continue this process recursively. If the base case, position (7, 12), is reached, the maze has been solved.

The recursive method in the `Maze` class is called `traverse`. It returns a `boolean` value that tells us whether a solution was found. First the method determines if a move to that row and column is valid. A move is valid if it stays within the grid boundaries and if the grid contains a 1 in that location, indicating that direction is not blocked. The first call to `traverse` passes in the upper-left location (0, 0).

Listing 6.2

```
//********************************************************************
//  Maze.java          Authors: Lewis/Chase
//
//  Represents a maze of characters. The goal is to get from the
//  top left corner to the bottom right, following a path of 1s.
//********************************************************************

public class Maze
{
   private final int TRIED = 3;
   private final int PATH = 7;

   private int[][] grid = { {1,1,1,0,1,1,0,0,0,1,1,1,1},
                            {1,0,1,1,1,0,1,1,1,1,0,0,1},
                            {0,0,0,0,1,0,1,0,1,0,1,0,0},
                            {1,1,1,0,1,1,1,0,1,0,1,1,1},
                            {1,0,1,0,0,0,0,1,1,1,0,0,1},
                            {1,0,1,1,1,1,1,1,0,1,1,1,1},
                            {1,0,0,0,0,0,0,0,0,0,0,0,0},
                            {1,1,1,1,1,1,1,1,1,1,1,1,1} };

   //-----------------------------------------------------------------
   //  Attempts to recursively traverse the maze. Inserts special
   //  characters indicating locations that have been tried and that
   //  eventually become part of the solution.
   //-----------------------------------------------------------------
   public boolean traverse (int row, int column)
   {
      boolean done = false;

      if (valid (row, column))
      {
         grid[row][column] = TRIED;  // this cell has been tried
```

Listing 6.2   **continued**

```java
      if (row == grid.length-1 && column == grid[0].length-1)
         done = true;   // the maze is solved
      else
      {
         done = traverse (row+1, column);     // down
         if (!done)
            done = traverse (row, column+1);  // right
         if (!done)
            done = traverse (row-1, column);  // up
         if (!done)
            done = traverse (row, column-1);  // left
      }

      if (done)  // this location is part of the final path
         grid[row][column] = PATH;
   }

   return done;
}

//---------------------------------------------------------------
//  Determines if a specific location is valid.
//---------------------------------------------------------------
private boolean valid (int row, int column)
{
   boolean result = false;

   // check if cell is in the bounds of the matrix
   if (row >= 0 && row < grid.length &&
       column >= 0 && column < grid[row].length)

      //  check if cell is not blocked and not previously tried
      if (grid[row][column] == 1)
         result = true;

   return result;
}

//---------------------------------------------------------------
//  Returns the maze as a string.
//---------------------------------------------------------------
public String toString ()
{
   String result = "\n";

   for (int row=0; row < grid.length; row++)
```

Listing 6.2 **continued**

```
    {
        for (int column=0; column < grid[row].length; column++)
            result += grid[row][column] + "";
        result += "\n";
    }

    return result;
    }
}
```

If the move is valid, the grid entry is changed from a 1 to a 3, marking this location as visited so that later we don't retrace our steps. Then the traverse method determines if the maze has been completed. So, there are three possibilities of the base case for this problem that will terminate any particular recursive path:

> An invalid move because the move is out of bounds or blocked

> An invalid move because the move has been tried before

> A move that arrives at the final location, completing the maze

If the location is not the bottom-right corner (completing the maze), we search for a solution in each of the four directions. First, we look down by recursively calling the traverse method and passing in the new location. The logic of the traverse method starts all over again using this new position. If we can't move down, we try moving right. If that fails, we try up. Finally, if no other direction works, we try left. If that doesn't work, there is no path from this location, and traverse returns false.

If a solution *is* found from the current location, then the grid entry is changed to a 7. The first 7 is placed in the bottom-right corner. The next 7 is placed in the location that led to the bottom-right corner, and so on until the final 7 is placed in the upper-left corner. Therefore, when the final maze is printed, the 0s still indicate a blocked path, a 1 indicates an open path that was never tried, a 3 indicates a path that was tried but failed to yield a correct solution, and a 7 indicates a part of the final solution of the maze.

There are several opportunities for recursion in each call to the traverse method. Any or all of them might be followed, depending on the maze configuration. Although there may be many paths through the maze, the recursion terminates when a path is found. Carefully trace the execution of this code while following the maze array to see how the recursion solves the problem. Then imagine trying to solve the maze without recursion.

The Towers of Hanoi

The *Towers of Hanoi* puzzle was invented in the 1880s by Edouard Lucas, a French mathematician. It has become a favorite among computer scientists because it is an excellent way to show how recursion works.

Imagine three pegs and a set of disks with holes in the middle so that they slide onto the pegs. Each disk is a different size. To start, all of the disks are stacked on one peg in order of size so that the largest disk is on the bottom, as shown in Figure 6.6.

The goal of the puzzle is to move all of the disks from the first peg to the third peg. We can use the middle peg as a temporary place to put disks, but we must obey the following three rules:

> We can move only one disk at a time.

> We cannot place a larger disk on top of a smaller disk.

> We cannot take a disk off a peg and put it aside—we have to put it on a peg.

This means we must move smaller disks "out of the way," onto the middle peg, in order to move a larger disk from one peg to another. Figure 6.7 shows the step-by-step solution for the Towers of Hanoi puzzle using three disks. In order to move all three disks from the first peg to the third peg, we first have to put the smaller two disks out of the way on the second peg so that we can move the largest disk from the first peg to the third peg.

The first three moves shown in Figure 6.7 move the smaller disks out of the way. The fourth move puts the largest disk in its final place. Then the last three moves put the smaller disks to their final places on top of the largest one.

Let's use this idea to form a general strategy. To move a stack of N disks from the first peg to the third peg:

1.   Move the top N–1 disks from the original peg to the middle peg.

2.   Move the largest disk from the first peg to the third peg.

3.   Move the N–1 disks from the second peg to the third peg.

This strategy lends itself nicely to a recursive solution. The step to move the N–1 disks out of the way is a familiar problem: moving a stack of disks. For this

FIGURE 6.6   The Towers of Hanoi puzzle

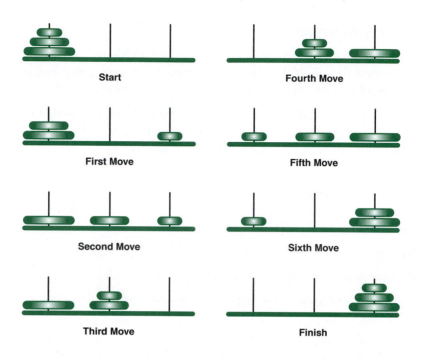

FIGURE 6.7 A solution to the three-disk Towers of Hanoi puzzle

subtask, though, there is one less disk, and our destination peg is what we were originally calling the second peg. The same thing happens after we've moved the largest disk, and we have to move the original N–1 disks again.

The base case for this problem is moving a "stack" of only one disk, because we don't need recursion to move just one disk.

The program in Listing 6.3 creates a `TowersOfHanoi` object and invokes its `solve` method. The output is a step-by-step list of instructions that describes how the disks should be moved to solve the puzzle. This example uses four disks (see the parameter to the `TowersOfHanoi` constructor). Figure 6.8 shows the UML description for this solution.

Listing 6.3

```
//*****************************************************************
//  SolveTowers.java        Authors: Lewis/Chase
//
//  Demonstrates recursion.
//*****************************************************************
```

Listing 6.3   continued

```java
public class SolveTowers
{
    //-----------------------------------------------------------------
    //  Creates a TowersOfHanoi puzzle and solves it.
    //-----------------------------------------------------------------
    public static void main (String[] args)
    {
        TowersOfHanoi towers = new TowersOfHanoi (4);

        towers.solve();
    }
}
```

Output

```
Move one disk from 1 to 2
Move one disk from 1 to 3
Move one disk from 2 to 3
Move one disk from 1 to 2
Move one disk from 3 to 1
Move one disk from 3 to 2
Move one disk from 1 to 2
Move one disk from 1 to 3
Move one disk from 2 to 3
Move one disk from 2 to 1
Move one disk from 3 to 1
Move one disk from 2 to 3
Move one disk from 1 to 2
Move one disk from 1 to 3
Move one disk from 2 to 3
```

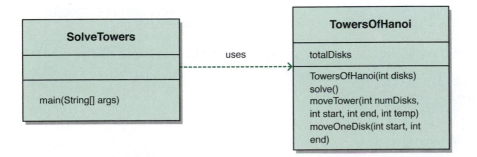

FIGURE 6.8 UML description of the `SolveTowers` and `TowersOfHanoi` classes

The `TowersOfHanoi` class, shown in Listing 6.4, uses the `solve` method to make the first call to `moveTower`, the recursive method. The first call says that all of the disks should be moved from peg 1 to peg 3, using peg 2 as the extra position.

Listing 6.4

```java
//********************************************************************
//  TowersOfHanoi.java        Authors: Lewis/Chase
//
//  Represents the classic Towers of Hanoi puzzle.
//********************************************************************

public class TowersOfHanoi
{
    private int totalDisks;

    //-----------------------------------------------------------------
    //  Sets up the puzzle with the specified number of disks.
    //-----------------------------------------------------------------
    public TowersOfHanoi (int disks)
    {
        totalDisks = disks;
    }

    //-----------------------------------------------------------------
    //  Performs the initial call to moveTower to solve the puzzle.
    //  Moves the disks from tower 1 to tower 3 using tower 2.
    //-----------------------------------------------------------------
    public void solve ()
    {
        moveTower (totalDisks, 1, 3, 2);
    }

    //-----------------------------------------------------------------
    //  Moves the specified number of disks from one tower to another
    //  by moving a subtower of n-1 disks out of the way, moving one
    //  disk, then moving the subtower back. Base case of 1 disk.
    //-----------------------------------------------------------------
    private void moveTower (int numDisks, int start, int end, int temp)
    {
        if (numDisks == 1)
            moveOneDisk (start, end);
        else
        {
            moveTower (numDisks-1, start, temp, end);
```

Listing 6.4   **continued**

```
        moveOneDisk (start, end);
        moveTower (numDisks-1, temp, end, start);
    }
}

//------------------------------------------------------------
//  Prints instructions to move one disk from the specified start
//  tower to the specified end tower.
//------------------------------------------------------------
private void moveOneDisk (int start, int end)
{
    System.out.println ("Move one disk from " + start + " to " +
                        end);
}
}
```

The moveTower method first considers the base case (a "stack" of one disk). If it finds the base case, it calls the moveOneDisk method, which prints a single line describing that move. If the stack contains more than one disk, we call moveTower again to get the N–1 disks out of the way, then move the largest disk, then move the N–1 disks to their final destination with yet another call to moveTower.

Notice that the parameters describing the pegs are switched around as needed to move the partial stacks. This code follows our general strategy, and uses the moveTower method to move all partial stacks. Look through the code for a stack of three disks and compare the processing steps to Figure 6.8.

6.4 ANALYZING RECURSIVE ALGORITHMS

In Chapter 1 we learned to analyze an algorithm to determine its complexity (usually its time complexity) and express it as a growth function. The growth function gave us the order of the algorithm, which we can use to compare it to other algorithms that do the same thing.

When analyzing a loop, we determined the order of the body of the loop and multiplied it by the number of times the loop was executed. Analyzing a recursive algorithm uses similar thinking. We can determine the order of a recursive algorithm by determining the order of the recursion (the number of times the recursive definition is followed) and multiplying that by the time complexity of the code inside the recursive method.

Consider the recursive method in Section 6.2 that adds up the integers from 1 to some positive value:

```java
// This method returns the sum of 1 to num
public int sum (int num)
{
    int result;
    if (num == 1)
        result = 1;
    else
        result = num + sum (num-1);
    return result;
}
```

We are very interested in the number of values to be added. Because we are adding the integers from 1 to num, the number of values to be added up is num. First we need to know how to add two values together. The body of the recursive method does one addition, and therefore is $O(1)$. Each time the recursive method is invoked, we subtract 1 from the value of num. So, the recursive method is called num times, so the recursive iterator is $O(n)$. And that means the order of the whole algorithm is $O(n)$.

In some algorithms each recursive step uses half as much data as the previous call in order to complete its execution, thus creating an order of recursion of $O(\log n)$. If the body of the method is $O(1)$, then the whole algorithm is $O(\log n)$. If the body of the method is $O(n)$, then the whole algorithm is $O(n \log n)$.

Now consider the Towers of Hanoi puzzle. The size of the puzzle is naturally the number of disks, and the processing operation of interest is the step of moving one disk from one peg to another. Except for the base case, each recursive call results in calling itself *twice more*, and each call operates on a stack of disks that is only one less than the stack that is passed in as the parameter.

In fact, the solution to the Towers of Hanoi puzzle is not very efficient. To solve the puzzle with a stack of N disks, we have to make $2^N - 1$ moves. Therefore, the Towers of Hanoi algorithm is $O(2^n)$. As the number of disks increases, the number of required moves increases exponentially.

Legend has it that priests of Brahma are working on this puzzle in a temple at the center of the world. They are using 64 gold disks, moving them between pegs of pure diamond. The bad news is that when the priests finish the puzzle, the world will end. The good news is that even if they move one disk every second of every day, it will take them over 584 billion years to complete it. That's with a puzzle of only 64 disks!

Summary of Key Concepts

> Recursion is a programming technique in which a method calls itself. To program recursively we must be able to think recursively.

> Any recursive definition must have a base case so the recursion will eventually end.

> We often use recursion to express mathematical problems and formulas.

> Each recursive call to a method creates new local variables and parameters.

> When we carefully trace recursive processing we can see how it it is used to solve a problem.

> Recursion may be the best way to solve some problems, but for others iteration works better.

> We can determine the order of a recursive algorithm by using techniques similar to analyzing iterative processing.

> The Towers of Hanoi solution has exponential complexity, which is very inefficient. Yet the implementation of the solution is incredibly short and elegant.

Self-Review Questions

6.1   What is recursion?

6.2   What is infinite recursion?

6.3   When is a base case needed for recursive processing?

6.4   Is recursion necessary?

6.5   When should recursion be avoided?

6.6   What is indirect recursion?

6.7   Explain how to solve the Towers of Hanoi puzzle. What does this have to do with recursion?

Exercises

6.1   Write a recursive definition of a valid Java identifier.

6.2   Write a recursive definition of x^y (x raised to the power y), where x and y are integers and y > 0.

6.3   Write a recursive definition of i * j (integer multiplication), where i > 0. Define the multiplication process in terms of integer addition. For example, 4 * 7 is equal to 7 added to itself 4 times.

6.4   Write a recursive definition of the Fibonacci numbers. The Fibonacci numbers are a sequence of integers, each of which is the sum of the previous two numbers. The first two numbers in the sequence are 0 and 1. Explain why you would not normally use recursion to solve this problem.

6.5   Find the method that calculates the sum of the integers between 1 and N shown in this chapter. Create a new version with the following recursive definition: The sum of 1 to N is the sum of 1 to (N/2) plus the sum of (N/2 + 1) to N. Trace your solution using an N of 7.

6.6   Write a recursive method that returns the value of N! (N factorial) using the definition given in this chapter. Explain why you would not normally use recursion to solve this problem.

6.7   Write a recursive method to reverse a string. Explain why you would not normally use recursion to solve this problem.

6.8   Create a new maze for the MazeSearch program in this chapter and rerun the program. Explain how the program solved the new maze, giving examples.

6.9   Number the lines of output of the SolveTowers program in this chapter to show the recursive steps.

6.10   Make a chart showing how many moves would be needed to solve the Towers of Hanoi puzzle using the following number of disks: 2, 3, 4, 5, 6, 7, 8, 9, 10, 15, 20, and 25.

6.11   Determine and explain the order of your solution to Exercise 6.4.

6.12   Determine and explain the order of your solution to Exercise 6.5.

6.13   Determine and explain the order of your solution to Exercise 6.6.

6.14   Determine the order of the recursive maze solution presented in this chapter.

Programming Projects

6.1   Design a program that works out Euclid's algorithm for finding the greatest common divisor of two positive integers. The greatest common divisor is the largest integer that divides both numbers without a remainder. In a class called DivisorCalc, define a static method called gcd that accepts two integers, num1 and num2. Create a driver to test your program. The recursive algorithm is defined as follows:

```
gcd (num1, num2) is num2 if num2 <= num1 and num2 divides num1
gcd (num1, num2) is gcd (num2, num1) if num1 < num2
gcd (num1, num2) is gcd (num2, num1%num2) otherwise
```

6.2   Change the `Maze` class so that it prints out the path of the final solution as it is discovered without storing it.

6.3   Design a program that traverses a 3D maze.

6.4   Design a recursive program that solves the Non-attacking Queens problem. That is, write a program to determine how eight queens can be positioned on an eight-by-eight chessboard so that none of them are in the same row, column, or diagonal as any other queen. There are no other chess pieces on the board.

6.5   In the language of an alien race, all words take the form of Blurbs. A Blurb is a Whoozit followed by one or more Whatzits. A Whoozit is the character 'x' followed by zero or more 'y's. A Whatzit is a 'q' followed by either a 'z' or a 'd', followed by a Whoozit. Design a recursive program that generates random Blurbs in this alien language.

6.6   Design a recursive program to determine if a string is a valid Blurb as defined in Project 6.5.

6.7   Design a recursive program to determine and print the Nth line of Pascal's Triangle, as shown below. Each interior value is the sum of the two values above it. So, the second number from the left on the last line is the sum of the numbers above it, 1 and 7, that is, 8. (*Hint*: Use an array to store the values on each line.)

```
                          1
                      1       1
                  1       2       1
              1       3       3       1
          1       4       6       4       1
      1       5      10      10       5       1
  1       6      15      20      15       6       1
1       7      21      35      35      21       7       1
1   8      28      56      70      56      28       8       1
```

6.8   Design and implement a graphic version of the Towers of Hanoi puzzle. Allow the user to set the number of disks used in the puzzle. The user should be able to interact with the puzzle in two main ways. The user can move the disks from one peg to another using the mouse, in which case the program should ensure that each move is legal. The user can also watch a solution take place as an animation, with pause/resume buttons. Permit the user to control the speed of the animation.

Answers to Self-Review Questions

6.1   Recursion is a programming technique in which a method calls itself, solving a smaller version of the problem each time, until the terminating condition is reached.

6.2   Infinite recursion occurs when there is no base case that serves as a terminating condition, or when the base case is improperly specified. The recursive path is followed forever. In a recursive program, infinite recursion will often result in an error that indicates that available memory has been exhausted.

6.3   A base case is always required to terminate recursion and begin the process of returning through the calling hierarchy. Without the base case, infinite recursion results.

6.4   Recursion is not necessary. Every recursive algorithm can be written in an iterative manner. However, some problem solutions are much more elegant and straightforward when written recursively.

6.5   Avoid recursion when the iterative solution is simpler and more easily understood and programmed. Recursion has the overhead of multiple method calls and is not always intuitive.

6.6   Indirect recursion occurs when a method calls another method, which calls another method, and so on until one of the called methods invokes the original. Indirect recursion is usually more difficult to trace than direct recursion, in which a method calls itself.

6.7   The Towers of Hanoi puzzle of N disks is solved by moving N–1 disks out of the way onto an extra peg, moving the largest disk to its destination, then moving the N–1 disks from the extra peg to the destination. This solution is inherently recursive because, to move the substack of N–1 disks, we can use the same process.

Searching and Sorting 7

CHAPTER OBJECTIVES

> Examine the linear
  search and binary
  search algorithms

> Study several sorting
  algorithms

Two common software development tasks are searching for an element in a group and sorting a group of elements into a particular order. There are several algorithms we can use to search and sort, and the differences between them are worth exploring.

7.1   SEARCHING

In software development, *searching* means looking for a *target element* in a group of items. The group of items to be searched is sometimes called the *search pool*.

This section looks at two approaches to searching: a linear search and a binary search. Later in this book other search techniques are presented that use the particular data structures to help speed up the search process.

Our goal is to search as efficiently as possible. We want to cut down the number of comparisons we have to make to find the target. In general, the more items there are in the search pool, the more comparisons it will take to find the target. So we are very interested in the number of items in the search pool.

To be able to search for an item, we must be able to tell one item from another— to be able to tell `Comparable` objects apart. For this we need to implement the `Comparable` interface.

Recall that the `Comparable` interface has one method, `compareTo`, that is designed to return an integer that is less than zero, equal to zero, or greater than zero (respectively) if the object is less than, equal to, or greater than the object to which it is being compared. So any class that implements the `Comparable` interface defines the order of any two objects of that class.

Linear Search

If the search pool is organized into a list, one way to search is to start at the beginning of the list and compare each value to the next until we find the target element. Eventually, either we will find the target or we will come to the end of the list and decide that the target isn't in the group. This approach is called a *linear search* because it searches from one end of a line of items to the other. Figure 7.1 shows how a linear search works.

The following method implements a linear search. It accepts the array to be searched and the target value. The method returns a `boolean` value that tells us whether or not the target element was found.

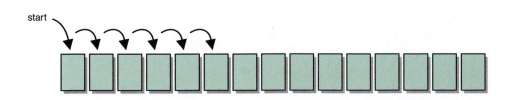

FIGURE 7.1 A linear search

```
//-----------------------------------------------------------------
//   Searches the specified array of objects for the target value
//   using a linear search algorithm.
//-----------------------------------------------------------------
public static boolean linearSearch (Comparable[] data,
                                       Comparable target)
{
    int index = 0;
    boolean found = false;

    while (!found && index < data.length)
    {
        if (data[index].compareTo(target) == 0)
            found = true;
        index++;
    }

    return found;
}
```

The while loop steps through the elements of the array, stopping when the element is found or when the end of the array is reached. The boolean variable found changes from false to true only if the target element is located.

We could also write this implementation so it returned the element if it was found and returned a null reference if it was not found. Or an exception could be thrown if the target element was not found.

We can make the linearSearch method part of any class. Our version of this method is defined as part of a class containing static methods that provide searching capabilities.

The linear search algorithm is easy to understand, but not very efficient. Note that a linear search doesn't need the elements to be in any particular order, as long as we can examine them one at a time. The binary search algorithm, described next, improves the efficiency of the search, but only works if the search pool is ordered.

Binary Search

If items in the search pool are sorted, then a binary search can be much more efficient than a linear search. Instead of starting the search at one end or the other, a *binary search* begins in the middle of the sorted list. If the target element is not found at that middle element, then the search continues. And because the list is sorted, we know that if the target is in the list, it will be on one side of the array or the other,

> **Key Concept**
>
> A binary search works only if the search pool is sorted.

depending on whether the target is less than or greater than the middle element. Thus, because the list is sorted, we eliminate half of the search pool with one comparison. The remaining half of the search pool represents the *viable candidates* in which the target element may yet be found.

The search now looks at the middle element of the viable candidates, eliminating half of them. Each comparison reduces the viable candidates by half until eventually the target element is found or there are no more viable candidates, which means the target element is not in the search pool. The process of a binary search is shown in Figure 7.2.

Let's look at an example. Consider the following sorted list of numbers:

10 12 18 22 31 34 40 46 59 67 69 72 80 84 98

Suppose we were trying to find the number 67 in the list. The target could be anywhere in the list (all items in the search pool are viable candidates).

The binary search begins by looking at the middle element, 46. That element is not our target, so we must continue searching. Because the list is sorted, we know that if 67 is in the list, it must be in the second half of the data, because all data to the left of the middle have values of 46 or less. This leaves the following (shown in bold):

10 12 18 22 31 34 40 46 **59 67 69 72 80 84 98**

Now we look at the middle value of the remaining numbers (72). Again, this is not our target, so we must continue the search. This time we can eliminate all values higher than 72, leaving:

10 12 18 22 31 34 40 46 **59 67 69** 72 80 84 98

In only two passes, we have cut the viable candidates from 15 items down to 3 items. Using the same approach, we select the middle element, and find the item we want, 67. If 67 hadn't been our target, we would have continued until we either found it or eliminated all possible data.

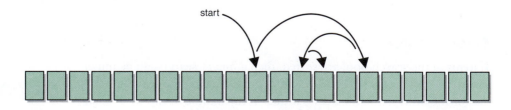

FIGURE 7.2 A binary search

With each pass, a binary search eliminates about half of the remaining data (and the middle element). That is, a binary search eliminates half of the data with the first pass, another quarter with the second pass, another eighth with the third pass, and so on.

The following method implements a binary search. Like the `linearSearch` method, it accepts an array of `Comparable` objects to be searched as well as the target value. It also takes integer values representing the minimum index and maximum index that define the part of the array to search (the viable candidates).

```java
//-----------------------------------------------------------------
//  Searches the specified array of objects for the target value
//  using a binary search algorithm.
//-----------------------------------------------------------------
public static boolean binarySearch (Comparable[] data, int min,
                                    int max, Comparable target)
{
    boolean found = false;
    int midpoint = (min + max) / 2;   // determine the midpoint

    if (data[midpoint].compareTo(target) == 0)
        found = true;
    else
        if (data[midpoint].compareTo(target) > 0)
            if (min <= midpoint-1)
                found = binarySearch(data, min, midpoint-1, target);
            else
                if (midpoint+1 <= max)
                    found = binarySearch(data, midpoint+1, max, target);

    return found;
}
```

Notice that the `binarySearch` method is implemented recursively. If the target element is not found, and there is more data to search, the method calls itself, passing parameters that shrink the size of the search pool. The `min` and `max` indexes are used to determine if there is still more data to search. That is, if the reduced search area does not contain at least one element, the method does not call itself and a value of false is returned.

When we have an even number of values to search, we have two "middle" values. As far as the algorithm goes, the midpoint used could be either of the two middle values; it doesn't matter which is chosen. This particular implementation picks the first of the two middle values.

Comparing Search Algorithms

For a linear search, the best case is when the target element happens to be the first item looked at—the midpoint. The worst case is when the target is not in the group, and we have to look at every element before we decide it isn't there. The expected case is that we would have to search half of the list before we find the element. That is, if there are n elements in the search pool, on average we would have to look at n/2 elements before finding the one we want.

Therefore, the linear search algorithm has a linear time complexity of $O(n)$. Because the elements are searched one at a time in turn, the complexity is linear—in direct proportion to the number of elements to be searched.

A binary search, on the other hand, is generally much faster. Because we can eliminate half of the remaining data with each pass, we can find the element much more quickly. The best case is that we find the target immediately—that is, that the target happens to be at the midpoint of the array. The worst case is that the element is not in the list, in which case we have to make approximately $\log_2 n$ comparisons before we eliminate all of the data. Thus, the expected case for finding an element that is in the search pool is approximately $(\log_2 n)/2$ comparisons.

A binary search is a *logarithmic algorithm* and has a time complexity of $O(\log_2 n)$. Compared to a linear search, a binary search is much faster for large arrays.

So if a logarithmic search is faster than a linear search, why would we ever use a linear search? First, a linear search is simpler than a binary search, and thus easier to program and debug. We don't need to sort the search pool ahead of time for a linear search.

> **Key Concept**
>
> A binary search is very efficient for a large search pool.

For small problems, there isn't much difference between a linear and a binary search. However, for large arrays, the binary search becomes attractive. Suppose a set of data contains one million elements. In a linear search, we'd have to look at each of the one million elements! In a binary search, we could find our target in roughly 20 passes.

7.2   SORTING

> **Key Concept**
>
> Sorting is putting a list of items in order.

Sorting is the process of putting items in order, either ascending or descending, based on some criteria. For example, you may want to put a list of names in alphabetical order or put a list of survey results into numeric order from greatest to least.

Many sorting algorithms have been developed over the years. In fact, sorting is a classic area of study in computer science. Like searching algorithms, sorting algorithms are divided into two categories: *sequential sorts,* which use a pair of nested loops and require roughly n^2 passes to sort n elements, and *logarithmic sorts,* which require roughly $n\log_2 n$ passes to sort n elements. As with the search algorithms, when n is small there is little difference between the two categories.

In this chapter we study three sequential sorts—selection sort, insertion sort, and bubble sort—and two logarithmic sorts—quick sort and merge sort. We look at other search techniques later in the book.

Let's start by solving a general sorting problem. The `SortPhoneList` program, shown in Listing 7.1, creates an array of `Contact` objects, sorts these objects, and then prints the sorted list. The `Contact` objects are sorted using a call to the `selectionSort` method, covered later in this chapter, but we could use any sorting method described in this chapter to get the same results.

Listing 7.1

```java
//********************************************************************
//  SortPhoneList.java        Authors: Lewis/Chase
//
//  Driver for testing an object selection sort.
//********************************************************************

public class SortPhoneList
{
   //-----------------------------------------------------------------
   //  Creates an array of Contact objects, sorts them, then prints
   //  them.
   //-----------------------------------------------------------------
   public static void main (String[] args)
   {
      Contact[] friends = new Contact[7];

      friends[0] = new Contact ("John", "Smith", "610-555-7384");
      friends[1] = new Contact ("Sarah", "Barnes", "215-555-3827");
      friends[2] = new Contact ("Mark", "Riley", "733-555-2969");
      friends[3] = new Contact ("Laura", "Getz", "663-555-3984");
      friends[4] = new Contact ("Larry", "Smith", "464-555-3489");
      friends[5] = new Contact ("Frank", "Phelps", "322-555-2284");
      friends[6] = new Contact ("Marsha", "Grant", "243-555-2837");

      Sort.selectionSort(friends);

      for (int index = 0; index < friends.length; index++)
         System.out.println (friends[index]);
   }
}
```

Output

```
Barnes, Sarah        215-555-3827
Getz, Laura          663-555-3984
Grant, Marsha        243-555-2837
```

Listing 7.1   continued

```
Phelps, Frank      322-555-2284
Riley, Mark        733-555-2969
Smith, John        610-555-7384
Smith, Larry       464-555-3489
```

Each Contact object represents a person with a last name, a first name, and a phone number. The Contact class is shown in Listing 7.2. The UML description of these classes is left as an exercise.

Listing 7.2

```java
//********************************************************************
//  Contact.java        Authors: Lewis/Chase
//
//  Represents a phone contact.
//********************************************************************

public class Contact implements Comparable
{
   private String firstName, lastName, phone;

   //-----------------------------------------------------------------
   //  Sets up this contact with the specified information.
   //-----------------------------------------------------------------
   public Contact (String first, String last, String telephone)
   {
      firstName = first;
      lastName = last;
      phone = telephone;
   }

   //-----------------------------------------------------------------
   //  Returns a description of this contact as a string.
   //-----------------------------------------------------------------
   public String toString ()
   {
      return lastName + ", " + firstName + "\t" + phone;
   }

   //-----------------------------------------------------------------
   //  Uses both last and first names to determine lexical ordering.
   //-----------------------------------------------------------------
   public int compareTo (Object other)
```

Listing 7.2   **continued**

```
    {
        int result;

        if (lastName.equals(((Contact)other).lastName))
            result = firstName.compareTo(((Contact)other).firstName);
        else
            result = lastName.compareTo(((Contact)other).lastName);

        return result;
    }
}
```

The `Contact` class implements the `Comparable` interface, which provides a definition of the `compareTo` method. In this case, the contacts are sorted by last name; if two contacts have the same last name, their first names are used.

Now let's look at several sorting algorithms and their implementations. We could use any of these to put the `Contact` objects in order.

Selection Sort

The *selection sort* algorithm sorts a list by putting each value into its final, sorted, position. In other words, for each position in the list, the algorithm picks the value that should go in that position and puts it there.

The selection sort algorithm works like this:

1. Scan the list to find the smallest value.

2. Swap that value with the value in the first position of the list.

3. Scan the rest of the list (all but the first value) to find the smallest value, and then swap it with the value in the second position.

4. Scan the rest of the list (all but the first two values) to find the smallest value, and then swap it with the value in the third position of the list.

5. Continue for each position in the list, until the list is sorted.

The selection sort process is illustrated in Figure 7.3.

The following method defines an implementation of the selection sort algorithm. It accepts an array of `Comparable` objects as a parameter. When it returns to the calling method, the elements within the array are sorted.

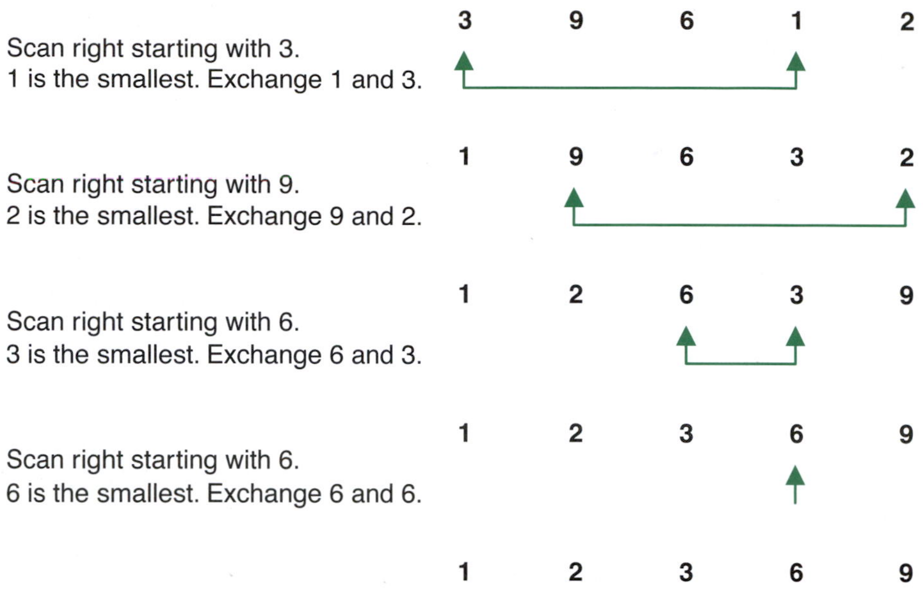
3 9 6 1 2
Scan right starting with 3.
1 is the smallest. Exchange 1 and 3.
1 9 6 3 2
Scan right starting with 9.
2 is the smallest. Exchange 9 and 2.
1 2 6 3 9
Scan right starting with 6.
3 is the smallest. Exchange 6 and 3.
1 2 3 6 9
Scan right starting with 6.
6 is the smallest. Exchange 6 and 6.
1 2 3 6 9

FIGURE 7.3 Selection sort processing

```
//-----------------------------------------------------------------
//  Sorts the specified array of objects using the selection
//  sort algorithm.
//-----------------------------------------------------------------
public static void selectionSort (Comparable[] data)
{
   int min;
   Comparable temp;
   for (int index = 0; index < data.length-1; index++)
   {
      min = index;
      for (int scan = index+1; scan < data.length; scan++)
         if (data[scan].compareTo(data[min])<0)
            min = scan;

      // Swap the values
      temp = data[min];
      data[min] = data[index];
      data[index] = temp;
   }
}
```

The implementation of the `selectionSort` method uses two loops to sort an array of integers. The outer loop controls where in the array the next smallest value will be stored. The inner loop finds the smallest value in the rest of the list by scanning all positions greater than or equal to the index specified by the outer loop. When it finds the smallest value, it *swaps* that value with the value stored at index. This swap is done by three assignment statements using an extra variable called temp.

Because this algorithm finds the smallest value during each pass, the array is sorted in ascending order (smallest to largest). But we can easily change the algorithm to put values in descending order (largest to smallest) by finding the largest value each time.

Insertion Sort

The *insertion sort* algorithm sorts a list by inserting each value into a subset of the list that it has already sorted. One at a time, it inserts each unsorted element in the right place in that sorted subset until the entire list is in order.

> **Key Concept**
>
> The insertion sort algorithm sorts a list by inserting each value into a subset of the list that it has already sorted.

The insertion sort algorithm works like this:

1. Sort the first two values in the list by swapping them if necessary.

2. Insert the third value into the correct position relative to the first two (sorted) values.

3. Insert the fourth value into its proper position relative to the first three values in the list. Each time an insertion is made, the number of values in the sorted subset increases by one.

4. Continue until all values in the list are sorted.

The insertion sort needs the other values in the array to shift to make room for the inserted element. Figure 7.4 shows the insertion sort process.

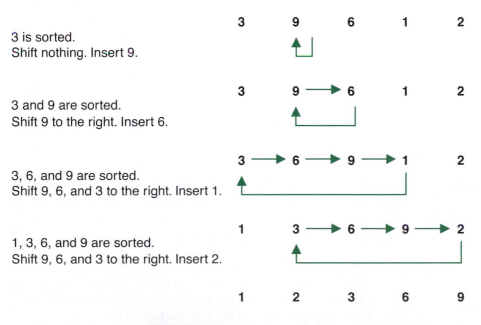

FIGURE 7.4 Insertion sort processing

The following method implements an insertion sort:

```
//-------------------------------------------------------------
//   Sorts the specified array of objects using an insertion
//   sort algorithm.
//-------------------------------------------------------------
public static void insertionSort (Comparable[] data)
{
   for (int index = 1; index < data.length; index++)
   {
      Comparable key = data[index];
      int position = index;

      // Shift larger values to the right
      while (position > 0 && data[position-1].compareTo(key) > 0)
      {
         data[position] = data[position-1];
         position--;
      }

      data[position] = key;
   }
}
```

Like the selection sort implementation, the `insertionSort` method uses two loops. In the insertion sort, however, the outer loop controls the index in the array of the next value to be inserted. The inner loop compares the current insert value with values stored at lower indexes (which make up the sorted subset). If the current insert value is less than the value at `position`, then that value is shifted to the right. Shifting continues until the correct position opens up. Each iteration of the outer loop adds one to the sorted subset of the list, until the entire list is sorted.

Bubble Sort

A *bubble sort* also uses two nested loops. It sorts values by comparing neighboring elements in the list and swapping them if they are not already in order.

The bubble sort algorithm works like this:

1. Scan the list, comparing neighboring elements and swapping them if they are not in order. This has the effect of "bubbling" the largest value to the last position in the list, which is its appropriate position in the final sorted list.

2. Scan the list again, bubbling up the second-to-last value.

3. Continue until all elements have been bubbled into their correct positions.

Each pass through the bubble sort algorithm moves the largest value to its final position. A pass may also reposition other elements as well. For example, if we started with the list

9 6 8 12 3 1 7

we would first compare 9 and 6. Because they are not in the correct order, we would swap them, getting

6 9 8 12 3 1 7

Then we would compare 9 and 8. Again, because they are not in the correct order, we would swap them, getting

6 8 9 12 3 1 7

Next we would compare 9 and 12. Because they are in the correct order, we don't swap them. Instead, we move to compare 12 and 3. Because they are not in order, we swap them, getting

6 8 9 3 12 1 7

Now we compare 12 and 1, and swap them, getting

6 8 9 3 1 12 7

And we compare 12 and 7, and swap them, getting

6 8 9 3 1 7 12

After this first pass, the largest value in the list (12) is in its correct position, but we can't be sure about any of the other numbers. Each new pass through the data guarantees that one more element ends up in the correct position. We make n−1 passes through the data, because if n−1 elements are in the correct positions, the nth item must also be in the correct location.

An implementation of the bubble sort algorithm is shown in the following method:

```
//----------------------------------------------------------------
//  Sorts the specified array of objects using a bubble sort
//  algorithm.
//----------------------------------------------------------------
public static void bubbleSort (Comparable[] data)
{
   int position, scan;
```

```
Comparable temp;

for (position = data.length-1; position >= 0; position--)
{
    for (scan = 0; scan <= position-1; scan++)
    {
        if (data[scan].compareTo(data[scan+1]) > 0)
        {
            // Swap the values
            temp = data[scan];
            data[scan] = data[scan + 1];
            data[scan + 1] = temp;
        }
    }
}
}
```

The outer `for` loop in the `bubbleSort` method represents the n–1 passes through the data. The inner `for` loop scans the data, compares the neighboring data, and swaps them if necessary.

Notice that the outer loop also has the effect of decreasing the position that represents the maximum index to examine in the inner loop. That is, after the first pass, which puts the last value in its correct position, there is no need to consider that value again. After the second pass, we can forget about the last two, and so on. Thus the inner loop examines one less value on each pass.

Quick Sort

The selection sort, insertion sort, and bubble sort algorithms are pretty simple, but inefficient. One more efficient sort is the *quick sort*.

The quick sort algorithm sorts a list by dividing a *partition element* and then recursively sorting the sublists on either side of the partition element. The quick sort algorithm works like this:

> **Key Concept**
>
> The quick sort algorithm sorts a list by dividing the list and then recursively sorting the two sublists.

1. Choose one element of the list to act as a partition element.

2. Divide the list so that all elements less than the partition element are to the left of that element and all elements greater than the partition element are to the right.

3. Apply this quick sort strategy (recursively) to both sides.

The choice of the partition element is random, so we can use the first element in the list. It would be nice if the partition element divided the list roughly in half, but the algorithm will work no matter what element is chosen as the partition.

Let's look at an example of creating a partition. If we started with the list

90   65   7   305   120   110   8

we could choose 90 as our partition element. We could then rearrange the list, swapping the elements that are less than 90 to the left side and those that are greater than 90 to the right side:

8   65   7   **90**   120   110   305

We would then apply the quick sort algorithm separately to both sides. We would keep going until one side contained only one element, which means the entire list is sorted. Once the first partition element is chosen and placed, it is never moved again.

The following method implements the quick sort algorithm. It accepts an array of Comparable data to sort and the minimum and maximum index values used for a particular call to the method. For the first call to the method, the values of min and max mark out the entire set of elements to be sorted.

```
//----------------------------------------------------------------
//   Sorts the specified array of objects using the quick sort
//   algorithm.
//----------------------------------------------------------------
public static void quickSort (Comparable[] data, int min, int max)
{
    int indexOfPartition;

    if (max-min  > 0)
    {
        // Create partitions
        indexOfPartition = findPartition (data, min, max);

        // Sort the left side
        quickSort (data, min, indexOfPartition-1);

        // Sort the right side
        quickSort (data, indexOfPartition+1, max);
    }
}
```

The quickSort method relies on the findPartition method, which it first calls to divide the sort area in two subsets. The findPartition method returns with the position (index) of the partition between the subsets. Then the quickSort method is called twice (recursively) to sort the two subsets. The base case of the recursion, represented by the `if` statement in the `quickSort` method, is a list of one element or less. The `findPartition` method is shown below:

```
//------------------------------------------------------------------
//   Rearranges the elements in the sort area into two partitions.
//------------------------------------------------------------------
private static int findPartition (Comparable[] data, int min, int max)
{
    int left, right;
    Comparable temp, partitionelement;

    // Use the first element as the partition element
    partitionelement = data[min];

    left = min;
    right = max;

    while (left < right)
    {
        // search for an element that is > the partition element
        while (data[left].compareTo(partitionelement) <=0 &&
                            left < right)
            left++;

        // search for an element that is < the partition element
        while (data[right].compareTo(partitionelement) > 0)
            right--;

        // swap the elements
        if (left < right)
        {
            temp = data[left];
            data[left] = data[right];
            data[right] = temp;
        }
    }

    // Move partition element to partition index
    temp = data[min];
    data[min] = data[right];
    data[right] = temp;

    return right;
}
```

The two inner `while` loops of the `findPartition` method find elements that need to be swapped. The first loop scans from left to right looking for an element that is greater than the partition element. The second loop scans from right to left looking for an element that is less than the partition element. When these two elements are found, they are swapped. This process continues until the right and left indexes meet in the "middle" of the list. Where they meet is also where the partition element (which isn't moved until the end) will finally be placed.

Merge Sort

The *merge sort* algorithm sorts a list by dividing the list in half and dividing the sublists in half, and so on until each sublist has one element. Then the sublists are put in order.

The merge sort algorithm works like this:

1. Divide the list in two roughly equal parts.

2. Divide each of the two lists into two lists, and so on until the list is divided into lists of one.

3. As control passes back up the recursive calling structure, merge into one sorted list the two sorted sublists resulting from the two recursive calls.

> **Key Concept**
>
> The merge sort algorithm sorts a list by dividing the list in half and dividing the sublists in half, and so on until each sublist has one element. Then it merges these sublists into a sorted list.

For example, if we started with the list from our example in the previous section, we would get the results shown in Figure 7.5. The merge portion of the algorithm would then recombine the list as shown in Figure 7.6.

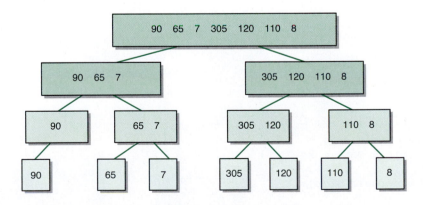

FIGURE 7.5 The decomposition of merge sort

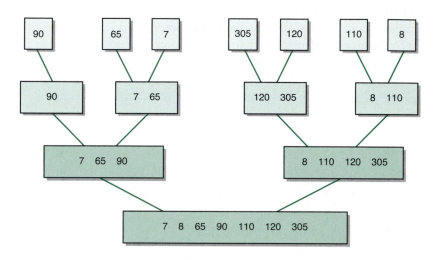

FIGURE 7.6 The merge portion of the merge sort algorithm

An implementation of the merge sort algorithm is shown below:

```
//-----------------------------------------------------------------
//  Sorts the specified array of objects using the merge sort
//  algorithm.
//-----------------------------------------------------------------
public static void mergeSort (Comparable[] data, int min, int max)
{
    Comparable temp[];
    int index1, left, right;

    // Return on list of length one
    if (min == max)
        return;

    // Find the length and the midpoint of the list
    int size = max - min + 1;
    int pivot = (min + max) / 2;

    temp = new Comparable[size];

    // Sort left half of list
    mergeSort(data, min, pivot);
```

```
    // Sort right half of list
    mergeSort(data, pivot + 1, max);

    // Copy sorted data into workspace
    for (index1 = 0; index1 < size; index1++)
        temp[index1] = data[min + index1];

    // Merge the two sorted lists
    left = 0;
    right = pivot - min + 1;
    for (index1 = 0; index1 < size; index1++)
    {
        if (right <= max - min)
            if (left <= pivot - min)
                if (temp[left].compareTo(temp[right]) > 0)
                    data[index1 + min] = temp[right++];
                else
                    data[index1 + min] = temp[left++];
            else
                data[index1 + min] = temp[right++];
        else
            data[index1 + min] = temp[left++];
    }
}
```

Summary of Key Concepts

> Searching is looking for a target in a group of items.

> An efficient search does as few comparisons as possible.

> A binary search works only if the search pool is sorted.

> A binary search eliminates half of the viable candidates with each pass.

> A binary search is very efficient for a large search pool.

> Sorting is putting a list of items in order.

> The selection sort algorithm sorts a list by putting each value into its final, sorted, position.

> The insertion sort algorithm sorts a list by inserting each value into a subset of the list that it has already sorted.

> The bubble sort algorithm sorts a list by comparing neighboring elements and swapping them if they are not already in order.

> The quick sort algorithm sorts a list by dividing the list and then recursively sorting the two sublists.

> The merge sort algorithm sorts a list by dividing the list in half and dividing the sublists in half and so on until each sublist has one element. It then merges these sublists into a sorted list.

Self-Review Questions

7.1   When would doing a linear search be better than doing a logarithmic search?

7.2   Which searching method needs the list sorted ahead of time?

7.3   When would a sequential sort work better than a recursive sort?

7.4   How does the insertion sort algorithm work?

7.5   How does the bubble sort algorithm work?

7.6   How does the selection sort algorithm work?

7.7   How does the quick sort algorithm work?

7.8   How does the merge sort algorithm work?

Exercises

7.1   How would a linear search algorithm search for the numbers 45 and 54 in the following list (3, 8, 12, 34, 54, 84, 91, 110)? How would a binary search do the search? Comare and contrast the two searches.

7.2   Make a table showing the number of passes needed to sort the list from Exercise 7.1 for each of the sort algorithms (selection sort, insertion sort, bubble sort, quick sort, and merge sort).

7.3   What happens to the number of comparisons for each of the sort algorithms if the list from Exercise 7.1 is already sorted?

7.4   Given the following list

     90   8   7   56   123   235   9   1   653

show a trace of execution for

   a. selection sort

   b. insertion sort

   c. bubble sort

   d. quick sort

   e. merge sort

7.5   After sorting the list from Exercise 7.4, show a trace of execution for a binary search, searching for the number 235.

7.6   Draw the UML description of the SortPhoneList example.

Programming Projects

7.1   The bubble sort algorithm shown in this chapter is less efficient than it could be. If a pass is made through the list without swapping any elements, the list is already sorted and there is no need to keep going. Change this algorithm so that it will stop as soon as it knows that the list is sorted. DO NOT use a break statement!

7.2   There is a kind of bubble sort algorithm called gap sort that, instead of comparing neighboring elements each time through the list, compares elements that are some number (i) of positions apart, where i is an integer less than n. For example, the first element would be compared to the (i + 1) element, the second element would be compared to the (i + 2) element, the nth element to the (n–i) element, and so on. A single pass is completed when all of the elements that can be compared have been compared. On the next pass, i is reduced by some number greater than 1 and the process continues until i is less than 1. Try writing a gap sort.

7.3   Change the sorts listed in the chapter (selection sort, insertion sort, bubble sort, quick sort, and merge sort) by adding code to each to count the total number of comparisons and time each algorithm takes to finish a sort. Execute the sort algorithms against the same list, writing down the total number of comparisons and time for each algorithm. Try different lists, including at least one that is already sorted.

Answers to Self-Review Questions

7.1   A linear search would be better for small, unsorted lists, and in languages that don't support recursion.

7.2   Binary search.

7.3   A sequential sort would be better for small data sets, and in languages that don't support recursion.

7.4   The insertion sort algorithm sorts a list by inserting each value into a subset of the list that has already been sorted.

7.5   The bubble sort algorithm sorts a list by comparing neighboring elements in the list and swapping them if they are not already in order.

7.6   The selection sort algorithm, which is an $O(n^2)$ sorting algorithm, sorts a list by putting each value into its final, sorted, position.

7.7   The quick sort algorithm divides the list using a partition element and then sorts the sublists on either side of the partition element.

7.8   The merge sort algorithm recursively divides the list in half until each sublist has one element. Then it puts these sublists in order to create the final sorted list.

Stacks 8

CHAPTER OBJECTIVES

> Examine stack processing

> Define a stack abstract data type

> Show how a stack can be used to solve problems

> Look at stack implementations

> Compare stack implementations

A stack may have been the first organized collection that we all learned about as children. From the very first time we stacked blocks one upon another, we learned that we usually should not try to get to the ones on the bottom of the stack without first removing the ones on top. The stack data structure we look at in this chapter works much the same way and has many uses in the world of computing.

8.1   A STACK ADT

A *stack* is a linear collection whose elements are added and removed from the same end. We call that *last in, first out* (LIFO): the last element to be put on a stack will be the first one that gets removed.

Stack processing is shown in Figure 8.1. Usually we call the end where elements are added and removed the *top* of the stack.

Recall from Chapter 3 that we define an abstract data type (ADT) using a set of operations that establish how we can manage the elements stored in the data structure. We always want to use ADTs to define the operations for a stack so we can cleanly separate the interface to the stack from any particular implementation technique we use to create it.

The operations for a stack ADT are listed in Figure 8.2. We say we *push* an element onto a stack and that we *pop* it off. We can also *peek* at the top element of a stack—looking at it or even using it—without actually removing it from the stack. There are also the general operations that allow us to determine if the stack is empty or, more specifically, how many elements it contains.

For a stack, the use of the terms *push* and *pop* are standard. The peek operation is sometimes referred to as *top*.

Not everyone defines *collection* the same way. You will find differences in how operations are defined from one book to another. We've been very careful in this book to define the operations on each data structure so that they match its purpose.

For example, note that none of the stack operations in Figure 8.2 let us reach down into the stack to remove or reorganize the elements in the stack. That is the

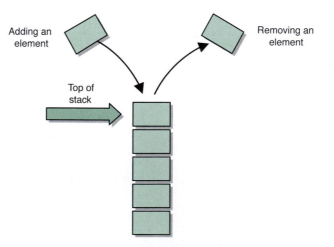

FIGURE 8.1   A conceptual view of a stack

Operation	Description
push	Adds an element to the top of the stack.
pop	Removes an element from the top of the stack.
peek	Examines the element at the top of the stack.
isEmpty	Determines if the stack is empty.
size	Determines the number of elements on the stack.

FIGURE 8.2   The operations on a stack

whole idea of a stack—everything happens at one end. If we find that we need to get the elements in the middle or bottom of the stack, then a stack is not the right data structure to use.

> **Key Concept**
>
> Choose the structure that works best for your data.

As we did with the set collection in Chapters 3 and 4, we provide a `toString` operation for the collection. This is not a classic operation defined for a stack, but it gives us a convenient way to traverse and display its contents without allowing us to change anything in the stack. Notice that we did not provide an `iterator` method. An iterator would need to access elements that were *not* at the top of the stack.

The operations on a stack can be defined in a Java interface, such as the one shown in Listing 8.1. Any class that implements the `StackADT` interface must give a definition for the methods listed in the interface. Note that the methods of this interface refer to generic `Object` reference variables, which lets a stack store any kind of object. Later in this chapter we look at two classes that implement these methods in different ways. For now, we can just explore the way stacks help us solve particular problems.

The `StackADT` interface in UML is shown in Figure 8.3.

Listing 8.1

```
//********************************************************************
//   StackADT.java        Authors: Lewis/Chase
//
//   Defines the interface to a stack collection.
//********************************************************************

package jss2;

public interface StackADT
{
```

Listing 8.1   **continued**

```
    public void push (Object element);

    public Object pop();

    public Object peek();

    public boolean isEmpty();

    public int size();

    public String toString();
}
```

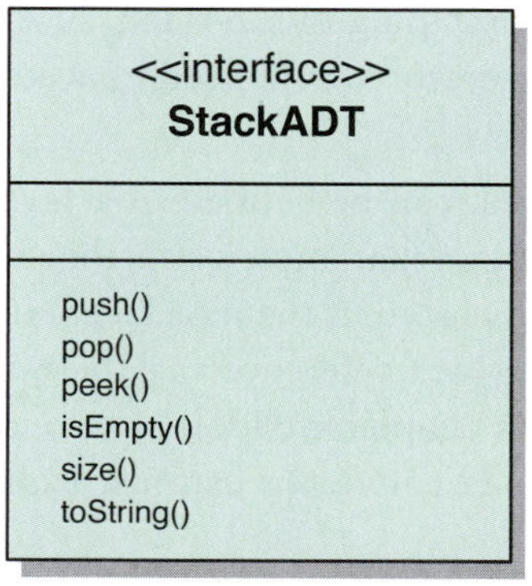

```
        <<interface>>
        StackADT


        push()
        pop()
        peek()
        isEmpty()
        size()
        toString()
```

FIGURE 8.3 The StackADT interface in UML

Stacks are used a lot in computing. For example, the undo operation in a word processor usually uses a stack. As we make changes to a document (add words, delete words, change the format, etc.), the word processor keeps track of each operation by pushing a representation of it onto a stack. If we want to undo an operation, the word processing software pops the most recent operation off the stack and reverses it. If we want to undo again (undoing the second-to-last operation we performed), another element is popped from the stack. In most word processors, many operations can be reversed in this way.

> **Key Concept**
>
> Some data structures work better for particular kinds of problems.

The following sections explore other examples of using stacks to solve problems.

8.2 USING STACKS: EVALUATING POSTFIX EXPRESSIONS

Traditionally, arithmetic expressions are written in an *infix* notation, meaning that the operator is placed between its operands:

<operand> <operator> <operand>

such as in the expression

    4 + 5

When an infix expression is evaluated, precedence rules determine the order of operator evaluation. For example, the expression

    4 + 5 * 2

equals 14, not 18, because the precedence rule says that, if there are no parentheses, we do multiplication before addition.

In a *postfix* expression, the operator comes *after* its two operands. Therefore a postfix expression takes the form

<operand> <operand> <operator>

For example, the postfix expression

    6 9 -

means the same thing as the infix expression

    6 - 9

A postfix expression is easier to work with than an infix expression because we don't have to worry about precedence rules and parentheses. The order of the values and operators in the expression are all we need to get a result. Programming language compilers and runtime environments often use postfix expressions for this reason.

With a postfix expression we simply scan from left to right, applying each operation to the two operands immediately before it. At the end we are left with the final value of the expression.

Consider the infix expression we looked at earlier:

    4 + 5 * 2

In postfix notation, this expression would be written

    4 5 2 * +

Let's use our evaluation rule to work this out. We scan from the left until we get to the multiplication (*) operator. We apply this operator to the two operands immediately before it (5 and 2) and replace them with the result (10), leaving us with

```
4 10 +
```

Continuing our scan from left to right, we get to the plus (+) operator. We apply this operator to the two operands immediately before it (4 and 10) to get 14, the final value.

Let's look at a more complicated example, the following infix expression:

```
(3 * 4 − (2 + 5)) * 4 / 2
```

The postfix version is

```
3 4 * 2 5 + − 4 * 2 /
```

Applying our evaluation rule results in:

	12 2 5 + − 4 * 2 /
then	12 7 − 4 * 2 /
then	5 4 * 2 /
then	20 2 /
then	10

> ### Key Concept
> A stack is the best data structure to use for evaluating a postfix expression.

Now let's think about designing a program that will evaluate a postfix expression. First, it would have to be able to retrieve the previous two operands whenever it gets to an operator. Also, a large postfix expression will have many operators and operands to manage. It turns out that a stack is the perfect data structure to use in this case. The stack operations match nicely with the process of evaluating a postfix expression.

Here's how it would work: Scan the postfix expression from left to right, identifying each token (operator or operand) in turn. If the token is an operand, push it onto the stack. If it is an operator, pop the top two elements off of the stack, apply the operation to them, and push the result onto the stack. When we reach the end of the expression, the element on top of the stack will be the result of the expression. Figure 8.4 illustrates the process.

The program in Listing 8.2 evaluates several postfix expressions entered by the user. It uses the PostfixEvaluator class shown in Listing 8.3.

To keep things simple, this program assumes that the operands to the expression are integers and that they are real values (not variables). When it runs, the program accepts and evaluates postfix expressions until the user chooses not to continue.

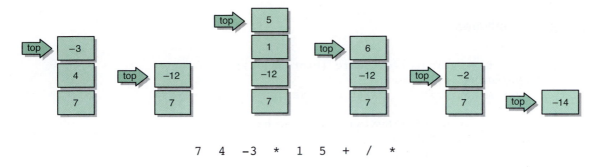

7   4   -3   *   1   5   +   /   *

FIGURE 8.4   Using a stack to evaluate a postfix expression

Listing 8.2

```
//********************************************************************
//   Postfix.java        Authors: Lewis/Chase
//
//   Demonstrates the use of a stack to evaluate postfix expressions.
//********************************************************************

import java.util.StringTokenizer;
import java.io.*;

public class Postfix
{
   //-----------------------------------------------------------------
   //   Reads and evaluates multiple postfix expressions.
   //-----------------------------------------------------------------
   public static void main (String[] args)
   {
      String expression, again;
      int result;

      try
      {
         BufferedReader in = new
             BufferedReader( new InputStreamReader(System.in));

         PostfixEvaluator evaluator = new PostfixEvaluator();

         do
         {
            System.out.println ("Enter a valid postfix expression: ");
            expression = in.readLine();
```

Listing 8.2 **continued**

```
            result = evaluator.evaluate (expression);
            System.out.println();
            System.out.println ("That expression equals " + result);

            System.out.print ("Evaluate another expression [Y/N]? ");
            again = in.readLine();
            System.out.println();
         }
         while (again.equalsIgnoreCase("y"));
      }
      catch (Exception IOException)
      {
         System.out.println("Input exception reported");
      }
   }
}
```

Output

```
Enter a valid postfix expression:
20 5 - 3 *

That expression equals 45
Evaluate another expression [Y/N]? y

Enter a valid postfix expression:
99 3 / 2 * 3 +

That expression equals 69
Evaluate another expression [Y/N]? n
```

Listing 8.3

```
//********************************************************************
//   PostfixEvaluator.java      Authors: Lewis/Chase
//
//   Represents an evaluator of postfix expressions. Assumes the
//   operands are integer literals.
//********************************************************************

import jss2.ArrayStack;
import java.util.StringTokenizer;
```

Listing 8.3 **continued**

```java
public class PostfixEvaluator
{
    private final char ADD = '+', SUBTRACT = '-';
    private final char MULTIPLY = '*', DIVIDE = '/';

    private ArrayStack stack;

    //----------------------------------------------------------------
    //  Sets up this evalutor by creating a new stack.
    //----------------------------------------------------------------
    public PostfixEvaluator()
    {
        stack = new ArrayStack();
    }

    //----------------------------------------------------------------
    //  Evaluates the specified postfix expression. If an operand is
    //  encountered, it is pushed onto the stack. If an operator is
    //  encountered, two operands are popped, the operation is
    //  evaluated, and the result is pushed onto the stack.
    //----------------------------------------------------------------
    public int evaluate (String expr)
    {
        int op1, op2, result = 0;
        String token;
        StringTokenizer tokenizer = new StringTokenizer (expr);

        while (tokenizer.hasMoreTokens())
        {
            token = tokenizer.nextToken();

            if (isOperator(token))
            {
                op2 = ((Integer)stack.pop()).intValue();
                op1 = ((Integer)stack.pop()).intValue();
                result = evalSingleOp (token.charAt(0), op1, op2);
                stack.push (new Integer(result));
            }
            else
                stack.push (new Integer(Integer.parseInt(token)));
        }

        return result;
    }
```

Listing 8.3   **continued**

```java
//-----------------------------------------------------------------
//  Determines if the specified token is an operator.
//-----------------------------------------------------------------
private boolean isOperator (String token)
{
    return ( token.equals("+") || token.equals("-") ||
             token.equals("*") || token.equals("/") );
}


//-----------------------------------------------------------------
//  Evaluates a single expression consisting of the specified
//  operator and operands.
//-----------------------------------------------------------------
private int evalSingleOp (char operation, int op1, int op2)
{
    int result = 0;

    switch (operation)
    {
        case ADD:
            result = op1 + op2;
            break;
        case SUBTRACT:
            result = op1 - op2;
            break;
        case MULTIPLY:
            result = op1 * op2;
            break;
        case DIVIDE:
            result = op1 / op2;
    }

    return result;
}
}
```

The `evaluate` method does the evaluation, supported by the `isOperator` and `evalSingleOp` methods. Note that in the `evaluate` method, only operands are pushed onto the stack. Operators are never put on the stack. An operand is put on the stack as an `Integer` object, instead of as an `int` primitive value, because the stack data structure is designed to store objects. Also, because the stack's `pop` operation returns a generic `Object` reference, we must turn the value returned from the `pop` method into an `Integer` before invoking the `intValue` method.

When we get to an operator, the most recent two operands are popped off of the stack. The first operand popped is actually the second operand in the expression, and the second operand popped is the first operand in the expression. The order doesn't matter in the cases of addition and multiplication, but it matters for subtraction or division.

The program also assumes that the postfix expression is valid, meaning that it has a correctly organized set of operators and operands. A postfix expression is invalid if either (1) two operands are not available on the stack when an operator is encountered or (2) there is more than one value on the stack when the tokens in the expression are used up. Either situation indicates that there was something wrong with the format of the expression, and both can be caught by looking at the stack. Checking for these problems is left as a programming project.

Perhaps the most important part of this program is the class that defined the stack collection. At this point, we don't know how the stack was implemented. We simply trusted the class to do its job. In this example, we used the class `ArrayStack`, but we could have used any class that implemented a stack as long as it correctly performed the stack operations (defined by the `StackADT` interface). From the point of view of evaluating postfix expressions, how the stack is implemented hardly matters. Figure 8.5 shows a UML class diagram for our postfix program.

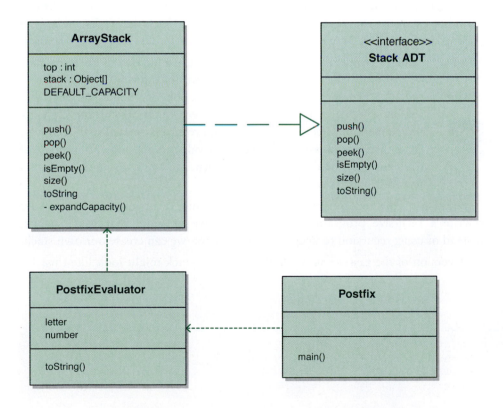

FIGURE 8.5 A UML class diagram for the postfix program

8.3   USING STACKS: SIMULATING RECURSION

A stack data structure is also used when the runtime environment executes a program. A *program stack* (or *runtime stack*) keeps track of methods that are called. Every time a method is called, an *activation record* is created and pushed onto the program stack. The elements on the stack represent the series of method calls used to reach a particular point in an executing program.

For example, when the `main` method of a program is called, an activation record for it is created and pushed onto the program stack. When `main` calls another method (say m2), an activation record for m2 is created and pushed onto the stack. When m2 calls method m3, an activation record for m3 is created and pushed onto the stack. When method m3 terminates, its activation record is popped off of the stack and control returns to the calling method (m2), which is now on the top of the stack.

If an exception occurs during a Java program, the programmer can look at the *call stack trace* to see where the problem is.

An activation record contains administrative data to help manage the execution of the program. It also contains a copy of the method's data (local variables and parameters).

The program stack works the same way when recursive calls are made. As discussed in Chapter 6, a recursive method calls itself, and each time it does it keeps a copy of the local data. Actually, it's the program stack that keeps track of the data.

Recall the maze problem in Chapter 6. The `traverse` method of the `Maze` class is a recursive method that keeps track of three pieces of information: the current row in the grid, the current column in the grid, and a `boolean` flag called `done` that

> **Key Concept**
>
> Recursive processing can use a stack to keep track of the appropriate data.

tells us whether or not a solution has been found. Each time the `traverse` method calls itself, an activation record is created with a copy of these three variables and their current values. Each time an instance of the `traverse` method completes execution, the associated activation record is popped off the stack.

Because of the relationship between stacks and recursion, we can always rewrite a recursive program into a nonrecursive program that uses a stack. Instead of using recursion to keep track of the data, we can create our own stack.

A version of the `traverse` method that uses a stack might look like this:

```
//-----------------------------------------------------------------
//  Attempts to iteratively traverse the maze.  It inserts special
//  characters indicating locations that have been tried.
//-----------------------------------------------------------------
```

```
public boolean traverse ()
{
    boolean done = false;
    Position pos = new Position();
    Stack stack = new Stack();
    stack.push(pos);

    while (!(done))
    {
        pos = (Position)stack.pop();
        grid[pos.getx()][pos.gety()] = TRIED;  // this cell has been tried
        if (pos.getx() == grid.length-1 && pos.gety() == grid[0].length-1)
            done = true;   // the maze is solved
        else
        {
            stack = pushNewPos (pos.getx(), pos.gety() - 1, stack);
            stack = pushNewPos (pos.getx(), pos.gety() + 1, stack);
            stack = pushNewPos (pos.getx() - 1, pos.gety(), stack);
            stack = pushNewPos (pos.getx() + 1, pos.gety(), stack);
        }
    }

    return done;
}
```

This solution does not behave exactly like the recursive solution from Chapter 6. It uses a class called Position to keep track of a position within the maze. The traverse method loops, popping the top position off of the stack, marking it as tried, and then testing to see whether we are done. If we are not done, then all of the valid moves from this position are pushed onto the stack and the loop continues. A private method called pushNewPos has been created to put the valid moves from the current position onto the stack:

```
private Stack pushNewPos (int x, int y, Stack stack)
{
    Position npos = new Position();
    npos.setx(x);
    npos.sety(y);
    if (valid(npos.getx(),npos.gety()))
        stack.push(npos);
    return stack;
}
```

This solution does not mark the successful path, the way that our traverse method from Chapter 6 did. This is left as a programming project.

8.4   IMPLEMENTING STACKS: WITH LINKS

Like the linked implementation of the set collection in Chapter 3, we can define a class called `LinkedStack` that represents a linked implementation of a stack. And we can reuse the `LinearNode` class defined in Chapter 3 to keep a linked list of nodes that represent the stack. We will use a reference variable called `top` to point to the top of the stack. Each node has a reference to the element stored at that point in the stack, and a reference to the next node (below it) in the stack.

> **Key Concept**
>
> A lined implementation of a stack adds and removes elements from one end of the linked list.

Figure 8.6 shows what this would look like for a stack of four elements, A, B, C, and D, that have been pushed onto the stack in that order.

Let's look at the `LinkedStack` class and how it works.

The push Operation

Every time a new element is pushed onto the stack, a new `LinearNode` object must be created to store it in the linked list. To put the newly created node at the top of the stack, we must set its `next` reference to the current top of the stack, and reset the `top` reference to point to the new node. We must also increase the `count` variable by one.

This results in the following code:

```
//-----------------------------------------------------------------
//  Adds the specified element to the top of the stack.
//-----------------------------------------------------------------
public void push (Object element)
{
    LinearNode temp = new LinearNode (element);

    temp.setNext(top);
    top = temp;
    count++;
}
```

Figure 8.7 shows the result of pushing the element E onto the stack shown in Figure 8.6.

The pop Operation

We implement the `pop` operation when we return a reference to the element currently stored at the top of the stack and adjust the `top` reference to the new top of the stack. Before returning any element, however, we must first ensure that there is at least one element to return. This is fairly simple:

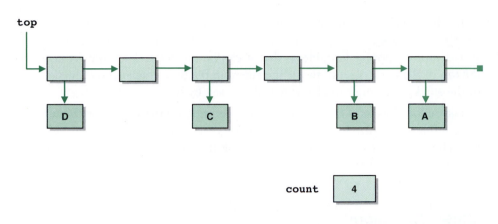

FIGURE 8.6   A linked implementation of a stack

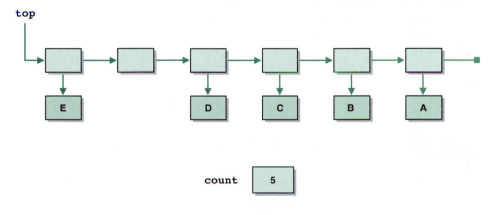

FIGURE 8.7   The stack after pushing element E

```
//-----------------------------------------------------------------
//   Removes the element at the top of the stack and returns a
//   reference to it. Throws an EmptyStackException if the stack
//   is empty.
//-----------------------------------------------------------------
public Object pop() throws EmptyStackException
{
    if (isEmpty())
        throw new EmptyStackException();

    Object result = top.getElement();
    top = top.getNext();
    count--;

    return result;
}
```

If the stack is empty, as determined by the isEmpty method, an EmptyStackException is thrown. If there is at least one element to pop, it is stored in a temporary variable so that it can be returned. Then the reference to the top of the stack is set to the next element in the list, which is now the new top of the stack. The count of elements is decreased by one as well.

Figure 8.8 illustrates the result of a pop operation on the stack from Figure 8.7. Notice that this figure is the same as our original configuration, shown in Figure 8.6. This makes sense when you stop to think that the pop operation is the opposite of the push operation.

Other Operations

In linked implementation, the peek operation is implemented by returning a reference to the element pointed to by the node pointed to by the top pointer. The isEmpty operation returns true if there are no elements (the count of elements is 0), and false otherwise. The size operation simply returns the number of elements in the stack. We can implement the iterator and toString operations using an approach like the one used in the set collection in Chapter 3. These operations are left as programming projects.

8.5   IMPLEMENTING STACKS: WITH ARRAYS

We can design an array implementation of a stack, defined by a class called ArrayStack. We start with four assumptions:

1.   The array is an array of object references.
2.   The bottom of the stack is always at index 0 of the array.

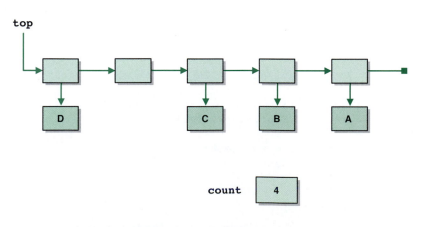

FIGURE 8.8 The stack after a pop operation

3. The elements of the stack are stored in order, one after the other, in the array.

4. An integer variable `top` stores the index of the array right after the top element in the stack.

Figure 8.9 illustrates this for a stack of A, B, C, and D elements, assuming that they have been pushed on in that order. To keep things simple, the elements are shown in the array rather than as objects referenced from the array. The variable `top` represents both the next cell into which a pushed element should be stored and the number of elements currently in the stack.

In this implementation, the bottom of the stack is always held at index 0 of the array, and the stack grows and shrinks at the higher indexes. This is more efficient than if the stack were reversed in the array. Consider the processing that would be necessary if the top of the stack were kept at index 0.

> **Key Concept**
>
> An array-based stack keeps the bottom of the stack at index 0.

The push Operation

To push an element on the stack, we insert it in the next available position in the array. The next available position is always specified by the current value of `top`. Before we can push an element on the stack, however, we need to know if the array is full and to expand it if it is. After storing the value, we update the value of `top` so that it continues to represent the number of elements in the stack.

Implementing these steps results in the following code:

```
//---------------------------------------------------------------
//   Adds the specified element to the top of the stack, expanding
//   the capacity of the stack array if necessary.
//---------------------------------------------------------------
public void push (Object element)
{
    if (size() == stack.length)
        expandCapacity();

    stack[top] = element;
    top++;
}
```

The `expandCapacity` method is implemented much the same way it was in Chapter 3 with the set collection. It serves as a support method of the class and can be implemented with private visibility.

Figure 8.10 illustrates the result of pushing an element E onto the stack that was shown in Figure 8.9. Notice that `top` now contains the value 5.

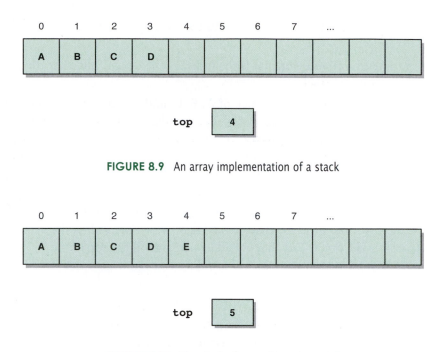

FIGURE 8.9   An array implementation of a stack

FIGURE 8.10   The stack after pushing element E

The pop Operation

The pop operation removes and returns the element at the top of the stack. For an array, that means returning the element at index top − 1. Before we can return an element, however, we must be sure there is at least one element in the stack.

The array-based version of the pop operation can be implemented as follows:

```
//-----------------------------------------------------------------
//  Removes the element at the top of the stack and returns a
//  reference to it. Throws an EmptyStackException if the stack
//  is empty.
//-----------------------------------------------------------------
public Object pop() throws EmptyStackException
{
   if (isEmpty())
      throw new EmptyStackException();

   top--;
   Object result = stack[top];
   stack[top] = null;

   return result;
}
```

If the stack is empty when the `pop` method is called, an `EmptyStack-Exception` is thrown. If the stack is not empty, the value of `top` is decreased by one (`top – 1`). Then the element at that location is stored in a temporary variable so that it can be returned. The now-empty cell in the array is then set to null. Note that the value of `top` ends up with the correct value for the now smaller stack.

Figure 8.11 illustrates the results of a `pop` operation on the stack from Figure 8.10, which brings it back to its earlier state (identical to Figure 8.9).

Other Operations

The `peek`, `isEmpty`, `size`, and `iterator` operations are left as programming projects.

8.6 IMPLEMENTING STACKS: THE `java.util.Stack` CLASS

Class `java.util.Stack` is an implementation of a stack provided in the Java Collections framework. The `java.util.Stack` class gives us the operations we have been discussing:

> The `push` operation places an object on the stack.

> The `pop` operation removes the object on top of the stack and returns a reference to it.

> The `peek` operation returns a reference to the object on top of the stack.

> The `empty` operation behaves like the `isEmpty` operation that we have been discussing.

> The `size` operation returns the number of elements in the stack.

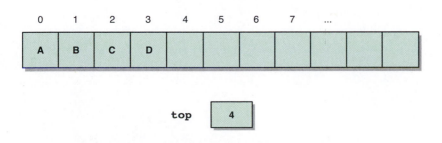

FIGURE 8.11   The stack after popping the top element

The `java.util.Stack` class is derived from the `Vector` class and uses its inherited capabilities to store the elements in the stack. Because it is built on a vector, `java.util.Stack` has the characteristics of both of these collections. It keeps track of the top of the stack using an index like the array implementation, so it does not need to store a `next` reference in each node. Plus, like the linked implementation, the `java.util.Stack` implementation only allocates additional space as needed.

Unique Operations

The `java.util.Stack` class also gives us an operation called `search`. The

> **Key Concept**
>
> The `java.util.stack` class is derived from `Vector`, which gives a stack operations it doesn't need.

search operation tells us how far from the top of the stack an object is on the stack. If the object is at the top of the stack, `search` returns the value 1. If the object is not found on the stack, `search` returns the value −1.

Unfortunately, because `java.util.Stack` is derived from the `Vector` class, quite a number of other operations inherited from the `Vector` class are available. In some cases, these additional capabilities violate the basic assumptions of a stack. Most software engineers consider this a bad use of inheritance. Because a stack is not everything a vector is, the `Stack` class should not be derived from the `Vector` class. A good developer, of course, will use only the operations appropriate to a stack.

Inheritance and Implementation

The class `java.util.Stack` is an extension of the class `java.util.Vector`, which is an extension of `java.util.AbstractList`, which is an extension of `java.util.AbstractCollection`, which is an extension of `java.lang.Object`. The `java.util.Stack` implements the `cloneable`, `collection`, `list`, and `serializable` interfaces. These relationships are shown in the UML diagram in Figure 8.12.

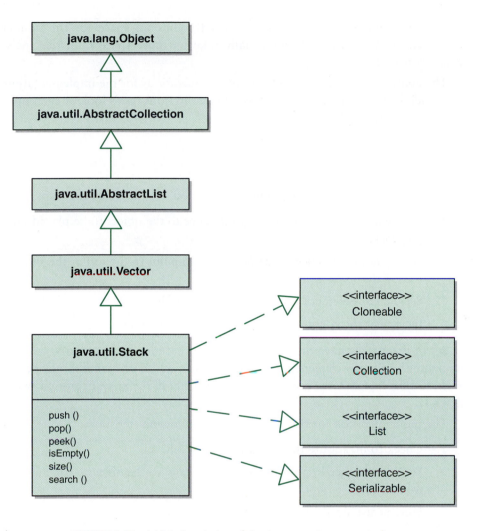

FIGURE 8.11   A UML description of the `java.util.Stack` class

8.7   ANALYSIS OF STACK IMPLEMENTATIONS

There is a space problem with the stack implementations we have discussed. The linked implementation needs more space per node because it has to store both the object and the link to the next object. However, it only takes space as it needs it, and it can store as many elements as needed up to the limitations of the hardware.

The array implementation does not need additional space for the pointer. However, array implementations usually take up more space than they need, which is wasteful.

The analysis of the time complexity of the operations for the implementations of a stack is quite simple compared to other collections. Let's look at each operation separately.

Analysis of push

The `push` operation for the linked implementation has the following steps:

1. Create a new node containing a reference to the object to be placed on the stack.
2. Set the `next` reference of the new node to point to the top of the stack (null if the stack is empty).
3. Set the `top` reference to point to the new node.
4. Increment the count of elements in the stack by one.

All of these steps have time complexity O(1) because they only take one step no matter how many elements are already in the stack. Each step is done once for each of the elements to be pushed. Using this method, the `push` operation would be O(1).

The `push` operation for the array takes the following steps:

1. Check to make sure that the array is not full.
2. Set the reference in position `top` of the array to the object being added to the stack.
3. Increment the values of `top` and `count` by one.

As with the steps for the `push` operation in the linked representation, each of these steps is O(1). Thus the operation is O(1).

The `push` operation for the `java.util.Stack` implementation is pretty much the same as it is for the array implementation: O(1).

From a time complexity point of view, there is no major difference between the `push` operations for the three implementations.

Analysis of pop

The `pop` operation for the linked implementation takes the following steps:

1. Check to make sure the stack is not empty.
2. Set a temporary reference equal to the element on top of the stack.

3. Set the `top` reference equal to the `next` reference of the node at the top of the stack.

4. Decrement the count of elements in the stack by one.

5. Return the element pointed to by the temporary reference.

Each of these operations is a single comparison or a simple assignment, so it is O(1). Thus, the pop operation for the linked implementation is O(1).

The pop operation for the array takes the following steps:

1. Check to make sure the stack is not empty.

2. Decrement the `top` counter by one.

3. Set a temporary reference equal to the element in `stack[top]`.

4. Set `stack[top]` equal to null.

5. Return the temporary reference.

All of these steps are also O(1). Thus, the pop operation for the array implementation has time complexity O(1).

The `pop` operation for `java.util.Stack` is just about the same as the `pop` operation in the array implementation, which is O(1).

So there is no real difference in the time complexity of the three implementations of the `pop` operation.

> **Key Concept**
>
> The order of every operation in every implementation of a stack collection is O(1).

The `front`, `isEmpty`, and `size` operations for all three implementations are O(1).

The `search` operation for `java.util.Stack` goes from the top to the bottom of the stack looking for the particular object. In the best case, the object we are looking for is on top of the stack. In the worst case, the object we are looking for is not on the stack, so we end up looking at all the objects on the stack, or n objects. The expected case would be roughly n/2 comparisons. This operation would be O(n).

Summary of Key Concepts

> The last element on a stack is the first one that gets removed: last in, first out (LIFO).

> Choose the structure that works best for your data.

> Some data structures work better for particular kinds of problems.

> A stack is the best data structure to use for evaluating a postfix expression.

> Recursive processing can use a stack to keep track of the appropriate data.

> A linked implementation of a stack adds and removes elements from one end of the linked list.

> An array-based stack keeps the bottom of the stack at index 0.

> The `java.util.Stack` class is derived from `Vector`, which gives a stack operations it doesn't need.

> The order of every operation in every implementation of a stack collection is O(1).

Self-Review Questions

8.1   How does a stack work?

8.2   What are the five basic operations on a stack?

8.3   What are some of the other operations that might be used on a stack?

8.4   What are the advantages to using a linked implementation instead of an array?

8.5   What are the advantages to using an array instead of a linked implementation?

8.6   What are the advantages of the `java.util.Stack` implementation of a stack?

8.7   What is the problem with the `java.util.Stack` implementation?

8.8   What is the advantage of postfix notation?

8.9   Why wouldn't you use a set to implement a stack?

Exercises

8.1 Hand-trace a stack X through the following operations:

```
X.push(new Integer(4));
X.push(new Character('T'));
Object Y = X.pop();
X.push(new Character('b'));
X.push(new Integer(2));
X.push(new Integer(5));
X.push(new Character('j'));
Object Y = X.pop();
X.push(new Character('q'));
X.push(new Integer(9));
```

8.2 Given the resulting stack X from the previous exercise, what would be the result of each of the following?

    a. `Y = X.peek();`

    b. `Y = X.pop();`

       `Z = X.peek();`

    c. `Y = X.pop();`

       `Z = X.peek();`

8.3 What would be the time complexity of the `size` operation for the linked implementation if there were no `count` variable?

8.4 Show how the undo operation in a word processor can use a stack. Give examples and draw a diagram of the stack after various actions are taken.

8.5 In the postfix expression evaluation example, the two most recent operands are popped after an operator, so that the subexpression can be evaluated. The first operand popped is treated as the second operand in the subexpression, and the second operand popped is the first. Give and explain an example that shows why this is important.

8.6 Draw an example using five integers (12, 23, 1, 45, 9) showing how a stack could be used to reverse the order (9, 45, 1, 23, 12) of these elements.

8.7 Explain what would happen to the algorithms and the time complexity of an array implementation of the stack if the top of the stack were at position 0.

Programming Projects

8.1   Finish the implementation of the `LinkedStack` class in this chapter. Complete the implementations of the `peek`, `isEmpty`, `size`, `iterator`, and `toString` methods.

8.2   Finish the implementation of the `ArrayStack` class in this chapter. Complete the implementations of the `peek`, `isEmpty`, `size`, `iterator`, and `toString` methods.

8.3   Design and implement an application that reads a sentence from the user and prints the sentence with the characters of each word backwards. Use a stack to reverse the characters of each word.

8.4   Change the solution to the postfix expression evaluation problem so that it checks to make sure the expression entered by the user is valid. Issue an error message when the expression is not valid.

8.5   Finish the solution to the iterative maze solver. Be sure that your solution marks the successful path the way that it was done in Chapter 6.

8.6   The linked implementation in this chapter uses a count variable to keep track of the number of elements in the stack. Rewrite the linked implementation without a count variable.

8.7   The array implementation in this chapter keeps the top variable pointing to the next array position above the actual top of the stack. Rewrite the array implementation so that `stack[top]` is the actual top of the stack.

8.8   There is a data structure called a drop-out stack that behaves like a stack in every way except that if the stack size is n, when the n + 1 element is pushed, the first element is lost. Implement a drop-out stack using links.

8.9   Implement the drop-out stack from the previous project using an array implementation. (*Hint:* A circular array implementation would make sense.)

8.10   Implement an integer adder using three stacks.

8.11   Implement an infix-to-postfix translator using stacks.

8.12   Implement a search operation like the one in `java.util.Stack` for the linked implementation.

8.13   Implement a search operation like the one in `java.util.Stack` for the array implementation.

8.14   Implement a class called `reverse` that uses a stack to accept elements from a user and output them in reverse order.

8.15   Create a graphical application that provides a button for push and pop from a stack, a text field to accept a string as input for push, and a text area to display the contents of the stack after each operation.

Answers to Self-Review Questions

8.1   A stack is a last in, first out (LIFO) structure.

8.2   The operations are

push—adds an element to the end of the stack

pop—removes an element from the front of the stack

peek—returns a reference to the element at the front of the stack

isEmpty—returns true if the stack is empty, returns false otherwise

wsize—returns the number of elements in the stack

8.3   makeEmpty(), destroy(), full()

8.4   A linked implementation only takes the space it needs and is only limited by the size of the hardware.

8.5   An array implementation uses less space per object because it only has to store the object and not an extra pointer. However, the array implementation will use much more space than it needs at first.

8.6   Because the java.util.Stack implementation is derived from the Vector class, it can keep track of the positions of elements in the stack using an index and does not need additional pointers. This implementation also only uses space as it is needed, like the linked implementation.

8.7   The java.util.Stack implementation is derived from the Vector class, so it inherits many operations that violate the basic assumptions of a stack.

8.8   Postfix notation lets us do without precedence rules.

8.9   First of all, sets, like stacks, are abstract data types. You would still need a particular implementation (ArraySet) in order to use the set. Second, sets are unordered collections and stacks must be ordered.

Queues 9

CHAPTER OBJECTIVES

> Look at queue processing

> Define a queue abstract data type

> Show how a queue can be used to solve problems

> Learn types of queue implementations

> Compare queue implementations

> Explore priority queues

A queue is another kind of collection. A queue is a waiting line, such as the line of customers waiting in a bank for their opportunity to talk to a teller. In many countries, a person might say "join the queue" rather than "get in line." In any queue, an item enters on one end and leaves from the other. Queues have many uses in computer algorithms.

9.1   A QUEUE ADT

A *queue* is a linear collection where the elements are added on one end and removed from the other. That is, queue elements are processed in a *first in, first out* (FIFO) manner rather than the last in, first out (LIFO) manner of a stack. Elements are removed from a queue in the same order in which they are placed on the queue.

This is basically the same as a waiting line. When a customer enters a bank, he or she begins waiting at the end of the line. When a teller is free, the customer at the beginning of the line goes to that teller. Eventually every customer who started out at the end of the line moves to the front of the line and leaves. For any given set of people, the first person to get in line is the first person to leave it.

The queue process is pictured in Figure 9.1. Usually a queue is drawn horizontally. One end is the *front* of the queue and the other is the *rear* of the queue. Elements go onto the rear of the queue and come off of the front. Sometimes the front of the queue is called the *head* and the rear of the queue the *tail*.

Let's look at queue processing compared to the LIFO (last in, first out) processing of a stack, discussed in Chapter 8. In a stack, the processing occurs at only one end of the collection. In a queue, processing occurs at both ends.

The queue ADT operations are listed in Figure 9.2. *Enqueue* is the process of adding a new element to the end of a queue. Likewise, *dequeue* is the process of removing the element at the front of a queue. The `first` operation lets the user look at the element at the front of the queue without removing it from the collection.

Remember that naming conventions are not the same for all collection operations. Sometimes enqueue is simply called `add` or `insert`. The dequeue operation is sometimes called `remove` or `serve`. The `first` operation is sometimes called `front`.

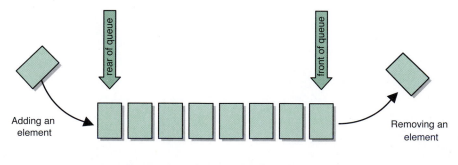

FIGURE 9.1   A conceptual view of a queue

Operation	Description
enqueue	Adds an element to the rear of the queue.
dequeue	Removes an element from the front of the queue.
first	Examines the element at the front of the queue.
isEmpty	Determines if the queue is empty.
size	Determines the number of elements on the queue.
toString	Returns a string representation of the queue.

FIGURE 9.2 The operations on a queue

The operations of a queue and a stack are similar. The enqueue, dequeue, and first operations are like the stack operations push, pop, and peek. Similar to a stack, there are no operations that allow the user to "reach into" the middle of a queue and reorganize or remove elements. If we need to do that we should use a different kind of collection, a generic list of some kind, such as those discussed in the next chapter.

As we did with stacks, we define a QueueADT interface that represents the queue operations, separating the general purpose of the operations from the ways they could be used. A Java version of the QueueADT interface is shown in Listing 9.1, and its UML description is shown in Figure 9.3.

Listing 9.1

```
//********************************************************************
//   QueueADT.java          Authors: Lewis/Chase
//
//   Defines the interface to a queue collection.
//********************************************************************

package jss2;

import java.util.Iterator;

public interface QueueADT
{
    //  Adds one element to the rear of the queue
    public void enqueue (Object element);

    //  Removes and returns the element at the front of the queue
    public Object dequeue();
```

Listing 9.1   **continued**

```java
//  Returns without removing the element at the front of the queue
public Object first();

//  Returns true if the queue contains no elements
public boolean isEmpty();

//  Returns the number of elements in the queue
public int size();

//  Returns a string representation of the queue
public String toString();
}
```

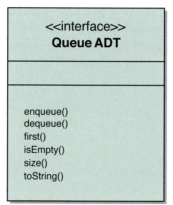

FIGURE 9.3 The QueueADT interface in UML

In addition to the standard queue operations, we have also included a toString method. The toString method is not a classic operation on a queue. Also, we have deliberately left out an iterator because the whole idea of a queue is one thing at a time, in order.

Queues can be used in many ways. Before we explore the ways to use a queue, let's look at how a queue can be used to solve problems.

9.2   USING QUEUES: CODE KEYS

A *Caesar cipher* is a simple way to encode messages by shifting each letter in a message along the alphabet by a constant number of letters. For example, if we shift by 3, then in an encoded message, each letter is shifted three characters forward: a is replaced with d, b with e, c with f, and so on. The end of the alphabet wraps back around to the beginning. Thus, w is replaced with z, x with a, y with b, and z with c.

To decode the message, each letter is shifted the same number of characters back. Therefore, the encoded message

```
vlpsolflwb iroorzv frpsohalwb
```

would be decoded into

```
simplicity follows complexity
```

Julius Caesar actually used this type of code in some of his secret government messages (hence the name). Unfortunately, the Caesar cipher is easy to break. There are only 26 possibilities for shifting the characters and the code can be broken by trying various key values (a shift of 1, a shift of 2, a shift of 3, and so on) until one works.

A better way of encoding uses a *repeating key*. Instead of shifting each character by a constant number, we can shift each character by a different number using a list of key values. If the message is longer than the list of key values, we just start using the key over again from the beginning. For example, if the key values are

```
3  1  7  4  2  5
```

then the first character is shifted by three, the second character by one, the third character by seven, and so on. After shifting the sixth character by five, we start using the key over again. The seventh character is shifted by three, the eighth by one, and so on.

Figure 9.4 shows the message "knowledge is power" encoded using this repeating key. Note that this approach encodes the same letter into different characters, depending on where it is in the message and which key value is used to encode it.

The program in Listing 9.2 uses a repeating key to encode and decode a message. The key is stored in a queue. After a key value is used, it is put back on the end of the queue so that the key repeats as needed for long messages. The key in this example uses both positive and negative values. Figure 9.5 illustrates the UML description of the Codes class.

> **Key Concept**
>
> A queue is a good collection for storing a repeating code key.

Encoded Message:	n	o	v	a	n	j	g	h	l		m	u		u	r	x	l	v
Key:	3	1	7	4	2	5	3	1	7		4	2		5	3	1	7	4
Decoded Message:	k	n	o	w	l	e	d	g	e		i	s		p	o	w	e	r

FIGURE 9.4   An encoded message using a repeating key

Listing 9.2

```java
//*****************************************************************
//  Codes.java         Authors: Lewis/Chase
//
//  Demonstrates the use of queues to encrypt and decrypt messages.
//*****************************************************************

import jss2.LinkedQueue;

public class Codes
{
   //---------------------------------------------------------------
   //  Encode and decode a message using a key of values stored in
   //  a queue.
   //---------------------------------------------------------------
   public static void main ( String[] args)
   {
      int[] key = {5, 12, -3, 8, -9, 4, 10};
      int keyValue;

      String encoded = "", decoded = "";

      String message = "All programmers are playwrights and all " +
                       "computers are lousy actors.";

      LinkedQueue keyQueue1 = new LinkedQueue();
      LinkedQueue keyQueue2 = new LinkedQueue();

      // load key queue
      for (int scan=0; scan < key.length; scan++)
      {
         keyQueue1.enqueue (new Integer(key[scan]));
         keyQueue2.enqueue (new Integer(key[scan]));
      }
```

Listing 9.2   **continued**

```java
    // encode message
    for (int scan=0; scan < message.length(); scan++)
    {
        keyValue = ((Integer) keyQueue1.dequeue()).intValue();
        encoded += (char) ((int)message.charAt(scan) + keyValue);
        keyQueue1.enqueue (new Integer(keyValue));
    }

    System.out.println ("Encoded Message:\n" + encoded + "\n");

    // decode message
    for (int scan=0; scan < encoded.length(); scan++)
    {
        keyValue = ((Integer) keyQueue2.dequeue()).intValue();
        decoded += (char) ((int)encoded.charAt(scan) - keyValue);
        keyQueue2.enqueue (new Integer(keyValue));
    }

    System.out.println ("Decoded Message:\n" + decoded);
    }
}
```

Output

```
Encoded Message:
Fxi(gvyl~^udi|x,^z\$zqmv_imqm?p(Xrn%mit_gyr|r|\v}%mom_pyz_v(Xg~t~p6

Decoded Message:
All programmers are playwrights and all computers are lousy actors.
```

This program actually uses two copies of the key stored in two separate queues. The idea is that the person encoding the message has one copy of the key, and the person decoding the message has another. Two copies of the key are helpful in this program because the decoding process needs to match up the first character of the message with the first value in the key.

Also, note that this program doesn't bother to wrap around the end of the alphabet. It encodes any character in the Unicode character set by shifting it to some other position in the character set. Therefore we can encode any character, including uppercase letters, lowercase letters, and punctuation. Even spaces get encoded.

Using a queue to store the key makes it easy to repeat the key by putting each key value back onto the queue as soon as it is used. The queue keeps the key values in the proper order, and we don't have to worry about reaching the end of the key and starting over.

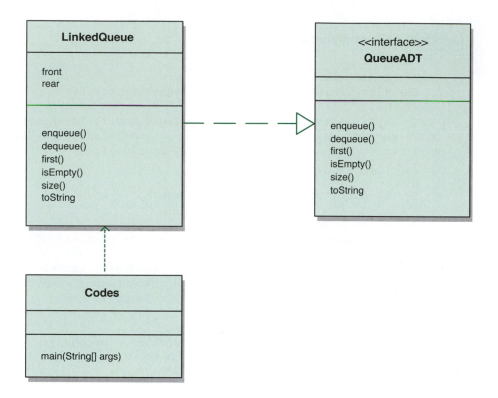

FIGURE 9.5   UML description of the Codes program

9.3   USING QUEUES: TICKET COUNTER SIMULATION

Imagine you are waiting in line to buy tickets to a movie. The more cashiers there are, the faster the line moves. The theatre manager wants to keep his customers happy, but doesn't want to employ any more cashiers than he has to. Suppose the

Key Concept

Queues are often used to represent waiting lines.

manager wants to keep the total time needed by a customer to less than seven minutes. Being able to *simulate* the effect of adding more cashiers during peak business hours helps the manager plan better. And, as we've discussed, a queue is the perfect collection for representing a waiting line.

Our simulated ticket counter will use the following assumptions:

> There is only one line and it is first-come first-served (a queue).

> Customers arrive about every 15 seconds (it is a popular movie).

> If there is a cashier available, people buy tickets as soon as they arrive.

> Selling a customer a ticket and getting them on their way takes on average two minutes (120 seconds) from the time they reach a cashier.

First we can create a `Customer` class, as shown in Listing 9.3. A `Customer` object keeps track of the time the customer arrives and the time the customer departs the ticket window and enters the theater after buying a ticket. The total time spent by the customer is therefore the departure time minus the arrival time. To keep things simple, we'll measure time in seconds, so a time value can be stored as a single integer. Our time will begin at 0.

Listing 9.3

```java
//********************************************************************
//  Customer.java        Authors: Lewis/Chase
//
//  Represents a waiting customer.
//********************************************************************

public class Customer
{
    private int arrivalTime, departureTime;

    //----------------------------------------------------------------
    //  Creates a new customer with the specified arrival time.
    //----------------------------------------------------------------
    public Customer (int arrives)
    {
        arrivalTime = arrives;
        departureTime = 0;
    }

    //----------------------------------------------------------------
    //  Returns the arrival time of this customer.
    //----------------------------------------------------------------
    public int getArrivalTime()
    {
        return arrivalTime;
    }

    //----------------------------------------------------------------
    //  Sets the departure time for this customer.
    //----------------------------------------------------------------
```

Listing 9.3   **continued**

```java
public void setDepartureTime (int departs)
{
    departureTime = departs;
}

//------------------------------------------------------------------
//  Returns the departure time of this customer.
//------------------------------------------------------------------
public int getDepartureTime()
{
    return departureTime;
}

//------------------------------------------------------------------
//  Computes and returns the total time spent by this customer.
//------------------------------------------------------------------
public int totalTime()
{
    return departureTime - arrivalTime;
}
}
```

Next we will create a queue of customers, then see how long it takes those customers to get through the queue if there is only one cashier. Then we'll process the same queue of customers with two cashiers. Then we'll do it again with three cashiers. We'll continue up to ten cashiers. At the end we'll compare the average time it takes to process a customer.

Because of our assumption that customers arrive every 15 seconds (on average), we can preload a queue with customers. We will process 100 customers.

In the program shown in Listing 9.4 the outer loop determines how many cashiers are used. For each pass, the customers are taken from the queue in turn and processed by a cashier. The total elapsed time is tracked, and at the end of each pass we figure the average time. Figure 9.6 shows the UML description of the TicketCounter and Customer classes.

The results are shown in Figure 9.7. Note that with eight cashiers, the customers do not wait at all. The time of 120 seconds is only the time it takes to walk up and buy the ticket. Increasing the number of cashiers to nine or ten or more will not give us a better time. Because the manager wants to keep the total average time to less than seven minutes (420 seconds), the simulation tells him that he should have six cashiers.

Listing 9.4

```java
//********************************************************************
//  TicketCounter.java       Authors: Lewis/Chase
//
//  Demonstrates the use of a queue for simulating a waiting line.
//********************************************************************

import jss2.*;

public class TicketCounter
{
   final static int PROCESS = 120;
   final static int MAX_CASHIERS = 10;
   final static int NUM_CUSTOMERS = 100;

   public static void main ( String[] args)
   {
      Customer customer;
      LinkedQueue customerQueue = new LinkedQueue();
      int[] cashierTime = new int[MAX_CASHIERS];
      int totalTime, averageTime, departs;

      // process the simulation for various number of cashiers
      for (int cashiers=1; cashiers <= MAX_CASHIERS; cashiers++)
      {
         // set each cashier's time to zero initially
         for (int count=0; count < cashiers; count++)
            cashierTime[count] = 0;

         // load customer queue
         for (int count=1; count <= NUM_CUSTOMERS; count++)
            customerQueue.enqueue(new Customer(count*15));

         totalTime = 0;

         // process all customers in the queue
         while (!(customerQueue.isEmpty()))
         {
            for (int count=0; count < cashiers; count++)
            {
               if (!(customerQueue.isEmpty()))
               {
                  customer = (Customer) customerQueue.dequeue();
                  if (customer.getArrivalTime() > cashierTime[count])
                     departs = customer.getArrivalTime() + PROCESS;
                  else
                     departs = cashierTime[count] + PROCESS;
                  customer.setDepartureTime (departs);
```

Listing 9.4   **continued**

```
                    cashierTime[count] = departs;
                    totalTime += customer.totalTime();
                }
            }
        }

        // output results for this simulation
        averageTime = totalTime / NUM_CUSTOMERS;
        System.out.println ("Number of cashiers: " + (cashiers));
        System.out.println ("Average time: " + averageTime + "\n");
    }
    }
}
```

Output

```
Number of cashiers: 1
Average time: 5317

Number of cashiers: 2
Average time: 2325

Number of cashiers: 3
Average time: 1332

Number of cashiers: 4
Average time: 840

Number of cashiers: 5
Average time: 547

Number of cashiers: 6
Average time: 355

Number of cashiers: 7
Average time: 219

Number of cashiers: 8
Average time: 120

Number of cashiers: 9
Average time: 120

Number of cashiers: 10
Average time: 120
```

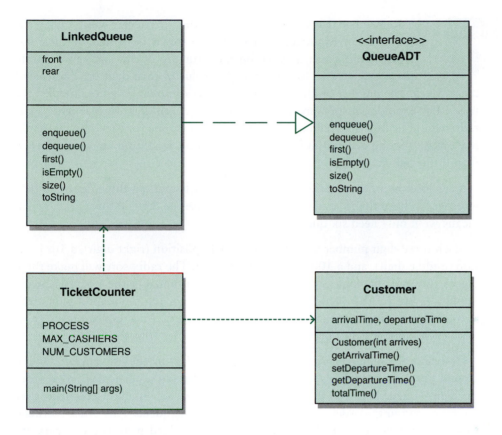

FIGURE 9.6   UML description of the `TicketCounter` program

Number of Cashiers:	1	2	3	4	5	6	7	8	9	10
Average Time (sec):	5317	2325	1332	840	547	355	219	120	120	120

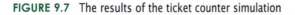

FIGURE 9.7   The results of the ticket counter simulation

9.4   USING QUEUES: RADIX SORT

Another interesting application of queues is a *radix sort*. We looked at several sorting algorithms in Chapter 5, but we didn't cover radix sort for two reasons. First, radix sort is not a comparison sort and doesn't have much in common with the techniques that we discussed in Chapter 5. Second, a radix sort needs to use a queue (several of them in fact) or a similar collection.

Remember that a sort is based on some particular value, called the *sort key*. For example, a set of people might be sorted by their last name. A radix sort is based on the structure of the sort key. Separate queues are created for each possible value of each digit or character of the sort key. The number of queues, or the number of possible values, is called the *radix*. For example, if we were sorting strings made up of lowercase letters, the radix would be 26. We would use 26 separate queues, one for each possible letter. If we were sorting decimal numbers, then the radix would be ten, one for each digit 0 through 9.

Let's look at an example that uses a radix sort to put ten three-digit numbers in order. To keep things manageable, we'll only use the digits 0 through 5, which means we'll only need six queues.

Each three-digit number to be sorted has a 1s position (right digit), a 10s position (middle digit), and a 100s position (left digit). The radix sort will make three passes through the values, one for each digit position. On the first pass, each number is put on the queue according to its 1s digit. On the second pass, each number is put on the queue according to its 10s digit. And finally, on the third pass, each number is put on the queue according to its 100s digit.

To begin, the numbers are loaded into the queues from the original list. On the second pass, the numbers are taken from the queues in a particular order: from the digit 0 queue first, and then the digit 1 queue, and so on. For each queue, they are processed in the order in which they come off the queue. This order is crucial to the operation of a radix sort. Likewise, on the third pass, the numbers are again taken from the queues in the same way. When the numbers are pulled off of the queues after the third pass, they will be completely sorted.

Figure 9.8 shows the processing of a radix sort for ten three-digit numbers. The number 442 is taken from the original list and put onto the digit 2 queue (the third row from the top), because the number in the 1s place is a 2. Then 503 is put onto the digit 3 queue. Then 312 is put onto the digit 2 queue (following 442). This continues for all values, resulting in the set of queues for the 1s position.

Imagine, as we begin the second pass, that we have a fresh set of six empty digit queues. (In reality, the queues can be used over again if processed carefully.) To begin the second pass, the numbers are taken from the 0 digit queue first. The number 250 is put onto the digit 5 queue, and then 420 is put onto the digit 2 queue. Then we can move to the next queue, taking 341 and putting it onto the queue for digit 4. This continues until all numbers have been taken off of the 1s position queues, resulting in the set of queues for the 10s position.

For the third pass, the process is again repeated. First, 102 is put onto the digit 1 queue, then 503 is put onto the digit 5 queue, then 312 is put onto the digit 3 queue. This continues until we have the final set of digit queues for the 100s position. These numbers are now in sorted order: 102, 143, 145, 250, 312, and so on.

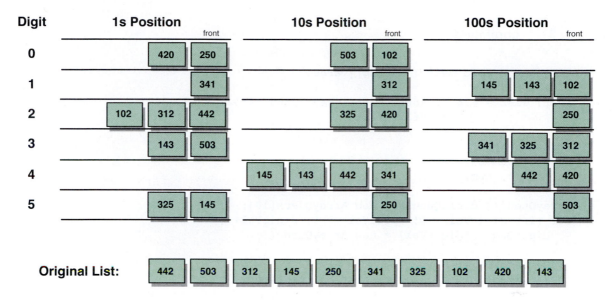

FIGURE 9.8   A radix sort of ten three-digit numbers

Let's now look at a program that uses the radix sort. For this example, we will sort four-digit numbers, and we'll use all ten digits. Listing 9.5 shows the RadixSort class, which contains a single main method. Using an array of ten queue objects (one for each digit 0 through 9), this method processes the radix sort. Figure 9.9 shows the UML description of the RadixSort class.

Listing 9.5

```
//********************************************************************
//  RadixSort.java        Authors: Lewis/Chase
//
//  Demonstrates the use of queues in the execution of a radix sort.
//********************************************************************

import jss2.ArrayQueue;

public class RadixSort
{
    //----------------------------------------------------------------
    //  Perform a radix sort on a set of numeric values.
    //----------------------------------------------------------------
```

Listing 9.5   **continued**

```java
public static void main ( String[] args)
{
    int[] list = {7843, 4568, 8765, 6543, 7865, 4532, 9987, 3241,
                  6589, 6622, 1211};

    String temp;
    Integer numObj;
    int digit, num;

    ArrayQueue[] digitQueues = new ArrayQueue[10];
    for (int digitVal = 0; digitVal <= 9; digitVal++)
        digitQueues[digitVal] = new ArrayQueue();

    // sort the list
    for (int position=0; position <= 3; position++)
    {
        for (int scan=0; scan < list.length; scan++)
        {
            temp = String.valueOf (list[scan]);
            digit = Character.digit (temp.charAt(3-position), 10);
            digitQueues[digit].enqueue (new Integer(list[scan]));
        }

        // gather numbers back into list
        num = 0;
        for (int digitVal = 0; digitVal <= 9; digitVal++)
        {
            while (!(digitQueues[digitVal].isEmpty()))
            {
                numObj = (Integer) digitQueues[digitVal].dequeue();
                list[num] = numObj.intValue();
                num++;
            }
        }
    }

    // output the sorted list
    for (int scan=0; scan < list.length; scan++)
        System.out.println (list[scan]);
}
}
```

Output

```
1211
3241
4532
```

Listing 9.5   **continued**

```
4568
6543
6589
6622
7843
7865
8765
9987
```

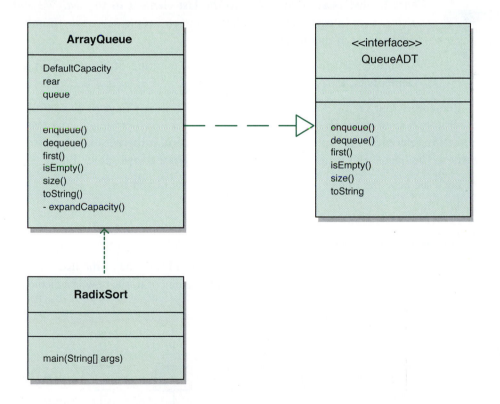

FIGURE 9.10   UML description of the RadixSort program

In the RadixSort program, the numbers are first stored in an array called list. After each pass, the numbers are pulled off of the queues and stored back in the list array in the right order. This lets the program reuse the original array of ten queues for each pass of the sort.

A radix sort can be used with any type of data as long as the sort key can be divided into well-defined positions. Note that unlike the sorts covered in Chapter 7, we can't create a generic radix sort for any object, because positioning the key values is a basic part of the process.

9.5   IMPLEMENTING QUEUES: WITH LINKS

Because it is a linear collection, we can implement a queue as a linked list of `LinearNode` objects, as we did with stacks. The main difference is that we will have to work on both ends of the list. So in addition to a reference (called `front`) pointing to the first element in the list, we will also keep track of a second reference (called `rear`) that points to the last element in the list. We will also use an integer variable called `count` to keep track of the number of elements in the queue.

> **Key Concept**
>
> A linked implementation of a queue uses references to the first and last elements of the linked list.

Figure 9.10 shows the linked list implemention of a queue with the elements A, B, C, and D, in that order.

Remember that Figure 9.10 is the general case. We always have to be careful to accurately maintain our references in special cases. For an empty queue, the `front` and `rear` references are both null and the `count` is zero. If there is exactly one element in the queue, the `front` and `rear` references point to the same object.

Let's see how the queue operations work with this linked list.

The enqueue Operation

For the `enqueue` operation we put the new element on the rear of the list. Usually that means setting the `next` reference of the old last element to the new last element,

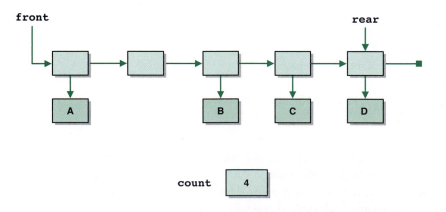

FIGURE 9.10   A linked implementation of a queue

and resetting the `rear` reference to the new last element. If the queue is empty, the `front` reference must also be set to the new (and only) element. This operation can be implemented as follows:

```
//--------------------------------------------------------------------
//  Adds the specified element to the rear of the queue.
//--------------------------------------------------------------------
public void enqueue (Object element)
{
    LinearNode node = new LinearNode(element);

    if (isEmpty())
        front = node;
    else
        rear.setNext (node);

    rear = node;
    count++;
}
```

Note that if the queue is empty, the `next` reference of the new node doesn't need to be set, because it has already been set to null in the `LinearNode` class. The `rear` reference is set to the new node in either case, and the `count` is increased by one.

Figure 9.11 shows the linked list implementation of the queue from Figure 9.10 after element E has been added.

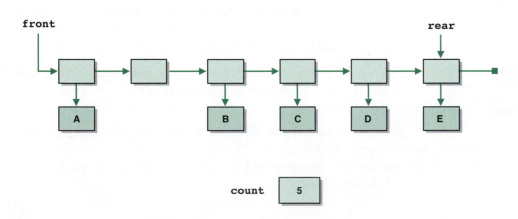

FIGURE 9.11   The queue after adding element E

The `dequeue` Operation

The first thing to do when implementing the `dequeue` operation is to make sure there is at least one element in the queue. If the queue is empty, an `EmptyCollectionException` is thrown. It makes sense to create a general `EmptyCollectionException` to which we can pass a parameter specifying which collection we are dealing with. If there is at least one element in the queue, the first element in the list is returned and the `front` reference is updated:

```
//-----------------------------------------------------------------
//   Removes the element at the front of the queue and returns a
//   reference to it. Throws an EmptyCollectionException if the
//   queue is empty.
//-----------------------------------------------------------------
public Object dequeue() throws EmptyCollectionException
{
    if (isEmpty())
        throw new EmptyCollectionException ("queue");

    Object result = front.getElement();
    front = front.getNext();
    count--;

    if (isEmpty())
        rear = null;

    return result;
}
```

For the `dequeue` operation, we have to think about what will happen if we return the only element in the queue. If, after we remove the front element, the queue is empty, the `rear` reference is set to null. In this case, the `front` will be null because it was set equal to the `next` reference of the last element in the list.

Figure 9.12 shows the result of a `dequeue` operation on the queue from Figure 9.11. The element A at the front of the list is removed and returned to the user.

Unlike the `pop` and `push` operations on a stack, the `dequeue` operation is not the opposite of `enqueue`. That is, Figure 9.12 is not identical to Figure 9.10, because the `enqueue` and `dequeue` operations are working on opposite ends of the collection.

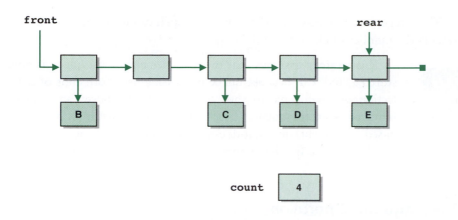

FIGURE 9.12   The queue after a dequeue operation

Other Operations

The other operations in the linked queue implementation are fairly straightforward. The `first` operation returns a reference to the element at the front of the queue. The `isEmpty` operation returns true if the count of elements is 0 (the queue is empty), and false otherwise. The `size` operation simply returns the count of elements in the queue. Finally, the `toString` operation returns a string made up of the `toString` results of each individual element (for example, element B could be represented as `"B"`). These operations are left as programming projects.

9.6   IMPLEMENTING QUEUES: WITH ARRAYS

One way to use an array with a queue is to fix one end of the queue (say, the front) at index 0 of the array. The elements are then stored one after another in the array. Figure 9.13 shows a queue stored this way: elements A, B, C, and D have been added to the queue in that order.

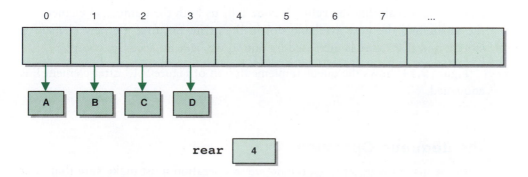

FIGURE 9.13   An array implementation of a queue

The integer variable `rear` indicates the next open cell in the array. It also represents the number of elements in the queue.

This strategy assumes that the first element in the queue is always stored at index 0. Because queue processing uses both ends of the collection, we will have to shift the elements whenever an element is removed from the queue. Later in this chapter, we look at an array-based implementation that doesn't need element shifting. But for now, let's look at the fixed-end approach.

The enqueue Operation

The `enqueue` operation adds a new element to the rear of the queue, which is stored at the high end of the array. As long as there is room in the array for another element, it can be stored in the location indicated by the integer `rear`. This operation can be implemented as follows:

```
//--------------------------------------------------------------
//  Adds the specified element to the rear of the queue, expanding
//  the capacity of the queue array if necessary.
//--------------------------------------------------------------
public void enqueue (Object element)
{
   if (size() == queue.length)
      expandCapacity();

   queue[rear] = element;
   rear++;
}
```

We expand the capacity of the queue array the same way we expanded other collections. Recall that the value of `rear` tells us both the number of elements in the queue and the next available slot in the array. So, first the new element is stored, and then `rear` is increased by one so we have an accurate count.

Figure 9.14 shows the queue implementation of Figure 9.13 after element E is enqueued.

The dequeue Operation

With the array queue strategy, the `dequeue` operation must make sure that after it removes the first element of the queue, the new first element (currently the second element in the list) is stored at index 0 of the array. Furthermore, because we

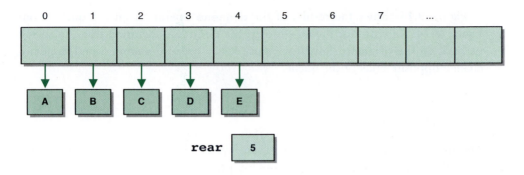

FIGURE 9.14   The queue after adding element E

cannot have gaps in the list, all elements must be shifted down one cell in the array. This operation can be implemented as follows:

```
//------------------------------------------------------------------
//   Removes the element at the front of the queue and returns a
//   reference to it. Throws an EmptyCollectionException if the
//   queue is empty.
//------------------------------------------------------------------
public Object dequeue() throws EmptyCollectionException
{
    if (isEmpty())
        throw new EmptyCollectionException ("queue");

    Object result = queue[0];

    // shift the elements
    for (int scan=0; scan < rear; scan++)
        queue[scan] = queue[scan+1];

    rear--;
    queue[rear] = null;

    return result;
}
```

This method first checks to see if the queue has at least one element. If not, it throws an `EmptyCollectionException`. If there is at least one element, the element is stored for return, the remaining elements (if any) are shifted, and the value of `rear` is decreased by one to show that we now have one less element in the queue. Finally, the copy of the reference to the last element in the queue is overwritten with `null`.

Figure 9.15 shows the results of the `dequeue` operation on the queue from Figure 9.14. As with our linked strategy, the `dequeue` operation does not bring us back to the original, shown in Figure 9.13, because `enqueue` and `dequeue` change opposite ends of the queue.

Other Operations

The implementation of the `first`, `isEmpty`, `size`, and `toString` operations using this strategy are left as programming projects.

9.7   PRIORITY QUEUES

Sometimes when items are put into a queue, it is important to handle a few of them first, regardless of when they entered the queue. For example, imagine an airport line where passengers whose planes are about to depart are allowed to cut in line. An agent of the airline will often walk through the line, moving these passengers to the front so they do not miss their planes. This situation is called a *priority queue*.

> **Key Concept**
>
> Priority queues store data sorted by a priority value.

There are several ways a priority queue can be implemented, but generally the queue is stored, sorted by priority. Figure 9.16 shows how a priority queue works. Items with the same priority follow the first in, first out processing of a regular queue.

Priorities for queues can be determined in many ways. Often elements will either implement the comparable interface for a natural ordering, or will have a priority method that will return an integer value—the larger the number the higher the priority.

For example, let's look at how an extension of the `LinkedQueue` class would handle this. Because the `dequeue` method would work the same with a priority queue as with a regular queue, all we would need to change would be the

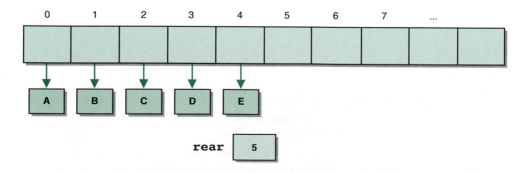

FIGURE 9.15   The queue after removing the first element

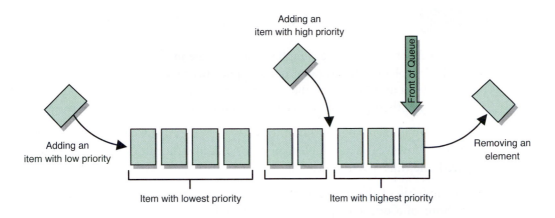

FIGURE 9.16 A priority queue

enqueue method. We will assume the element to be added implements a `PriorityElement` interface with the priority method used below.

```
//----------------------------------------------------------------------
// Adds the specified element to the rear of the items in the queue that share
// the same priority.
//----------------------------------------------------------------------
public void enqueue (PriorityElement element)
{
    LinearNode node = new LinearNode(element);

    if(isEmpty())
        front = node;
    else
        {
            // Search for the appropriate place to put the node
            if(front.value().priority() < element.priority())
            {
                element.setNext(front);
                front = element;
            }
            else
            {
                LinearNode temp = front;
                while(temp.next() != null && temp.next().value().priority() >
                    element.priority())
                    temp = temp.next();
                element.setNext(temp.next());
                temp.setNext(element);
            }
        }
}
```

9.8   ANALYSIS OF QUEUE IMPLEMENTATIONS

There is a difference in space complexity among the implementations of a queue. The linked implementations require more space per node since they have to store both the object and the link to the next object. However, they only allocate space as needed and then can store elements up to the limitations of the hardware.

The array implementation does not need the extra space per element for the reference. However, array implementations usually allocate more space than is required and thus may be wasteful.

The analysis of the time complexity of the operations for the various implementations of a queue is quite simple. Let's take each operation for each of the three implementations in turn.

enqueue

The `enqueue` operation for the linked implementation has the following steps:

1. Create a new node with the `element` reference pointing to the object to be added to the queue and with the `next` reference set to null.
2. Set the `next` reference of the current node at the rear of the queue to point to the new object.
3. Set the `rear` reference to point to the new object.
4. Increase the `count` of elements in the queue by one.

All of these steps have time complexity O(1) because they require only one processing step no matter how many elements are already in the queue. Each of these steps has to be taken once for each of elements enqueued. Thus, using this method, the `enqueue` operation is O(1).

The `enqueue` operation for the array implementation takes the following steps:

1. Check to make sure that the array is not full (if it is, throw an exception).
2. Set the reference at the rear of the queue to point to the object being added.
3. Increase the values of `rear` and `count` by one.

Like the steps for the `enqueue` operation, each of these steps is O(1), so the operation is O(1).

The `enqueue` operation for a linked priority queue takes the following steps:

1. Create a new node with the element reference, pointing to the object to be added to the queue. Set the next reference to null.

2. Check to see if the new item has a higher priority than the front of the list. If so, make the new item the new front of the list and exit the method.

3. Search the list of nodes to find the last node with a priority higher than the new element, then insert the element after the higher-priority node.

The first two steps in this process are O(1). However, the third step could be O(n). Therefore, the complexity of the enqueue operation for a linked priority queue is O(n).

dequeue

The `dequeue` operation for both linked implementations takes the following steps:

1. Check to make sure the queue is not empty (throw an exception if it is).

2. Set a temporary reference to the node pointed to by `front`.

3. Set the `front` reference equal to the `next` reference of the node at the head of the queue.

4. Decrease the `count` of elements in the queue by one.

5. Return the element pointed to by the temporary reference.

As with our earlier examples, each of these operations is a single comparison or a simple assignment and is therefore O(1). Thus, the `dequeue` operation for the linked implementation is O(1).

The `dequeue` operation for the array implementation has the following steps:

1. Check to make sure the queue is not empty (throw an exception if it is).

2. Set a temporary object equal to the first element in the array.

3. Shift all of the elements in the array one position to the left.

4. Decrease the values of `rear` and `count` by one.

5. Return the temporary object.

All of these steps are O(1), with the exception of shifting all of the remaining elements in the array to the left, which is O(n). So the `dequeue` operation for the array implementation has time complexity O(n).

> **Key Concept**
>
> The shifting of elements in an array implementation creates an O(n) complexity.

The `front`, `isEmpty`, and `size` operations for all three implementations are O(1).

As you can see, we do pay a time complexity penalty for `dequeue` operations on the array implementation.

Summary of Key Concepts

> Queue elements are processed on a first in, first out (FIFO) basis.

> A queue is a good collection for storing a repeating code key.

> Queues are often used to represent waiting lines.

> A radix sort is based on queue processing.

> A linked implementation of a queue uses references to the first and last elements of the linked list.

> The enqueue and dequeue operations work on opposite ends of the queue.

> Because queue operations change both ends of the collection, fixing one end at index 0 means that the elements must be shifted.

> Priority queues store data sorted by a priority value.

> The shifting of elements in an array implementation creates an O(n) complexity.

Self-Review Questions

9.1   What is the difference between a queue and a stack?

9.2   What are the five basic operations on a queue?

9.3   What are some of the other queue operations?

9.4   How many queues would it take to use a radix sort to sort names stored as all lowercase letters?

9.5   Can the front and rear references in a linked implementation be equal?

9.6   Can the front and rear references in an array implementation be equal?

9.7   Can the front and rear references in a priority queue be equal?

9.8   Which implementation has the worst time complexity?

9.9   Which implementation has the worst space complexity?

Exercises

9.1   Hand-trace a queue X through the following operations:

```
X.enqueue(new Integer(4));
X.enqueue(new Character('T'));
Object Y = X.dequeue();
X.enqueue(new Character('b'));
```

```
X.enqueue(new Integer(2));
X.enqueue(new Integer(5));
X.enqueue(new Character('j'));
Object Y = X.dequeue();
X.enqueue(new Character('q'));
X.enqueue(new Integer(9));
```

9.2   Given queue X from Exercise 9.1, what would be the result of each
       of the following?

   a. `X.front();`

   b. `Y = X.dequeue();`

       `X.front();`

   c. `Y = X.dequeue();`

       `X.front();`

9.3   What would be the time complexity of the `size` operation for each
       of the three implementations if there were no `count` variable?

9.4   Under what circumstances could the `front` and `rear` references be
       equal for each of the three implementations?

9.5   Hand-trace the ticket counter problem for 22 customers and 4
       cashiers. Graph the total process time for each person. What do
       these results tell you?

9.6   Hand-trace a radix sort for the following list of five-digit student ID
       numbers (each digit must be between 1 and 5):

       13224

       32131

       54355

       12123

       22331

       21212

       33333

       54312

9.7   What is the time complexity of a radix sort compared to the sorting
       algorithms discussed in Chapter 7?

9.8   Compare and contrast the `enqueue` method of the `LinkedQueue`
       class to the `push` method of the `LinkedStack` class from Chapter 8.

9.9   Describe two different ways the `isEmpty` method of the
       `LinkedQueue` class could be implemented.

9.10   Name five everyday examples of a queue other than those discussed
       in this chapter.

9.11   Explain why elements don't need to be shifted in the array implementation of a stack but they do in the array implementation of a queue.

Programming Projects

9.1   Complete the implementation of the `LinkedQueue` class presented in this chapter. Be sure you complete the implementations of the `first`, `isEmpty`, `size`, and `toString` methods.

9.2   Complete the implementation of the `ArrayQueue` class presented in this chapter. Be sure you complete the implementations of the `first`, `isEmpty`, `size`, and `toString` methods.

9.3   Write a version of the `ArrayQueue` class that keeps the rear of the queue fixed at index 0.

9.4   All of the implementations in this chapter use a `count` variable to keep track of the number of elements in the queue. Rewrite the linked implementation without a `count` variable.

9.5   All of the implementations in this chapter use a `count` variable to keep track of the number of elements in the queue. Rewrite the array implementation without a `count` variable.

9.6   A data structure called a *deque* (pronounced "deck") is closely related to a queue. The name *deque* stands for double-ended queue. The difference between a queue and a deque is that with a deque, you can insert or remove from either end of the queue. Implement a deque using arrays.

9.7   Implement the deque from Programming Project 9.6 using links. (*Hint*: Each node will need a `next` and a `previous` reference.)

9.8   Implement the `front`, `isEmpty`, and `size` operations for the array implementation of a queue.

9.9   Create a graphical application that provides buttons for `enqueue` and `dequeue` from a queue, a text field to accept a string as input for enqueue, and a text area to display the contents of the queue after each operation.

9.10   Create an application that simulates a hotel with VIP registration. Start with the application you wrote for Programming Project 9.9, and change it so it uses a priority queue for this situation.

Answers to Self-Review Questions

9.1   A queue is a first in, first out (FIFO) collection, whereas a stack is a last in, first out (LIFO) collection.

9.2   The basic queue operations are:

enqueue—adds an element to the end of the queue

dequeue—removes an element from the front of the queue

first—returns a reference to the element at the front of the queue

isEmpty—returns true if the queue is empty, and false if it is not

size—returns the number of elements in the queue

9.3   makeEmpty(), destroy(), full()

9.4   27, one for each of the 26 letters in the alphabet and 1 to store the whole list before, during, and after sorting

9.5   Yes, it happens when the queue is empty (both front and rear are null) and when there is only one element on the queue.

9.6   There is no front reference in this implementation. The first element in the queue is always in position 0 of the array. However, when the queue is empty, the rear also points to position 0.

9.7   Yes, it can happen under two circumstances: when the queue is empty, and when there is only one element in the queue.

9.8   The noncircular array implementation with an O(n) dequeue operation has the worst time complexity.

9.9   Both of the array implementations waste space for unfilled elements in the array. The linked implementation uses more space per element stored.

Lists 10

CHAPTER OBJECTIVES

> Examine list processing and ordering techniques

> Define a list abstract data type

> Show how a list can be used to solve problems

> Learn about list implementations

> Compare list implementations

The idea of a list is very familiar. We make "to-do" lists, and grocery lists, and lists of friends to invite to a party. We may number the items in a list or we may keep them in alphabetical order in, say, an e-mail address book. For other lists we may keep the items in an order that simply makes the most sense to us. This chapter explores the list collection and how it works.

9.1   A LIST ADT

There are three types of list collections:

> *Ordered lists,* whose elements are ordered by some characteristic of the elements in the list: alphabetically, numbered, by date, or in some other way

> *Unordered lists,* whose elements are kept in an order chosen by the client

> *Indexed lists,* whose elements can be referenced using a numeric index

The order of an ordered list is based on some characteristic of the elements in the list. For example, you may keep a list of names ordered alphabetically, or you may keep an inventory list ordered by part number. The list is sorted based on some key value: a letter of the alphabet, a number, and so on. Any element added to an ordered list has one correct location in the list, given its key value and the key values of the elements already in the list: The number 54 must go after 49 and before 57, for example, as shown in Figure 10.1. To add a value to the list we must find its correct position among the other elements.

An unordered list is not based on any characteristic of the elements. But don't let the name mislead you. The elements in an unordered list can be kept in a particular order, but that order is not based on the elements themselves. The client using the list chooses the order of the elements. Figure 10.2 shows an unordered list. A new element can be put on the front or rear of the list, or it can be inserted after a particular element already in the list.

An indexed list is like an unordered list in that the client using the list chooses the order of the elements. However, in an indexed list each element can be referenced by a numeric index that begins at 0 at the front of the list and continues to the end of the list. Figure 10.3 shows an indexed list. A new element can be inserted into the list anywhere, including at the front or rear of the list. Every time there's a change in the list, the indexes are adjusted to stay in order, with no gaps.

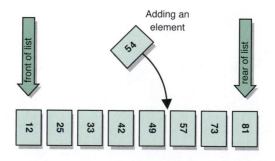

FIGURE 10.1 A conceptual view of an ordered list

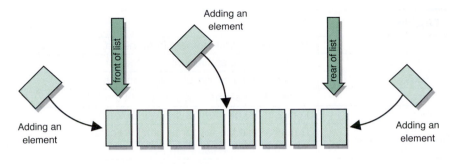

FIGURE 10.2   A conceptual view of an unordered list

The main difference between an indexed list and an array is that an indexed list does not allow gaps. If an element is removed, the indexes of other elements push together to fill in the gap. When an element is inserted, the indexes of other elements are shifted to make room.

> **Key Concept**
>
> An indexed list maintains a numeric index for its elements.

Keep in mind that these are overviews of lists. As with any collection, lists can be implemented in many ways. List implementations don't have to play by all the rules, though it is easier if they do.

All three types of lists share a set of operations, shown in Figure 10.4. They include operations to remove and look at elements, as well as classic operations such as `isEmpty` and `size`. The `contains` operation lets the user determine if a list contains a particular element. We saw a similar operation defined for a set collection in Chapter 3.

> **Key Concept**
>
> All list types share some operations. The differences between the types of lists center on how elements are added.

The differences in the types of lists center on how elements are added to the list. In an ordered list, the position of a new element in the list is based on its key value. This operation is shown in Figure 10.5.

An unordered list has three variations of the `add` operation. Elements can be added to the front or rear of the list, or after a particular element that is already in the list. These operations are shown in Figure 10.6.

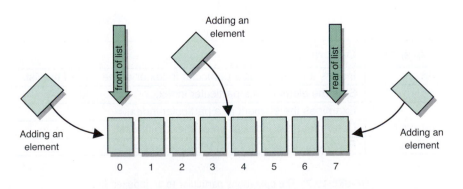

FIGURE 10.3   A conceptual view of an indexed list

Operation	Description
removeFirst	Removes the first element from the list.
removeLast	Removes the last element from the list.
remove	Removes a particular element from the list.
first	Looks at the element at the front of the list.
last	Looks at the element at the rear of the list.
contains	Determines if the list contains a particular element.
isEmpty	Determines if the list is empty.
size	Determines the number of elements on the list.

FIGURE 10.4 The common operations on a list

Operation	Description
add	Adds an element to the list.

FIGURE 10.5 The operation particular to an ordered list

Operation	Description
addToFront	Adds an element to the front of the list.
addToRear	Adds an element to the rear of the list.
addAfter	Adds an element after a particular element already in the list.

FIGURE 10.6 The operations particular to an unordered list

The operations particular to an indexed list use its ability to reference elements by their index. These operations are shown in Figure 10.7. A new element can be inserted into the list at a particular index, or it can be added to the rear of the list

Operation	Description
add	Inserts an element at a particular index or at the rear of the list.
set	Sets the element at a particular index.
get	Examines the element at a particular index.
indexOf	Determines the index of an element in the list.
remove	Removes the element at a particular index.

FIGURE 10.7 The operations particular to an indexed list

without specifying an index at all. If an element is inserted, the elements at higher indexes are shifted up to make room. Or the element at a particular index can be set, which overwrites the element at that index and therefore does not make other elements shift. In addition, the get operation returns the element stored at that index without removing it from the list. The indexOf operation determines the index of a particular element, if it exists. Also, an indexed list has its own remove operation, in which the element to be removed is specified by its index.

The common set of list operations need to be defined only once. So we will define four list interfaces: one with the common operations and three with the operations particular to each list type. Inheritance can be used with interfaces just as it can with classes. The interfaces of the particular list types extend the common list definition. This relationship is shown in Figure 10.8.

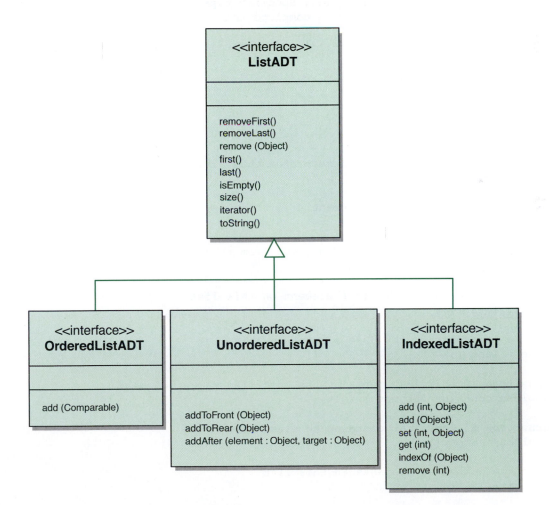

FIGURE 10.8 The list interfaces

When interfaces are inherited, the child interface contains all the abstract methods defined in the parent. Therefore, any class implementing a child interface must implement all methods from both the parent and the child.

Listings 10.1 through 10.4 show the Java interfaces for the UML diagram in Figure 10.8.

Listing 10.1

```
//********************************************************************
//  ListADT.java         Authors: Lewis/Chase
//
//  Defines the interface to a general list. Specific types
//  of lists will extend this interface to complete the
//  set of necessary operations.
//********************************************************************

package jss2;

import java.util.Iterator;

public interface ListADT
{
    //  Removes and returns the first element from this list
    public Object removeFirst ();

    //  Removes and returns the last element from this list
    public Object removeLast ();

    //  Removes and returns the specified element from this list
    public Object remove (Object element);

    //  Returns a reference to the first element on this list
    public Object first ();

    //  Returns a reference to the last element on this list
    public Object last ();

    //  Returns true if this list contains the specified target element
    public boolean contains (Object target);

    //  Returns true if this list contains no elements
    public boolean isEmpty();

    //  Returns the number of elements in this list
    public int size();
```

Listing 10.1   continued

```java
    //  Returns an iterator for the elements in this list
    public Iterator iterator();

    //  Returns a string representation of this list
    public String toString();
}
```

Listing 10.2

```java
//********************************************************************
//  OrderedListADT.java        Authors: Lewis/Chase
//
//  Defines the interface to an ordered list. Only comparable
//  elements are stored, kept in the order determined by
//  the relationship among the elements.
//********************************************************************

package jss2;

public interface OrderedListADT extends ListADT
{
    //  Adds the element to this list at the correct location
    public void add (Comparable element);
}
```

Listing 10.3

```java
//********************************************************************
//  UnorderedListADT.java        Authors: Lewis/Chase
//
//  Defines the interface to an unordered list collection. Elements
//  can be stored in any order the user wants.
//********************************************************************

package jss2;

public interface UnorderedListADT extends ListADT
{
```

Listing 10.3   **continued**

```java
    //  Adds the element to the front of this list
    public void addToFront (Object element);

    //  Adds the element to the rear of this list
    public void addToRear (Object element);

    //  Adds the element after the target
    public void addAfter (Object element, Object target);
}
```

Listing 10.4

```java
//********************************************************************
//   IndexedListADT.java        Authors: Lewis/Chase
//
//   Defines the interface to an indexed list collection.
//   Elements are referenced by numeric indexes.
//********************************************************************

package jss2;

public interface IndexedListADT extends ListADT
{
    //  Inserts the element at the specified index
    public void add (int index, Object element);

    //  Sets the element at the specified index
    public void set (int index, Object element);

    //  Adds the element to the rear of this list
    public void add (Object element);

    //  Returns a reference to the element at the specified index
    public Object get (int index);

    //  Returns the index of the element
    public int indexOf (Object element);

    //  Removes and returns the element at the index
    public Object remove (int index);
}
```

Before exploring how these lists can be implemented, let's see how they might be used.

10.2 USING ORDERED LISTS: TOURNAMENT MAKER

Sporting tournaments, such as the NCAA basketball tournament or a championship tournament at a local bowling alley, are often organized by the team's number of wins during the regular season. Ordered lists can be used to help organize the tournament. A list of teams can be ordered by number of wins. To form the match-ups for the first round of the tournament, teams can be selected from the front and back of the list in pairs.

> **Key Concept**
>
> An ordered list is a good collection to use when creating a tournament schedule.

For example, consider the eight bowling teams listed in Figure 10.9. This table shows each team's number of wins during the regular season.

To create the first-round tournament matches, we would sort the teams in a list ordered by the number of wins. The first team on the list (the team with the best record) is removed from the list and matched up with the last team on the list (the team with the worst record) to form the first game of the tournament. The process continues, matching up the team with the next-best record with the team with the next-worst record to form the second game and so on, until the list is empty. The same process would be used to form the second-round match-ups, only for the second round, the teams would be ordered by game number from the first round. For the third round, the teams would be ordered by game number from the second round. This process would continue with half as many games per round until there was only one game left. From our example in Figure 10.9 we would end up with the tournament as laid out in Figure 10.10.

To design a program to create the first-round tournament match-ups, we would create a `Team` class. The `Team` class will store the name of the team and the

Team Name	Wins
GutterBalls	9
KingPins	8
PinDoctors	7
Scorecards	10
Spares	5
Splits	4
Tenpins	3
Woodsplitters	2

FIGURE 10.9 Bowling league team names and number of wins

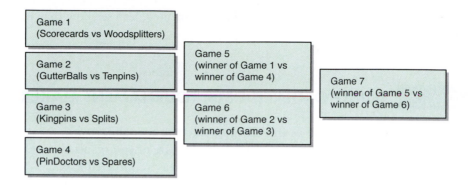

FIGURE 10.10   Sample tournament layout for a bowling league tournament

number of wins. The class will also provide us with some sort of comparison operation. Let's say we create an interface called `Comparable`, which the `Team` class will implement. This interface provides for a `compareTo` operation, which is different from the traditional `compareTo` operation. The `compareTo` operation will return −1 if the new element, the one being inserted in the list, is less than the element already in the list. For example, if two teams have the same number of wins, the team that is entered first will be higher in the list. Figure 10.11 illustrates the UML relationships among the classes used to solve this problem. Listing 10.5 shows the `Tournament` class and sample output. Listing 10.6 shows the `Team` class, and Listing 10.7 illustrates the `TournamentMaker` class.

Listing 10.5

```
//********************************************************************
//   Tournament.java        Authors: Lewis/Chase
//
//   Demonstrates the use of an ordered list to create the match-ups
//   in a sporting tournament.
//********************************************************************
public class Tournament
{
    //-----------------------------------------------------------------
    //   Determines and prints the tournament organization.
    //-----------------------------------------------------------------
    public static void main (String[] args)
    {
```

Listing 10.5   **continued**

```
    try
    {
        TournamentMaker temp = new TournamentMaker();
        temp.make();
    }
    catch (Exception IOException)
    {
        System.out.println("Invalid input reported");
    }
  }
}
```

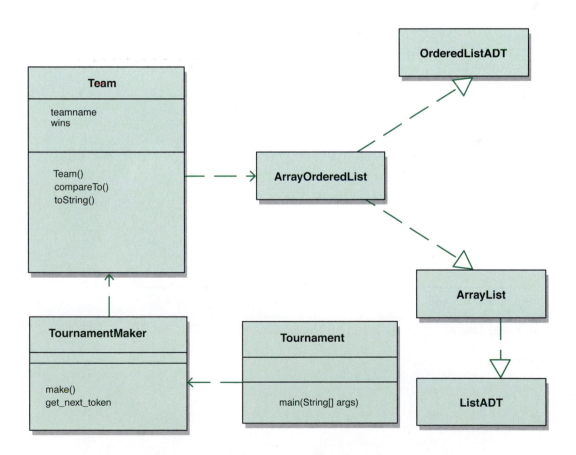

FIGURE 10.11   UML description of the Tournament class

Listing 10.6

```
//*****************************************************************
//  Team.java          Authors: Lewis/Chase
//
//  Represents a sports team and its wins.
//*****************************************************************

import java.util.*;

//-----------------------------------------------------------------
//  Returns the number of wins.
//-----------------------------------------------------------------
public int numWins()
{
   return winds;
}


//-----------------------------------------------------------------
//  Records a win.
//-----------------------------------------------------------------
public void recordWin()
{
   return wins;
}
   wins ++
{
   if (this.numWins() < (((Team)other).numWins()))
      return -1;
   else
     if (this.numWins == (((Team)other).numWins))
        return 0;
     else
        return 1;
}


//-----------------------------------------------------------------
//  Returns the name of the team.
//-----------------------------------------------------------------
public String toString()
{
   return teamname;
}
}
```

Listing 10.7

```java
//**********************************************************************
//   TournamentMaker.java        Authors: Lewis/Chase
//
//   Supports the generation of tournaments.
//**********************************************************************

import jss2.*;
import jss2.exceptions.*;
import java.util.StringTokenizer;
import java.io.*;

public class TournamentMaker
{
    //------------------------------------------------------------
    //   Gets the next token from the input stream.
    //------------------------------------------------------------
    private String getNextToken() throws IOException
    {
        String temptoken, instring;
        StringTokenizer tokenizer;
        BufferedReader in = new
            BufferedReader(new InputStreamReader(System.in));

        instring = in.readLine();
        tokenizer = new StringTokenizer(instring);
        temptoken = (tokenizer.nextToken());
        return temptoken;
    }


    //------------------------------------------------------------
    //   Determines and prints the tournament organization.
    //------------------------------------------------------------
    public void make( ) throws IOException
    {
        ArrayOrderedList tournament = new ArrayOrderedList();
        String team1, team2, teamname;
        int numwins, numteams = 0;

        System.out.println("Tournament Maker");

        while (((numteams % 2) != 0) || (numteams == 0))
        {
            System.out.println ("Enter the number of teams (must be even):");
            numteams = Integer.parseInt(get_next_token());
        }
```

Listing 10.7   continued

```
    System.out.println ("Enter " + numteams + " team names and number "
                         + "of wins:");
    System.out.println("Teams may be entered in any order ");

    for (int count=1; count <= numteams; count++)
    {
        System.out.println("Enter team name: ");
        teamname = getNextToken();
        System.out.println("Enter number of wins: ");
        numwins = Integer.parseInt(getNextToken());
        tournament.add(new Team(teamname, numwins));
    }

    System.out.println("The first round match-ups are: ");

    for (int count=1; count <= (numteams/2); count++)
    {
        team1 = ((Team)(tournament.removeFirst())).teamname;
        team2 = ((Team)(tournament.removeLast())).teamname;
        System.out.println ("Game " + count + " is " + team1 +
            " against " + team2);
        System.out.println ("with the winner to play the winner of game "
            + (((numteams/2)+1) - count));
    }

    }
}
```

Output

```
Enter the number of teams (must be even):
4
Enter 4 team names and number of wins:
Teams may be entered in any order
Enter team name:
PinDoctors
Enter number of wins:
11
Enter team name:
GutterBalls
Enter number of wins:
5
Enter team name:
Spares
Enter number of wins:
8
```

Listing 10.7	**continued**

```
Enter team name:
FirstStrikes
Enter number of wins:
12
The first round match-ups are:
Game 1 is GutterBalls against FirstStrikes
with the winner to play the winner of game 2
Game 2 is Spares against PinDoctors
with the winner to play the winner of game 1
```

10.3 USING INDEXED LISTS: THE JOSEPHUS PROBLEM

Flavius Josephus was a Jewish historian of the first century. Legend has it that he was one of a group of 41 Jewish rebels trapped by the Romans who decided to kill themselves rather than surrender. They decided to form a circle and to kill every third person until no one was left. Josephus, not wanting to die, calculated where he needed to stand so that he would be the last one alive and thus would not have to die. Thus was born a class of problems referred to as the Josephus problem. These problems involve finding the order of events when events in a list are not taken in order, but rather are taken every nth element until there are none left.

> **Key Concept**
>
> The Josephus problem is a classic computing problem that can be solved with indexed lists.

For example, let us suppose that we have a list of seven elements numbered from 1 to 7:

1 2 3 4 5 6 7

If we were to remove every third element from the list, the first element to be removed would be number 3, leaving the list:

1 2 4 5 6 7

The next element to be removed would be number 6:

1 2 4 5 7

The elements are thought of as in a *continuous cycle*, so that when we reach the end of the list, we continue counting at the beginning. Therefore, the next element to be removed would be number 2, leaving:

1 4 5 7

The next element to be removed would be number 7:

1   4   5

The next element to be removed would be number 5:

1   4

The next-to-last element to be removed would be number 1, leaving the number 4 as the last element on the list.

Listing 10.8 illustrates the Josephus problem, allowing the user to input the number of items in the list and the gap between elements. Note that the original list is placed in an indexed list. Each element is then removed from the list one at a time. The one complication is computing the next index position to be removed. This is particularly interesting because the list collapses on itself as elements are removed. For example, the element number 6 from our previous example should be the second element removed from the list. However, once element 3 has been removed from the list, element 6 is no longer in its original position. Instead of being at index position 5 in the list, it is now at index position 4. Figure 10.12 illustrates the UML for the Josephus problem. Notice that we are using the `ArrayList` implementation from the Java Collections API, which is actually an indexed list implementation.

Listing 10.8

```
//********************************************************************
//   Josephus.java          Authors: Lewis/Chase
//********************************************************************

import java.util.ArrayList;
import java.util.StringTokenizer;
import java.io.*;

public class Josephus
{

    //----------------------------------------------------------------
    //   Continue around the list eliminating every nth soldier
    //   until all of the soldiers have been eliminated
    //----------------------------------------------------------------
    public static void main ( String[] args) throws IOException
    {
        String instring;
        int numpeople, gap, newgap, counter;
```

Listing 10.8   continued

```java
        StringTokenizer tokenizer;
        ArrayList list = new ArrayList();
        Object tempelement;
        BufferedReader in = new
            BufferedReader(new InputStreamReader(System.in));

        // get the initial number of soldiers
        System.out.println("Enter the number of soldiers: ");
        instring = in.readLine();
        tokenizer = new StringTokenizer(instring);
        numpeople = Integer.parseInt (tokenizer.nextToken());

        // get the gap between soldiers
        System.out.println("Enter the gap between soldiers: ");
        instring = in.readLine();
        tokenizer = new StringTokenizer(instring);
        gap = Integer.parseInt (tokenizer.nextToken());

        // load the initial list of soldiers
        for (int count=1; count <= numpeople; count++)
        {
           list.add(new Integer(count));
        }
        counter = gap - 1;
        newgap = gap;

        //  Treating the list as if it were circular, remove every
        //  nth element until the list is empty

        System.out.println("The order is: ");


        while (!(list.isEmpty()))
        {
           tempelement = list.remove(counter);
           numpeople = numpeople - 1;
           if (numpeople > 0)
              counter = (counter + gap - 1) % numpeople;
           System.out.println(tempelement);
        }
    }
}
```

Output

```
Enter the number of soldiers:
11
Enter the gap between soldiers:
```

Listing 10.8 **continued**

```
3
The order is:
3
6
9
1
5
10
4
11
8
2
7
```

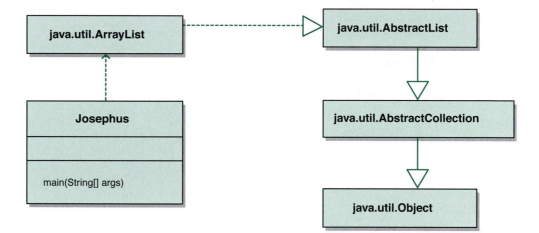

FIGURE 10.12 UML description of the Josephus program

10.4 IMPLEMENTING LISTS: WITH ARRAYS

An array-based implementation of a list could fix one end of the list at index 0 and shift elements as needed, like the array-based implementation of a queue we studied in Chapter 9. The main difference is that we will also insert elements into the middle of the list.

Figure 10.13 shows an array list with the front fixed at index 0. The integer variable `rear` is the number of elements in the list and the next available slot for adding an element to the rear.

Figure 10.13 applies to all three variations of the list. Now let's explore the common operations.

The remove Operation

The `remove` operation searches for the element and removes it from the list. Then any remaining elements are shifted to fill in the gap. This operation can be implemented as follows:

```
//---------------------------------------------------------------
//  Removes and returns the specified element.
//---------------------------------------------------------------
public Object remove (Object element)
{
   Object result;
   int index = find (element);

   if (index == NOT_FOUND)
      throw new NoSuchElementException("list");

   result = list[index];

   // shift the appropriate elements
   for (int scan=index; scan < rear; scan++)
      list[scan] = list[scan+1];

   rear--;
   list[rear] = null;

   return result;
}
```

The `remove` method uses a method called `find`, which finds the element, if it exists in the list, and returns its index. The `find` method returns a constant called `NOT_FOUND` if the element is not in the list. The `NOT_FOUND` constant is equal to −1 and is defined in the `ArrayList` class. If the element is not found, a `NoSuchElementException` is generated. If it is found, the elements at higher indexes are shifted down, the `rear` value is updated, and the element is returned.

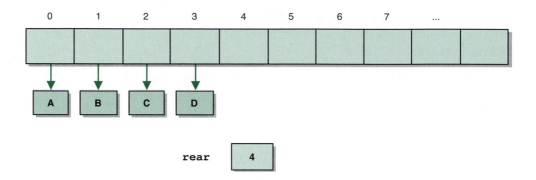

FIGURE 10.13 An array implementation of a list

The `find` method supports a public operation, instead of defining its own operation. Therefore, the `find` method should be declared with private visibility. The `find` method can be implemented as follows:

```
//------------------------------------------------------------------
//   Returns the array index of the element, or the
//   constant NOT_FOUND if it is not found.
//------------------------------------------------------------------
private int find (Object target)
{
    int scan = 0, result = NOT_FOUND;
    boolean found = false;

    if (! isEmpty())
        while (! found && scan < rear)
            if (target.equals(list[scan])
                found = true;
            else
                scan++;

    if (found)
        result = scan;

    return result;
}
```

The `find` method uses the `equals` method to determine whether the target has been found. The object passed into the method could be an exact copy of the target element. In fact, it may be an alias of the element in the list. However, if the parameter is a separate object, it may not contain all aspects of the target element. Only the key characteristics on which the `equals` method is based are important.

The logic of the `find` method could have been made part of the `remove` method, though that would have made the `remove` method complicated. Instead support methods should be defined to keep each method readable. In this case, the `find` support method helps us implement the `contains` operation, as we will now explore.

The contains Operation

The `contains` operation determines whether a particular element is in the list. We saw a similar operation in the set collection in Chapter 3. This time, however, we can make use of the `find` support method:

```
//------------------------------------------------------------------
//  Returns true if this list contains the target element.
//------------------------------------------------------------------
public boolean contains (Object target)
{
    return (find(target) != NOT_FOUND)
}
```

If the target element is not found, the `contains` method returns false. If the target element is found, the `contains` method returns true. If we are careful when we create the `return` statement, we can be sure we have the correct return value.

The remaining common list operations are left as programming projects. Let's look at the operations that are particular to a type of list now.

The add Operation for an Ordered List

The `add` operation is the only way an element can be added to an ordered list. We don't have to give a location in the call because the elements themselves determine their order. The `add` operation can be implemented as follows:

```
//------------------------------------------------------------------
//  Adds the specified Comparable element to the list, keeping
//  the elements in sorted order.
//------------------------------------------------------------------
public void add (Comparable element)
{
```

```
   if (size() == list.length)
      expandCapacity();

   int scan = 0;
   while (scan < rear && element.compareTo(list[scan]) > 0)
      scan++;

   for (int scan2=rear; scan2 > scan; scan2--)
      list[scan2] = list[scan2-1];

   list[scan] = element;
   rear++;
}
```

The parameter to the method is a Comparable object. Only Comparable objects can be stored in an ordered list. This guarantees that the objects in the list can be compared to each other so that we can put them in order.

Remember that the Comparable interface defines the compareTo method. The compareTo method returns a negative, zero, or positive integer value if the executing object is less than, equal to, or greater than the parameter, respectively. The Comparable interface is very important in sorting, so it makes sense that we need it for an ordered list collection, because we are keeping the elements in the list in sorted order.

Unordered and indexed lists do not need Comparable objects. In object-oriented programming the classes that implement these lists are not bothered by these differences.

Operations Particular to Unordered Lists

The three add operations for an unordered list are left as programming projects. The addToFront and addToRear operations are like operations from other collections. Keep in mind that the addToFront operation must shift the elements in the list first to make room at index 0 for the new element.

The addAfter operation accepts two Object objects: one for the element to be added and one for the target element, where the new element will be placed. The addAfter method must first find the target element, and then insert the new element after it.

Operations Particular to Indexed Lists

The Java Collections API provides two implementations for lists: `ArrayList` and `LinkedList`. Both of these classes extend the abstract class `java.util.Abstract-List`, which implements the `java.util.List` interface. These are part of the Java class library and are different from the interfaces and classes we've discussed so far in this chapter. The `java.util.AbstractList` class is an extension of the `java.util.AbstractCollection` class, which implements the `java.util.Collection` interface. Both of the Java Collections list implementations are indexed lists, even though the class names do not spell that out.

> **Key Concept**
>
> The Java Collections API has two implementations of an indexed list.

The `ArrayList` implementation of an indexed list is an array-based implementation. Many of the issues discussed in the array implementations of stacks, queues, unordered lists, and ordered lists apply here. For example, using an array implementation of a list, an `add` operation that specifies an index in the middle of the list will need all of the elements above that position in the list to be shifted one position higher in the list. Likewise, a `remove` operation that removes an element from the middle of the list needs all of the elements above that position in the list to be shifted one position lower in the list.

If adding a new element would overflow the `ArrayList`, the underlying array is automatically resized. The `ArrayList` class has two additional operations for this: `ensureCapacity` increases the size of the array to a size of the user's choosing if it is not already that large or larger, and `trimToSize` trims the array to the actual current size of the list.

One advantage of the `ArrayList` implementation is that we can access all elements in the list in the same amount of time. The downside is the added cost of shifting elements whenever we insert or delete an item.

10.5   IMPLEMENTING LISTS: WITH LINKS

A linked list can be a convenient way to implement a linear collection. The common operations that apply for all three types of a list collection, as well as the particular operations for the three types, can be implemented with techniques like the ones we've used before. We will look at a couple of the more interesting operations, but most of the rest will be left as programming projects.

The `remove` Operation

The `remove` operation is part of the `LinkedList` class shared by all three implementations: unordered, ordered, and indexed lists. The `remove` operation checks to make sure that the list is not empty, finds the element to be removed, and then handles one of four cases: the element to be removed is the only element in the list, the element to be removed is the first element in the list, the element to be removed is the last element in the list, or the element to be removed is in the middle of the list. In all cases, the count is decreased by one. An implementation of the remove operation is shown below.

```java
//================================================================
//  Removes the first instance of the specified element from the
//  list if it is found in the list and returns a reference to it.
//  Throws an EmptyListException if the list is empty.  Throws a
//  NoSuchElementException if the specified element is not found
//  on the list.
//================================================================
public Object remove (Object targetElement) throws
   EmptyCollectionException, ElementNotFoundException
{
   if (isEmpty())
      throw new EmptyCollectionException ("List");

   boolean found = false;

   LinearNode previous = null;
   LinearNode current = head;

   while (current != null && !found)
      if (targetElement.equals (current.getElement()))
         found = true;
      else
      {
         previous = current;
         current = current.getNext();
      }

   if (!found)
      throw new ElementNotFoundException ("List");

   if (size() == 1)
      head = tail = null;
   else
      if (current.equals (head))
         head = current.getNext();
      else
         if (current.equals (tail))
         {
            tail = previous;
            tail.setNext(null);
         }
```

```
        else
            previous.setNext(current.getNext());

    count--;

    return current.getElement();
}
```

Doubly Linked Lists

Note how much code in this method is devoted to finding the target element and keeping track of a `current` and a `previous` reference. This seems like a chance to reuse code. After all, we already have a `find` method in the `LinkedList` class. What if this list were *doubly linked,* meaning that each node stores a reference to the next element, as well as to the previous element? Would this make the `remove` operation simpler? First, we would need a `DoubleNode` class, as shown in Listing 10.9.

Listing 10.9

```java
//********************************************************************
//  DoubleNode.java        Authors: Lewis/Chase
//
//  Represents a node in a doubly linked list.
//********************************************************************

public class DoubleNode
{
    private DoubleNode next;
    private Object element;
    private DoubleNode previous;

    //-----------------------------------------------------------------
    //  Creates an empty node.
    //-----------------------------------------------------------------
    public DoubleNode()
    {
        next = null;
        element = null;
        previous = null;
    }
```

Listing 10.9   **continued**

```java
//-----------------------------------------------------------------
//  Creates a node storing the specified element.
//-----------------------------------------------------------------
public DoubleNode (Object elem)
{
   next = null;
   element = elem;
   previous = null;
}

//-----------------------------------------------------------------
//  Returns the node that follows this one.
//-----------------------------------------------------------------
public DoubleNode getNext()
{
   return next;
}

//-----------------------------------------------------------------
//  Returns the node that precedes this one.
//-----------------------------------------------------------------
public DoubleNode getPrevious()
{
   return previous;
}

//-----------------------------------------------------------------
//  Sets the node that follows this one.
//-----------------------------------------------------------------
public void setNext (DoubleNode dnode)
{
   next = dnode;
}

//-----------------------------------------------------------------
//  Sets the node that follows this one.
//-----------------------------------------------------------------
public void setPrevious (DoubleNode dnode)
{
   previous = dnode;
}

//-----------------------------------------------------------------
//  Returns the element stored in this node.
//-----------------------------------------------------------------
```

Listing 10.9   continued

```
    public Object getElement()
    {
        return element;
    }

    //-------------------------------------------------------------
    //  Sets the element stored in this node.
    //-------------------------------------------------------------
    public void setElement (Object elem)
    {
        element = elem;
    }
}
```

The `remove` operation can now be implemented using a doubly linked list. We can also use the `find` operation to locate the target, and we don't need to keep track of a `previous` reference. In this example, we also use the `removeFirst` and `removeLast` operations to handle the special cases of removing either the first or last element.

```
    //-------------------------------------------------------------
    //  Removes and returns the specified element.
    //-------------------------------------------------------------
    public Object remove (Object element)
    {
        Object result;
        DoubleNode nodeptr = find (element);

        if (nodeptr == null)
            throw new ElementNotFoundException ("list");

        result = nodeptr.getElement();

        // check to see if front or rear
        if (nodeptr == front)
            result = this.removeFirst();
        else
            if (nodeptr == rear)
                result = this.removeLast();
```

```
      else
      {
         nodeptr.getNext().setPrevious(nodeptr.getPrevious());
         nodeptr.getPrevious().setNext(nodeptr.getNext());
         count--;
      }

   return result;
}
```

Figure 10.14 illustrates a doubly linked list. The implementations of the other operations for doubly linked lists are left as exercises.

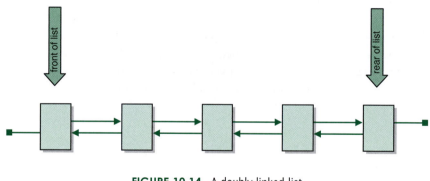

FIGURE 10.14   A doubly linked list

10.6   ANALYSIS OF LIST IMPLEMENTATIONS

Because each type of list collection has its own unique issues, we'll cover the analysis of each type separately.

Analysis of Ordered List Implementations

The difference in space complexity between the linked and array implementations of an ordered list is pretty much the same as what we've seen with unordered lists, stacks, and queues. The linked implementation needs more space per object to be inserted in the list simply because of the space allocated for the `next` reference. However, the array implementation must start with some space, to store the objects in the list, and whatever space is not used in the array is wasted.

The analysis of the time complexity of most of the operations for the list implementations has already been covered in this chapter. Only the `addElement` operation is different.

The two `addElement` operations are almost identical. One difference between the two is that once the insertion location is found, the array implementation must shift all of the elements up one position. Like the `insertAfter` operation for unordered lists, the `addElement` operation for the array implementation of ordered lists will always result in a total of n + 1 comparison-plus shifts. You may be confused by the fact that the shift happens in a `while` loop, so this looks like an $O(n^2)$ algorithm. However, notice that in the same part of the algorithm, the `found` flag is set to true so that the `while` loop will end after the shift.

Analysis of Unordered List Implementations

The difference in space complexity between the linked and array implementations of an unordered list is pretty much the same as with stacks and queues. The linked implementation needs more space per object simply because it needs space for the `next` reference. The array implementation, on the other hand, must allocate all the space at the beginning, and whatever space is not used is wasted.

The analysis of the time complexity of the operations for the implementations of a list is simple. We will address each operation for each of the three implementations.

addToFront

The `addToFront` operation for the linked implementation takes the following steps:

1. Create a new node with the `element` reference pointing to the object to be added to the list. Set the `next` reference to null.

2. If the list is empty, set the `tail` reference to point to the new object.

3. Set the `next` reference of the new object to the head of the list.

4. Set the `head` reference to point to the new object.

5. Increase the `count` by one.

All of these steps are O(1). So the `addToFront` operation for the linked implementation is O(1).

The `addToFront` operation for the array implementation takes the following steps:

1. Check to make sure that the array is not full (if it is, throw an exception).
2. Set the reference in position `[(head-1 + length) % length]` of the array to point to the object being added to the list.
3. Set `head` to `(head-1 + length) % length`.
4. Increase the `count` by one.

Because all of these steps are O(1), the `addToFront` operation for the array implementation is O(1). There is no real difference in time complexity for the `addToFront` operations.

addToRear

The `addToRear` operation for the linked implementation takes the following steps:

1. Create a new node with the `element` reference pointing to the object to be added to the list. Set the `next` reference to null.
2. If the list is empty, set the `head` and `tail` references to point to the new object.
3. Set the `next` reference of the node at the tail of the list to point to the new object.
4. Set the `tail` reference equal to the new object.
5. Increase the `count` by one.

Because all of these steps are O(1), the `addToRear` operation for the linked implementation is O(1).

The `addToRear` operation for the array implementation includes the following steps:

1. Check to make sure that the array is not full (if it is, throw an exception).
2. Set the `tail` reference to point to the object being added to the list.
3. Set `tail` to `(tail+1) % length` where `length` is the fixed length of the array.
4. Increase the `count` by one.

Because all of these steps are O(1), the `addToRear` operation for the array implementation is O(1). There is no real difference in the time complexity of the `addToRear` operations.

insertAfter

The insertAfter operation for the linked implementation consists of the following steps:

1. Set a boolean flag found to false.

2. Set a temporary reference current to point to the head of the list.

3. If the current node equals the target element, then set found to true or current to current.next.

4. If the target element was not found, throw an exception.

5. Create a new node, storing the element to be inserted.

6. Set the next reference of the new node to point to the same object pointed to by the next reference of the current node.

7. Set the next reference of the current node to point to the new object.

8. If the current object is also the tail, set the tail reference to point to the new object.

9. Increase the count by one.

All of these steps are O(1) except for the search for the target element, which is O(n). The best case is that the target element is the first element of the list, the worst case is that the target element is the last element, and the expected case is that the target element is in the middle of the list.

The insertAfter operation for the array implementation takes the following steps:

1. If the list is full, throw an exception.

2. Set a temporary index value to the head of the list.

3. Set a boolean flag found to false.

4. Set a boolean flag firstelement to true.

5. Set firstelement to false.

6. If the current element is the target element, set found to true.

7. If the target element was not found, throw an exception.

8. Shift all of the reference values from the current (index + 1) to the tail of the list up one position.

9. Set the next reference in the (index) position in the array to point to the object to be inserted.

10. Set the tail equal to (tail+1)%length.

11. Increase the count by one.

The `insertAfter` operation for the array implementation takes two O(n) steps, the `while` loop to find the target element and the process of shifting all of the elements above the target one position to the right. The best case for the search component is finding the target element at the head of the list. However, the best case for the shift component is finding the target element at the tail of the list. The expected case either way is n/2, which is O(n). In fact, the combination of the two always results in n total steps between comparisons and shifts, because no matter where we find our target location in the array, we have to shift all of the elements we did not compare. The `insertAfter` operation is O(n) for both implementations. The array implementation takes two O(n) operations, the search and the shift, as opposed to only one O(n) operation, the search, in the linked implementation.

removeElement

The `removeElement` operation for the linked implementation takes the following steps:

1. If the list is empty, throw an exception.
2. Initialize `found` to false, `previous` to null, and `current` to the head of the list.
3. If the current node equals the target element, then set `found` to true. If it does not, set `previous` equal to `current` and then set `current` equal to `current.next`.
4. If the target element was not found, throw an exception.
5. If there is only one element in the list, set `head` and `tail` to null.
6. If the target element is at the head of the list, set `head` equal to `head.next`.
7. If the target element is at the tail of the list, set `tail` equal to `previous` and set `tail.next` to null.
8. Set `previous.next` equal to `current.next`.
9. Decrement the number of objects in the list.
10. Return `current.element`.

All of these steps are O(1) except for the search, which is O(n). Thus the `removeElement` operation for the linked implementation is O(n).

The `removeElement` operation for the array implementation takes the following steps:

1. If the list is empty, throw an exception.
2. Set a temporary index value to the head of the list.
3. Set a boolean flag `found` to false.

4. Set a boolean flag `firstelement` to true.

5. Set `firstelement` to false.

6. If the current element is the target element, set `found` to true.

7. Increase the index by one.

8. If the target element was not found, throw an exception.

9. Set a temporary object reference equal to the `element` reference of the position `index` of the array.

10. Shift all of the reference values in the list from the current position (`index + 1`) to the tail of the list down one position.

11. Set the `tail` index equal to (`tail-1+length`) `% length`.

12. Lower the `count` of objects in the list.

13. Return the temporary object.

The `removeElement` operation takes only two O(n) steps, the search and the shift, so the operation is O(n).

The `firstelement` and `lastelement` operations for both implementations are O(1). The `removeFirst` operation is O(1) for both implementations. The `removeLast` operation is O(1) for the array implementation, but O(n) for the linked implementation. This is because the entire list must be traversed to reach the element before the last element. The `isEmpty` and `size` operations are O(1) for both implementations. The `contains` and `find` operations are just linear searches in both implementations, so they are O(n).

Analysis of Indexed List Implementations

The difference in space complexity between the linked and array implementations of an indexed list is pretty much the same as with the other data structures. The linked implementation needs more space simply because of the references. Keep in mind that the `LinkedList` class is actually a doubly linked list, so it needs twice the number of references. The `ArrayList` class is more efficient at managing space because it is resizable, and can add or subtract space as needed.

The analysis of the time complexity for the operations for the `ArrayList` and `LinkedList` implementations generally falls into one of three categories: access to objects, insertion of objects, and removal of objects.

Access to objects includes operations such as `contains`, `get`, and `indexof`. In an `ArrayList`, if the index of the object we want is already known, then the access to the object is O(1), because we can get to any object in the list by using the index value—the time to get the object is always the same. If the index of the object is not already known, then the access to the object is O(n), where n is the number of objects in the list. That's because each object on the list must be compared with the target object (best case is one comparison, worst case is n comparisons, expected case is n/2 comparisons).

Access to objects in a `LinkedList` tends to be more costly. No matter whether or not the index of the object is already known, access to the object is O(n). If we know the index, the operations will still have to start at one end or the other, whichever is closer, and traverse their way to the particular index location (best case is no traversal if the index we are looking for is one of our endpoints, worst case is n/2 traversals if the index we are looking for is in the middle of the list, expected case is n/4 traversals). Traversing the list looking for an object is O(n) with best, worst, and expected cases the same as the `ArrayList` implementation.

We can insert objects into an `ArrayList` at the end of the list, which is an O(1) operation, or into a particular index value in the list, which is an O(n) operation. This is because all of the positions above the insertion location must be shifted one position. The best case for this type of insert is one shift if we are inserting into the last index in the array, the worst case is n shifts if we are inserting into the first index in the array, and the expected case is n/2 shifts. One complication is capacity. The insertion may cause the `ArrayList` to have to be resized. While this could have an effect on the completion time of a particular `insert` operation, it does not affect the analysis of the time complexity. Averaged across all insertions, this time to resize is very small.

We can insert an object into a `LinkedList` at either end of the list. Because this is a doubly linked list, insertion is O(1) in both cases. We can also insert into a particular position in the list, which, like the analysis of the `ArrayList` implementation, is O(n), but for a very different reason. In the `LinkedList` implementation, we do not need to shift all of the elements above the insertion point; however, we do not have direct access to the particular index position in the list, so we must traverse the list from one end or the other. So the best case is no traversal, if the insertion point is one of the endpoints; the worst case is n/2 traversals, if the insertion point is in the middle of the list; and the expected case is n/4 traversals.

The analysis of the deletion of objects from the list is like insertions. For an `ArrayList`, the best case is that the element is at the end of the list so we don't need to shift any elements. The worst case is that we are removing the element at the beginning of the list and must shift all of the remaining (n–1) elements. The expected case is n/2 shifts. So deletion from an `ArrayList` is an O(n) operation.

Deletion from a `LinkedList` is similar. The best case is that we are deleting one of the two ends of the list and do not have to traverse the list at all. The worst case is that we are deleting an element in the middle of the list and must traverse n/2 elements to reach the middle. The expected case is n/4 traversals. So deletion from a `LinkedList` is an O(n) operation. Of course, the `removeFirst` and `removeLast` operations are O(1) because they are always dealing with the ends of the list and require no traversals.

Summary of Key Concepts

> List collections can be ordered, unordered, or indexed.

> The order of an ordered list is based on some characteristic of the elements in the list.

> The elements of an unordered list are kept in whatever order the client chooses.

> An indexed list maintains a numeric index for its elements.

> All list types share some common operations. The differences between the types of lists center on how elements are added.

> Interfaces can be derived from other interfaces. The child interface contains all abstract methods of the parent.

> An ordered list is a good collection to use when creating a tournament schedule.

> The Josephus problem is a classic computing problem that can be solved with indexed lists.

> Only `Comparable` objects can be stored in an ordered list.

> The Java Collections API has two implementations of an indexed list.

Self-Review Questions

10.1   What is the difference between an indexed list, an ordered list, and an unordered list?

10.2   What are the basic methods of accessing an indexed list?

10.3   What additional operations are part of the Java Collections framework?

10.4   What are the trade-offs in space complexity between an `ArrayList` and a `LinkedList`?

10.5   What are the trade-offs in time complexity between an `ArrayList` and a `LinkedList`?

10.6   What is the time complexity of the `contains` operation and the `find` operation for both implementations?

10.7   What would happen if a `LinkedList` implementation used a singly linked list instead of a doubly linked list?

10.8   Why is the time to increase the size of the array on an `add` operation considered hardly worth noting for the `ArrayList` implementation?

Exercises

10.1   Hand-trace an ordered list X through the following operations:

```
X.add(new Integer(4));
X.add(new Integer(7));
Object Y = X.first();
X.add(new Integer(3));
X.add(new Integer(2));
X.add(new Integer(5));
Object Y = X.removeLast();
Object Y = X.remove(new Integer(7));
X.add(new Integer(9));
```

10.2   Given the resulting list X from Exercise 10.1, what would be the result of each of the following?

a.   `X.last();`

b.   `z = X.contains(new Integer(3));`

   `X.first();`

c.   `Y = X.remove(new Integer(2));`

   `X.first();`

10.3   What would be the time complexity of the `size` operation for each of the implementations if there were no `count` variable?

10.4   In the array implementation, under what circumstances could the `head` and `tail` references be equal?

10.5   In the linked implementation, could the `head` and `tail` references be equal?

10.6   If there were no `count` variable in the array implementation, how could you figure out whether the list was empty?

10.7   If there were no `count` variable in the array implementation, how could you figure out whether the list was full?

Programming Projects

10.1   Implement a stack using a `LinkedList`.

10.2   Implement a stack using an `ArrayList`.

10.3   Implement a queue using a `LinkedList`.

10.4   Implement a queue using an `ArrayList`.

10.5   Implement the Josephus problem using a queue. Compare the performance of your algorithm to the `ArrayList` implementation from this chapter.

10.6   Implement an `OrderedList` using a `LinkedList`.

10.7   Implement an `OrderedList` using an `ArrayList`.

10.8   Finish the implementation of the `ArrayList` class.

10.9   Finish the implementation of the `ArrayOrderedList` class.

10.10 Finish the implementation of the `ArrayUnorderedList` class.

10.11 Write an implementation of the `LinkedList` class.

10.12 Write an implementation of the `LinkedOrderedList` class.

10.13 Write an implementation of the `LinkedUnorderedList` class.

10.14 Create an implementation of a doubly linked `DoubleOrderedList`
       class. You will need to create a `DoubleNode` class, a `DoubleList`
       class, and a `DoubleIterator` class.

10.15 Create a graphical application that provides a button for `add` and
       `remove` from an ordered list, a text field to accept a string as input
       for `add`, and a text area to display the contents of the list after each
       operation.

10.16 Create a graphical application that provides a button for
       `addToFront`, `addToRear`, `addAfter`, and `remove` from an unordered
       list. Your application must provide a text field to accept a string as
       input for any of the `add` operations. The user should be able to select
       the element to be added after, and select the element to be removed.

Answers to Self-Review Questions

10.1   An indexed list is a collection of objects that are ordered by
       index value. An ordered list is a collection of objects ordered by
       value. An unordered list is a collection of objects ordered as the
       client chooses.

10.2   We can access the list one of three ways: by index position, by ends
       of the list, or by object value.

10.3   All Java Collections framework classes implement the `Collections`
       interface, the `Serializable` interface, and the `Cloneable` interface.

10.4   The linked implementation requires more space per inserted object
       because of the space needed for the references. The `LinkedList` class
       is actually a doubly linked list, requiring twice as much space for ref-
       erences. The `ArrayList` class is more efficient at managing space
       than the other array-based implementations because `ArrayList` col-
       lections are resizable.

10.5 The major difference between the two is access to a particular index position of the list. The `ArrayList` implementation can access any element of the list in equal time if the index value is known. The `LinkedList` implementation needs to traverse the list from one end or the other to reach a particular position.

10.6 The `contains` and `find` operations will be O(n) because they are simply linear searches.

10.7 This would change the time complexity for the `addLast` and `removeLast` operations because they would now require traversal of the list.

10.8 Averaged over the total number of insertions into the list, the time to enlarge the array has little effect on the total time.

Trees 11

In this chapter we explore nonlinear collections and data structures. We discuss the use and implementation of trees, define the terms associated with trees, analyze possible tree implementations, and look at examples of implementing and using trees.

11.1   TREES

The collections we've examined earlier in the book (stacks, queues, and lists) are all linear data structures, meaning their elements are arranged in a line, one after another. A *tree* is a nonlinear structure. In a tree the elements are organized into a hierarchy like the branches of a tree. This section describes trees and the terms we use to describe them.

A tree has *nodes* (think of the leaves or fruit on a real tree) in which elements are stored. The actual branches of the tree, called *edges*, connect one node to another. Each node is at a particular *level* in the tree hierarchy. The *root* of the tree is the only node at the top level of the tree. There is only one root node in a tree. Figure 11.1 shows a tree.

The nodes at lower levels of the tree are the *children* of nodes at the level above. In Figure 11.1, the nodes labeled B, C, D, and E are the children of A. Nodes F and G are the children of B. A node can only have one parent, but a node may have many children. Nodes that have the same parent are called *siblings*. Nodes H, I, and J in Figure 11.1 are siblings because they are all children of D.

The root node is the only node in a tree that does not have a parent. A node that does not have any children is called a *leaf*. A node that is not the root and has at least one child is called an *internal node*. Remember that the tree is upside-down. Our trees "grow" from the root at the top of the tree to the leaves toward the bottom of the tree.

The root is the entry point into a tree structure. We can follow a *path* through the tree from parent to child. For example, the path from node A to N

in Figure 11.1 is A, D, I, N. A node is the *ancestor* of another node if it is above it on the path from the root. So the root is the ancestor of all nodes in a tree. Nodes that can be reached by following a path from a particular node are the *descendants* of that node.

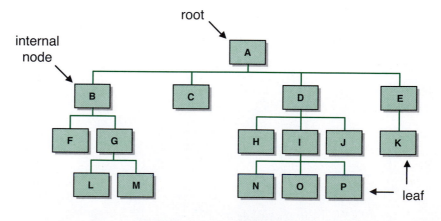

FIGURE 11.1   Tree terminology

The level of a node is also the length of the path from the root to the node. This *path length* is determined by counting the number of edges that must be followed to get from the root to the node. The root is level 0, the children of the root are at level 1, the grandchildren of the root are at level 2, and so on. Path length and level are shown in Figure 11.2.

The *height* of a tree is the length of the longest path from the root to a leaf. So the height of the tree in Figure 11.2 is 3, because the path length from the root to leaf F is 3. The path length from the root to leaf C is 1.

Types of Trees

Trees can be classified in many ways. The most important way we classify trees is by the number of children any node in the tree may have. This value is sometimes called the *order* of the tree. A tree that has no limit to the number of children a node may have is called a *general tree*. A tree that limits each node to no more than n children is called an *n-ary tree*.

A tree in which nodes may have at most two children is called a *binary tree*. This type of tree is helpful in many situations. Much of our exploration of trees will focus on binary trees.

Another way to classify a tree is by whether it is balanced or not. A tree is *balanced* if all of the leaves of the tree are on the same level or at least within one level of each other. So the tree shown on the left in Figure 11.3 is balanced, but the one on the right is not.

A *complete* tree is balanced and all of the leaves at the bottom level are on the left side of the tree. That may seem random, but we'll see later that this has to do with how a tree is stored.

Another related term is *full tree*. A tree is full if all of the leaves of the tree are at the same level and every node is either a leaf or is full of children. The balanced tree from Figure 11.3 is not complete, but all of the 3-ary (or tertiary) trees shown in Figure 11.4 are complete. Only the third tree in Figure 11.4 is full.

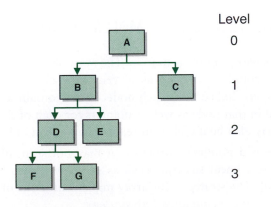

FIGURE 11.2 Path length and level

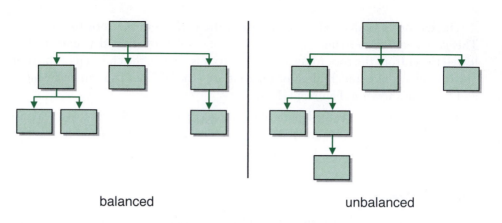

balanced   unbalanced

FIGURE 11.3 Balanced and unbalanced trees

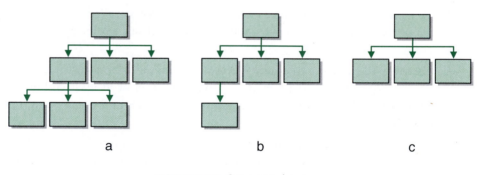

a   b   c

FIGURE 11.4 Some complete trees

11.2 STRATEGIES FOR IMPLEMENTING TREES

Let's look at ways we can implement trees. The most obvious way is a linked structure. Each node could be defined as a `TreeNode` class, as we did with the `LinearNode` class for linked lists. Each node would contain a pointer to the element to be stored in that node as well as pointers for each of the possible children of the node. It may also be useful to store, in each node, a pointer to its parent.

Because a tree is a nonlinear structure, it may not seem like a good idea to implement it using a linear structure such as an array. However, sometimes that approach is useful. The strategies for array implementations of a tree are a *computational strategy* and a *simulated link strategy*.

Computational Strategy for Array Implementation of Trees

A computational strategy can be used for storing binary trees using an array. For example, for any element stored in position n of the array, that element's left child will be stored in position $(2 * n + 1)$ and that element's right child will be stored in position $(2 * (n + 1))$. This strategy is illustrated in Figure 11.5. This strategy works very well, partly because it lets us manage capacity in much the same way that we managed capacity for the array implementations of lists, queues, and stacks. However, this strategy also has drawbacks. For example, if the tree is not complete, we may be wasting large amounts of memory in the array for positions of the tree that do not contain data.

> **Key Concept**
>
> One strategy puts the left child of element n at position $(2 * n + 1)$ and the right child at position $(2 * (n + 1))$.

Simulated Link Strategy for Array Implementation of Trees

Another array implementation of trees is based on the way operating systems manage memory. Instead of giving elements of the tree array positions by location in the tree, we can assign array positions on a first-come first-served basis. Each element of the array will be a node class like the `TreeNode` class that we discussed earlier. However, instead of storing object reference variables as pointers to its children (and perhaps its parent), each node would store the array index of each child (and perhaps its parent). This lets us store elements without any gaps, so that space is not wasted. On the flip side, elements will have to be shifted whenever an element is deleted. This strategy is illustrated in Figure 11.6. The order of the elements in the array is determined simply by their entry order into the tree. In this case, the entry order was A, C, B, E, D, F.

We can also use this strategy when we need to store tree structures on disk using a direct I/O approach. In this case, instead of an array index being used as a pointer, each node will store the position of its children in the file so that we can calculate an offset from the base address of the file.

> **Key Concept**
>
> The simulated link strategy lets us assign array positions one after another, without gaps, no matter how complete the tree is.

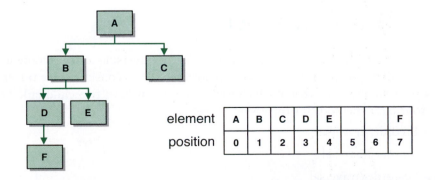

element	A	B	C	D	E			F
position	0	1	2	3	4	5	6	7

FIGURE 11.5 Computational strategy for array implementation of trees

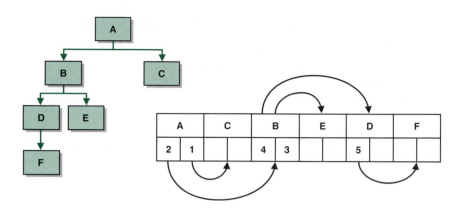

FIGURE 11.6 Simulated link strategy for array implementation of trees

Analysis of Trees

As we discussed earlier, trees are a useful way to implement other collections. Let's take an ordered list for example. When we talked about list implementations in Chapter 10, we described the `find` operation as expected case n/2 or O(n). However, if we implemented an ordered list using a balanced *binary search tree*—a binary tree in which the left child is always less than the parent, which is always less than or equal to the right child—then we could improve the efficiency of the `find` operation to O(log n). We will discuss binary search trees in detail in Chapter 12.

> **Key Concept**
>
> A balanced search tree with n elements will have height $\log_2 n$.

This order of complexity is due to the fact that the height or order of a balanced binary search tree with n elements will always be $\log_2 n$. This is very similar to the binary search discussed in Chapter 7. With the added ordering property of a binary search tree, the worst that can happen is that have to search one path from the root to a leaf.

11.3 TREE TRAVERSALS

Because a tree is a nonlinear structure, the idea of traversing a tree is more interesting than the idea of traversing a linear structure. Let's consider some traversals of a binary tree (i.e., a tree in which each node has at most two children). There are four basic methods for traversing a tree:

> Preorder traversal

> Inorder traversal

> Postorder traversal

> Level-order traversal

Preorder traversal is done by visiting each node (starting at the root), then visiting each of its children (left then right). *Inorder traversal* is done by visiting the left child of the node, then the node, then the right-hand child of the node, starting with the root. *Postorder traversal* is done by visiting the children (left then right), then the node, starting with the root. *Level-order traversal* is done by visiting all the nodes in each level, one level at a time, starting with the root. While these definitions are given for binary search trees, they can be expanded to encompass all trees. Let us examine each traversal in more detail in the context of printing values stored by the nodes.

> **Key Concept**
>
> There are four basic methods for traversing a tree: preorder, inorder, postorder, and level-order.

Preorder Traversal

Let's start with the tree shown in Figure 11.7. A preorder traversal of this tree would produce the sequence A, B, D, E, C. Remember that preorder traversal is done by visiting each node, followed by its children. So, we start by visiting the root, which writes A to the output. Next, we visit the node writing B, and then its children, which would write D and E. When we get to D, we discover there are no children. We then visit any other children of B. This brings us to E, and since E has no children, we visit any other children of A. This brings us to C, where we use the same algorithm, first visiting the node, ouputting C, and then visiting any children. Since there are no children of C and no more children of A, the traversal is complete.

Stated in pseudocode, the algorithm for a preorder traversal is

```
Visit node
Traverse(left child)
Traverse(right child)
```

Inorder Traversal

For the tree shown in Figure 11.7, an inorder traversal would produce D, B, E, A, C. Our definition says that inorder traversal is done by visiting the left child of the node, then the node, then the right child of the node, starting with the root.

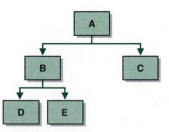

FIGURE 11.7 A complete tree

So, starting with the root, we go to the left child of the root, B. We then go to the left child of B, which is D. We have not yet outputted any nodes. When we try to go to the left child of D, we discover there is not one, so we print the current node, D. Next, we try to go to any children of D. Since there are none, we then visit the previous node, printing B. When we try to go to any remaining children of B, we find the node containing E. Because E does not have a left child, we visit the node, printing E. Because E has no right child, we then visit the previous node, printing A. We then go to any remaining children of A, which takes us to C. Using the same algorithm, we try to go to the left child of C, but there is none, so we visit the current node, printing C. We try to go to any remaining children of C, but again there are none, so we return to the previous node, which happens to be the root. There are no more children of the root, and the traversal is complete.

Stated in pseudocode, the algorithm for an inorder traversal is

```
Traverse(left child)
Visit node
Traverse(right child)
```

Postorder Traversal

For the tree shown in Figure 11.7, a postorder traversal would produce D, E, B, C, A. We defined postorder traversal as starting at the root, visiting the children, then visiting the node. So, starting from the root, we traverse to the left child, the node containing B. Next we traverse to the left child again, the node containing D. D does not have any children, so we visit that node, printing D. Returning to node B, we visit the right child, the node containing E. Because this node does not have any children, we visit the node, printing E, and then return to the previous node and visit it, printing B. Returning to the previous node, in this case the root, we find that it has a right child, so we traverse to the right child, the node containing C. Because this node does not have any children, we visit it, printing C. The previous node (the root) has no remaining children, so we visit it, printing A, and we are done.

Stated in pseudocode, the algorithm for a postorder traversal is

```
Traverse(left child)
Traverse(right child)
Visit node
```

Level-Order Traversal

For the tree shown in Figure 11.7, a level-order traversal would produce A, B, C, D, E. Our definition says that a level-order traversal is done by visiting all of the nodes at each level, one level at a time, starting with the root. Using this definition, we first visit the root, printing A. Next we visit the left child of the root, printing B, then the right child of the root, printing C, and then the children of B, printing D and E.

Stated in pseudocode, an algorithm for a level-order traversal is

```
Create two queues: nodes and result

Enqueue the root onto the nodes queue

While the nodes queue is not empty

{

  Dequeue the first element from the queue

  If that element is not null

      Enqueue that element on the result queue

      Enqueue the children of the element on the nodes queue

  Else

      Enqueue null on the result queue

}

Return an iterator for the result queue
```

This algorithm for a level-order traversal is only one of many possible solutions. However, it does have some interesting properties. First, note that we are using a collection, a queue, to solve a problem within another collection, a binary tree. Second, remember that iterators can't react if a collection is modified while the iterator is in use. When we store elements in a queue in order and then return an iterator over the queue, the iterator can only take a snap-shot of the binary tree and is not affected by any changes. This can be either a good thing or a bad thing, depending on how the iterator is used.

11.4   IMPLEMENTING BINARY TREES

Let's take a look at a simple binary tree implementation. In Section 11.6, we will illustrate an example using this implementation. One possible set of operations for a binary tree ADT is listed in Figure 11.8. Keep in mind that you will find variations in the operations defined for specific data structures from one book to another. We've been very careful in this book to define the operations on each data structure so that they are consistent with its purpose.

Notice that in all of the operations listed, there are no operations to add elements to the tree. This is because until we know what the binary tree is for, we can't know how to add an element to the tree other than through a constructor.

Operation	Description
removeLeftSubtree	Removes the left subtree of the root.
removeRightSubtree	Removes the right subtree of the root.
removeAllElements	Removes all of the elements from the tree.
isEmpty	Determines if the tree is empty.
size	Determines the number of elements in the tree.
contains	Determines if the target is in the tree.
find	Returns a reference to the target if it is found.
tostring	Returns a string representation of the tree.
iteratorInOrder	Returns an iterator for an inorder traversal of the tree.
iteratorPreOrder	Returns an iterator for a preorder traversal of the tree.
iteratorPostOrder	Returns an iterator for a postorder traversal of the tree.
iteratorLevelOrder	Returns an iterator for a level-order traversal of the tree.

FIGURE 11.8   The operations on a binary tree

It is also interesting to note that there is no removeElement method in our BinaryTreeADT. That's because we do not yet have enough information to know how to remove an element. When we were dealing with sets in Chapter 3, we could picture the state of the set after we removed an element. The same can be said of stacks and queues because we could only remove an element from one end. Even with lists, where we could remove an element from the middle, it was easy to picture the resulting list. With a tree, however, we have many issues to handle. What happens to the children and other descendants of an element that is removed? Where does the child pointer of the element's parent now point? What if the element we are removing is the root? As we will see in our example later in this chapter, for some trees we just plain can't remove an element. Once we know how the tree will be used, we may decide that a removeElement method is appropriate. A good example of this is binary search trees, as we will see in Chapter 12.

Listing 11.1 shows the BinaryTreeADT interface. Figure 11.9 shows the UML description for the BinaryTreeADT interface.

We will look at how some of these methods might be implemented. Others will be left as exercises. The BinaryTree class implementing the BinaryTreeADT interface will need to keep track of the root node and the number of elements on the tree. The BinaryTree instance data could be declared as

```
private int count;
protected BinaryTreeNode root;
```

The constructors for the BinaryTree class should handle three cases: a binary tree with nothing in it, a binary tree with a single element but no children, and

Listing 11.1

```java
//*********************************************************************
//  BinaryTreeADT.java        Authors:  Lewis/Chase
//
//  Defines the interface to a binary tree data structure.
//*********************************************************************

package jss2;

import java.util.Iterator;

public interface BinaryTreeADT
{
   public void removeLeftSubtree();
   public void removeRightSubtree();
   public void removeAllElements();
   public boolean isEmpty();
   public int size();
   public boolean contains (Object targetElement);
   public Object find (Object targetElement);
   public String toString();
   public Iterator iteratorInOrder();
   public Iterator iteratorPreOrder();
   public Iterator iteratorPostOrder();
   public Iterator iteratorLevelOrder();
}
```

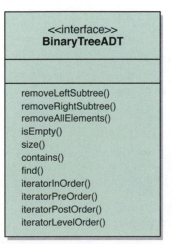

FIGURE 11.9 UML description of the `BinaryTreeADT` interface

a binary tree with an element and two subtrees. The `BinaryTree` class might have the following constructors. Each of the constructors must include the `root` and `count` attributes, and the last constructor must take into account the possibility that either or both of the subtrees might be null.

```java
//------------------------------------------------------------
//   Creates an empty binary tree.
//------------------------------------------------------------
public BinaryTree()
{
   count = 0;
   root = null;
}


//------------------------------------------------------------
//   Creates a binary tree with the specified element as its root.
//------------------------------------------------------------
public BinaryTree (Object element)
{
   count = 1;
   root = new BinaryTreeNode (element);
}


//------------------------------------------------------------
//   Constructs a binary tree from the two specified binary trees.
//------------------------------------------------------------
public BinaryTree (Object element, BinaryTree leftSubtree,
                                   BinaryTree rightSubtree)
{
   root = new BinaryTreeNode (element);
   count = 1;

   if (leftSubtree != null)
   {
      count = count + leftSubtree.size();
      root.left = leftSubtree.root;
   }
   else
      root.left = null;

   if (rightSubtree !=null)
   {
      count = count + rightSubtree.size();
      root.right = rightSubtree.root;
   }
   else
      root.right = null;
}
```

Notice that the instance data and the constructors use a class called `BinaryTreeNode`. This class keeps track of the element stored at each location as well as pointers to the left and right subtree or children of each node. In this implementation, we don't include a pointer back to the parent of each node. Listing 11.2 shows the `BinaryTreeNode` class. The `BinaryTreeNode` class also includes a recursive method to return the number of children of the given node.

Listing 11.2

```java
//********************************************************************
//  BinaryTreeNode.java         Authors: Lewis/Chase
//
//  Represents a node in a binary tree with a left and right child.
//********************************************************************
package jss2;

class BinaryTreeNode
{
    protected Object element;
    protected BinaryTreeNode left, right;

    //-----------------------------------------------------------------
    //  Creates a new tree node with the specified data.
    //-----------------------------------------------------------------
    BinaryTreeNode (Object obj)
    {
        element = obj;
        left = null;
        right = null;
    }

    //-----------------------------------------------------------------
    //  Returns the number of non-null children of this node.
    //  This method may be able to be written more efficiently.
    //-----------------------------------------------------------------
    public int numChildren()
    {
        int children = 0;

        if (left != null)
            children = 1 + left.numChildren();

        if (right != null)
            children = children + 1 + right.numChildren();

        return children;
    }
}
```

There are several other ways we could implement a tree node or binary tree node class. For example, we could include methods to test whether the node is a leaf (i.e., does not have any children), to test whether the node is an internal node (i.e., has at least one child), to test how far (deep) the node is from the root, or to calculate the height of the left and right subtrees.

We could also use polymorphism so that, rather than testing a node to see if it has data, or has children, we would create implementations such as an `emptyTreeNode`, `innerTreeNode`, and `leafTreeNode`.

The `removeLeftSubtree` Method

To remove the left subtree of a binary tree, we must set the left child pointer of the root to null and subtract the total number of nodes in the left subtree from the count:

```java
//----------------------------------------------------------------
//  Removes the left subtree of this binary tree.
//----------------------------------------------------------------
public void removeLeftSubtree()
{
    if (root.left != null)
        count = count - root.left.numChildren() - 1;
    root.left = null;
}
```

The other `remove` operations are very similar and are left as exercises. Because we are maintaining a `count` variable, the `isEmpty` and `size` operations are the same as the methods we developed in our earlier collections.

The `find` Method

Our `find` method traverses the tree using the `equals` method. This puts the definition of equality under the control of the class being stored in the tree. The `find` method throws an exception if the target element is not found.

Many tree methods may be written either recursively or iteratively. When written recursively, these methods usually require a private support method because the signature and/or the behavior of the first call and later calls may not be the same. The `find` method is an excellent example of this strategy.

We have chosen to use a recursive `findAgain` method. The first call to `find` will start at the root of the tree. If that instance of the `find` method does not find the target, we need to throw an exception. The private `findAgain` method lets us distinguish between the first instance of the `find` method and later calls.

```java
//-------------------------------------------------------------
//  Returns a reference to the target element if it is found
//  in the binary tree.  Throws a NoSuchElementException if
//  the target element is not found in the binary tree.
//-------------------------------------------------------------
public Object find (Object targetElement) throws
                    ElementNotFoundException
{

   BinaryTreeNode current = root;
   BinaryTreeNode temp = current;

   if (!(current.element.equals(targetElement)) &&
       (current.left != null))
   current = findAgain( targetElement, current.left);

   if (!(current.equals(targetElement)))
      current = temp;

   if (!(current.element.equals(targetElement)) &&
       (current.right != null))
      current = findAgain(targetElement, current.right);

   if (!(current.element.equals(targetElement)))
      throw new ElementNotFoundException ("binarytree");

   return current.element;
}

//-------------------------------------------------------------
//  Returns a reference to the target element if it is
//  found in the binary tree.
//-------------------------------------------------------------
private BinaryTreeNode findAgain (Object targetElement,
                                  BinaryTreeNode next)
{
   BinaryTreeNode current = next;
   if (!(next.element.equals(targetElement)) && (next.left !=null))
      next = findAgain (targetElement, next.left);

   if (!(next.equals(targetElement)))
      next = current;

   if (!(next.element.equals(targetElement)) &&
       (next.right != null))
   next = findAgain (targetElement, next.right);

   return next;
}
```

The contains method, as in earlier examples, can use the find method. It is left as an exercise.

The iteratorInOrder Method

The iteratorInOrder method creates an iterator object that will let a user class step through the elements of the tree in an inorder traversal. Again, we can use one collection to build another. We simply traverse the tree using a definition of "visit" (from earlier pseudocode) that enqueues the contents of the node onto a queue. We then return the queue iterator as the result of the iterator method for our tree. The linear nature of a queue and the way that we implemented the iterator method for a queue and the LinkedIterator class make this possible. The iterator method for a queue returns a LinkedIterator that starts with the element at the front of the queue and steps through the queue linearly. It is important to understand that the iterator does this simply because we chose to implement the iterator method for a queue and the LinkedIterator class.

Like the find operation, we use a private helper method in our recursion.

```
//-------------------------------------------------------------
//  Performs an inorder traversal on the binary tree by calling a
//  recursive inorder method that starts with the root.
//-------------------------------------------------------------
public Iterator iteratorInOrder()
{
   LinkedQueue queue = new LinkedQueue();
   inorder (root, queue);
   return queue.iterator();
}


//-------------------------------------------------------------
//  Performs a recursive inorder traversal.
//-------------------------------------------------------------
protected void inorder (BinaryTreeNode node, LinkedQueue queue)
{
   if (node != null)
   {
      inorder (node.left, queue);
      queue.enqueue(node.element);
      inorder (node.right, queue);
   }
}
```

The other iterator operations are left as exercises.

11.5   USING BINARY TREES: EXPRESSION TREES

In Chapter 8, we used a stack algorithm to evaluate postfix expressions. In this section, we use a stack algorithm to create a kind of binary tree called an *expression tree*. The term *expression* here means a math expression. Figure 11.10 illustrates an expression tree. Notice that the root and all of the internal nodes of an expression tree contain operations (+, *, −) and that all of the leaves contain operands (9, 4, 5, 3). An expression tree is evaluated from the bottom up.

1.   We start with the (5 − 3) term, which gives us 2.

2.   Then we multiply that result, 2, by 4, which gives us 8.

3.   Finally, we add 8 to 9, getting 17.

Listing 11.3 illustrates our `ExpressionTree` class. This class extends the `BinaryTree` class, giving us constructors that reference the constructors for the `BinaryTree` class and giving us an `evaluate` method to recursively evaluate an expression tree once it has been built.

The `evaluateTree` method calls the recursive `evaluateNode` method. The `evaluateNode` method either returns a number, if the node contains a number, or returns the result of the operation, if the node contains an operation. The `ExpressionTree` class stores the `ExpressionTreeObj` class at each node of the tree. The `ExpressionTreeObj` class helps us keep track of whether the element is a number or an operator, and which operator or what value is stored there. The `ExpressionTreeObj` class is illustrated in Listing 11.4.

The `Postfix` and `PostfixEvaluator` classes let the user enter a postfix expression from the keyboard. Consider the following pseudocode:

```
The user enters a term
If it is an operand then

    A new ExpressionTreeObj is created with the given value
    and an ExpressionTree is built using that element as the
    root and with no children.

    The new expression tree is then pushed onto a stack.
If the term entered is an operator then

    The top two expression trees are popped off.

    A new expression tree is created with the given operator
    value as its root, and the two expression trees as its left
    and right subtrees.
Continue this process until there are no more terms entered.
```

Figure 11.11 illustrates this process for the expression tree from Figure 11.10. The top of the expression tree stack is on the right.

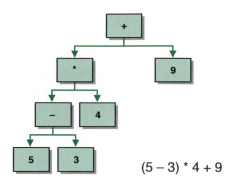

$$(5 - 3) * 4 + 9$$

FIGURE 11.10 An example expression tree

Listing 11.3

```java
//********************************************************************
//  ExpressionTree.java        Authors: Lewis/Chase
//
//  Represents an expression tree of operators and operands.
//********************************************************************

package jss2;

public class ExpressionTree extends BinaryTree
{
   //-----------------------------------------------------------
   //  Creates an empty expression tree.
   //-----------------------------------------------------------
   public ExpressionTree()
   {
      super();
   }

   //-----------------------------------------------------------
   //  Builds an expression tree from the two trees.
   //-----------------------------------------------------------
   public ExpressionTree (Object element, ExpressionTree leftSubtree,
                          ExpressionTree rightSubtree)
   {
      super(element, leftSubtree, rightSubtree);
   }
```

Listing 11.3   **continued**

```
//------------------------------------------------------------
//  Evaluates the expression tree using the recursive evaluateNode
//  method.
//------------------------------------------------------------
public int evaluateTree()
{
   return evaluateNode(root);
}


//------------------------------------------------------------
//  Recursively evaluates each node of the tree.
//------------------------------------------------------------
public int evaluateNode (BinaryTreeNode root)
{
   int result, operand1, operand2;
   ExpressionTreeObj temp;
   if (root == null)
      result = 0;
   else
   {
      temp = (ExpressionTreeObj)root.element;
      if (temp.isOperator())
      {
         operand1 = evaluateNode(root.left);
         operand2 = evaluateNode(root.right);
         result = computeTerm(temp.getOperator(), operand1, operand2);
      }
      else
         result = temp.getValue();
   }

   return result;
}


//------------------------------------------------------------
//  Evaluates an operator and two operands.
//------------------------------------------------------------
private static int computeTerm (char operator, int operand1,
                                int operand2)
{
   int result = 0;
```

Listing 11.3 **continued**

```
      if (operator == '+')
         result = operand1 + operand2;
      else if (operator == '-')
         result = operand1 - operand2;
      else if (operator == '*')
         result = operand1 * operand2;
      else
         result = operand1 / operand2;

      return result;
   }
}
```

Listing 11.4

```
//********************************************************************
//  ExpressionTreeObj.java        Authors: Lewis/Chase
//
//  Represents an element in an expression tree.
//********************************************************************

package jss2;

public class ExpressionTreeObj
{
   private int termtype;
   private char operator;
   private int value;

   //-----------------------------------------------------------------
   //  Creates a new expression tree object with the specified data.
   //-----------------------------------------------------------------
   public ExpressionTreeObj (int type, char op, int val)
   {
      termtype = type;
      operator = op;
      value = val;
   }

   //-----------------------------------------------------------------
   //  Returns true if this object is an operator and false
   //  if it is not.
   //-----------------------------------------------------------------
```

Listing 11.4   **continued**

```java
public boolean isOperator()
{
    return (termtype == 1);
}

//------------------------------------------------------------
//  Returns the operator.
//------------------------------------------------------------
public char getOperator()
{
    return operator;
}

//------------------------------------------------------------
//  Returns the value.
//------------------------------------------------------------
public int getValue()
{
    return value;
}
}
```

Input in Postfix: 5 3 – 4 * 9 +

Token	Processing Steps	Expression Tree Stack (top at right)
5	push(new ExpressionTree(5, null, null)	5
3	push(new ExpressionTree(3, null, null)	5 3

FIGURE 11.11 Building an expression tree from a postfix expression (continued on next page)

–	op2 = pop op1 = pop push(new ExpressionTree(–, op1, op2))	
4	push(new ExpressionTree(4, null, null)	
*	op2 = pop op1 = pop push(new ExpressionTree(*, op1, op2))	
9	push(new ExpressionTree(9, null, null)	
+	op2 = pop op1 = pop push(new ExpressionTree(+, op1, op2))	

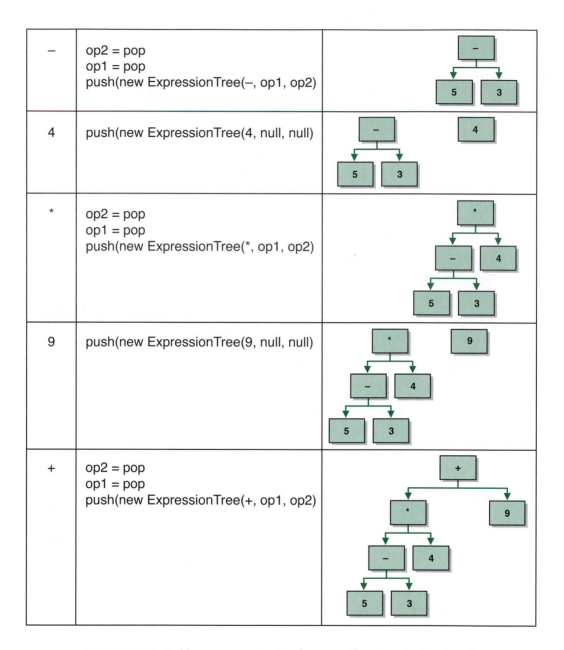

FIGURE 11.11 Building an expression tree from a postfix expression (continued)

The Postfix class is shown in Listing 11.5 and the PostfixEvaluator class is shown in Listing 11.6. The UML description of the Postfix class is shown in Figure 11.12.

Listing 11.5

```
//********************************************************************
//  Postfix.java         Authors: Lewis/Chase
//
//  Uses the PostfixEvaluator class to solve a postfix expression.
//********************************************************************

public class Postfix
{
   public static void main (String[] args)
   {
      PostfixEvaluator temp = new PostfixEvaluator();
      temp.solve();
   }
}
```

Output

```
Enter a valid postfix expression one token at a time.
Enter an integer, an operator (+,-,*,/) or ! to quit
3
4
+
5
/
4
5
-
*
!
The result is -1
```

Listing 11.6

```
//********************************************************************
//  PostfixEvaluator.java        Authors:  Lewis/Chase
//
//  A pair of stacks create an expression tree from a
//  valid postfix expression. Then a recursive method
//  from the ExpressionTree class evaluates the tree.
//********************************************************************

import jss2.*;
import jss2.exceptions.*;
import java.util.StringTokenizer;
```

Listing 11.6   continued

```java
import java.util.Iterator;
import java.io.*;

public class PostfixEvaluator
{
    //----------------------------------------------------------------
    //  Retrieves and returns the next operand from the tree stack.
    //----------------------------------------------------------------
    private ExpressionTree getOperand(LinkedStack treeStack)
    {
        ExpressionTree temp;
        temp = (ExpressionTree)treeStack.pop();
        return temp;
    }

    //----------------------------------------------------------------
    //  Retrieves the next token.
    //----------------------------------------------------------------
    private String getNextToken()
    {
        String tempToken = "0", instring;
        StringTokenizer tokenizer;

        try
        {
            BufferedReader in = new
            BufferedReader(new InputStreamReader(System.in));
            instring = in.readLine();
            tokenizer = new StringTokenizer(instring);
            tempToken = (tokenizer.nextToken());
        }
        catch (Exception IOException)
        {
            System.out.println("An I/O exception has occurred");
        }

        return tempToken;
    }

    //----------------------------------------------------------------
    //  Asks the user to enter a valid postfix expression.
    //  Converts it to an expression tree using a two-stack method.
    //  Then calls a recursive method to evaluate the expression.
    //----------------------------------------------------------------
```

Listing 11.6   **continued**

```
public void solve()
{
   ExpressionTree operand1, operand2;
   char operator;
   String tempToken;
   LinkedStack treeStack = new LinkedStack();

   System.out.println("Enter a valid postfix expression " +
                   "one token at a time.");
   System.out.println("Enter an integer, an operator (+,-,*,/) " +
                   "or ! to quit ");

   tempToken = getNextToken();
   operator = tempToken.charAt(0);

   while (!(operator == '!'))
   {
      if ((operator == '+') || (operator == '-') ||
         (operator == '*') || (operator == '/'))
      {
         operand1 = getOperand(treeStack);
         operand2 = getOperand(treeStack);
         treeStack.push (new ExpressionTree(new ExpressionTreeObj
                     (1, operator, 0), operand2, operand1));
      }
      else
         treeStack.push (new ExpressionTree(new ExpressionTreeObj
            (2, ' ', Integer.parseInt(tempToken)), null, null));

      tempToken = getNextToken();
      operator = tempToken.charAt(0);
   }

   System.out.print ("The result is ");
   System.out.println (((ExpressionTree) treeStack.peek()
                   ).evaluateTree());
}
}
```

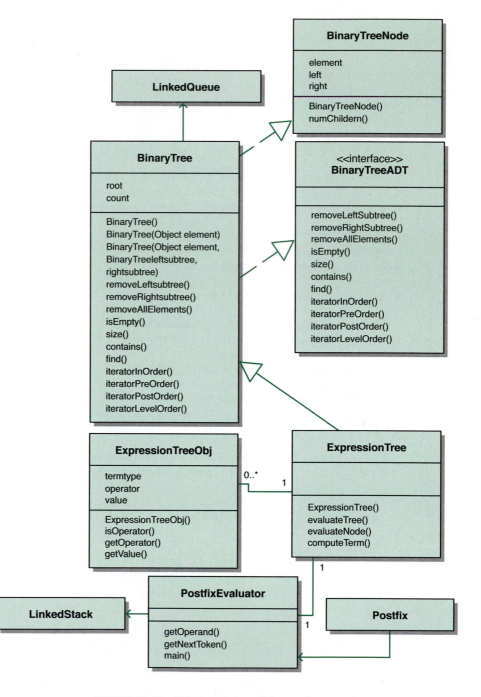

FIGURE 11.12 UML description of the postfix example

Summary of Key Concepts

> A tree is a nonlinear structure in which the elements are organized into a hierarchy.

> Trees are described by a large set of related terms.

> One strategy puts the left child of element n at position (2 * n + 1) and the right child at position (2 * (n + 1)).

> The simulated link strategy lets us assign array positions one after another without a gap, no matter how complete the tree is.

> A balanced search tree with n elements will have height $\log_2 n$.

> There are four basic methods for traversing a tree: preorder, inorder, postorder, and level-order.

Self-Review Questions

11.1   What is a tree?

11.2   What is a node?

11.3   What is a root?

11.4   What is a leaf?

11.5   What is an internal node?

11.6   Define the height of a tree.

11.7   Define the level of a node.

11.8   What are the advantages and disadvantages of the computational strategy?

11.9   What are the advantages and disadvantages of the simulated link strategy?

11.10 What attributes should be stored in the `TreeNode` class?

11.11 Which method of traversing a tree would result in a sorted list for a binary search tree?

11.12 We used a queue to implement the iterator methods for a binary tree. What must be true for this strategy to work?

Exercises

11.1   Write the pseudocode for a level-order traversal of a binary tree.

11.2   Draw a family tree for a couple of generations of your own family or a well-known family such as the Tudors (British) or the Barrymores (Hollywood). Write the pseudocode algorithm to insert a person into their proper place in the tree.

11.3   Write a pseudocode algorithm to build an expression tree from a prefix expression.

11.4   Write a pseudocode algorithm to build an expression tree from an infix expression.

11.5   What is the time complexity of the `find` method?

11.6   What is the time complexity of the `iteratorinorder` method?

11.7   Write the pseudocode for the `size` method, assuming that there is no `count` variable.

11.8   Write the pseudocode for the `isEmpty` operation, assuming that there is no `count` variable.

11.9   Draw an expression tree for the expression $(9 + 4) * 5 + (4 - (6 - 3))$.

Programming Projects

11.1   Complete the implementation of the `removeRightSubtree` and `removeAllElements` operations of a binary tree.

11.2   Complete the implementation of the `size` and `isEmpty` operations of a binary tree, without a `count` variable.

11.3   Create boolean methods for our `BinaryTreeNode` class that will tell us whether the node is a leaf or an internal node.

11.4   Create a method called `depth` that will return an `int` for the level (depth) of a node from the root.

11.5   Complete the implementation of the `contains` method for a binary tree.

11.6   Implement the `contains` method for a binary tree without using the `find` operation.

11.7   Complete the implementation of the iterator methods for a binary tree.

11.8   Implement the iterator methods for a binary tree without using a queue.

11.9   Change the `ExpressionTree` class to create a method called `draw` that will draw a diagram of an expression tree.

11.10 We use postfix notation in the example in this chapter because it doesn't need precedence rules and parentheses. Some infix expressions also do not need parentheses. Implement a method for the `ExpressionTree` class that will tell us if an integer expression would need parentheses when written as an infix notation.

11.11 Create an array-based implementation of a binary tree using the computational strategy.

11.12 Create an array-based implementation of a binary tree using the simulated link strategy.

Answers to Self-Review Questions

11.1   A *tree* is a nonlinear structure. Each node in the tree, other than the root node, has exactly one parent.

11.2   A *node* is where an element is stored in a tree.

11.3   A *root* is the node at the base of the tree, the one node in the tree that does not have a parent.

11.4   A *leaf* is a node that does not have any children.

11.5   An *internal node* is any node that is not a root and that has at least one child.

11.6   The *height* of the tree is the longest path from the root to a leaf.

11.7   The *level* of a node is measured by the number of links between a node and the root.

11.8   The computational strategy does not have to store links from parent to child because that relationship is fixed by position. However, this strategy may waste space.

11.9   The simulated link strategy stores array index values as pointers between parent and child and allows the data to be stored without a gap no matter how balanced and/or complete the tree. However, this strategy means we have to shift elements in the array.

11.10 The `TreeNode` class must store a pointer to the element stored in that position as well as pointers to each of the children of that node. The class may also contain a pointer to the parent of the node.

11.11 In-order traversal of a binary search tree would result in a sorted list in ascending order.

11.12 The iterator for a queue must return the elements in the order in which they were enqueued (first in, first out). For this implementation of a queue, we know this is the case.

Binary Search Trees

12

CHAPTER OBJECTIVES

> Define a binary search tree abstract data structure

> Demonstrate how a binary search tree can be used

> Examine a binary search tree implementation

> Compare binary search tree implementations

In this chapter, we explore binary search trees. We examine algorithms for adding and removing elements from binary search trees and for keeping them balanced. We also analyze these implementations and learn how binary search trees are used.

12.1   A BINARY SEARCH TREE

A *binary search tree* is a binary tree in which each left child is less than the parent, which is less than or equal to the right child. The operations on a binary search tree are listed in Figure 12.1.

Keep in mind that the definition of a binary search tree is an extension of the definition of a binary tree that we discussed in the last chapter. So the operations in Figure 12.1 are in addition to the ones defined for a binary tree. At this point we are simply discussing binary search trees, but as we will see shortly, the interface for a balanced binary search tree will be the same. Listing 12.1 and Figure 12.2 describe a `BinarySearchTreeADT`.

Listing 12.1

```
//********************************************************************
//   BinarySearchTree.java          Authors: Lewis/Chase
//
//   Defines the interface to a binary search tree.
//********************************************************************
package jss2;
public interface BinarySearchTreeADT extends BinaryTreeADT
{
    public void addElement (Comparable element);
    public Comparable removeElement (Comparable targetElement);
    public void removeAllOccurrences (Comparable targetElement);
    public Comparable removeMin();
    public Comparable removeMax();
    public Comparable findMin();
    public Comparable findMax();
}
```

Operation	Description
`addElement`	Add an element to the tree.
`removeElement`	Remove an element from the tree.
`removeAllOccurrences`	Remove all occurrences of element from the tree.
`removeMin`	Remove the minimum element in the tree.
`removeMax`	Remove the maximum element in the tree.
`findMin`	Return a reference to the minimum element in the tree.
`findMax`	Return a reference to the maximum element in the tree.

FIGURE 12.1   The operations on a binary search tree

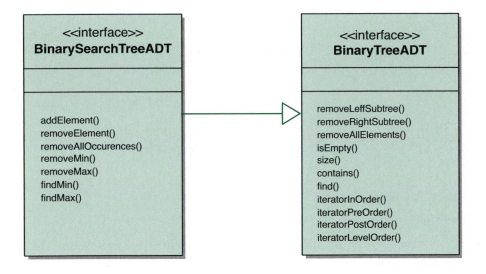

FIGURE 12.2   UML description of the `BinarySearchTreeADT`

12.2   IMPLEMENTING BINARY SEARCH TREES: WITH LINKS

In Chapter 11, we introduced a simple `BinaryTree` class and used a `BinaryTreeNode` class to represent each node of the tree. Each `BinaryTreeNode` object has a reference to the element stored at that node as well as references to each of the node's children. We can extend that definition with a `BinarySearchTree` class implementing the `BinarySearchTreeADT` interface. Since we are extending the `BinaryTree` class, all of the methods we discussed in Chapter 11 are still supported, including the traversals.

> **Key Concept**
>
> Each `BinaryTreeNode` object has a reference to the element stored at that node, as well as references to each of the node's children.

Our `BinarySearchTree` class offers two constructors: one to create an empty `BinarySearchTree` and the other to create a `BinarySearchTree` with a particular element at the root. Both of these constructors refer to the constructors of the super class (i.e., the `BinaryTree` class).

```
//----------------------------------------------------------------
//  Creates an empty binary search tree.
//----------------------------------------------------------------
public BinarySearchTree()
{
    super();
}
```

```
//------------------------------------------------------------
//  Creates a binary search with the given element as its
//  root.
//------------------------------------------------------------
public BinarySearchTree (Comparable element)
{
    super (element);
}
```

The addElement Operation

The addElement method adds a Comparable element to the tree. Where the element goes depends on its value:

1. If the tree is empty, the new element becomes the root.

2. If the tree is not empty, the new element is compared with the element at the root. If it is less than the element at the root and the left child of the root is null, then the new element becomes the left child.

3. If the left child of the root is not null, then we compare the element with the left child, and so on.

4. If, on the other hand, the new element is greater than or equal to the root and the right child of the root is null, then the new element becomes the right child.

5. If the new element is greater than or equal to the root and the right child of the root is not null, then we traverse to the right child of the root and compare again.

In a nutshell, greater-than adds to the right and less-than adds to the left. It may be easier if you remember that *less* and *left* begin with *L*. The following code and Figure 12.3 lay out this process.

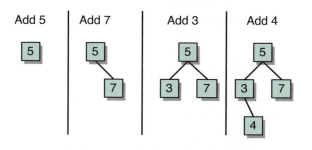

FIGURE 12.3 Adding elements to a binary search tree

```java
//-----------------------------------------------------------------
//  Adds an object to the binary search tree
//  according to its key value.  Note that
//  equal elements are added to the right.
//-----------------------------------------------------------------
public void addElement (Comparable element)
{
    BinaryTreeNode temp = new BinaryTreeNode (element);

    if (isEmpty())
        root = temp;
    else
    {
        BinaryTreeNode current = root;
        boolean added = false;

        while (!added)
        {
            if (element.compareTo(current.element) < 0)

                if (current.left == null)
                {
                    current.left = temp;
                    added = true;
                }
            else
                current = current.left;
            else
                if (current.right == null)
                {
                    current.right = temp;
                    added = true;
                }
                else
                    current = current.right;
        }
    }

    count++;
}
```

The removeElement Operation

The removeElement method removes the Comparable element from a binary search tree or throws an ElementNotFoundException if the element is not found in the tree. Unlike linear structures, in a binary search tree we can't remove the node just by pointing to it. Instead, we have to *promote*, or push forward, another node to replace the one being removed. The protected method replacement returns a reference to a node that will replace the one being removed. There are three ways replacing a node can be handled:

> If the node has no children, replacement returns null.

> If the node has only one child, replacement returns that child.

> If the node has two children, replacement will return the inorder predecessor of the node to be removed.

Listing 12.2 illustrates the replacement method. Figure 12.4 shows how elements are removed from a binary search tree.

```java
//-----------------------------------------------------------------
//  Removes the first element that matches the target
//  element and returns a reference to it.
//  Throws an ElementNotFoundException if the specified target
//  element is not found in the binary search tree.
//-----------------------------------------------------------------
public Comparable removeElement (Comparable targetElement) throws
ElementNotFoundException
{
    Comparable result = null;

    if (!isEmpty())

        if (targetElement.equals(root.element))
        {
            result = (Comparable) root.element;
            root = replacement (root);
            count--;
        }
    else
    {
        BinaryTreeNode current, parent = root;
        boolean found = false;

        if (targetElement.compareTo(root.element) < 0)
            current = root.left;
        else
            current = root.right;

        while (current != null && !found)
        {
            if (targetElement.equals(current.element))
            {
                found = true;
                count--;
```

```java
                result = (Comparable) current.element;

                if (current == parent.left)
                   parent.left = replacement (current);
                else
                   parent.right = replacement (current);
             }
          else
          {
             parent = current;

             if (targetElement.compareTo(current.element) < 0)
                current = current.left;
             else
                current = current.right;
          }
       }
       if (!found)
          throw new ElementNotFoundException("binary tree");
    }

    return result;
}
```

```java
//-----------------------------------------------------------------
//  Returns a reference to a node that will replace the one
//  being removed.  If the removed node has two children,
//  the inorder predecessor is used as its replacement.
//-----------------------------------------------------------------
protected BinaryTreeNode replacement (BinaryTreeNode node)
{
   BinaryTreeNode result = null;

   if ((node.left == null)&&(node.right==null))
      result = null;
   else
      if ((node.left != null)&&(node.right==null))
         result = node.left;
      else
         if ((node.left == null)&&(node.right != null))
            result = node.right;
         else
         {
            BinaryTreeNode current = node.left;
            BinaryTreeNode parent = node;
```

```
            while (current.right != null)
            {
                parent = current;
                current = current.right;
            }

            parent.right = current.left;
            result = current;
        }

    return result;
}
```

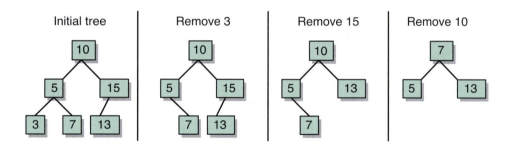

FIGURE 12.4   Removing elements from a binary search tree

The `removeAllOccurrences` Operation

The `removeAllOccurrences` method removes all occurrences of a `Comparable` element from a binary search tree or throws an `ElementNotFoundException` if the given element is not found. This method calls the `removeElement` method once, guaranteeing that the exception will be thrown if there is not at least one occurrence of the element in the tree. The `removeElement` method is then called again and again until the tree no longer contains the target element. This can be useful when you are removing an element from a larger collection—for example, a tree of students in a class: If a student leaves the school they will need to be removed from the class lists.

```
//-------------------------------------------------------------
//  Removes elements that match the target element
//  from the binary search tree. Throws an
//  ElementNotFoundException if the specified target element
//  is not found.
//-------------------------------------------------------------
public void removeAllOccurrences (Comparable targetElement) throws
ElementNotFoundException
{
    removeElement(targetElement);

    while (contains(targetElement))
        removeElement(targetElement);
}
```

The removeMin Operation

Sometimes in an ordered collection it is useful to remove the minimum item in the list; for example, if a to-do list was stored in a tree it would be good to be able to get the next item on the list to do. There are three ways to locate and remove the element with the lowest value in a binary search tree:

> If the root has no left child, then the root is the minimum element and the right child of the root becomes the new root.

> If the leftmost node of the tree is a leaf, then it is the minimum element and we simply set its parent's left child reference to null.

> If the leftmost node of the tree is an internal node, then we set its parent's left child reference to point to the right child of the node to be removed.

> ### Key Concept
> The leftmost node in a binary search tree will contain the minimum element and the rightmost node will contain the maximum element.

Figure 12.5 illustrates these possibilities, and the code below implements the method described.

```
//-------------------------------------------------------------
//  Removes the node with the least value from the binary search
//  tree and returns a reference to its element.  Throws an
//  EmptyBinarySearchTreeException if the binary search tree is
//  empty.
//-------------------------------------------------------------
public Comparable removeMin() throws EmptyCollectionException
{
    Comparable result = null;

    if (isEmpty())
        throw new EmptyCollectionException ("binary tree");
```

```
        else
        {
            if (root.left == null)
            {
                result = (Comparable) root.element;
                root = root.right;
            }
            else
            {
                BinaryTreeNode parent = root;
                BinaryTreeNode current = root.left;
                while (current.left != null)
                {
                    parent = current;
                    current = current.left;
                }
                result = (Comparable) current.element;
                parent.left = current.right;
            }

            count--;
        }

        return result;
    }
```

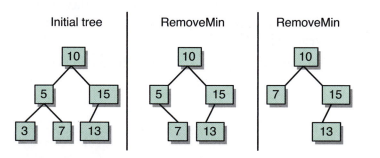

FIGURE 12.5 Removing the minimum element from a binary search tree

The removeMax, findMin, and findMax operations are left as exercises.

12.3   USING BINARY SEARCH TREES: IMPLEMENTING ORDERED LISTS

As we discussed in Chapter 11, one main use of trees is to implement other collections. The `OrderedList` collection from Chapter 10 is an excellent example. Figure 12.6 is the common operations for lists, and Figure 12.7 is the operation particular to an ordered list. We can combine these with a binary search tree to create an implementation called `BinarySearchTreeOrderedList`, a more efficient implementation than those we discussed in Chapter 10.

> **Key Concept**
>
> One of the main uses of trees is to provide efficient implementations of other collections.

To keep things simple, we have implemented both the `ListADT` and the `OrderedListADT` interfaces with the `BinarySearchTreeOrderedList` class as shown in Listing 12.2. In some cases, the same method from either the `BinaryTree` or `BinarySearchTree` classes will work. This is true for the contains, isEmpty, and size operations. For the rest of the operations, the `BinaryTree` method or `BinarySearchTree` class has an `OrderedList` equivalent. Thus, each of these methods can be implemented simply by calling the associated method for a `BinarySearchTree`. This works for the add, removeFirst, removeLast, remove, first, last, and iterator methods.

Operation	Description
removeFirst	Removes the first element from the list.
removeLast	Removes the last element from the list.
remove	Removes a particular element from the list.
first	Examines the element at the front of the list.
last	Examines the element at the rear of the list.
contains	Determines if the list contains a particular element.
isEmpty	Determines if the list is empty.
size	Determines the number of elements on the list.

FIGURE 12.6   The common operations on a list

Operation	Description
add	Adds an element to the list.

FIGURE 12.7   The operation particular to an ordered list

Analysis of the **BinarySearchTreeOrderedList** Implementation

Let's assume that the `BinarySearchTree` implementation used in the `BinarySearchTreeOrderedList` implementation is a balanced binary search tree. Let's also assume that the maximum depth of any node is $\log_2(n)$, where n is the number of elements stored in the tree. Figure 12.8 compares a singly linked implementation of an ordered list and our `BinarySearchTreeOrderedList` implementation.

Notice that the `add` and `remove` operations could cause the tree to become unbalanced. Rebalancing the tree could affect the analysis, depending on the algorithm used. Also notice that some operations are more efficient in the tree implementation—such as `removeLast`, `last`, and `contains`—and others, such as `removeFirst` and `first`, are less efficient.

Listing 12.2

```
//*********************************************************************
//  BinarySearchTreeOrderedList.java        Authors: Lewis/Chase
//
//  Represents an ordered list implemented using a binary search
//  tree.
//*********************************************************************

package jss2;
import jss2.exceptions.*;
import java.util.Iterator;

public class BinarySearchTreeOrderedList extends BinarySearchTree
implements ListADT, OrderedListADT
{
   //----------------------------------------------------------------
   //  Creates an empty list.
   //----------------------------------------------------------------
   public BinarySearchTreeOrderedList()
   {
      super();
   }

   //----------------------------------------------------------------
   //  Adds the specified element to the list.
   //----------------------------------------------------------------
```

Listing 12.2   **continued**

```java
public void add (Comparable element)
{
   addElement(element);
}

//----------------------------------------------------------------
//  Removes and returns the first element from this list.
//----------------------------------------------------------------
public Object removeFirst ()
{
   return removeMin();
}

//----------------------------------------------------------------
//  Removes and returns the last element from this list.
//----------------------------------------------------------------
public Object removeLast ()
{
   return removeMax();
}

//----------------------------------------------------------------
//  Removes and returns the specified element from this list.
//----------------------------------------------------------------
public Object remove (Object element)
{
   return removeElement((Comparable)element);
}

//----------------------------------------------------------------
//  Returns a reference to the first element on this list.
//----------------------------------------------------------------
public Object first ()
{
   return findMin();
}

//----------------------------------------------------------------
//  Returns a reference to the last element on this list.
//----------------------------------------------------------------
public Object last ()
{
   return findMax();
}
```

Listing 12.2   **continued**

```
//-------------------------------------------------------------
//  Returns an iterator for the list.
//-------------------------------------------------------------
public Iterator iterator()
{
    return iteratorInOrder();
}

}
```

Operation	LinkedList	BinarySearchTreeOrderedList
removeFirst	O(1)	O(log n)
removeLast	O(n)	O(log n)
remove	O(n)	O(log n)*
first	O(1)	O(log n)
last	O(n)	O(log n)
contains	O(n)	O(log n)
isEmpty	O(1)	O(1)
size	O(1)	O(1)
add	O(n)	O(log n)*
*Both the add and remove operations may cause the tree to become unbalanced.		

FIGURE 12.8 Analysis of linked list and binary search tree implementations of an ordered list

12.4 BALANCED BINARY SEARCH TREES

In the previous section we assumed that our tree was balanced. What would happen to our analysis if the tree were not balanced? Suppose we read the following list of integers from a file and added them to a binary search tree:

    3   5   9   12   18   20

Figure 12.9 shows the result. This binary tree, called a *degenerate tree,* looks like a linked list, but it is less efficient than a linked list.

Because this tree is not balanced, the addElement operation has worst-case time complexity of O(n) instead of O(log n) because of the possibility that the root is the smallest element in the tree and the element we are inserting might be the largest element. This makes the tree very inefficient because you have lost the benefit of having two possible paths to take in order to reach an element. With a tree that looks like the tree in Figure 12.9 it is no more efficient than a list.

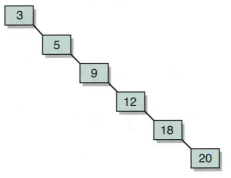

FIGURE 12.9   A degenerate binary tree

Our goal is to keep the maximum path length in the tree at or near $\log_2 n$. There are several algorithms available for balancing or maintaining balance in a tree. There are brute-force methods, which are not elegant or efficient, but get the job done. For example, we could write an inorder traversal of the tree to an array and then use a recursive method (much like binary search) to insert the middle element of the array as the root, then build balanced left and right subtrees. This would work, but there are more elegant solutions, such as AVL trees and red/black trees.

First we need to understand some additional terms. The methods described here will work for any subtree of a binary search tree as well. We simply replace the reference to root with whatever reference points to the root of the subtree.

Right Rotation

Figure 12.10 shows a binary search tree that is not balanced and the processing steps needed to rebalance it. The maximum path length in this tree is 3 and the minimum path length is 1. With only 6 elements in the tree, the maximum path length should be $\log_2 6$ or 2. To get this tree into balance, we need to do the following. Look at Figure 12.10 as you read.

A. Make the left child element (7) of the root (13) the new root element.

B. Make the old root element (13) the right child element of the new root (7).

C. Make the right child (10) of what was the left child (7) of the old root (13) the new left child of the old root.

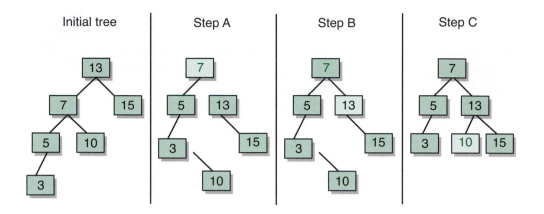

FIGURE 12.10 Unbalanced tree and balanced tree after a right rotation

This is called *right rotation*. The last image in Figure 12.10 shows the tree after a right rotation. The rotation can be done at any level of the tree. This single rotation to the right will solve the imbalance if the imbalance is caused by a long path in the left subtree of the left child of the root.

Left Rotation

Figure 12.11 shows another binary search tree that is not balanced. Again, the maximum path length is 3 and the minimum path length is 1. However, this time the longer path is in the right subtree of the right child of the root. Figure 12.11 traces the steps we take to get this tree into balance:

A. Make the right child element of the root the new root element.

B. Make the former root element the left child element of the new root.

C. Make the left child of what was the right child of the former root the new right child of the former root.

This is called *left rotation*. The left rotation can be done at any level of the tree. This single rotation to the left will solve the imbalance if the imbalance is caused by a longer path on the right.

Rightleft Rotation

Unfortunately, not all imbalances can be solved by single rotations. If the imbalance is caused by a long path in the left subtree of the right child of the root, we must first perform a right rotation of the left child of the right child of the root

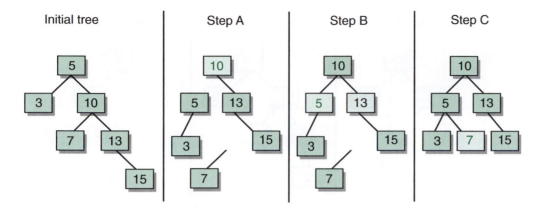

FIGURE 12.11   Unbalanced tree and balanced tree after a left rotation

around the right child of the root, and then perform a left rotation of the resulting right child of the root around the root. Figure 12.12 illustrates a rightleft rotation.

Leftright Rotation

If the imbalance is caused by a long path in the right subtree of the left child of the root, we must first perform a left rotation of the right child of the left child of the root around the left child of the root, and then perform a right rotation of the resulting left child of the root around the root. Figure 12.13 illustrates a left-right rotation.

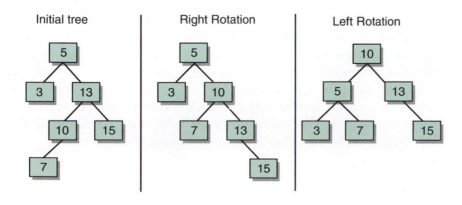

FIGURE 12.12   A rightleft rotation

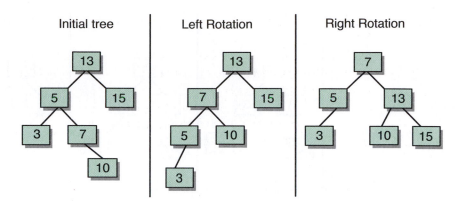

FIGURE 12.13   A leftright rotation

12.5   IMPLEMENTING BINARY SEARCH TREES: THE JAVA COLLECTIONS API

The Java Collections API provides two implementations of balanced binary search trees: `TreeSet` and `TreeMap`. In order to understand these implementations, we must first discuss the difference between a *set* and a *map* in the Java Collections API.

> **Key Concept**
>
> The Java Collections API provides two implementations of balanced binary search trees: `TreeSet` and `TreeMap`.

Tables 12.1 and 12.2 show the operations for a `TreeSet` and `TreeMap`. Note that these implementations use (and allow the use of) a `Comparator` instead of `Comparable`, as we did in our earlier implementations. The `Comparator` interface describes a method, `compare`, that, like `compareTo`, returns –1, 0, or 1, representing less than, equal, or greater than. However, unlike `compareTo`, `compare` takes two arguments and does not need to be implemented within the class be stored in the collection.

In this way, we only have to deal with the key, name, and reference, so we need a much smaller piece of our system's memory than if we were manipulating all of the data associated with an employee. Also, the same employee data could be referenced by multiple maps without our having to make multiple copies. So if for one application we want to represent employees in a set collection and for another application we needed to represent employees as an ordered list, we could load keys into a set and load matching keys into an ordered list yet only have one instance of the actual data. The only drawback is that we must be careful that changes to an object through one reference affect the object referenced by all of the other references, because there is only one instance of the object.

Operation	Description
`TreeSet()`	Constructs a new, empty set, sorted according to the elements' natural order.
`TreeSet(Collection c)`	Constructs a new set containing the elements in the collection, sorted according to the elements' natural order.
`TreeSet(Comparator c)`	Constructs a new, empty set, sorted according to the given comparator.
`TreeSet(SortedSet s)`	Constructs a new set containing the same elements as the given sorted set, sorted according to the same ordering.
`boolean add(Object o)`	Adds the specified element to this set if it is not already present.
`boolean addAll(Collection c)`	Adds all of the elements in the specified collection to this set.
`void clear()`	Removes all of the elements from this set.
`Object clone()`	Returns a shallow copy of this `TreeSet` instance.
`Comparator comparator()`	Returns the comparator used to order this sorted set, or null if this `TreeSet` uses its elements' natural ordering.
`boolean contains(Object o)`	Returns true if this set contains the target element.
`Object first()`	Returns the first (lowest) element currently in this sorted set.
`SortedSet headSet(Object toElement)`	Returns a view of the portion of this set whose elements are strictly less than `toElement`.
`boolean isEmpty()`	Returns true if this set contains no elements.
`Iterator iterator()`	Returns an iterator over the elements in this set.
`Object last()`	Returns the last (highest) element currently in this sorted set.
`boolean remove(Object o)`	Removes the given element from this set if it is present.
`int size()`	Returns the number of elements in this set (its cardinality).
`SortedSet subSet(Object fromElement, (Object toElement)`	Returns a view of the portion of this set whose elements range from `fromElement`, inclusive, to `toElement`, exclusive.
`SortedSet tailSet(Object fromElement)`	Returns a view of the part of this set whose elements are greater than or equal to `fromElement`.

TABLE 12.1   Operations on a `TreeSet`

Operation	Description
`TreeMap()`	Constructs a new, empty map, sorted according to the keys' natural order.
`TreeMap(Comparator c)`	Constructs a new, empty map, sorted according to the given comparator.
`TreeMap(Map m)`	Constructs a new map containing the same mappings as the given map, sorted according to the keys' natural order.
`TreeMap(SortedMap m)`	Constructs a new map containing the same mappings as the given `SortedMap`, sorted according to the same ordering.
`void clear()`	Removes all mappings from this `TreeMap`.
`Object clone()`	Returns a shallow copy of this `TreeMap` instance.
`Comparator comparator()`	Returns the comparator used to order this map, or null if this map uses its keys' natural order.
`boolean containsKey(Object key)`	Returns true if this map contains a mapping for the specified key.
`boolean containsValue(Object value)`	Returns true if this map maps one or more keys to the specified value.
`Set entrySet()`	Returns a set view of the mappings contained in this map.
`Object firstKey()`	Returns the first (lowest) key in the sorted map.
`Object get(Object key)`	Returns the value to which this map maps the specified key.
`SortedMap headMap(Object toKey)`	Returns a view of the portion of this map whose keys are strictly less than `toKey`.
`Set keySet()`	Returns a set view of the keys contained in this map.
`Object lastKey()`	Returns the last (highest) key in the sorted map.
`Object put(Object key, Object value)`	Associates the specified value with the specified key in this map.
`void putAll(Map map)`	Copies all of the mappings from the specified map to this map.
`Object remove(Object key)`	Removes the mapping for this key from this `TreeMap`, if it is there.
`int size()`	Returns the number of key-value mappings in this map.
`SortedMap subMap(Object fromKey, Object toKey)`	Returns a view of the portion of this map whose keys range from `fromKey`, inclusive, to `toKey`, exclusive.
`SortedMap tailMap(Object fromKey)`	Returns a view of the portion of this map whose keys are greater than or equal to `fromKey`.
`Collection values()`	Returns a collection view of the values contained in this map.

FIGURE 12.2   Operations on a `TreeMap`

Summary of Key Concepts

> A binary search tree is a binary tree in which the left child is less than the parent, which is less than or equal to the right child.

> The definition of a binary search tree is an extension of the definition of a binary tree.

> Each `BinaryTreeNode` object has a reference to the element stored at that node, as well as references to each of the node's children.

> When an element is removed from a binary search tree, another node must be promoted to replace the one being removed.

> The leftmost node in a binary search tree will contain the minimum element, and the rightmost node will contain the maximum element.

> One of the main uses of trees is to provide efficient implementations of other collections.

> If a binary search tree is not balanced, it may be less efficient than a linear structure.

> The Java Collections API provides two implementations of balanced binary search trees: `TreeSet` and `TreeMap`.

Self-Review Questions

12.1   What is the difference between a binary tree and a binary search tree?

12.2   Why can we use `addElement` and `removeElement` operations for a binary search tree but not for a binary tree?

12.3   If a binary search tree is balanced, what is the time complexity (order) of the `addElement` operation?

12.4   If a binary search tree is not balanced, what is the time complexity (order) of the `addElement` operation?

12.5   Why might a degenerate tree be less efficient than a linked list?

12.6   Our `removeElement` operation uses the inorder predecessor as the replacement for a node with two children. What would be another choice for replacement?

12.7   The `removeAllOccurences` operation uses the `contains` and `removeElement` operations. What is the time complexity (order) for this operation?

12.8   `RemoveFirst` and `first` were O(1) operations for our earlier ordered list. Why are they less efficient for our `BinarySearchTreeOrderedList`?

12.9   Why does the `BinarySearchTreeOrderedList` class have to define the `iterator` method? Why can't it just rely on the `iterator` method of its parent class, like it does for `size` and `isEmpty`?

12.10   What is the difference between a `TreeSet` and a `TreeMap`?

Exercises

12.1   Draw the binary search tree that results from adding the following integers (34 45 3 87 65 32 1 12 17). Use our simple implementation with no balancing mechanism.

12.2   Starting with the tree from Exercise 12.1, draw the tree that results from removing (45 12 1), again using our simple implementation with no balancing mechanism.

Programming Projects

12.1   The `BinarySearchTree` class is using the `find` and `contains` methods of the `BinaryTree` class. Implement these methods for the `BinarySearchTree` class so that they will be more efficient by using the ordering property of a binary search tree.

12.2   Implement the `removeMax`, `findMin`, and `findMax` operations for our binary search tree implementation.

12.3   Implement a balance tree method using the brute-force method described in Section 12.4.

12.4   Develop an array implementation of a binary search tree built on an array implementation of a binary tree. Use the simulated link strategy. Each element of the array will need to a reference to the data element stored there as well as the array positions of the left and right child. You will also need to maintain a list of available array positions where elements have been removed in order to reuse those positions.

12.5   Develop an array implementation of a binary search tree built on an array implementation of a binary tree. Use the computational strategy.

12.6   Create a binary search tree implementation of a set.

12.7   Create a binary search tree implementation of a bag.

Answers to Self-Review Questions

12.1   In a binary search tree the left child of any node is less than the node, and the node is less than or equal to its right child.

12.2   Because of the ordering property of a binary search tree, we can define what the state of the tree should be after an `add` or `remove`. We couldn't define that state for a binary tree.

12.3   If the tree is balanced, it will take at worst log n steps to find the insertion point for the new element. Because inserting the element is simply a matter of setting the value of one reference, the operation is Order(log n).

12.4   Without the balance assumption, the worst case would be a degenerate tree, which is basically a linked list. Therefore the `addElement` operation would be O(n).

12.5   A degenerate tree will waste space with unused references, and many of the algorithms will check for null references before following the degenerate path, which adds steps that the linked list implementation does not have.

12.6   The two best choices are the inorder predecessor and the inorder successor. There is little or no difference between them in this regard.

12.7   The `contains` operation uses the `find` operation, which will be rewritten in the binary search tree class to take advantage of the ordering property and will be O(log n). The `removeElement` operation is O(log n). The `while` loop will iterate some constant (k) number of times, depending on how many times the element occurs in the tree. The worst case would be that all the elements of the tree are the element to be removed, which would make the tree degenerate, so the complexity would be n*2*n or O(n^2). However, the expected case would be some small constant (0<=k<n) occurrences of the element in a balanced tree, for a complexity of k*2*log n or O(log n).

12.8   In our earlier linked implementation of an ordered list, we had a reference that kept track of the first element in the list, which made it easy to remove it or return it. With a binary search tree, we have to traverse to get to the leftmost element before we even know we have the first element in the ordered list.

12.9   The iterators for a binary tree are all followed by which traversal order to use. That is why the iterator method for the `BinarySearchTreeOrderedList` class calls the `iteratorInOrder` method of the `BinaryTree` class.

12.10 Both are implementations of a binary search tree. The difference is that in a `TreeSet`, all of the data are stored with an element, and with a `TreeMap`, a separate key is created and stored in the collection while the data are stored separately.

References

Adel'son-Vel'skii, G. M., and E. M. Landis. "An Algorithm for the Organization of Information." *Soviet Mathematics* 3(1962): 1259–1263.

Bayer, R. "Symmetric Binary B-trees: Data Structure and Maintenance Algorithms." *Acta Informatica* (1972): 290–306.

Collins, W. J. *Data Structures and the Java Collections Framework*. New York: McGraw-Hill, 2002.

Cormen, T., C. Leierson, and R. Rivest. *Introduction to Algorithms*. New York: McGraw-Hill, 1992.

Guibas, L., and R. Sedgewick. "A Diochromatic Framework for Balanced Trees." *Proceedings of the 19th Annual IEEE Symposium on Foundations of Computer Science* (1978): 8–21.

Basic Concept Review A

A.1 STRING LITERALS

In Java, a character string is an object defined by the class `String`. Because strings are such an important part of computer programming, Java provides something called a *string literal*, which appears inside double quotation marks. We explore the `String` class and its methods in more detail later in this appendix. For now, let's explore two other useful details about strings: concatenation and escape sequences.

String Concatenation

The program called `Facts` shown in Listing A.1 contains several `println` statements. The first one prints a sentence that will not fit on one line. A character string in double quotation marks cannot be split between two lines of code. One way to get around this problem is to use the *string concatenation* operator, the plus sign (+). String concatenation joins one string to another. The string concatenation operation in the first `println` statement results in one large string that is passed to the method and printed, as shown in the output.

We don't *have* to pass any information to the `println` method. Look at the second line of the `Facts` program: `System.out.printLn ();`. This call does not print characters that you can see, but it does move to the next line of output. In this case, the call to `println` that passes in no parameters (that is, empty parentheses) makes it "print" a blank line.

The rest of the calls to `println` in the `Facts` program show strings concatenated with numbers. The numbers in those lines (12, 672, 1515, 40) are not enclosed in double quotes, so they are not character strings. In these cases, the number is automatically converted to a string, and then the two strings are concatenated, that

Listing A.1

```
//**************************************************************
//  Facts.java          Author: Lewis/Loftus/Cocking
//
//  Demonstrates the use of the string concatenation operator and the
//  automatic conversion of an integer to a string.
//**************************************************************
```

Listing A.1   **continued**

```java
public class Facts
{
   //-----------------------------------------------------------------
   //   Prints various facts.
   //-----------------------------------------------------------------
   public static void main (String[] args)
   {
      // Strings can be concatenated into one long string
      System.out.println ("We present the following facts for your "
                            + "extracurricular edification:");

      System.out.println ();

      // A string can contain numeric digits
      System.out.println ("Letters in the Hawaiian alphabet: 12");

      // A numeric value can be concatenated to a string
      System.out.println ("Dialing code for Antarctica: " + 672);

      System.out.println ("Year in which Leonardo da Vinci invented "
                            + "the parachute: " + 1515);

      System.out.println ("Speed of ketchup: " + 40 + " km per year");
   }
}
```

Output

```
We present the following facts for your extracurricular edification:

Letters in the Hawaiian alphabet: 12
Dialing code for Antarctica: 672
Year in which Leonardo da Vinci invented the parachute: 1515
Speed of ketchup: 40 km per year
```

is, joind together. Because we are printing particular values, we simply could have included the numeric value as part of the string literal, such as

```
"Speed of ketchup: 40 km per year"
```

Digits are characters, of course, and can be included in strings. We have only separated them in the Facts program to show how to concatenate a string and a number.

Because the plus sign (+) is also used for arithmetic, what the + operator does depends on what kind of data it gets. If the + operator gets strings, it does string concatenation.

The `Addition` program shown in Listing A.2 shows the difference between string concatenation and addition. The `Addition` program uses the + operator four times. In the first call to `println`, both + operations perform string concatenation. This is because the operators execute left to right. The first operator concatenates the string with the first number (24), creating a larger string. Then that string is concatenated with the second number (45), creating an even larger string, which gets printed.

In the second call to `println`, parentheses are used to group the + operation with the two numbers. This forces that operation to happen first. Because both operands are numbers, the numbers are added together, producing the result 69. That number is then concatenated with the string, producing a larger string that gets printed.

We'll come back to this later, when we learn the rules about which operators get evaluated when.

Listing A.2

```java
//********************************************************************
//   Addition.java        Author: Lewis/Loftus/Cocking
//
//   Demonstrates the difference between the addition and string
//   concatenation operators.
//********************************************************************

public class Addition
{
    //-----------------------------------------------------------------
    //   Concatenates and adds two numbers and prints the results.
    //-----------------------------------------------------------------
    public static void main (String[] args)
    {
        System.out.println ("24 and 45 concatenated: " + 24 + 45);

        System.out.println ("24 and 45 added: " + (24 + 45));
    }
}
```

Output

```
24 and 45 concatenated: 2445
24 and 45 added: 69
```

Escape Sequences

Because the double quotation mark (") is used in the Java language to show the beginning and end of a string, we need a special way to print a quotation mark. If we simply put a quotation mark in a string ("""), the compiler gets confused because it thinks the second quotation character is the end of the string and doesn't know what to do with the third one. This results in a compile-time error.

So Java defines several *escape sequences* to represent special characters. An escape sequence begins with the backslash character (\), which tells us that the character or characters that follow should be interpreted in a special way. Figure A.1 lists the Java escape sequences.

The program in Listing A.3, called `Roses`, prints some text resembling a poem. It uses only one `println` statement, even though the poem is several lines long. Note the escape sequences used throughout the string. The \n escape sequence forces the output to a new line, and the \t escape sequence represents a tab character. The \" escape sequence makes sure that the quotation mark before and after *commitment issues* is included as part of the string, not the end of it, so it can be printed as part of the output.

A.2   VARIABLES AND ASSIGNMENT

Most of the information in a program is represented by variables. Let's look at how we declare and use them in a program.

Key Concept

A variable is a name for a memory location used to hold a value.

Variables

A *variable* is a name for a location in memory used to hold a data value. A variable declaration tells the compiler to set aside part of main

Escape Sequence	Meaning
\n	new line
\"	double quote
\\	backslash
\b	backspace
\t	tab
\r	carriage return
\'	single quote

FIGURE A.1   Java escape sequences

Listing A.3

```
//********************************************************************
//   Roses.java         Author: Lewis/Loftus/Cocking
//
//   Demonstrates the use of escape sequences.
//********************************************************************

public class Roses
{
    //-----------------------------------------------------------------
    //   Prints a poem (of sorts) on multiple lines.
    //-----------------------------------------------------------------
    public static void main (String[] args)
    {
        System.out.println ("Roses are red,\n\tViolets are blue,\n" +
            "Sugar is sweet,\n\tBut I have \"commitment issues\",\n\t" +
            "So I'd rather just be friends\n\tAt this point in our " +
            "relationship.");
    }
}
```

Output

```
Roses are red,
        Violets are blue,
Sugar is sweet,
        But I have "commitment issues",
        So I'd rather just be friends
        At this point in our relationship.
```

memory space large enough to hold the value. It also tells the compiler what to call the location.

Consider the program `PianoKeys`, shown in Listing A.4. The first line of the `main` method is the declaration of a variable named `keys` that holds a number, or an integer (`int`), value. The declaration also gives `keys` an initial value of 88. If you don't give an initial value for a variable, the value is undefined. Most Java compilers give errors or warnings if you try to use a variable before you've given it a value.

In the `PianoKeys` program, the string passed to the `println` method is formed from three pieces. The first and third are string literals, and the second is the variable `keys`. When the program gets to the variable it uses the currently stored value. Because the value of `keys` is an integer, it is automatically changed into a string so it can be concatenated with the first string. Then the concatenated string is passed to `println` and printed.

Listing A.4

```
//*****************************************************************
//  PianoKeys.java         Author: Lewis/Loftus/Cocking
//
//  Demonstrates the declaration, initialization, and use of an
//  integer variable.
//*****************************************************************

public class PianoKeys
{
    //------------------------------------------------------------
    //  Prints the number of keys on a piano.
    //------------------------------------------------------------
    public static void main (String[] args)
    {
        int keys = 88;

        System.out.println ("A piano has " + keys + " keys.");
    }
}
```

Output

```
A piano has 88 keys.
```

Note that a variable declaration can have many variables of the same type on one line. Each variable on the line can be declared with or without an initializing value. For example, the following declaration declares two variables, weight and total, and gives total a beginning value of 0.

```
int weight, total = 0:
```

The Assignment Statement

Let's look at a program that changes the value of a variable. Listing A.5 shows a program called Geometry. This program first declares an integer variable called sides and initializes it to 7. It then prints out the current value of sides.

The next line in main changes the value stored in the variable sides:

```
sides = 10;
```

This is called an *assignment statement* because it gives or *assigns* a value to a variable. When the statement is executed, the expression on the right-hand side of the assignment operator (=) is evaluated, and the result is stored in the memory

Listing A.5

```java
//********************************************************************
//   Geometry.java         Author: Lewis/Loftus/Cocking
//
//   Demonstrates the use of an assignment statement to change the
//   value stored in a variable.
//********************************************************************

public class Geometry
{
    //----------------------------------------------------------------
    //  Prints the number of sides of several geometric shapes.
    //----------------------------------------------------------------
    public static void main (String[] args)
    {
        int sides = 7;   // declaration with initialization
        System.out.println ("A heptagon has " + sides + " sides.");

        sides = 10;   // assignment statement
        System.out.println ("A decagon has " + sides + " sides.");

        sides = 12;
        System.out.println ("A dodecagon has " + sides + " sides.");
    }
}
```

Output

```
A heptagon has 7 sides.
A decagon has 10 sides.
A dodecagon has 12 sides.
```

location indicated by the variable on the left-hand side. In this example, the expression is simply a number, 10.

A variable can store only one value of its declared type. A new value overwrites the old one. In this case, when the value 10 is assigned to sides, the original value 7 is overwritten and lost forever. However, when a reference is made to a variable, such as when it is printed, the value of the variable is not changed.

The Java language is *strongly typed*, meaning that we can't assign the wrong type of value to a variable. Assigning the wrong type of value (such as assigning the letter 'J' to a double (number with decimal value) variable will cause an error when you try to compile the program. So, the expression on the right-hand side of an assignment statement must have the same type as the variable on the left-hand side.

> **Key Concept**
>
> A variable can store only one value of its declared type.

> **Key Concept**
>
> Java is a strongly typed language. Each variable has a declared type and we cannot assign a value of one type to a variable of another type.

Constants

Sometimes we use data that never changes—we say it is *constant* throughout a program. For instance, we might write a program for a theater that can hold no more than 427 people. This number never changes, so it is a *constant*. It is often helpful to give a constant value a name, such as MAX_OCCUPANCY, instead of using a literal value, such as 427, throughout the code. Literal values such as 427 are sometimes referred to as "magic" numbers because their meaning in a program is a mystery to anyone trying to read the code.

Constants are identifiers and are like variables except that they always have the same value. In Java, if you write the reserved word final before a declaration, the identifier is made a constant. Uppercase letters are used for constant names to help us tell them apart from regular variables, and words are separated by the underscore character. For example, the constant describing the maximum occupancy of a theater could be

```
final int MAX_OCCUPANCY = 427;
```

> **Key Concept**
>
> Constants are like variables, but they have the same value throughout the program.

You'll get an error message if you try to change the value of a constant. This is another good reason to use constants. Constants keep us from making simple coding mistakes because the only place you can change their value is in the initial assignment.

There is a third good reason to use constants. If you've used a constant throughout a program and suddenly need to change its value (the theater added a balcony section), then you only have to change the value in one place. For example, if the balcony changes the theater capacity from 427 to 535, then you have to change only one declaration, and all uses of MAX_OCCUPANCY will automatically change. If you had used the literal 427 throughout the code, you would have had to find and change each use. If you were to miss one or two, you'd be sure to have problems.

A.3   PRIMITIVE DATA TYPES

There are eight primitive data types in Java: four kinds of integers, two kinds of floating point numbers, a character data type, and a boolean data type. Everything else is represented using objects. Of the eight primitive types, three are a part of the AP subset. We look at these three (int, double, and boolean) plus a fourth (char), in more detail below.

Integers and Floating Points

Java has two kinds of numeric values: integers, which have no fractional part, and floating points, which do. The primitive type int is an integer data type and double is a floating-point data type. The numeric types are *signed*, meaning they have either a negative (–) sign or a positive (+) sign.

The int data type can be used to represent numbers between −2,147,483,648 and 2,147,483,647. The double data type can represent numbers from approximately −1.7E+308 to 1.7E+308 with 15 significant digits.

> **Key Concept**
>
> Java has two kinds of numeric values: integers and floating point. The primitive type int is an integer data type and the type double is a floating-point data type.

A *literal* is a specific data value used in a program. The numbers used in programs such as Facts (Listing A.1), Addition (Listing A.2), and PianoKeys (Listing A.4) are all *integer literals*. Java assumes all integer literals are of type int. Likewise, Java assumes that all *floating-point literals* are of type double. The following are examples of numeric variable declarations in Java:

```
int answer = 42;
int number1, number2;
double delta = 453.523311903;
```

The numbers used, 42 and 453.523311903, are literals.

Booleans

A boolean value, defined in Java using the reserved word boolean, has only two values: true and false. A boolean variable tells whether a condition is true or false, but it can also represent any situation that has two states, such as a lightbulb being on or off.

A boolean value cannot be changed to any other data type, and no other data type be changed to a boolean value. The words true and false are called *boolean literals* and cannot be used for anything else.

Here are some examples of boolean variable declarations in Java:

```
boolean flag = true;
boolean tooHigh, tooSmall, tooRough;
boolean done = false;
```

Characters

Characters are another type of data. However, they are not part of the AP subset. Individual characters such as letters can be treated as separate data items (d, o, g), or they can be combined to form character strings (dog).

A *character literal* is expressed in a Java program with single quotes, such as 'b' or 'J' or ';'. Remember that *string literals* come in double quotation marks, and that the String type is not a primitive data type in Java, it is a class name. We discuss the String class in detail later in this appendix.

Note the difference between a digit as a character (or part of a string) and a digit as a number (or part of a larger number). The number 602 is a numeric value that we can use in math: 602 + 50 = 652. But in the string "602 Greenbriar Court" the 6, 0, and 2 are characters, just like the letters in the string: We can't add 602 Greenbriar Court and 50 Washington Street!

The characters are defined by a *character set*, which is just a list of characters in a particular order. Each programming language has its own character set, and many use the same character set, such as the *ASCII character set*. ASCII stands for the American Standard Code for Information Interchange. The basic ASCII set supports 128 different characters, including:

> uppercase letters, such as 'A', 'B', and 'C'

> lowercase letters, such as 'a', 'b', and 'c'

> punctuation, such as the period ('.'), semicolon (';'), and comma (',')

> the digits '0' through '9'

> the space character, ' '

> special symbols, such as the ampersand ('&'), vertical bar ('|'), and back-slash ('\')

> control characters, such as the carriage return, null, and end-of-text marks

The *control characters* are sometimes called nonprinting or invisible characters. They can be stored and used in the same way as any other character.

As computers became more popular all over the world, users needed character sets that included other language alphabets. ASCII was changed so the number of characters in the set doubled to 256. The new ASCII has many characters not used in English.

But even with 256 characters, the ASCII character set can't represent all the world's alphabets, especially the Asian alphabets, which have many thousands of characters, called *ideograms*. So the developers of the Java programming language chose the *Unicode character set,* which supports 65,536 characters. The characters and symbols from many languages are included in the Unicode definition. ASCII is a subset of the Unicode character set. Appendix B discusses the Unicode character set in more detail.

In Java, the data type `char` represents a single character. The following are some examples of character variable declarations in Java:

```
char topGrade = 'A';
char symbol1, symbol2, symbol3;
char terminator = ';', separator = ' ';
```

A.4   INVOKING CLASS METHODS

Some methods can be invoked through their class name, without having to instantiate an object of the class first. These are called *class methods* or *static methods.* Let's look at some examples.

The Math Class

The Math class lets us do many basic math functions. The Math class is part of the Java standard class library and is defined in the `java.lang` package. Figure A.2 lists several of its methods.

The reserved word `static` tells us that the method can be invoked through the name of the class. For example, a call to `Math.abs(total)` will return the absolute (`abs`) value of the number stored in `total`. A call to `Math.pow(7, 4)` will

AP→ ```
static int abs (int num)
```
AP→ ```
static double abs (double num)
```
Returns the absolute value of num.

```
static double acos (double num)

static double asin (double num)

static double atan (double num)
```
Returns the arc cosine, arc sine, or arc tangent of num.

```
static double cos (double angle)

static double sin (double angle)

static double tan (double angle)
```
Returns the angle cosine, sine, or tangent of angle, which is measured in radians.

```
static double ceil (double num)
```
Returns the ceiling of num, which is the smallest whole number greater than or equal to num.

```
static double exp (double power)
```
Returns the value e raised to the specified power.

```
static double floor (double num)
```
Returns the floor of num, which is the largest whole number less than or equal to num.

AP→ ```
static double pow (double num, double power)
```
Returns the value num raised to the specified power.

```
static double random ()
```
Returns a random number between 0.0 (inclusive) and 1.0 (exclusive).

AP→ ```
static double sqrt (double num)
```
Returns the square root of num, which must be positive.

FIGURE A.2   Some methods of the Math class

return 7 raised to the fourth power (`pow`). You can pass integer values to a method that accepts a `double` parameter. This is a form of assignment conversion, which we discussed earlier.

A.5   CONTROL FLOW

The order in which statements are executed is called the *flow of control*. Most of the time, a running program starts at the first programming statement and moves down one statement at a time until it is done. A Java application begins with the first line of the `main` method and goes step by step until it gets to the end of the `main` method.

Calling a method changes the flow of control. When a method is called, control jumps to the code for that method. When the method finishes, control returns to the place where the method was called and processing continues from there.

> **Key Concept**
>
> Conditionals and loops let us control the flow of execution through a method.

Within a method, we can change the flow of control through the code by using certain types of programming statements. Statements that control the flow through a method fall into two categories: conditionals and loops.

A *conditional statement* is sometimes called a *selection statement* because it lets us choose which statement will be executed next. The conditional statements in Java that we will study are the `if` statement and the `if-else` statement. These statements let us decide which statement to execute next. Each decision is based on a *boolean expression* (also called a *condition*), which says whether something is true or false. The result of the expression determines which statement is executed next.

For example, the cost of life insurance might depend on whether the insured person is a smoker. If the person smokes, we calculate the cost using one formula; if not, we calculate it using another. The conditional statement evaluates a boolean condition (whether the person smokes or not) and then to execute the calculation for that condition.

A *loop*, or *repetition statement*, lets us execute the same statement over and over again. Like a conditional, a loop is based on a boolean expression.

For example, suppose we wanted to calculate the grade point average of every student in a class. The calculation is the same for each student; it is just the data that is different. We would set up a loop that repeats the calculation for each student until there are no more students to process.

Java has three types of loop statements:

> the `while` statement

> the `do` statement

> the `for` statement

We will study the while and for statements in this appendix. Information on the do statement (which is not in the AP subset) can be found on the Web site.

The *if statement* is a conditional statement found in many programming languages, including Java. The following is an example of an if statement:

```
if (total > amount)
    total = total + (amount + 1);
```

An if statement starts with the reserved word if. This is followed by a boolean expression, or condition, which is followed by a statement. The condition is enclosed in parentheses and must be either true or false. In our example, the condition is (total > amount). If the condition is true, the statement is executed and we move on to the next statement. If the condition is false, the statement is skipped and we move immediately with the next statement. In this example, if the value in total is greater than the value in amount, the assignment statement total = total + (amount + 1) is executed; otherwise, the assignment statement is skipped. Figure A.3 shows how this works.

> **Key Concept**
>
> An if statement lets a program choose whether to execute a particular statement.

Note that the assignment statement in this example is indented. This means that the assignment statement is part of the if statement. Indentation makes a program easier to read.

The example in Listing A.6 reads the age of the user and then decides which sentence to print.

> **Key Concept**
>
> Indentation makes a program easier to read. It shows the relationship between one statement and another.

The Age program in Listing A.6 echoes (reads back) the age value the user entered. If the age is less than the value of the constant MINOR, the statement about youth is printed. If the age is equal to or greater than the value of MINOR, the println statement is skipped. In either case, the sentence about age being a state of mind is printed.

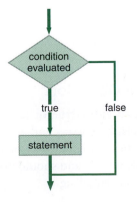

FIGURE A.3 The logic of an if statement

Listing A.6

```
//***********************************************************************
//   Age.java          Author: Lewis/Loftus/Cocking
//
//   Demonstrates the use of an if statement.
//***********************************************************************

import cs1.Keyboard;

public class Age
{
   //-----------------------------------------------------------------
   //   Reads the user's age and prints comments accordingly.
   //-----------------------------------------------------------------
   public static void main (String[] args)
   {
      final int MINOR = 21;

      System.out.print ("Enter your age: ");
      int age = Keyboard.readInt();

      System.out.println ("You entered: " + age);

      if (age < MINOR)
         System.out.println ("Youth is a wonderful thing. Enjoy.");

      System.out.println ("Age is a state of mind.");
   }
}
```

Output

```
Enter your age: 35
You entered: 35
Age is a state of mind.
```

Equality and Relational Operators

Boolean expressions evaluate to either true or false. Java has several operators that produce a true or false result. The == and != operators are called *equality operators*; they test if two values are equal (==) or not equal (!=). The equality operator is two equal signs side by side and should not be mistaken for the assignment operator that uses only one equal sign.

The following `if` statement prints a sentence only if the variables `total` and `sum` contain the same value:

```
if (total == sum)
    System.out.println ("total equals sum");
```

Likewise, the following `if` statement prints a sentence only if the variables `total` and `sum` do *not* contain the same value:

```
if (total != sum)
    System.out.println ("total does NOT equal sum");
```

In the `Age` program in Listing A.6 we used the < operator to decide whether one value was less than another. The "less than" operator is a *relational opera-tor*. Relational operators let us decide the relationships between values. Figure A.4 lists the Java equality and relational operators.

The equality and relational operators have a lower precedence than the arith-metic operators. This means that arithmetic operations are done first, before equality and relational operations. We can use parentheses to change the order of evaluation.

Let's look at a few more examples of basic `if` statements.

```
if (size >= MAX)
    size = 0;
```

This `if` statement sets the variable `size` to zero if its current value is greater than or equal to the value in the constant `MAX`.

The condition of the following `if` statement first adds three values together, then compares the result to the value stored in `numBooks`.

```
if (numBooks < stackCount + inventoryCount + duplicateCount)
    reorder = true;
```

If `numBooks` is less than the other three values combined, the boolean variable `reorder` is set to `true`. The addition operations are done before the less than operator because the arithmetic operators have a higher precedence than the rela-tional operators.

Operator	Meaning
==	equal to
!=	not equal to
<	less than
<=	less than or equal to
>	greater than
>=	greater than or equal to

FIGURE A.4 Java equality and relational operators

The following `if` statement compares the value returned by `nextInt` to the result of dividing the constant `HIGH` by 5. The odds of this code picking a winner are 1 in 5.

```
if (generator.nextInt(HIGH) < HIGH / 5)
    System.out.println ("You are a randomly selected winner!");
```

The `if-else` Statement

Sometimes we want to do one thing if a condition is true and another thing if that condition is false. We can add an *else clause* to an `if` statement, making it an *if-else statement*, to handle this kind of situation. The following is an example of an `if-else` statement:

```
if (height <= MAX)
    adjustment = 0;
else
    adjustment = MAX - height;
```

> **Key Concept**
>
> An if-else statement tells a program to do one thing if a condition is true and another thing if the condition is false.

If the condition is true, the first assignment statement (`adjustment = 0`) is executed; if the condition is false, the second statement (`adjustment = MAX — height`) is executed. Only one or the other will be executed because a boolean will give us either true or false. Note that we indented to show that the statements are part of the `if` statement.

The `Wages` program shown in Listing A.7 uses an `if-else` statement to compute the payment for an employee.

In the `Wages` program, if an employee works over 40 hours in a week, the payment amount includes the overtime hours. An `if-else` statement is used to decide whether the number of hours entered by the user is greater than 40. If it is, the extra hours are paid at one and a half times the normal rate. If there are no overtime hours, the total payment is based on the standard rate.

Let's look at another example of an `if-else` statement:

```
if (roster.getSize() == FULL)
    roster.expand();
else
    roster.addName (name);
```

This example uses an object called `roster`. Even without knowing what `roster` is, we can see that it has at least three methods: `getSize`, `expand`, and `addName`. The condition of the `if` statement calls `getSize` and compares the result to the constant `FULL`. If the condition is true, the `expand` method is invoked (probably to expand the size of the roster). If the roster is not yet full, the variable `name` is passed as a parameter to the `addName` method.

If Statement

An if statement tests the boolean Expression. If it is true, the program executes the first Statement. The optional else clause shows the Statement that should be executed if the Expression is false.

Examples:

```
if (total < 7)
    System.out.println ("Total is less than 7.");

if (firstCh != 'a')
    count++;
else
    count = count / 2;
```

Listing A.7

```java
//************************************************************
//   Wages.java         Author: Lewis/Loftus/Cocking
//
//   Demonstrates the use of an if-else statement.
//************************************************************

import java.text.NumberFormat;
import cs1.Keyboard;

public class Wages
{
    //-----------------------------------------------------------
    //   Reads the number of hours worked and calculates wages.
    //-----------------------------------------------------------
    public static void main (String[] args)
    {
        final double RATE = 8.25;   // regular pay rate
        final int STANDARD = 40;    // standard hours in a work week

        double pay = 0.0;

        System.out.print ("Enter the number of hours worked: ");
        int hours = Keyboard.readInt();
```

Listing A.7   continued

```java
        System.out.println ();

        // Pay overtime at "time and a half"
        if (hours > STANDARD)
            pay = STANDARD * RATE + (hours-STANDARD) * (RATE * 1.5);
        else
            pay = hours * RATE;

        NumberFormat fmt = NumberFormat.getCurrencyInstance();
        System.out.println ("Gross earnings: " + fmt.format(pay));
    }
}
```

Output

```
Enter the number of hours worked: 46

Gross earnings: $404.25
```

Using Block Statements

We may want to do more than one thing after evaluating a boolean condition. In Java, we can replace any statement with a *block statement*. A block statement is a collection of statements enclosed in braces ({}). We've already seen these braces used with the main method and a class definition. The program called Guessing, shown in Listing A.8, uses an if-else statement with the statement of the else clause in a block statement.

If the user's guess equals the answer, the sentences "You got it! Good guessing" are printed. If the guess doesn't match, two statements are printed, one that says that the guess is wrong and one that prints the correct answer.

If we didn't use the block braces, the sentence stating that the guess is incorrect would be printed if the guess was wrong, but the sentence revealing the correct answer would be printed in all cases. That is, only the first statement would be part of the else clause.

Remember that indentation is only for people reading the code. Not indenting can cause the programmer to misunderstand how the code will execute. For example, the following code is misleading:

```java
if (depth > 36.238)
    delta = 100;
else
    System.out.println ("WARNING: Delta is being reset to ZERO");
    delta = 0;   // not part of the else clause!
```

Listing A.8

```java
//********************************************************************
//  Guessing.java        Author: Lewis/Loftus/Cocking
//
//  Demonstrates the use of a block statement in an if-else.
//********************************************************************

import cs1.Keyboard;
import java.util.Random;

public class Guessing
{
    //-----------------------------------------------------------------
    //  Plays a simple guessing game with the user.
    //-----------------------------------------------------------------
    public static void main (String[] args)
    {
        final int MAX = 10;
        int answer, guess;

        Random generator = new Random();
        answer = generator.nextInt(MAX) + 1;

        System.out.print ("I'm thinking of a number between 1 and "
                          + MAX + ". Guess what it is: ");
        guess = Keyboard.readInt();

        if (guess == answer)
            System.out.println ("You got it! Good guessing!");
        else
        {
            System.out.println ("That is not correct, sorry.");
            System.out.println ("The number was " + answer);
        }
    }
}
```

Output

```
I'm thinking of a number between 1 and 10. Guess what it is: 7
That is not correct, sorry.
The number was 4
```

The indentation (not to mention the logic of the code) seems to mean that the variable delta is reset only when depth is less than 36.238. However, because a block wasn't used, the assignment statement that resets delta to zero is not ruled by the `if-else` statement at all. It is executed in either case, which is clearly not what the programmer meant it to do.

A block statement can be used anywhere a single statement is called for in Java syntax. For example, the `if` part of an `if-else` statement could be a block, or the `else` part could be a block (as we saw in the `Guessing` program), or both parts could be block statements. For example:

```java
if (boxes != warehouse.getCount())
{
    System.out.println ("Inventory and warehouse do NOT match.");
    System.out.println ("Beginning inventory process again!");
    boxes = 0;
}
else
{
    System.out.println ("Inventory and warehouse MATCH.");
    warehouse.ship();
}
```

In this `if-else` statement, the value of `boxes` is compared to a value that we got by calling the `getCount` method of the `warehouse` object (whatever that is). If they do not match exactly, the two statements are printed and an assignment statement is executed. If they do match, the message "Inventory and warehouse MATCH." is printed and the `ship` method of `warehouse` is invoked.

Nested `if` Statements

It is sometimes useful to make another decision based on the results of an earlier decision. For example, if you have decided to eat a salad for lunch instead of a sandwich, you must then decide on a type of salad dressing. In a program, the statement executed as the result of an `if` statement could be another `if` statement. This is called a *nested if*. The program in Listing A.9, called `MinOfThree`, uses nested `if` statements to find the smallest of three values entered by the user.

Carefully trace the logic of the `MinOfThree` program in Listing A.9, using different sets of numbers, with the smallest number in a different position each time, to see how the program chooses the lowest value.

An important situation arises with nested `if` statements when one or more is an `if-else` statement. It may seem that an `else` clause after a nested `if` could apply to either `if` statement. For example:

```java
if (code == 'R')
    if (height <= 20)
        System.out.println ("Situation Normal");
    else
        System.out.println ("Bravo!");
```

Listing A.9

```java
//********************************************************************
//  MinOfThree.java        Author: Lewis/Loftus/Cocking
//
//  Demonstrates the use of nested if statements.
//********************************************************************

import cs1.Keyboard;

public class MinOfThree
{
    //----------------------------------------------------------------
    //  Reads three integers from the user and decides which is the
    //  smallest value.
    //----------------------------------------------------------------
    public static void main (String[] args)
    {
        int num1, num2, num3, min = 0;

        System.out.println ("Enter three integers: ");
        num1 = Keyboard.readInt();
        num2 = Keyboard.readInt();
        num3 = Keyboard.readInt();

        if (num1 < num2)
            if (num1 < num3)
                min = num1;
            else
                min = num3;
        else
            if (num2 < num3)
                min = num2;
            else
                min = num3;

        System.out.println ("Minimum value: " + min);
    }
}
```

Output

```
Enter three integers:
45    22    69
Minimum value: 22
```

Is the `else` clause matched to the inner `if` statement or the outer `if` statement? The indentation seems to mean that it is part of the inner `if` statement, and that is correct. An `else` clause is always matched to the closest unmatched `if` that came before it. However, if we're not careful, we can cause confusion by misaligning indentation. This is one reason why indentation is so important.

Braces can be used to show which `if` statement belongs with which `else` clause. For example, if our example had been written so that the string `"Bravo!"` would be printed if `code` did not equal `'R'`, we could force that relationship (and properly indent) this way:

```java
if (code == 'R')
{
    if (height <= 20)
        System.out.println ("Situation Normal");
}
else
    System.out.println ("Bravo!");
```

By using the block statement in the first `if` statement, we make it clear that the `else` clause belongs to it.

A.7 THE `while` STATEMENT

Remember that a repetition statement (or loop) lets us execute a statement as many times as we need to. A `while` *statement* is a loop that evaluates a boolean condition—just like an `if` statement does—and executes a statement (called the body of the loop) if the condition is true. However, unlike the `if` statement, after the body is executed, the condition is evaluated again. If it is still true, the body is executed again. This repeats until the condition becomes false; then processing continues with the statement after the body of the `while` loop. Figure A.5 shows this processing.

The `Counter` program shown in Listing A.10 prints the values from 1 to 5. Each turn through the loop prints one value, then increases the counter by one. A constant called `LIMIT` holds the maximum value that `count` is allowed to reach. The condition of the `while` loop, (`count <= LIMIT`), means that the loop will keep going as long as `count` is less than or equal to `LIMIT`. When `count` reaches `LIMIT`, the condition is false and the loop quits.

The body of the `while` loop is a block containing two statements. Because the value of `count` is increased by one each time, we can be sure that `count` will eventually reach the value of `LIMIT`.

Let's look at another program that uses a `while` loop. The `Average` program, shown in Listing A.11, reads integer values from the user, adds them up, and computes their average.

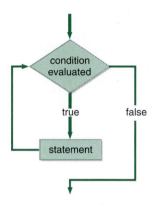

FIGURE A.5   The logic of a while loop

Listing A.10

```java
//********************************************************************
//   Counter.java          Author: Lewis/Loftus/Cocking
//
//   Demonstrates the use of a while loop.
//********************************************************************

public class Counter
{
    //-----------------------------------------------------------------
    //   Prints integer values from 1 to a specific limit.
    //-----------------------------------------------------------------
    public static void main (String[] args)
    {
        final int LIMIT = 5;
        int count = 1;

        while (count <= LIMIT)
        {
            System.out.println (count);
            count = count + 1;
        }

        System.out.println ("Done");
    }
}
```

Output

```
1
2
3
4
5
Done
```

Listing A.11

```java
//***********************************************************************
//   Average.java         Author: Lewis/Loftus/Cocking
//
//   Demonstrates the use of a while loop, a sentinel value, and a
//   running sum.
//***********************************************************************

import java.text.DecimalFormat;
import cs1.Keyboard;

public class Average
{
   //----------------------------------------------------------------
   //   Computes the average of the values entered by the user.
   //   The running sum is printed as the numbers are entered.
   //----------------------------------------------------------------
   public static void main (String[] args)
   {
      int sum = 0, value, count = 0;
      double average;

      System.out.print ("Enter an integer (0 to quit): ");
      value = Keyboard.readInt();

      while (value != 0)  // sentinel value of 0 to terminate loop
      {
         count++;

         sum += value;
         System.out.println ("The sum so far is " + sum);

         System.out.print ("Enter an integer (0 to quit): ");
         value = Keyboard.readInt();
      }

      System.out.println ();
      System.out.println ("Number of values entered: " + count);

      average = (double)sum / count;

      DecimalFormat fmt = new DecimalFormat ("0.###");
      System.out.println ("The average is " + fmt.format(average));
   }
}
```

Listing A.11 **continued**

Output

```
Enter an integer (0 to quit): 25
The sum so far is 25
Enter an integer (0 to quit): 164
The sum so far is 189
Enter an integer (0 to quit): -14
The sum so far is 175
Enter an integer (0 to quit): 84
The sum so far is 259
Enter an integer (0 to quit): 12
The sum so far is 271
Enter an integer (0 to quit): -35
The sum so far is 236
Enter an integer (0 to quit): 0
Number of values entered: 6
The average is 39.333
```

While Statement

The `while` loop executes the Statement over and over as long as the boolean Expression is true. The Expression is evaluated first; so the Statement might not be executed at all. The Expression is evaluated again after each execution of Statement until the Expression becomes false.

Example:

```
while (total > max)
{
    total = total / 2;
    System.out.println ("Current total: " + total);
}
```

We don't know how many values the user may enter, so we need a way to know that the user is done. In this program, we pick zero to be a *sentinel value*, which is a value that shows the end of the input the way a sentinel stands guard at the gate of a fort. The `while` loop keeps processing input values until the user enters zero. This means that the user cannot enter zero until he or she is done. A sentinel value can never be a valid input number.

In the `Average` program in Listing A.11, a variable called `sum` is used to keep a *running sum*. A running sum is the total of the values entered so far. The variable `sum` starts at zero, and each value read is added to and stored in `sum`.

We also have to count how many values are entered so that after the loop finishes we can divide by that number to get the average. Now, we don't count the sentinel value. But what if the user enters the sentinel value before entering any other values? The value of `count` in this case will still be zero and trying to compute the average will give us a runtime error.

Let's look at another program that uses a `while` loop. The `WinPercentage` program shown in Listing A.12 figures the winning percentage of a sports team based on the number of games won.

We use a `while` loop in the `WinPercentage` program to *validate the input,* meaning we guarantee that the user enters a value that we consider to be valid. In this example, the number of games won must be greater than or equal to zero and less than or equal to the total number of games played. The `while` loop keeps asking the user for input until the user enters a valid number.

Validating input data, avoiding errors such as dividing by zero, and other actions that guarantee proper processing are important design steps. We generally want our programs to be *robust,* which means that they handle errors—even user errors—well.

Infinite Loops

The programmer must make sure that the condition of a loop will eventually become false. If it doesn't, the loop will keep going forever, or at least until we shut the program down. This common mistake is called an *infinite loop.*

> **Key Concept**
>
> We must carefully avoid infinite loops. The loop condition must eventually become false.

The program shown in Listing A.13 has an infinite loop. If you execute this program, you will have to interrupt it to make it stop. On most systems, pressing the Control-C keyboard combination (hold down the Control key and press C) stops a running program.

In the `Forever` program in Listing A.13, the starting value of `count` is 1. Then we subtract from that value in the loop body. The `while` loop will continue as long as `count` is less than or equal to 25. Because `count` gets smaller with each iteration, the condition will always be true.

Let's look at some other examples of infinite loops:

```
int count = 1;
while (count != 50)
    count += 2;
```

In this code, the variable `count` begins at 1 and increases by 2 each time. This loop will never end because `count` will never equal 50. It begins at 1 and then changes to 3, then 5, and so on. Eventually it reaches 49, then changes to 51, then 53, and continues forever.

Listing A.12

```java
//***********************************************************************
//  WinPercentage.java       Author: Lewis/Loftus/Cocking
//
//  Demonstrates the use of a while loop for input validation.
//***********************************************************************

import java.text.NumberFormat;
import cs1.Keyboard;

public class WinPercentage
{
   //----------------------------------------------------------------
   //  Computes the percentage of games won by a team.
   //----------------------------------------------------------------
   public static void main (String[] args)
   {
      final int NUM_GAMES = 12;
      int won;
      double ratio;

      System.out.print ("Enter the number of games won (0 to "
                        + NUM_GAMES + "): ");
      won = Keyboard.readInt();

      while (won < 0 || won > NUM_GAMES)
      {
         System.out.print ("Invalid input. Please reenter: ");
         won = Keyboard.readInt();
      }

      ratio = (double)won / NUM_GAMES;

      NumberFormat fmt = NumberFormat.getPercentInstance();

      System.out.println ();
      System.out.println ("Winning percentage: " + fmt.format(ratio));
   }
}
```

Output

```
Enter the number of games won (0 to 12): -5
Invalid input. Please reenter: 13
Invalid input. Please reenter: 7

Winning percentage: 58%
```

Listing A.13

```
//************************************************************************
//   Forever.java          Author:  Lewis/Loftus/Cocking
//
//   Demonstrates an INFINITE LOOP.   WARNING!!
//************************************************************************

public class Forever
{
    //-------------------------------------------------------------
    //   Prints ever-decreasing integers in an INFINITE LOOP!
    //-------------------------------------------------------------
    public static void main (String[] args)
    {
        int count = 1;

        while (count <= 25)
        {
            System.out.println (count);
            count = count - 1;
        }

        System.out.println ("Done");   // this statement is never reached
    }
}
```

Output

```
1
0
-1
-2
-3
-4
-5
-6
-7
-8
-9
and so on until interrupted
```

Now consider the following situation:

```
double num = 1.0;
while (num != 0.0)
    num = num — 0.1;
```

Once again, the value of the loop control variable seems to be moving in the right direction. And, in fact, it seems like num will eventually take on the value 0.0. However, this loop is infinite (at least on most systems) because num will never have a value *exactly* equal to 0.0.

Nested Loops

The body of a loop can contain another loop. This is called a *nested loop*. Keep in mind that each time the outer loop executes once, the inner loop executes completely. Consider the following code fragment. How many times does the string "Here again" get printed?

```java
int count1, count2;
count1 = 1;
while (count1 <= 10)
{
    count2 = 1;
    while (count2 <= 50)
    {
        System.out.println ("Here again");
        count2++;
    }
    count1++;
}
```

The println statement is inside the inner loop. The outer loop executes 10 times, as count1 iterates between 1 and 10. The inner loop executes 50 times, as count2 iterates between 1 and 50. Each time the outer loop executes, the inner loop executes completely. So the println statement is executed 500 times.

As with any loop, we must study the loops and variables. Let's consider some small changes to this code. What if the condition of the outer loop were (count1 < 10) instead of (count1 <= 10)? How would that change the total number of lines printed? Well, the outer loop would execute 9 times instead of 10, so the println statement would be executed 450 times. What if the outer loop were left as it was originally, but count2 were initialized to 10 instead of 1 before the inner loop? The inner loop would then execute 40 times instead of 50, so the total number of lines printed would be 400.

Let's look at another example of a nested loop. A *palindrome* is a string of characters that reads the same forward or backward. For example, the following strings are palindromes:

> radar

> drab bard

> ab cde xxxx edc ba

> kayak

> deified

> able was I ere I saw elba

Some palindromes have an even number of characters, and others have an odd number of characters. The `PalindromeTester` program shown in Listing A.14 tests to see whether a string is a palindrome. Users may test as many strings as they want.

The code for `PalindromeTester` has two loops, one inside the other. The outer loop controls how many strings are tested, and the inner loop scans through each string, character by character, until it decides whether the string is a palindrome.

The variables `left` and `right` store the indexes of two characters. At first they show the characters on either end of the string. Each pass of the inner loop compares the two characters, `left` and `right`. We fall out of the inner loop when either the characters don't match, meaning the string is not a palindrome, or when the value of `left` is equal to or greater than the value of `right`, which means the entire string has been tested and it is a palindrome.

Listing A.14

```
//********************************************************************
//   PalindromeTester.java         Author: Lewis/Loftus/Cocking
//
//   Demonstrates the use of nested while loops.
//********************************************************************

import cs1.Keyboard;

public class PalindromeTester
{
    //-----------------------------------------------------------------
    //   Tests strings to see if they are palindromes.
    //-----------------------------------------------------------------
    public static void main (String[] args)
    {
        String str, another = "y";
        int left, right;

        while (another.equalsIgnoreCase("y")) // allows y or Y
        {
            System.out.println ("Enter a potential palindrome:");
            str = Keyboard.readString();

            left = 0;
            right = str.length() - 1;
```

Listing A.14   continued

```
        while (str.charAt(left) == str.charAt(right) && left < right)
        {
            left++;
            right--;
        }

        System.out.println();

        if (left < right)
            System.out.println ("That string is NOT a palindrome.");
        else
            System.out.println ("That string IS a palindrome.");

        System.out.println();
        System.out.print ("Test another palindrome (y/n)? ");
        another = Keyboard.readString();
        }
    }
}
```

Output

```
Enter a potential palindrome:
radar

That string IS a palindrome.

Test another palindrome (y/n)? y
Enter a potential palindrome:
able was I ere I saw elba

That string IS a palindrome.

Test another palindrome (y/n)? y
Enter a potential palindrome:
abcddcba

That string IS a palindrome.

Test another palindrome (y/n)? y
Enter a potential palindrome:
abracadabra

That string is NOT a palindrome.

Test another palindrome (y/n)? n
```

The `StringTokenizer` Class

Let's look at another useful class from the Java standard class library. The types of problems this class helps us solve are repetitious, so the solutions almost always use loops. Note that the `StringTokenizer` class is not in the AP subset.

Often we want to use just part of a string. Taking data out of a string so we can work with it is a common programming activity. The parts of the string are called *tokens*, so taking them out is called *tokenizing* the string. The characters used to separate one token from another are called *delimiters*.

For example, we may want to separate a sentence into words:

```
"The quick brown fox jumped over the lazy dog"
```

In this case, each word is a token and the space character is the delimiter. As another example, we may want to separate the elements of a URL such as:

```
"www.csc.villanova.edu/academics/courses"
```

The delimiters are the period (`.`) and the slash (`/`). In another situation we may want to get data values from a string, such as:

```
"75.43 190.49 69.58 140.77"
```

The delimiter is again the space character. First we change the token strings into numeric values. This kind of processing is done by the code in the `Keyboard` class. When we invoke a `Keyboard` method such as `readDouble` or `readInt`, the data is first read as a string, then tokenized, and finally changed into numeric form. If there are several values on one line, the `Keyboard` class keeps track of them, and takes them out and uses them as needed.

The `StringTokenizer` class, which is part of the `java.util` package in the Java standard class library, is used to separate a string into tokens. The `StringTokenizer` class uses the space, tab, carriage return, and newline characters as default delimiters. Figure A.6 lists some methods of the `StringTokenizer` class. The second constructor in the list gives us a way to pick another set of delimiters for separating tokens. Once the `StringTokenizer` object is created, a call to the `nextToken` method returns the next token from the string. The `hasMoreTokens` method, which returns a `boolean` value, is often used in the condition of a loop to determine whether more tokens are left to process in the string.

The `CountWords` program, shown in Listing A.15, uses the `StringTokenizer` class and a nested `while` loop to analyze several lines of text. The user types in lines of text, ending with a line of only the word `"DONE"`. The outer loop processes one line of text at a time. The inner loop gets and processes the tokens in the current line. The program counts the number of words and the number of characters in the words. After the user enters the sentinel value `"DONE"` (which is not counted), the results are displayed.

Note that the punctuation characters in the strings are included with the tokenized words because the program uses only the default delimiters of the `StringTokenizer` class.

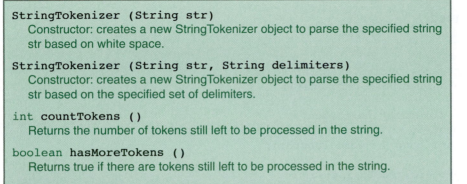

StringTokenizer (String str)
    Constructor: creates a new StringTokenizer object to parse the specified string
    str based on white space.

StringTokenizer (String str, String delimiters)
    Constructor: creates a new StringTokenizer object to parse the specified string
    str based on the specified set of delimiters.

int countTokens ()
    Returns the number of tokens still left to be processed in the string.

boolean hasMoreTokens ()
    Returns true if there are tokens still left to be processed in the string.

String nextToken ()
    Returns the next token in the string.

FIGURE A.6   Some methods of the StringTokenizer class

Listing A.15

```java
//********************************************************************
//   CountWords.java        Author: Lewis/Loftus/Cocking
//
//   Demonstrates the use of the StringTokenizer class and nested
//   loops.
//********************************************************************

import cs1.Keyboard;
import java.util.StringTokenizer;

public class CountWords
{
    //-----------------------------------------------------------
    //   Reads several lines of text, counting the number of words
    //   and the number of non-space characters.
    //-----------------------------------------------------------
    public static void main (String[] args)
    {
        int wordCount = 0, characterCount = 0;
        String line, word;
        StringTokenizer tokenizer;

        System.out.println ("Please enter text (type DONE to quit):");

        line = Keyboard.readString();
        while (!line.equals("DONE"))
```

Listing A.15   continued

```
    {
        tokenizer = new StringTokenizer (line);
        while (tokenizer.hasMoreTokens())
        {
            word = tokenizer.nextToken();
            wordCount++;
            characterCount += word.length();
        }
        line = Keyboard.readString();
    }

    System.out.println ("Number of words: " + wordCount);
    System.out.println ("Number of characters: " + characterCount);
    }
}
```

Output

```
Please enter text (type DONE to quit):
Mary had a little lamb; its fleece was white as snow.
And everywhere that Mary went, the fleece shed all
over and made quite a mess. Little lambs do not make
good house pets.
DONE
Number of words: 34
Number of characters: 141
```

A.8   THE for STATEMENT

Key Concept

We use a for statement when we know
how many times a loop will be executed.

The while statement is good to use when you don't know how many times you want to execute the loop body. The for *statement* is a repetition statement that works well when you *do* know exactly how many times you want to execute the loop.

The Counter2 program shown in Listing A.16 also prints the numbers 1 through 5, except this time we use a for loop to do it.

The header of a for loop has three parts, separated by semicolons. Before the loop begins, the first part of the header, called the *initialization,* is executed. The second part of the header is the boolean condition. If the condition is true, the body of the loop is executed, followed by the third part of the header, which is called the *increment.* The initialization part is executed only once, but the increment part is executed each time. Figure A.7 shows this processing.

Listing A.16

```java
//************************************************************
//   Counter3.java          Author: Lewis/Loftus/Cocking
//
//   Demonstrates the use of a for loop.
//************************************************************

public class Counter3
{
    //----------------------------------------------------------
    //  Prints integer values from 1 to a specific limit.
    //----------------------------------------------------------
    public static void main (String[] args)
    {
        final int LIMIT = 5;

        for (int count=1; count <= LIMIT; count++)
            System.out.println (count);

        System.out.println ("Done");
    }
}
```

Output

```
1
2
3
4
5
Done
```

A for loop can be a bit tricky to read until you get used to it. The execution of the code doesn't read "top to bottom, left to right." The increment code executes after the body of the loop, even though it is in the header.

Note how the three parts of the for loop header map to the equivalent parts of the original Counter program that uses a while loop. The initialization part of the for loop header declares the variable count and gives it a beginning value. We don't have to declare a variable there, but we usually do, unless the variable is needed outside of the loop. Because count is declared in the for loop header, it exists only inside the loop body and can't be referenced anywhere else. The loop control variable is set up, checked, and changed by the actions in the loop header. It can be referenced inside the loop body, but it should not be changed except by the actions defined in the loop header.

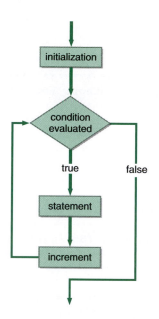

FIGURE A.7   The logic of a `for` loop

The increment part of the `for` loop header can decrement (subtract 1 from) a value rather than increment it. For example, the following loop prints the integer values from 100 down to 1:

```
for (int num = 100; num > 0; num--)
    System.out.println (num);
```

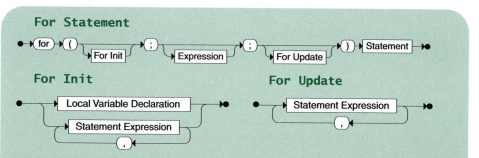

The `for` statement executes Statement over and over, as long as the boolean Expression is true. The For Init part of the header is executed only once, before the loop begins. The For Update part executes after each execution of Statement.

Examples:

```
for (int value=1; value < 25; value++)
    System.out.println (value + " squared is " + value*value);

for (int num=40; num > 0; num-=3)
    sum = sum + num;
```

In fact, the increment part of the for loop can do any calculation, not just a simple adding or subtracting 1 from the value. Look at the program in Listing A.17, which prints multiples of a particular value up to a limit.

Listing A.17

```java
//************************************************************
//  Multiples.java        Author: Lewis/Loftus/Cocking
//
//  Demonstrates the use of a for loop.
//************************************************************

import cs1.Keyboard;

public class Multiples
{
    //----------------------------------------------------------
    //  Prints multiples of a user-specified number up to a user-
    //  specified limit.
    //----------------------------------------------------------
    public static void main (String[] args)
    {
        final int PER_LINE = 5;
        int value, limit, mult, count = 0;

        System.out.print ("Enter a positive value: ");
        value = Keyboard.readInt();

        System.out.print ("Enter an upper limit: ");
        limit = Keyboard.readInt();

        System.out.println ();
        System.out.println ("The multiples of " + value + " between " +
                            value + " and " + limit + " (inclusive) are:");

        for (mult = value; mult <= limit; mult += value)
        {
            System.out.print (mult + "\t");

            // Print a specific number of values per line of output
            count++;
            if (count % PER_LINE == 0)
                System.out.println();
        }
    }
}
```

Listing A.17   **continued**

Output

```
Enter a positive value: 7
Enter an upper limit: 400

The multiples of 7 between 7 and 400 (inclusive) are:
7          14         21         28         35
42         49         56         63         70
77         84         91         98         105
112        119        126        133        140
147        154        161        168        175
182        189        196        203        210
217        224        231        238        245
252        259        266        273        280
287        294        301        308        315
322        329        336        343        350
357        364        371        378        385
392        399
```

The increment part of the `for` loop adds the value entered by the user, in this case 7. The number of values printed per line is controlled by counting the values printed and then moving to the next line whenever `count` is evenly divisible by the `PER_LINE` constant, in this case 5.

The `Stars` program in Listing A.18 uses nested `for` loops. The output is a triangle made of asterisks. The outer loop executes exactly 10 times, each time printing one line of asterisks. The inner loop has a different number of iterations depending on the line value, which is controlled by the outer loop. Each time it executes, the inner loop prints one star on the current line.

Comparing Loops

The `while` and `for` loop statements are about the same: any loop written using one type of loop statement can be written using the other loop type. Which type of statement we use depends on the situation.

A `for` loop is like a `while` loop in that the condition is evaluated before the loop body is executed. Figure A.8 shows the general structure of `for` and `while` loops.

We usually use a `for` loop when we know how many times we want to go through a loop. Most of the time it is easier to put the code that sets up and controls the loop in the `for` loop header.

Listing A.18

```java
//************************************************************************
//   Stars.java          Author: Lewis/Loftus/Cocking
//
//   Demonstrates the use of nested for loops.
//************************************************************************

public class Stars
{
    //---------------------------------------------------------------
    //  Prints a triangle shape using asterisk (star) characters.
    //---------------------------------------------------------------
    public static void main (String[] args)
    {
        final int MAX_ROWS = 10;

        for (int row = 1; row <= MAX_ROWS; row++)
        {
            for (int star = 1; star <= row; star++)
                System.out.print ("*");

            System.out.println();
        }
    }
}
```

Output

```
*
**
***
****
*****
******
*******
********
*********
**********
```

```
for (initialization; condition; increment)      initialization;
    statement;                                   while (condition)
                                                 {
                                                     statement;
                                                     increment;
                                                 }
```

FIGURE A.8   The general structure of equivalent for and while loops

 **ARRAYS**

An *array* is a simple but powerful way to organize data. When we have a large amount of information, such as a list of 100 names, it is not practical to declare separate variables for each piece of data. Arrays solve this problem by letting us declare one variable that can hold many values.

Array Indexing

An array is a list of values. Each value is stored at a numbered position in the array. The number for each position is called an *index* or a *subscript*. Figure A.9 shows an array of integers and the indexes for each position. The array is called `height` and the integers are several peoples' heights in inches.

In Java, array indexes always begin at zero. So the value stored at index 5 is actually the sixth value in the array. The array shown in Figure A.9 has 11 values, indexed from 0 to 10.

To get a value that's in an array, we use the name of the array followed by the index in square brackets. For example, the following expression refers to the ninth value in the array `height`:

```
height[8]
```

If you look at Figure A.9, you'll see that `height[8]` (pronounced "height-sub-eight") contains the value 79. Don't confuse the value of the index, in this case 8, with the value stored in the array at that index, in this case 79.

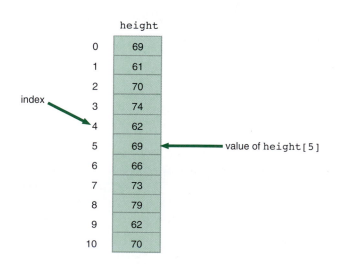

FIGURE A.9 An array called `height` containing integer values

The expression `height[8]` refers to a single integer stored at a particular memory location. You can use it wherever you would use an integer variable. This means you can assign a value to it, use it in calculations, print its value, and so on. Furthermore, because array indexes are integers, you can use integer expressions to specify the index used to access an array. For example, in the following lines of code we see the index in the `height` array given by a number (2), a variable (`count`), and an expression (`MAX/2` and `rand.nextInt(11)`).

```
height[2] = 72;
height[count] = feet * 12;
average = (height[0] + height[1] + height[2]) / 3;
System.out.println ("The middle value is " + height[MAX/2]);
pick = height[rand.nextInt(11)];
```

Declaring and Using Arrays

In Java, arrays are objects. To create an array, we must declare the reference to the array. We can then instantiate the array using the `new` operator, which reserves memory space to store values. The following code is the declaration for the array shown in Figure A.9:

> **Key Concept**
>
> In Java, an array is an object. Memory space for the array elements is reserved by instantiating the array using the `new` operator.

```
int[] height = new int[11];
```

In this declaration the variable `height` is an array of integers whose type is written as `int[]`. All values stored in an array have the same type (or are at least compatible). For example, we can create an array that can hold integers or an array that can hold strings, but not an array that can hold *both* integers and strings. An array can hold any primitive type or any object (class) type. A value stored in an array is sometimes called an *array element*, and the type of values that an array holds is called the *element type* of the array.

The type of the array variable (`int[]`) does not include the size of the array. When we instantiated `height`, using the `new` operator, we reserved the memory space to store 11 integers, indexed from 0 to 10. Once we declare an array is to be a certain size, we can't change the number of values it can hold.

The example shown in Listing A.9 creates an array called `list` that can hold 15 integers. It then changes the value of the sixth element in the array (at index 5). Finally, it prints all values stored in the array.

Figure A.10 shows the array as it changes during the execution of the `BasicArray` program. It's a good idea to use `for` loops with arrays because the number of positions in the array doesn't change: It is constant. A constant called `LIMIT` is used in several places in the `BasicArray` program. We use this constant to declare the size of the array, to control the `for` loop that initializes the array values, and to control the `for` loop that prints the values. Using constants in this way is a good practice. It makes a program more readable and easier to change. For instance, if you needed to change the size of the array, you would only have to change one line of code (the constant declaration).

Listing A.19

```java
//********************************************************************
//  BasicArray.java          Author: Lewis/Loftus/Cocking
//
//  Demonstrates basic array declaration and use.
//********************************************************************

public class BasicArray
{
    final static int LIMIT = 15;
    final static int MULTIPLE = 10;

    //-----------------------------------------------------------
    //  Creates an array, fills it with various integer values,
    //  modifies one value, then prints them out.
    //-----------------------------------------------------------
    public static void main (String[] args)
    {
        int[] list = new int[LIMIT];

        //  Initialize the array values
        for (int index = 0; index < LIMIT; index++)
            list[index] = index * MULTIPLE;

        list[5] = 999;   // change one array value

        for (int index = 0; index < LIMIT; index++)
            System.out.print (list[index] + "   ");

        System.out.println ();
    }
}
```

Output

```
0   10   20   30   40   999   60   70   80   90   100   110   120   130   140
```

The square brackets around the index of an array are treated as an operator in Java. Just like the + operator or the <= operator, the index operator ([ ]) has a precedence. In fact, it has the highest precedence of all Java operators: It is always acted on first.

Whenever a reference to an array element is made, the index must be greater than or equal to zero and less than the size of the array. For example, suppose an array called prices is created with 25 elements. The valid indexes for the array are from 0 to 24. Whenever a reference is made to a particular element in the array (such as prices[count]), the value of the index is checked. If it is between zero and 24 inclusive, the

Key Concept

Bounds checking ensures that an index used to refer to an array element is in range. The Java index operator performs automatic bounds checking.

The array is created with 15 elements, indexed from 0 to 14

After three iterations of the first loop

After completing the first loop

After changing the value of `list[5]`

FIGURE A.10   The array `list` as it changes in the `BasicArray` program

reference is carried out. If the index is not valid, if for example it is 25, the exception `ArrayIndexOutOfBoundsException` is thrown. The index operator does *automatic bounds checking*. Bounds checking makes sure that the index is within the range for the array being referenced.

Because array indexes begin at zero it is easy to create *off-by-one errors* in a program. When you reference array elements, make sure that the index stays within the array bounds.

The size of a Java array is held in a constant called `length` in the array object. It is a public constant and so it can be referenced directly. For example, if we create an array called `prices` with 25 elements, the constant `prices.length` will contain the value 25. Its value is set once when the array is created and cannot be changed.

Let's look at another example. The `ReverseOrder` program, shown in Listing A.20, reads 10 integers into an array called `numbers` and then prints them in reverse order. The array `numbers` is declared to have 10 elements, so it is indexed from 0 to 9. The index range is controlled in the two `for` loops by using the `length` field of the array object. You should carefully set the initial value of loop control variables and the conditions that end loops to make sure that all elements are processed and only valid indexes are used to reference an array element. For example, you do not want to miss the element at index 0 or 9, but you also do not want to try to process index 10.

Listing A.20

```java
//********************************************************************
//   ReverseOrder.java          Author: Lewis/Loftus/Cocking
//
//   Demonstrates array index processing.
//********************************************************************

import cs1.Keyboard;

public class ReverseOrder
{
    //-----------------------------------------------------------
    //   Reads a list of numbers from the user, storing them in an
    //   array, then prints them in reverse order.
    //-----------------------------------------------------------
    public static void main (String[] args)
    {
        double[] numbers = new double[10];

        System.out.println ("The size of the array: " + numbers.length);

        for (int index = 0; index < numbers.length; index++)
        {
            System.out.print ("Enter number " + (index+1) + ": ");
            numbers[index] = Keyboard.readDouble();
        }

        System.out.println ("The numbers in reverse order:");

        for (int index = numbers.length-1; index >= 0; index--)
            System.out.print (numbers[index] + "   ");

        System.out.println ();
    }
}
```

Output

```
The size of the array: 10
Enter number 1:    18.36
Enter number 2:    48.9
Enter number 3:    53.5
Enter number 4:    29.06
Enter number 5:    72.404
Enter number 6:    34.8
Enter number 7:    63.41
Enter number 8:    45.55
Enter number 9:    69.0
Enter number 10: 99.18
The numbers in reverse order:
99.18   69.0   45.55   63.41   34.8   72.404   29.06   53.5   48.9   18.36
```

The `LetterCount` example, shown in Listing A.21, uses two arrays and a `String` object. The array called `upper` stores the number of times each uppercase letter is found in the string. The array called `lower` stores the number of times each lowercase letter is found.

Listing A.21

```java
//************************************************************
//  LetterCount.java        Author: Lewis/Loftus/Cocking
//
//  Demonstrates the relationship between arrays and strings.
//************************************************************

import cs1.Keyboard;

public class LetterCount
{
    //---------------------------------------------------------
    //  Reads a sentence from the user and counts the number of
    //  uppercase and lowercase letters contained in it.
    //---------------------------------------------------------
    public static void main (String[] args)
    {
        final int NUMCHARS = 26;

        int[] upper = new int[NUMCHARS];
        int[] lower = new int[NUMCHARS];

        char current;    // the current character being processed
        int other = 0;   // counter for non-alphabetics

        System.out.println ("Enter a sentence:");
        String line = Keyboard.readString();

        //  Count the number of each letter occurence
        for (int ch = 0; ch < line.length(); ch++)
        {
            current = line.charAt(ch);
            if (current >= 'A' && current <= 'Z')
                upper[current-'A']++;
            else
                if (current >= 'a' && current <= 'z')
                    lower[current-'a']++;
                else
                    other++;
        }
```

Listing A.21   **continued**

```
        //  Print the results
        System.out.println ();
        for (int letter=0; letter < upper.length; letter++)
        {
            System.out.print ( (char) (letter + 'A') );
            System.out.print (": " + upper[letter]);
            System.out.print ("\t\t" + (char) (letter + 'a') );
            System.out.println (": " + lower[letter]);
        }

        System.out.println ();
        System.out.println ("Non-alphabetic characters: " + other);
    }
}
```

Output

```
Enter a sentence:
In Casablanca, Humphrey Bogart never says "Play it again, Sam."
A: 0          a: 10
B: 1          b: 1
C: 1          c: 1
D: 0          d: 0
E: 0          e: 3
F: 0          f: 0
G: 0          g: 2
H: 1          h: 1
I: 1          i: 2
J: 0          j: 0
K: 0          k: 0
L: 0          l: 2
M: 0          m: 2
N: 0          n: 4
O: 0          o: 1
P: 1          p: 1
Q: 0          q: 0
R: 0          r: 3
S: 1          s: 3
T: 0          t: 2
U: 0          u: 1
V: 0          v: 1
W: 0          w: 0
X: 0          x: 0
Y: 0          y: 3
Z: 0          z: 0

Non-alphabetic characters: 14
```

Because there are 26 letters in the English alphabet, the `upper` and `lower` arrays are each declared with 26 elements. Each element contains zero to start with. The `for` loop scans through the string one character at a time. Each time it finds a letter—lowercase *a*, for example—it increases the count in the array element by one. It also counts all the nonalphabet characters, such as word spaces and punctuation.

Both of the counter arrays are indexed from 0 to 25. We have to match each character to a counter. A logical way to do this is to use `upper[0]` to count the number of `'A'` characters found, `upper[1]` to count the number of `'B'` characters found, and so on. Likewise, `lower[0]` is used to count `'a'` characters, `lower[1]` is used to count `'b'` characters, and so on. A variable called `other` is used to count the nonalphabetic characters.

We use the current character to calculate which index in the array to reference. Remember that each character has a numeric value based on the Unicode character set, and that the uppercase and lowercase letters are continuous and in order. So we use the numeric value of an uppercase letter such as `'E'` (which is 69) and subtract the numeric value of the character `'A'` (which is 65) to get 4, which is the correct index for the counter of the character `'E'` as shown in Figure A.11. Nowhere in the program do we actually need to know the specific numeric values for each letter.

Initializer Lists

Another way to instantiate arrays is to use an *initializer list*, which lists the initial values for the elements of the array. The items in an initializer list are separated by commas and enclosed in braces (`{}`). When an initializer list is used, the new

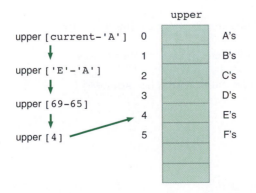

FIGURE A.11   When current is `'E'`, `upper[current-'A']` is the array cell where the number of `E`s is stored

operator is not used. The size of the array is the same as the number of items in the initializer list. For example, the following declaration instantiates the array scores as an array of eight integers, indexed from 0 to 7 with these initial values:

```
int[] scores = {87, 98, 69, 54, 65, 76, 87, 99};
```

We can use an initializer list only when we first declare an array.

The type of each value in an initializer list must match the type of the array elements. Let's look at another example:

```
char[] letterGrades = {'A', 'B', 'C', 'D', 'F'};
```

Key Concept

An initializer list can be used to instantiate an array object. The size of the array is the same as the number of items the list.

In this case, letterGrades is declared to be an array of five characters, and the initializer list contains the letters A, B, C, D, and F. The program shown in Listing A.22 shows an initializer list used to instantiate an array.

Listing A.22

```java
//*****************************************************************
//   Primes.java         Author: Lewis/Loftus/Cocking
//
//   Demonstrates the use of an initializer list for an array.
//*****************************************************************

public class Primes
{
    //-------------------------------------------------------------
    //   Stores some prime numbers in an array and prints them.
    //-------------------------------------------------------------
    public static void main (String[] args)
    {
        int[] primeNums = {2, 3, 5, 7, 11, 13, 17, 19};

        System.out.println ("Array length: " + primeNums.length);

        System.out.println ("The first few prime numbers are:");

        for (int scan = 0; scan < primeNums.length; scan++)
            System.out.print (primeNums[scan] + "   ");

        System.out.println ();
    }
}
```

Output

```
Array length: 8
The first few prime numbers are:
2   3   5   7   11   13   17   19
```

Arrays as Parameters

An entire array can be passed as a parameter to a method. Because an array is an object, we can actually pass a copy of the reference to the original array. We discussed objects passed as parameters in Chapter 2.

A method that gets an array as a parameter can permanently change an element of the array because it is referring to the original element value. The method cannot permanently change the reference to the array itself because only a copy of the original reference is sent to the method. These are the same as the rules for any object type.

> **Key Concept**
>
> An array can be passed as a parameter, making the formal parameter a copy of the original.

An element of an array can be passed to a method as well. If the element is a primitive type, a copy of the value is passed. If the element is a reference to an object, a copy of the object reference is passed. As always, what impact the changes have depends on the type of the parameter. We discuss arrays of objects further in the next section.

A.10   ARRAYS OF OBJECTS

In our examples so far, the arrays stored primitive types, such as integers and characters. Arrays can also store references to objects. Complicated information management structures can be created using only arrays and other objects. For example, an array could contain objects, and each of those objects could have several variables and the methods that use them. Those variables could themselves be arrays, and so on.

Arrays of String Objects

Consider the following declaration:

```
String[] words = new String[25];
```

The variable `words` is an array of references to `String` objects. The `new` operator in the declaration instantiates the array and reserves space for 25 `String` references. This declaration does not create any `String` objects; it just creates an array that holds references to `String` objects.

The program called `GradeRange` creates an array of `String` objects called `grades`, which stores letter grades for a course. The `String` objects are created using string literals in the initializer list. This array could not have been declared as an array of characters because the plus and minus grades create two-character strings. The output for the `GradeRange` program lists letter grades and their cutoff values (the lowest score you can have to get an A is 95, for example), which have been stored in a corresponding array of integers.

Sometimes two arrays like this are called *parallel arrays*. Parallel arrays can be tricky because they can get out of synch with each other. You are usually better off creating one array that holds all the necessary information. For example, the GradeRange program could be changed to use a single array that contains both the grade string and the numeric cutoff value.

Filling Arrays of Objects

> **Key Concept**
>
> Instantiating an array of objects just reserves room to store references. We must create the objects that will be stored in each element separately.

There is something else you need to know about object arrays: Creating the array and creating the objects that we store in the array are two separate steps. When we declare an array of String objects, for example, we create an array that holds String references. We have to create the String objects separately. In earlier examples, we created the String objects using string literals in an initializer list or, in the case of command-line arguments, they were created by the Java runtime environment.

This is shown in the Tunes program in Listing A.23. Listing A.23 shows the Tunes class, which has a main method that creates, changes, and looks at a compact disc (CD) collection. Each CD added to the collection has a title, artist, purchase price, and number of tracks.

Listing A.23

```java
//********************************************************************
//   Tunes.java          Author: Lewis/Loftus/Cocking
//
//   Driver for demonstrating the use of an array of objects.
//********************************************************************

public class Tunes
{
   //----------------------------------------------------------------
   //  Creates a CDCollection object and adds some CDs to it. Prints
   //  reports on the status of the collection.
   //----------------------------------------------------------------
   public static void main (String[] args)
   {
      CDCollection music = new CDCollection ();

      music.addCD ("By the Way", "Red Hot Chili Peppers", 14.95, 10);
      music.addCD ("Come On Over", "Shania Twain", 14.95, 16);
      music.addCD ("Soundtrack", "The Producers", 17.95, 33);
      music.addCD ("Play", "Jennifer Lopez", 13.90, 11);
```

Listing A.23 **continued**

```
        System.out.println (music);

        music.addCD ("Double Live", "Garth Brooks", 19.99, 26);
        music.addCD ("Greatest Hits", "Stone Temple Pilots", 15.95, 13);

        System.out.println (music);
    }
}
```

Output

```
*********************************************
My CD Collection

Number of CDs: 4
Total value: $61.75
Average cost: $15.44

CD List:

$14.95   10      By the Way      Red Hot Chili Peppers
$14.95   16      Come On Over    Shania Twain
$17.95   33      Soundtrack      The Producers
$13.90   11      Play            Jennifer Lopez


*********************************************
My CD Collection

Number of CDs: 6
Total value: $97.69
Average cost: $16.28

CD List:

$14.95   10      By the Way      Red Hot Chili Peppers
$14.95   16      Come On Over    Shania Twain
$17.95   33      Soundtrack      The Producers
$13.90   11      Play            Jennifer Lopez
$19.99   26      Double Live     Garth Brooks
$15.95   13      Greatest Hits   Stone Temple Pilots
```

Listing A.24 shows the CDCollection class. It contains an array of CD
objects representing the collection. It counts the CDs and their combined
value. It also keeps track of the size of the collection array so that a larger
array can be created if too many CDs are added to the collection.

Listing A.24

```java
//********************************************************************
//  CDCollection.java          Author: Lewis/Loftus
//
//  Represents a collection of compact discs.
//********************************************************************

import java.text.NumberFormat;

public class CDCollection
{
    private CD[] collection;
    private int count;
    private double totalCost;

    //-----------------------------------------------------------------
    //  Creates an initially empty collection.
    //-----------------------------------------------------------------
    public CDCollection ()
    {
        collection = new CD[100];
        count = 0;
        totalCost = 0.0;
    }

    //-----------------------------------------------------------------
    //  Adds a CD to the collection, increasing the size of the
    //  collection if necessary.
    //-----------------------------------------------------------------
    public void addCD (String title, String artist, double cost,
                       int tracks)
    {
        if (count == collection.length)
            increaseSize();

        collection[count] = new CD (title, artist, cost, tracks);
        totalCost += cost;
        count++;
    }

    //-----------------------------------------------------------------
    //  Returns a report describing the CD collection.
    //-----------------------------------------------------------------
    public String toString()
    {
        NumberFormat fmt = NumberFormat.getCurrencyInstance();
```

Listing A.24 continued

```
        String report = "*******************************************\n";
        report += "My CD Collection\n\n";

        report += "Number of CDs: " + count + "\n";
        report += "Total cost: " + fmt.format(totalCost) + "\n";
        report += "Average cost: " + fmt.format(totalCost/count);

        report += "\n\nCD List:\n\n";


        for (int cd = 0; cd < count; cd++)
            report += collection[cd].toString() + "\n";

        return report;
    }

    //-----------------------------------------------------------
    //  Doubles the size of the collection by creating a larger array
    //  and copying the existing collection into it.
    //-----------------------------------------------------------
    private void increaseSize ()
    {
        CD[] temp = new CD[collection.length * 2];

        for (int cd = 0; cd < collection.length; cd++)
            temp[cd] = collection[cd];

        collection = temp;
    }
}
```

The collection array is instantiated in the CDCollection constructor. Every time a CD is added to the collection (using the addCD method), a new CD object is created and a reference to it is stored in the collection array.

Each time a CD is added to the collection, we check to see whether we have filled up the collection array. If we didn't do this, we would get an exception when we tried to store a new CD object at an invalid index. If the array is full, the private increaseSize method is invoked. The increaseSize method creates an array that is twice as big as the current collection array. It then copies each CD in the collection into the new array. Finally, it sets the collection reference to the larger array. This means we never run out of room in our CD collection. The user of the CDCollection object (the main method) never has to worry about running out of space because it's all handled internally.

The toString method of the CDCollection class returns a report summarizing the collection. The report is created, in part, using calls to the toString method of each CD object stored in the collection. Listing A.25 shows the CD class.

Listing A.25

```java
//********************************************************************
//  CD.java           Author: Lewis/Loftus/Cocking
//
//  Represents a compact disc.
//********************************************************************

import java.text.NumberFormat;

public class CD
{
   private String title, artist;
   private double cost;
   private int tracks;

   //----------------------------------------------------------------
   //  Creates a new CD with the specified information.
   //----------------------------------------------------------------
   public CD (String name, String singer, double price, int numTracks)
   {
      title = name;
      artist = singer;
      cost = price;
      tracks = numTracks;
   }

   //----------------------------------------------------------------
   //  Returns a description of this CD.
   //----------------------------------------------------------------
   public String toString()
   {
      NumberFormat fmt = NumberFormat.getCurrencyInstance();

      String description;

      description = fmt.format(cost) + "\t" + tracks + "\t";
      description += title + "\t" + artist;

      return description;
   }
}
```

The Java Class Library

This appendix lists many of the classes in the Java standard class library. We list the variables, constants, constructors, and methods of each class. Items in a class are grouped by their purpose. The classes are listed in alphabetical order. The package each class is contained in is given in parentheses after the class name.

Applet (java.applet)

`Applet` is a public class, derived from `Panel`. It is used as a program running inside a Web page.

constructors

```
public Applet()
```
Creates a new instance of an applet to go in a Web page.

methods

```
public void destroy()
```
Destroys the applet and all of its resources. This method contains no functionality and should be overridden by subclasses.

```
public AppletContext getAppletContext()
```
Returns this applet's context (where it is running).

```
public String getAppletInfo()
```
Returns a string representation of information regarding this applet. This method contains no functionality and should be overridden by subclasses.

```
public AudioClip getAudioClip(URL audio)
public AudioClip getAudioClip(URL base, String filename)
```
Returns the `AudioClip` requested. The location of the audio clip can be given by the base URL and the filename relative to that base.

```
public URL getCodeBase()
public URL getDocumentBase()
public Locale getLocale()
```
Returns the URL of this applet, the document that contains this applet, or where this applet is located.

```
public Image getImage(URL image)
public Image getImage(URL base, String filename)
```
Returns the image requested. The location of the image can be given by the base URL and the filename relative to that base.

```
public String getParameter(String param)
public String[][] getParameterInfo()
```
Returns the value of the specified parameter for this applet. An array of string elements containing information about each parameter for this applet can also be obtained. Each element of the returned array should be comprised of three strings (parameter name, type, and description). This method contains no functionality and should be overridden by subclasses.

```
public void init()
```
This method provides a place for the programmer to set up initialization functionality to the applet before the applet is started for the first time. It is automatically called by the browser or the appletviewer program. This method contains no functionality as is and should be overridden by subclasses.

```
public boolean isActive()
```
Returns a true value if this applet is active. An applet is active just before execution of its start method and is no longer active just after execution of its stop method.

```
public void play(URL source)
public void play(URL base, String filename)
```
Plays the audio clip. The location of the audio clip can be given as a URL and filename.

```
public void resize(Dimension dim)
public void resize(int w, int h)
```
Resizes this applet.

```
public final void setStub(AppletStub stub)
```
Sets the interface between this applet and the browser or appletviewer.

```
public void showStatus(String message)
```
Prints the message in the browser's status window.

```
public void start()
```
This method gives the programmer a place for functionality relevant to the starting of this applet. It is called after the applet has been initialized (with the `init` method) and every time the applet is reloaded in the browser or appletviewer program. This method contains no functionality as is and should be overridden by subclasses.

```
public void stop()
```
This method gives the programmer a place for functionality relevant to the stopping of this applet. It is called by the browser (when the containing Web page is replaced) or appletviewer program. This method contains no functionality as is and should be overridden by subclasses.

ArrayList (java.util)

This is a public class, derived from `AbstractList`, that represents a resizable array implementation of a list. Similar to `Vector`, but unsynchronized.

constructors

`public ArrayList()`

`public ArrayList(int initialCapacity)`
  Creates a new list with the given initial capacity (ten by default).

`public ArrayList(Collection col)`
  Creates a new list containing the elements of the collection.

methods

`public void add(int index, Object element)`
  Inserts the element into this list at the given index.

`public boolean add(Object obj)`
  Adds the element to the end of this list.

`public boolean addAll(Collection col)`

`public boolean addAll(int index, Collection col)`
  Inserts all of the elements in the collection into the list at the index, or adds
  them to the end of the list if no index is specified.

`public void clear()`
  Removes all of the elements from this list.

`public boolean contains(Object obj)`
  Returns true if this list contains the object.

`public void ensureCapacity(int minimumCapacity)`
  Increases the size of this list to the given value.

`public Object get(int index)`
  Returns the element at the index. Throws `IndexOutOfBoundsException` if
  the index is out of range.

`public int indexOf(Object obj)`
  Returns the index of the first place the object was found (based on the `equals`
  method) or −1 if it was not found.

`public boolean isEmpty()`
  Returns true if this list is empty.

`public int lastIndexOf(Object obj)`
  Returns the index of the last place the object was found (based on the `equals`
  method) or −1 if it was not found.

`public Object remove(int index)`
  Removes and returns the object at the given index in this list. Throws
  `IndexOutOfBoundsException` if the index is out of range.

`protected void removeRange(int fromIndex, int toIndex)`
  Removes the elements at the indexes in the range, exclusive.

`public Object set(int index, Object obj)`
  Replaces the element at the given index with the specified object.

`public int size()`
  Returns the number of elements in this list.

```
public Object[] toArray()
```
   Returns an array containing the elements in this list.

```
public void trimToSize()
```
   Trims the size of this list.

BigDecimal (java.math)

This is a public class, derived from `Number`, that can be used to represent a decimal number with precision.

variables and constants

ROUND_CEILING

   A constant for rounding in which the value of the `BigDecimal` is rounded up (away from zero) if the number is positive, and down (closer to zero) if the number is negative.

ROUND_DOWN

   A constant that represents a rounding mode in which the value of the `BigDecimal` is rounded closer to zero (decreasing a positive number and increasing a negative number).

ROUND_FLOOR

   A constant for rounding in which the value of the `BigDecimal` is rounded down (closer to zero) if the number is positive, and up (away from zero) if the number is negative.

ROUND_HALF_DOWN

   A constant for rounding in which the value of the `BigDecimal` is rounded as in `ROUND_UP` if the fraction of the number is greater than 0.5 and as `ROUND_DOWN` in all other cases.

ROUND_HALF_EVEN

   A constant for rounding in which the value of the `BigDecimal` is rounded as in `ROUND_HALF_UP` if the number to the left of the decimal is odd and as `ROUND_HALF_DOWN` when the number is even.

ROUND_HALF_UP

   A constant for rounding in which the value of the `BigDecimal` is rounded as in `ROUND_UP` if the fraction of the number is greater than or equal to 0.5 and as in `ROUND_DOWN` in all other cases.

ROUND_UNNECESSARY

   A constant for rounding in which the value of the `BigDecimal` is not rounded (if possible) and an exact result is returned.

ROUND_UP

   A constant for rounding in which the value of the `BigDecimal` is rounded away from zero (increasing a positive number, and decreasing a negative number).

constructors

```
public BigDecimal(BigInteger arg)
public BigDecimal(BigInteger arg, int scale) throws
NumberFormatException
public BigDecimal(double arg) throws NumberFormatException
public BigDecimal(String arg) throws NumberFormatException
```

Creates an instance of `BigDecimal` from `arg`. The string argument should include a minus sign for a negative number. The resulting `BigDecimal`'s scale will be the number of integers to the right of the decimal point in the string, a given value, or 0 (zero) if none are present.

methods

```
public double doubleValue()
public float floatValue()
public int intValue()
public long longValue()
public BigInteger toBigInteger()
public String toString()
```

Converts this `BigDecimal` to either a Java primitive type or a `BigInteger`.

```
public BigDecimal abs()
```

Returns the absolute value of this `BigDecimal` with the same scale as this `BigDecimal`.

```
public BigDecimal add(BigDecimal arg)
public BigDecimal subtract(BigDecimal arg)
```

Returns the result of `arg` added to or subtracted from this `BigDecimal`, with the resulting scale equal to the larger of the two `BigDecimals`' scales.

```
public int compareTo(BigDecimal arg)
```

Compares this `BigDecimal` to `arg` and will return a –1 if this `BigDecimal` is less than `arg`, 0 if it is equal to `arg`, or a 1 if it is greater than `arg`. If the values of the two `BigDecimals` are the same and the scales are different, they are considered equal.

```
public BigDecimal divide(BigDecimal arg, int mode) throws
ArithmeticException, IllegalArgumentException
public BigDecimal divide(BigDecimal arg, int scale, int mode)
throws ArithmeticException, IllegalArgumentException
```

Returns the result of this `BigDecimal` divided by `arg`. If required, the rounding mode is used. The resulting `BigDecimal`'s scale is identical to this `BigDecimal`'s scale or a specified value.

```
public boolean equals(Object arg)
```

Returns a true value if this `BigDecimal`'s value and scale are equal to `arg`'s value and scale.

```
public int hashCode()
```
Returns the hash code of this BigDecimal.

```
public BigDecimal max(BigDecimal arg)
```

```
public BigDecimal min(BigDecimal arg)
```
Returns the greater or lesser of this BigDecimal and arg.

```
public BigDecimal movePointLeft(int num)
```

```
public BigDecimal movePointRight(int num)
```
Returns this BigDecimal with the decimal point moved num positions.

```
public BigDecimal multiply(BigDecimal arg)
```
Returns the result of this BigDecimal multiplied with the value of arg. The scale of the resulting BigDecimal is the result of the addition of the two BigDecimals' scales.

```
public BigDecimal negate()
```
Returns the negation of this BigDecimal's value with the same scale.

```
public int scale()
```
Returns the scale of this BigDecimal.

```
public BigDecimal setScale(int val) throws ArithmeticException,
IllegalArgumentException
```

```
public BigDecimal setScale(int val, int mode) throws
ArithmeticException, IllegalArgumentException
```
Returns a BigDecimal whose value is the same as this BigDecimal's and has a new scale specified by val. If rounding is necessary, a rounding mode can be specified.

```
public int signum()
```
Returns a −1 if this BigDecimal is negative, 0 if zero, and 1 if positive.

```
public static BigDecimal valueOf(long value)
```

```
public static BigDecimal valueOf(long value, int scale) throws
NumberFormatException
```
Returns a BigDecimal with a defined value. The scale of the returned number is either given or defaults to 0 (zero).

BigInteger (java.math)

This is a public class, derived from Number. It can be used to represent an integer in a two's complement format of any precision.

constructors

```
public BigInteger(byte[] arg) throws NumberFormatException
```

```
public BigInteger(int signum, byte[] magnitude) throws
NumberFormatException
```
Creates an instance of a BigInteger from the specified byte array. The sign of the number can be placed in signum (where −1 is negative, 0 is zero, and 1 is positive).

```
public BigInteger(String arg) throws NumberFormatException
public BigInteger(String arg, int radix) throws
NumberFormatException
```
Creates an instance of a `BigInteger` from the string `arg`, which can contain a minus sign and decimal numbers. The argument `radix` gives the base of the `arg` value.

```
public BigInteger(int size, Random rand) throws
IllegalArgumentException
public BigInteger(int size, int prob, Random rand)
```
Creates a (generally) prime instance of a `BigInteger` from a random integer, `rand`, of a given length, `size`. The certainty parameter (`prob`) is how likely it is that the generated number is a prime.

methods

```
public double doubleValue()
public float floatValue()
public int intValue()
public long longValue()
public String toString()
public String toString(int base)
```
Converts this `BigDecimal` either to a Java primitive type or to a `BigInteger`. The base can give the radix of the number value returned.

```
public BigInteger abs()
```
Returns the absolute value of this `BigInteger`.

```
public BigInteger add(BigInteger arg) throws ArithmeticException
public BigInteger subtract(BigInteger arg)
```
Adds the argument to, or subtracts `arg` from, this `BigInteger` and returns the result.

```
public BigInteger and(BigInteger arg)
public BigInteger andNot(BigInteger arg)
public BigInteger not()
public BigInteger or(BigInteger arg)
public BigInteger xor(BigInteger arg)
```
Returns the result of a logical operation of this `BigInteger` and the value of `arg`. The not method returns the logical not of this `BigInteger`.

```
public int bitCount()
```
Returns the number of bits from this `BigInteger` that are different from the sign bit.

```
public int bitLength()
```
Returns the number of bits from this `BigInteger`, excluding the sign bit.

```
public BigInteger clearBit(int index) throws ArithmeticException
```
Returns the modified representation of this `BigInteger` with the bit at the position `index` cleared.

```
public int compareTo(BigInteger arg)
```
Compares this `BigInteger` to the parameter `arg`. If this `BigInteger` is less than `arg`, a –1 is returned. If it is equal to `arg`, a 0 (zero) is returned. If it is greater than `arg`, a 1 is returned.

```
public BigInteger divide(BigInteger arg) throws
ArithmeticException
```

```
public BigInteger[] divideAndRemainder(BigInteger arg) throws
ArithmeticException
```
Returns the result of this `BigInteger` divided by `arg`. The `divideAndRemainder` method returns as the first element ([0]) the quotient, and the second element ([1]) the remainder.

```
public boolean equals(Object arg)
```
Returns true if this `BigInteger` is equal to the parameter `arg`.

```
public BigInteger flipBit(int index) throws ArithmeticException
```
Returns the modified representation of this `BigInteger` with the bit at position `index` flipped.

```
public BigInteger gcd(BigInteger arg)
```
Returns the greatest common denominator of the absolute value of this `BigInteger` and the absolute value of the parameter `arg`.

```
public int getLowestSetBit()
```
Returns the index of the rightmost bit that is equal to one from this `BigInteger`.

```
public int hashCode()
```
Returns the hash code of this `BigInteger`.

```
public boolean isProbablePrime(int prob)
```
Returns a true value if this `BigInteger` is probably a prime number. The parameter `prob` represents the certainty of the decision.

```
public BigInteger max(BigInteger arg)
```

```
public BigInteger min(BigInteger arg)
```
Returns the larger or smaller of this `BigInteger` or `arg`.

```
public BigInteger mod(BigInteger arg)
```

```
public BigInteger modInverse(BigInteger arg) throws
ArithmeticException
```

```
public BigInteger modPow(BigInteger exp, BigInteger arg)
```
Returns the result of this `BigInteger` mod arg. The `modInverse` returns the modular multiplicative inverse. `modPow` returns the result of this (`BigInteger` ^^ exp) mod arg.

```
public BigInteger multiply(BigInteger arg)
```
Returns the result of this `BigInteger` multiplied by `arg`.

```
public BigInteger negate()
```
Returns this `BigInteger` negated (this `BigInteger` * –1).

```
public BigInteger pow(int exp) throws ArithmeticException
```
Returns the result of this `BigInteger` ^^ exp.

```
public BigInteger remainder(BigInteger arg) throws
ArithmeticException
```
Returns the result of this `BigInteger` mod arg.

```
public BigInteger setBit(int index) throws ArithmeticException
```
Returns the result of this `BigInteger` with the bit at the given index set.

```
public BigInteger shiftLeft(int num)
```
```
public BigInteger shiftRight(int num)
```
Returns the result of this `BigInteger` shifted by num bits.

```
public int signum()
```
Returns a –1 if the value of this `BigInteger` is negative, 0 if zero, and 1 if positive.

```
public boolean testBit(int index) throws ArithmeticException
```
Returns a true value if the bit at the specified index is set.

```
public byte[] toByteArray()
```
Returns the two's complement of this `BigInteger` in an array of bytes.

```
public static BigInteger valueOf(long arg)
```
Returns a `BigInteger` from the value of arg.

Boolean (java.lang)

This is a public final class, derived from `Object` and implementing `Serializable`. It contains boolean logic operations, constants, and methods as a wrapper around the Java primitive type `boolean`.

variables and constructs

```
public final static Boolean TRUE
```
```
public final static Boolean FALSE
```
`Boolean` constant values of true or false.

```
public final static Class TYPE
```
The `Boolean` constant value of the boolean type class.

constructors

```
public Boolean(boolean arg)
```
```
public Boolean(String arg)
```
Creates an instance of the `Boolean` class from the parameter arg.

methods

```
public boolean booleanValue()
```
The boolean value of the current object.

```
public boolean equals(Object arg)
```
Returns the result of an equality comparison against arg. Here arg must be a boolean object with the same value as this `Boolean` for a resulting true value.

```
public static boolean getBoolean(String str)
```
Returns a Boolean representation of the system property named in str.

```
public int hashCode()
```
Returns the hash code for this object.

```
public String toString()
```
Returns the string representation of the state of the current object (i.e., "true" or "false").

```
public static Boolean valueOf(String str)
```
Returns a new Boolean initialized to the value of str.

BufferedReader (java.io)

This is a public class, derived from Reader. It provides a buffered stream of character-based input.

constructors

```
public BufferedReader(Reader rdr)
```

```
public BufferedReader(Reader rdr, int size)
```
Creates a BufferedReader from the given Reader, by using a given size (in characters). The default size is 8192 characters.

methods

```
public void close() throws IOException
```
Closes this BufferedReader.

```
public void mark(int readAheadLimit) throws IOException
```
Sets a mark in the stream where attempts to reset this BufferedReader will go. The readAheadLimit determines how far ahead the stream can be read before the mark expires.

```
public boolean markSupported()
```
An overridden method from Reader that determines if this stream supports the setting of a mark.

```
public int read() throws IOException
```

```
public String readLine() throws IOException
```
Reads a single character or an entire line from this BufferedReader stream. The character is returned as an int, the line as a string. A line of text is considered to be a series of characters ending in a carriage return (\r), a line feed (\n), or a carriage return followed by a line (\r\n).

```
public int read(char[] dest, int offset, int size) throws
IOException
```
Reads size characters from this BufferedReader stream. Reading will skip offset characters into the current location in the stream, and place them in the destination array. This method will return the number of characters read from the stream or a –1 if the end of the stream was reached.

```
public boolean ready() throws IOException
```
Returns a true value if this `BufferedReader` can be read from. This state can only be true if the buffer is not empty.

```
public void reset() throws IOException
```
Resets this `BufferedReader` to the last mark.

```
public long skip(long num) throws IOException
```
Skips forward num characters in the stream and returns the number of characters skipped.

BufferedWriter (java.io)

This is a public class, derived from `Writer`. It represents a character output stream that buffers characters for efficiency.

constructors

```
public BufferedWriter(Writer out)
```
```
public BufferedWriter(Writer out, int size)
```
Creates a buffered output stream using the specified `Writer` stream and a buffer of the specified size.

methods

```
public void close()
```
Closes this stream.

```
public void flush()
```
Flushes this stream.

```
public void newLine()
```
Writes a line separator to this stream.

```
public void write(int ch)
```
```
public void write(String str)
```
```
public void write(String str, int offset, int length)
```
```
public void write(char[] buffer)
```
```
public void write(char[] buffer, int offset, int length)
```
Writes a single character, string, or character array to this stream. A part of the string or character array can be given.

Calendar (java.util)

This is a public abstract class, derived from `Object` and implementing `Cloneable` and `Serializable`. It allows a `Date` object to be changed or deleted.

variables and constructs

```
public static final int AM
```

```
public static final int PM
```
   Constant values that represent before (ante) and after (post) noon (meridian).
```
public static final int ERA
public static final int YEAR
public static final int MONTH
public static final int WEEK_OF_YEAR
public static final int WEEK_OF_MONTH
public static final int DATE
public static final int DAY_OF_MONTH
public static final int DAY_OF_YEAR
public static final int DAY_OF_WEEK
public static final int DAY_OF_WEEK_IN_MONTH
public static final int AM_PM
public static final int HOUR
public static final int HOUR_OF_DAY
public static final int MINUTE
public static final int SECOND
public static final int MILLISECOND
public static final int ZONE_OFFSET
public static final int DST_OFFSET
```
   Constant values that represent the index to the field where time data (to millisecond precision) is stored. The combination of all of these fields gives us a full representation of a moment of time.
```
public static final int JANUARY
public static final int FEBRUARY
public static final int MARCH
public static final int APRIL
public static final int MAY
public static final int JUNE
public static final int JULY
public static final int AUGUST
public static final int SEPTEMBER
public static final int OCTOBER
public static final int NOVEMBER
public static final int DECEMBER
public static final int UNDECIMBER
```
   Constant values representing the months. UNDECIMBER represents the 13th month of a Gregorian calendar (lunar month).
```
public static final int SUNDAY
public static final int MONDAY
public static final int TUESDAY
public static final int WEDNESDAY
```

```
public static final int THURSDAY
public static final int FRIDAY
public static final int SATURDAY
```
Constant values representing the days of a week.

`protected boolean areFieldsSet`
A boolean flag that tells us whether the time fields have been set for this `Calendar`.

`public static final int FIELD_COUNT`
A constant value that represents the number of date/time fields stored by a `Calendar`.

`protected int fields[]`
The integer array that contains the `Calendar` values.

`protected boolean isSet[]`
The boolean array used to indicate if a time field has been set.

`protected boolean isTimeSet`
A boolean flag field used to tell if the time is set.

`protected long time`
A `long int` field that contains the time set for this `Calendar`.

methods

`public abstract void add(int field, int val)`
Adds or subtracts an amount of days or time from the specified `field`.

`public abstract boolean after(Object arg)`

`public abstract boolean before(Object arg)`
Returns a true value if this `Calendar` date is after or before the date given by arg.

`public final void clear()`

`public final void clear(int field)`
Clears the value from the given time `field`. The `clear` method will clear all of the values from this `Calendar`.

`public Object clone()`
Returns an exact copy of this `Calendar`.

`protected void complete()`
Tries to complete any empty date/time fields by calling the `completeTime()` and `completeFields()` methods of this `Calendar`.

`protected abstract void computeFields()`

`protected abstract void computeTime()`
Computes the values of the time fields based on the currently set time (`computeFields()`) or computes the time based on the currently set time fields (`computeTime()`) for this `Calendar`.

`public abstract boolean equals(Object arg)`
Returns true if this `Calendar` is equal to the value of arg.

```
public final int get(int fld)
```
Returns the value of the given time field.
```
public static synchronized Locale[] getAvailableLocales()
```
Returns the list of locales that are available.
```
public int getFirstDayOfWeek()
```
```
public void setFirstDayOfWeek(int val)
```
Returns or sets the first day of the week to val for this Calendar.
```
public abstract int getGreatestMinimum(int fld)
```
Returns the largest allowable minimum value for the specified field.
```
public static synchronized Calendar getInstance()
```
```
public static synchronized Calendar getInstance(Locale locale)
```
```
public static synchronized Calendar getInstance(TimeZone tz)
```
```
public static synchronized Calendar getInstance(TimeZone tz,
Locale locale)
```
Returns an instance of a Calendar based on the default time zone and locale, or from a given time zone and/or locale.
```
public abstract int getLeastMaximum(int fld)
```
Returns the smallest allowable maximum value for the given field.
```
public abstract int getMaximum(int fld)
```
```
public abstract int getMinimum(int fld)
```
Returns the largest or smallest allowable value for the given field.
```
public int getMinimalDaysInFirstWeek()
```
```
public void setMinimalDaysInFirstWeek(int val)
```
Returns or sets the smallest allowable number of days in the first week of the year, based on the locale.
```
public final Date getTime()
```
```
public final void setTime(Date dt)
```
Returns or sets the time for this Calendar.
```
protected long getTimeInMillis()
```
```
protected void setTimeInMillis(long ms)
```
Returns or sets the time in milliseconds for this Calendar.
```
public TimeZone getTimeZone()
```
```
public void setTimeZone(TimeZone val)
```
Returns or sets the time zone for this Calendar.
```
protected final int internalGet(int fld)
```
An internal method used to obtain field values to be used by subclasses of Calendar.
```
public boolean isLenient()
```
```
public void setLenient(boolean flag)
```
Returns or sets the flag indicating leniency for date/time input.
```
public final boolean isSet(int fld)
```
Returns true if a value is set for the given field.

```
public abstract void roll(int fld, boolean direction)
```
Adds one unit of time to the given date/time field. A true value for direction increases the field's value; false decreases it.

```
public final void set(int fld, int val)
```
Sets a single specified field to a value.

```
public final void set(int year, int month, int date)
```

```
public final void set(int year, int month, int date, int hour,
int min)
```

```
public final void set(int year, int month, int date, int hour,
int min, int sec)
```
Sets the year, month, date, hour, minute, and seconds of the time fields for this Calendar.

Character (java.lang)

This is a public class, derived from Object and implementing Serializable. It contains character constants and methods to convert and identify characters.

variables and constructs

```
public final static byte COMBINING_SPACING_MARK
public final static byte CONNECTOR_PUNCTUATION
public final static byte CONTROL
public final static byte CURRENCY_SYMBOL
public final static byte DASH_PUNCTUATION
public final static byte DECIMAL_DIGIT_NUMBER
public final static byte ENCLOSING_MARK
public final static byte END_PUNCTUATION
public final static byte FORMAT
public final static byte LETTER_NUMBER
public final static byte LINE_SEPARATOR
public final static byte LOWERCASE_LETTER
public final static byte MATH_SYMBOL
public final static byte MODIFIER_LETTER
public final static byte MODIFIER_SYMBOL
public final static byte NON_SPACING_MARK
public final static byte OTHER_LETTER
public final static byte OTHER_NUMBER
public final static byte OTHER_PUNCTUATION
public final static byte OTHER_SYMBOL
public final static byte PARAGRAPH_SEPARATOR
public final static byte PRIVATE_USE
```

```
public final static byte SPACE_SEPARATOR
public final static byte START_PUNCTUATION
public final static byte SURROGATE
public final static byte TITLECASE_LETTER
public final static byte UNASSIGNED
public final static byte UPPERCASE_LETTER
```
Constant values for character symbols and types.

```
public final static int MAX_RADIX
```
A constant value that represents the largest possible value of a radix (base).

```
public final static char MAX_VALUE
```
A constant value that represents the largest possible value of a character in Java = '\uffff'.

```
public final static int MIN_RADIX
```
A constant value that represents that smallest possible value of a radix (base).

```
public final static char MIN_VALUE
```
A constant value that represents the smallest possible value of a character in Java = '\u0000'.

```
public final static Class TYPE
```
The `Character` constant value of the character type class.

constructors

```
public Character(char prim)
```
Creates an instance of the `Character` class from the primitive parameter `prim`.

methods

```
public char charValue()
```
Returns the value of this `Character` as a primitive character.

```
public static int digit(char c, int base)
public static char forDigit(int c, int base)
```
Returns the numeric value or the character depiction of the parameter `c` in radix `base`.

```
public boolean equals(Object arg)
```
Returns a true value if this `Character` is equal to the parameter `arg`.

```
public static int getNumericValue(char c)
```
Returns the Unicode representation of the character parameter (c) as a nonnegative integer. If the character has no numeric representation, a −1 is returned. If the character cannot be represented as a nonnegative number, −2 will be returned.

```
public static int getType(char c)
```
Returns an integer value that represents the type of character the parameter `c` is.

```
public int hashCode()
```
Returns a hash code for this `Character`.

```
public static boolean isDefined(char c)
public static boolean isISOControl(char c)
```
Returns true if the parameter c has a defined meaning in Unicode or is an ISO control character.

```
public static boolean isIdentifierIgnorable(char c)
```
Returns true if the parameter c is a character that can be ignored in a Java identifier (such as control characters).

```
public static boolean isJavaIdentifierPart(char c)
public static boolean isJavaIdentifierStart(char c)
```
Returns true if the parameter c can be used in a valid Java identifier in any but the leading character. `isJavaIdentifierStart` returns true if the parameter c can be used as the leading character in a valid Java identifier.

```
public static boolean isDigit(char c)
public static boolean isLetter(char c)
public static boolean isLetterOrDigit(char c)
public static boolean isLowerCase(char c)
public static boolean isSpaceChar(char c)
public static boolean isTitleCase(char c)
public static boolean isUnicodeIdentifierPart(char c)
public static boolean isWhitespace(char c)
public static boolean isUnicodeIdentifierStart(char c)
public static boolean isUpperCase(char c)
```
Returns a true value if the parameter c is a digit; letter; letter or a digit; lowercase character; space character; titlecase character; can be used in a valid Unicode identifier in any but the leading character; a white space character; can be used as the leading character in a valid Unicode identifier or an uppercase character (respectively).

```
public static char toLowerCase(char c)
public String toString()
public static char toTitleCase(char c)
public static char toUpperCase(char c)
```
Returns a lowercase character, string representation, titlecase, or uppercase character of the parameter c.

Class (java.lang)

This is a public final class, derived from `Object` and implementing `Serializable`. It describes interfaces and classes in the currently running Java program.

methods

`public static Class forName(String class) throws ClassNotFoundException`

Returns a `Class` object that matches the named class. The name of the given class must be a fully qualified class name (such as `java.io.Reader`).

`public Class[] getClasses()`

`public Class[] getDeclaredClasses() throws SecurityException`

Returns an array of `Classes` that contains all of the interfaces and classes that are members of this Class (excluding superclasses). `getClasses` returns only the list of public interfaces and classes.

`public ClassLoader getClassLoader()`

Returns the `ClassLoader` for this Class.

`public Class getComponentType()`

Returns the `Component` type of the array that is represented by this Class.

`public Constructor getConstructor(Class[] types) throws NoSuchMethodException, SecurityException`

`public Constructor[] getConstructors() throws SecurityException`

Returns the `Constructor` object or an array containing the public constructors for this class. The signature of the public constructor that is returned must exactly match the types and sequence of the parameters given by the `types` array.

`public Constructor getDeclaredConstructor(Class[] types) throws NoSuchMethodException, SecurityException`

`public Constructor[] getDeclaredConstructors() throws SecurityException`

Returns the `Constructor` object or an array containing the constructors for this class. The signature of the public constructor that is returned must exactly match the types and sequence of the parameters specified by the `types` array parameter.

`public Field getDeclaredField(String field) throws NoSuchFieldException, SecurityException`

`public Field[] getDeclaredFields() throws SecurityException`

Returns the `Field` object or an array containing all of the fields for the specified matching `field` name for this Class.

`public Method getDeclaredMethod(String method, Class[] types) throws NoSuchMethodException, SecurityException`

`public Method[] getDeclaredMethods() throws SecurityException`

Returns a `Method` object or an array containing all of the methods for the specified `method` of this Class. The requested method's parameter list must match the types and sequence of the elements of the `types` array.

`public Class getDeclaringClass()`

Returns the declaring class of this `Class`, provided that this Class is a member of another class.

`public Field getField(String field) throws NoSuchFieldException, SecurityException` `public Field[] getFields() throws SecurityException`

Returns a `Field` object or an array containing all of the fields of a specified matching `field` name for this Class.

`public Class[] getInterfaces()`

Returns an array containing all of the interfaces of this Class.

`public Method getMethod(String method, Class[] types) throws NoSuchMethodException, SecurityException`

`public Method[] getMethods() throws SecurityException`

Returns a `Method` object or an array containing all of the public methods for the given public `method` of this Class. The method's parameter list must match the types and sequence of the elements of the `types` array.

`public int getModifiers()`

Returns the encoded integer visibility modifiers for this Class. The values can be decoded using the `Modifier` class.

`public String getName()`

Returns the string representation of the type name that this Class represents.

`public URL getResource(String arg)`

Returns a URL for the system resource for the class loader of this Class.

`public InputStream getResourceAsStream(String arg)`

Returns an input stream representing the system resource `arg` from the class loader of this Class.

`public Object[] getSigners()`

Returns an array of `Object`s that contains the signers of this Class.

`public Class getSuperclass()`

Returns the superclass of this Class, or null if this Class is an interface or of type `Object`.

`public boolean isArray()`

Returns true if this Class represents an array type.

`public boolean isAssignableFrom(Class other)`

Returns true if this Class is the same as a superclass or superinterface of the other class.

`public boolean isInstance(Object target)`

Returns true if the `target` object is an instance of this Class.

`public boolean isInterface()`

`public boolean isPrimitive()`

Returns a true value if this Class is an interface class or a primitive type in Java.

`public Object newInstance() throws InstantiationException, IllegalAccessException`

Creates a new instance of this Class.

`public String toString()`

Returns a string representation of this Class in the form of the word *class* or *interface*, followed by the fully qualified name of this Class.

Color (java.awt)

This is a public final class, derived from `Object` and implementing `Serializable`. It is used to represent colors. A color has three components: red, blue, and green. Each has a value from 0 to 255.

variables and constructs

```
public final static Color black
public final static Color blue
public final static Color cyan
public final static Color darkGray
public final static Color gray
public final static Color green
public final static Color lightGray
public final static Color magenta
public final static Color orange
public final static Color pink
public final static Color red
public final static Color white
public final static Color yellow
```
  A constant value that describes the colors `black` (0, 0, 0), `blue` (0, 0, 255), `cyan` (0, 255, 255), `darkGray` (64, 64, 64), `gray` (128, 128, 128), `green` (0, 255, 0), `lightGray` (192, 192, 192), `magenta` (255, 0, 255), `orange` (255, 200, 0), `pink` (255, 175, 175), `red` (255, 0, 0), `white` (255, 255, 255) and `yellow` (255, 255, 0) as a set of RGB values.

constructors

```
public Color(float r, float g, float b)
public Color(int rgb)
public Color(int r, int g, int b)
```
  Creates a new instance of the color described by the RGB value. When passed as a single integer value, the red component is represented in bits 16 to 23, green in 15 to 8, and blue in 0 to 7.

methods

```
public Color brighter()
public Color darker()
```
  Returns a brighter or darker version of this color.
```
public static Color decode(String str) throws
NumberFormatException
```
  Returns the color specified by `str`.

```
public boolean equals(Object arg)
```
Returns a true value if this color is equal to `arg`.

```
public int getBlue()
```
```
public int getGreen()
```
```
public int getRed()
```
Returns the blue, green, or red component value for this color.

```
public static Color getColor(String str)
```
```
public static Color getColor(String str, Color default)
```
```
public static Color getColor(String str, int default)
```
Returns the color represented in the string `str` (where its value is an integer). If the value is not determined, the color `default` is returned.

```
public static Color getHSBColor(float h, float s, float b)
```
Returns a color specified by the Hue-Saturation-Brightness model for colors, where `h` is the hue, `s` is the saturation, and `b` is the brightness of the desired color.

```
public int getRGB()
```
Returns an integer representation of the RGB value for this color.

```
public int hashCode()
```
Returns the hash code for this color.

```
public static int HSBtoRGB(float hue, float saturation, float
brightness)
```
Converts a hue, saturation, and brightness representation of a color to an RGB value.

```
public static float[] RGBtoHSB(int r, int g, int b, float[]
hsbvals)
```
Converts an RGB representation of a color to an HSB value, placing the converted values into the `hsbvals` array. The RGB value is represented via a red (`r`), green (`g`), and blue (`b`) value.

```
public String toString()
```
Returns a string representation of this color.

Date (java.util)

This is a public class, derived from `Object` and implementing `Serializable` and `Cloneable`. It creates and manipulates a moment of time.

constructors

```
public Date()
```
```
public Date(long date)
```
Creates a new instance of `Date` from a specified `date` (time in milliseconds since midnight, January 1, 1970 GMT) or by using the current time.

methods

```
public boolean after(Date arg)
public boolean before(Date arg)
```
   Returns true if this Date is after/before the date specified in arg.

```
public boolean equals(Object arg)
```
   Returns true if Date is equal to arg.

```
public long getTime()
public void setTime(long tm)
```
   Returns or sets the time specified by this Date. The time is represented as a long integer equal to the number of seconds since midnight, January 1, 1970 UTC.

```
public int hashCode()
```
   Returns the hash code for this Date.

```
public String toString()
```
   Returns a string representation of this Date.

DecimalFormat (java.text)

This is a public class, derived from NumberFormat. It is used to format decimal numbers to locale-based strings and vice versa.

constructors

```
public DecimalFormat()
public DecimalFormat(String str)
public DecimalFormat(String str, DecimalFormatSymbols sym)
```
   Creates a new instance of DecimalFormat from the given or default pattern and given or default symbols, and using the default locale.

methods

```
public void applyLocalizedPattern(String str)
public String toLocalizedPattern()
```
   Sets or returns the pattern of DecimalFormat. The specified pattern is in a locale-specific format.

```
public void applyPattern(String str)
public String toPattern()
```
   Sets or returns the pattern of DecimalFormat.

```
public Object clone()
```
   Returns a copy of DecimalFormat.

```
public boolean equals(Object arg)
```
   Returns a true value if DecimalFormat is equal to arg.

```
public StringBuffer format(double num, StringBuffer dest,
FieldPosition pos)
```

```
public StringBuffer format(long num, StringBuffer dest,
FieldPosition pos)
```
Formats the given Java primitive type starting at pos, according to DecimalFormat. Places the resulting string in the destination buffer. This method returns the value of the string buffer.

```
public DecimalFormatSymbols getDecimalFormatSymbols()
```

```
public void setDecimalFormatSymbols(DecimalFormatSymbols
symbols)
```
Returns or sets the decimal number format symbols for DecimalFormat.

```
public int getGroupingSize()
```

```
public void setGroupingSize(int val)
```
Returns or sets the size of groupings for DecimalFormat.

```
public int getMultiplier()
```

```
public void setMultiplier(int val)
```
Returns or sets the value of the multiplier for use in percent calculations.

```
public String getNegativePrefix()
```

```
public void setNegativePrefix(String val)
```
Returns or sets the prefix for negative numbers for DecimalFormat.

```
public String getNegativeSuffix()
```

```
public void setNegativeSuffix(String val)
```
Returns or sets the suffix for negative numbers for DecimalFormat.

```
public String getPositivePrefix()
```

```
public void setPositivePrefix(String val)
```
Returns or sets the prefix for positive numbers for DecimalFormat.

```
public String getPositiveSuffix()
```

```
public void setPositiveSuffix(String val)
```
Returns or sets the suffix for positive numbers for DecimalFormat.

```
public int hashCode()
```
Returns the hash code for DecimalFormat.

```
public boolean isDecimalSeparatorAlwaysShown()
```

```
public void setDecimalSeparatorAlwaysShown(boolean toggle)
```
Returns or sets the state value that allows/prevents the display of the decimal point when formatting integers.

```
public Number parse(String src, ParsePosition pos)
```
Parses the specified string as a long (if possible) or double, starting a position pos, and returns Number.

DecimalFormatSymbols (java.text)

This is a public class, derived from Object and implementing Serializable and Cloneable. It has the functionality for formatting decimals. This class is usually part of a DecimalFormat class (or subclass).

constructors

```
public DecimalFormatSymbols()
public DecimalFormatSymbols(Locale locale)
```
Creates a new instance of `DecimalFormatSymbols` using the given or default locale.

methods

```
public Object clone()
```
Returns a copy of `DecimalFormatSymbols`.

```
public boolean equals(Object arg)
```
Returns true if `DecimalFormatSymbols` is equal to arg.

```
public char getDecimalSeparator()
public void setDecimalSeparator(char separator)
```
Returns or sets the character used to separate decimal numbers.

```
public char getDigit()
public void setDigit(char num)
```
Returns or sets the character used as a digit placeholder.

```
public char getGroupingSeparator()
public void setGroupingSeparator(char separator)
```
Returns or sets the character used to separate groups of thousands.

```
public String getInfinity()
public void setInfinity(String str)
```
Returns or sets the infinity symbol.

```
public char getMinusSign()
public void setMinusSign(char minus)
```
Returns or sets the minus sign.

```
public String getNaN()
public void setNaN(String str)
```
Returns or sets a NaN (not-a-number) value.

```
public char getPatternSeparator()
public void setPatternSeparator(char separator)
```
Returns or sets the character used to separate positive and negative numbers in a pattern.

```
public char getPercent()
public void setPercent(char percent)
```
Returns or sets a percent sign.

```
public char getPerMill()
public void setPerMill(char perMill)
```
Returns or sets a mille percent sign.

```
public char getZeroDigit()
```

```
public void setZeroDigit(char zero)
```
Returns or sets zero.
```
public int hashCode()
```
Returns the hash code.

Double (java.lang)

This is a public final class, derived from `Number`. It contains floating-point math operations, constants, and methods to compute minimum and maximum numbers, and string manipulation routines related to the `double` primitive type.

variables and constructs

```
public final static double MAX_VALUE
```
```
public final static double MIN_VALUE
```
Constant values that contain the maximum (1.79769313486231570e+308d) and minimum (4.94065645841246544e2324d) possible values of an integer in Java.
```
public final static double NaN
```
A constant value that contains the representation of the not-a-number (NaN) double (0.0d).
```
public final static double NEGATIVE_INFINITY
```
```
public final static double POSITIVE_INFINITY
```
Constant values that contain the negative (–1.0d / 0.0d) and positive (1.0d / 0.0d) infinity double.
```
public final static Class TYPE
```
A constant value of the `Double` type class.

constructors

```
public Double(double arg)
```
```
public Double(String arg) throws NumberFormatException
```
Creates an instance of the `Double` class from the parameter `arg`.

methods

```
public byte byteValue()
```
```
public double doubleValue()
```
```
public float floatValue()
```
```
public int intValue()
```
```
public long longValue()
```
```
public short shortValue()
```
Returns the value of the current object as a Java primitive type.

```
public static long doubleToLongBits(double num)
public static double longBitsToDouble(long num)
```
Returns a long bit stream or a double representation of parameter num. Bit 63 of the returned long is the sign bit, bits 52 to 62 are the exponent, and bits 0 to 51 are the mantissa.

```
public boolean equals(Object param)
```
Returns a true value if this Double is equal to the specified parameter (param).

```
public int hashCode()
```
Returns a hash code for this Double.

```
public boolean isInfinite()
public static boolean isInfinite(double num)
```
Returns true if the current object or num is positive or negative infinity, false in all other cases.

```
public boolean isNaN()
public static boolean isNaN(double num)
```
Returns true if the current object or num is not-a-number (NaN), false in all other cases.

```
public static double parseDouble(String str) throws
NumberFormatException
```
Returns the double value represented by str.

```
public String toString()
public static String toString(double num)
```
Returns the string representation of the current object or num in base 10 (decimal).

```
public static Double valueOf(String str) throws
NumberFormatException
```
Returns a Double initialized to the value of str.

Exception (java.lang)

This is a public class, derived from Throwable. It catches conditions that are thrown by methods.

constructors

```
public Exception()
public Exception(String str)
```
Creates a new instance of an exception. A message can be provided via str.

Float (java.lang)

This is a public final class, derived from Number. It contains floating-point math operations, constants, and methods to compute minimum and maximum numbers, and string manipulation routines related to the primitive float type.

variables and constructs

```
public final static float MAX_VALUE
public final static float MIN_VALUE
```
Constant values that contain the maximum possible value (3.40282346638528860e+38f) or the minimum possible value (1.40129846432481707e245f) of a float in Java.

```
public final static float NaN
```
A constant value that contains the representation of the not-a-number (NaN) float (0.0f).

```
public final static float NEGATIVE_INFINITY
public final static float POSITIVE_INFINITY
```
Constant values that contain the representation of the negative (–1.0f / 0.0f) or positive (1.0f / 0.0f) infinity float.

```
public final static Class TYPE
```
The `Float` constant value of the float type class.

constructors

```
public Float(double arg)
public Float(float arg) throws NumberFormatException
public Float(String arg)
```
Creates an instance of the `Float` class from the parameter `arg`.

methods

```
public byte byteValue()
public float floatValue()
public double doubleValue()
public int intValue()
public long longValue()
public short shortValue()
```
Returns the value of the current object as a Java primitive type.

```
public boolean equals(Object arg)
```
Returns the result of an equality comparison against `arg`.

```
public static int floatToIntBits(float num)
public static float intBitsToFloat(int num)
```
Returns the bit stream or float equivalent of the parameter num as an `int`. Bit 31 of the `int` returned value is the sign bit; bits 23 to 30 are the exponent, while bits 0 to 22 are the mantissa.

```
public int hashCode()
```
Returns a hash code for this object.

```
public boolean isInfinite()
public static boolean isInfinite(float num)
```
Returns true if the current object or num is positive or negative infinity, false in all other cases.

```
public boolean isNaN()
```
```
public static boolean isNaN(float num)
```
Returns true if the current object or num is not-a-number (NaN), false in all other cases.

```
public static float parseFloat(String str) throws
NumberFormatException
```
Returns the float value represented by str.

```
public String toString()
```
```
public static String toString(float num)
```
Returns the string representation of the current object or num.

```
public static Float valueOf(String str) throws
NumberFormatException
```
Returns a Float initialized to the value of str.

HashMap (java.util)

This is a public class that provides a hash table implementation of the map interface.

constructors

```
public HashMap()
```
```
public HashMap(int initialCapacity)
```
Constructs a new map with the given initial capacity (16 by default).

```
public HashMap(int initialCapacity, float loadFactor)
```
Constructs an empty HashMap with the given initial capacity and load factor.

```
public HashMap(Map m)
```
Constructs a new HashMap with the same mappings as the specified Map.

methods

```
public void clear()
```
Removes all mappings from this map.

```
public boolean containsKey(Object key)
```
Returns true if this map contains a mapping for the given key.

```
public boolean containsValue(Object value)
```
Returns true if this map maps one or more keys to the given value.

```
public Object get(Object key)
```
Returns the value to which the given key is mapped or null if the map contains no mapping for this key.

```
public boolean isEmpty()
```
Returns true if this map contains no key-value mappings.

```
public Set keySet()
```
Returns a set view of the keys contained in this map.
```
public Object put(Object key, Object value)
```
Associates the given value with the given key in this map.
```
public void putAll(Map t)
```
Copies all of the mappings from the given map to this map. These mappings will replace any mappings that this map had for any of the keys currently in the given map.
```
public Object remove(Object key)
```
Removes the mapping for this key, if present.
```
public int size()
```
Returns the number of key-value mappings in this map.

HashSet (java.util)

This is a public class that implements the Set interface, backed by a hash table. It makes no guarantees as to the iteration order of the set; in particular, it does not guarantee that the order will remain constant over time.

constructors

```
public HashSet()
```
Constructs a new, empty set with an initial capacity of 16.
```
public HashSet(Collection c)
```
Constructs a new set containing the elements in the given collection.
```
public HashSet(int initialCapacity)
```
Constructs a new, empty set with the given initial capacity.

methods

```
public boolean add(Object o)
```
Adds the given element to this set if it is not already present.
```
public void clear()
```
Removes all of the elements from this set.
```
public boolean contains(Object o)
```
Returns true if this set contains the given element.
```
public boolean isEmpty()
```
Returns true if this set contains no elements.
```
public Iterator iterator()
```
Returns an iterator over the elements in this set.
```
public boolean remove(Object o)
```
Removes the given element from this set if it is present.
```
public int size()
```
Returns the number of elements in this set.

InputStream `(java.io)`

This is a public abstract class, derived from `Object`. It is the parent class of any type of input stream that reads bytes. The methods of this abstract class contain little or no functionality (as described below) and should be overridden by any subclass.

constructors

`public InputStream()`

Generally called only by subclasses, this constructor creates a new instance of an `InputStream`.

methods

`public int available() throws IOException`

Returns the number of available bytes that can be read. This method returns a 0 (zero) value and should be overridden by a subclass implementation.

`public void close() throws IOException`

Closes the input stream. This method has no functionality and should be overridden by a subclass implementation.

`public void mark(int size)`

Sets a mark in the input stream, allowing a rereading of the stream data to occur if the `reset` method is invoked. The `size` parameter indicates how many bytes may be read after the mark has been set, before the mark is considered invalid.

`public boolean markSupported()`

Returns true if this `InputStream` object supports the mark and reset methods. This method always returns a false value and should be overridden by a subclass implementation.

`public abstract int read() throws IOException`

Reads the next byte of data from this `InputStream` and returns it as an `int`. This method has no functionality and should be implemented in a subclass. Execution of this method will block until data is available to be read, the end of the input stream occurs, or an exception is thrown.

`public int read(byte[] dest) throws IOException`
`public int read(byte[] dest, int offset, int size) throws IOException`

Reads from this `InputStream` into the array `dest`, and returns the number of bytes read. `size` specifies the maximum number of bytes read from this `InputStream` into the array `dest[]` starting at index `offset`. This method returns the actual number of bytes read or −1, which means that the end of the stream was reached. To read `size` bytes and throw them away, call this method with `dest[]` set to null.

`public synchronized void reset() throws IOException`
   Resets the read point of this `InputStream` to the location of the last mark set.

`public long skip(long offset) throws IOException`
   Skips over `offset` bytes from this `InputStream`. Returns the actual number of bytes skipped, as it is possible to skip over less than `offset` bytes.

InputStreamReader (java.io)

This is a public class, derived from `Reader`. It is an input stream of characters.

constructors

`public InputStreamReader(InputStream input)`

`public InputStreamReader(InputStream input, String encoding)`
`throws UnsupportedEncodingException`
   Creates an instance of `InputStreamReader` from the `InputStream` input with a specified `encoding`.

methods

`public void close() throws IOException`
   Closes this `InputStreamReader`.

`public String getEncoding()`
   Returns the string representation of this `InputStreamReader`'s encoding.

`public int read() throws IOException`
   Reads a single character from this `InputStreamReader`. The character read is returned as an `int`, or a −1, which means that the end of this `InputStreamReader` was reached.

`public int read(char[] dest, int offset, int size) throws IOException`
   Reads no more than `size` bytes from this `InputStreamReader` into the array `dest[]` starting at index `offset`. This method returns the actual number of bytes read or −1, which means that the end of the stream was reached. To read `size` bytes and throw them away, call this method with `dest[]` set to null.

`public boolean ready() throws IOException`
   Returns true if this `InputStreamReader` can be read from. This state can only be true if the buffer is not empty.

Integer (java.lang)

This is a public final class, derived from `Number`. It contains the integer math operations, constants, and methods we need to compute minimum and maximum numbers. It also contains string manipulation routines related to the primitive `int` type.

variables and constructs

```
public final static int MAX_VALUE
public final static int MIN_VALUE
```
The maximum possible value (2147483647) or minimum possible value (–2174783648) of an integer in Java.
```
public final static Class TYPE
```
The `Integer` constant value of the integer type class.

constructors

```
public Integer(int num)
public Integer(String num) throws NumberFormatException
```
Creates an instance of the `Integer` class from the parameter `num`.

methods

```
public byte byteValue()
public double doubleValue()
public float floatValue()
public int intValue()
public long longValue()
public short shortValue()
```
Returns the value of this integer as a Java primitive type.
```
public static Integer decode(String str) throws
NumberFormatException
```
Decodes the given string (`str`) and returns it as an integer. The decode method can handle octal, hexadecimal, and decimal input values.
```
public boolean equals(Object num)
```
Returns the result of an equality comparison against `num`.
```
public static Integer getInteger(String str)
public static Integer getInteger(String str, int num)
public static Integer getInteger(String str, Integer num)
```
Returns an integer representation of the system property named in `str`. If there is no property for `num`, or the format of its value is incorrect, then the default `num` is returned as an `Integer` object.
```
public int hashCode()
```
Returns a hash code for this object.
```
public static int parseInt(String str) throws
NumberFormatException
public static int parseInt(String str, int base) throws
NumberFormatException
```
Evaluates the string `str` and returns the `int` equivalent in radix `base`.
```
public static String toBinaryString(int num)
public static String toHexString(int num)
```

```
public static String toOctalString(int num)
```
Returns the string representation of parameter num in base 2 (binary), 8 (octal), or 16 (hexadecimal).

```
public String toString()
```

```
public static String toString(int num)
```

```
public static String toString(int num, int base)
```
Returns the string representation of this integer or num. The radix of num can be given in base.

```
public static Integer valueOf(String str) throws
NumberFormatException
```

```
public static Integer valueOf(String str, int base) throws
NumberFormatException
```
Returns an Integer initialized to the value of str in radix base.

LinkedList (java.util)

This is a public class from the java.util package that implements the List interface. In addition to implementing the List interface, the LinkedList class provides methods to get, remove, and insert an element at the beginning and end of the list. LinkedList is a part of the Java Collections Framework.

constructors

```
public final static double E
```

```
public LinkedList()
```
Constructs an empty list.

```
public LinkedList(Collection c)
```
Constructs a list containing the elements of the given collection, in the order they are returned by the collection's iterator.

methods

```
public void add(int index, Object element)
```
Inserts the given element at the given position in the list.

```
public boolean add(Object o)
```
Adds the given element to the end of this list.

```
public boolean addAll(Collection c)
```
Adds all of the elements in the given collection to the end of this list, in the order that they are returned by the collection's iterator.

```
public boolean addAll(int index, Collection c)
```
Inserts all of the elements in the given collection into this list, starting at the position shown.

```
public void addLast(Object o)
```
Adds the given element to the end of this list.

```
public void clear()
```
Removes all of the elements from this list.

```
public boolean contains(Object o)
```
Returns true if this list contains the given element.

```
public Object get(int index)
```
Returns the element at the given position in the list.

```
public Object getFirst()
```
Returns the first element in the list.

```
public Object getLast()
```
Returns the last element in the list.

```
public int indexOf(Object o)
```
Returns the index of the first occurrence of the given element, or –1 if the list does not contain the element.

```
public int lastIndexOf(Object o)
```
Returns the index of the last occurrence of the given element, or –1 if the list does not contain the element.

```
public ListIterator listIterator(int index)
```
Returns a list iterator of the elements in this list (in sequence), starting at the given position in the list.

```
public Object remove(int index)
```
Removes the element at the given position in this list.

```
public boolean remove(Object o)
```
Removes the first occurrence of the given element in the list.

```
public Object removeFirst()
```
Removes and returns the first element from the list.

```
public Object removeLast()
```
Removes and returns the last element from the list.

```
public Object set(int index, Object element)
```
Replaces the element at the given position with the object element. Returns the object that had been stored at that index.

```
public int size()
```
Returns the number of elements in the list.

```
public Object[] toArray()
```
Returns an array containing all of the elements in the list, in the correct order.

Math (java.lang)

This is a public final class, derived from Object. It contains integer and floating-point constants. It has methods that do math operations, compute minimum and maximum numbers, and generate random numbers.

variables and constructs

```
public final static double E
```

```
public final static double PI
```
Constant values that contain the natural base of logarithms (2.7182818284590452354) and the ratio of the circumference of a circle to its diameter (3.14159265358979323846).

methods

```
public static double abs(double num)
public static float abs(float num)
public static int abs(int num)
public static long abs(long num)
```
Returns the absolute value of the given parameter.

```
public static double acos(double num)
public static double asin(double num)
public static double atan(double num)
```
Returns the arc cosine, arc sine, or arc tangent of num as a double.

```
public static double atan2(double x, double y)
```
Returns the component e of the polar coordinate {r, e} that matches the cartesian coordinate <x, y>.

```
public static double ceil(double num)
```
Returns the smallest integer value that is not less than num.

```
public static double cos(double angle)
public static double sin(double angle)
public static double tan(double angle)
```
Returns the cosine, sine, or tangent of parameter angle measured in radians.

```
public static double exp(double num)
```
Returns e to the num, where e is the base of natural logarithms.

```
public static double floor(double num)
```
Returns a double that is the largest integer value that is not greater than num.

```
public static double IEEEremainder(double arg1, double arg2)
```
Returns the mathematical remainder between arg1 and arg2, as defined by IEEE 754.

```
public static double log(double num) throws ArithmeticException
```
Returns the natural logarithm of num.

```
public static double max(double num1, double num2)
public static float max(float num1, float num2)
public static int max(int num1, int num2)
public static long max(long num1, long num2)
```
Returns the larger of num1 and num2.

```
public static double min(double num1, double num2)
public static float min(float num1, float num2)
public static int min(int num1, int num2)
public static long min(long num1, long num2)
```
Returns the smallest of parameters num1 and num2.

```
public static double pow(double num1, double num2) throws
ArithmeticException
```
Returns the result of num1 to num2.

```
public static double random()
```
Returns a random number between 0.0 and 1.0.

```
public static double rint(double num)
```
Returns the closest integer to num.

```
public static long round(double num)
```
```
public static int round(float num)
```
Returns the closest long or int to num.

```
public static double sqrt(double num) throws ArithmeticException
```
Returns the square root of num.

Number (java.lang)

This is a public abstract class, derived from Object and implementing Serializable. It is the parent class to the wrapper classes Byte, Double, Integer, Float, Long, and Short.

constructors

```
public Number()
```
Creates a new instance of Number.

methods

```
public byte byteValue()
```
```
public abstract double doubleValue()
```
```
public abstract float floatValue()
```
```
public abstract int intValue()
```
```
public abstract long longValue()
```
```
public short shortValue()
```
Returns the value of this Number as a Java primitive type.

NumberFormat (java.text)

This is a public abstract class, derived from Format and implementing Cloneable. It is used to turn number objects into strings, and vice versa.

variables and constructs

```
public static final int FRACTION_FIELD
```
```
public static final int INTEGER_FIELD
```
Constant values that indicate field locations in a NumberFormat.

constructors

```
public NumberFormat()
```
Creates a new instance of `NumberFormat`.

methods

```
public Object clone()
```
Returns a copy of `NumberFormat`.

```
public boolean equals(Object arg)
```
Returns true if `NumberFormat` is equal to `arg`.

```
public final String format(double num)
```
```
public final String format(long num)
```
Formats the Java primitive type according to `NumberFormat`, returning a string.

```
public abstract StringBuffer format(double num, StringBuffer
dest, FieldPosition pos)
```
```
public abstract StringBuffer format(long num, StringBuffer dest,
FieldPosition pos)
```
```
public final StringBuffer format(Object num, StringBuffer dest,
FieldPosition pos)
```
Formats the Java primitive type (or object) starting at `pos`, according to this `NumberFormat`, placing the resulting string in the destination buffer. This method returns the value of the string buffer.

```
public static Locale[] getAvailableLocales()
```
Returns the available locales.

```
public static final NumberFormat getCurrencyInstance()
```
```
public static NumberFormat getCurrencyInstance(Locale locale)
```
Returns the `NumberFormat` for currency for the default or given locale.

```
public static final NumberFormat getInstance()
```
```
public static NumberFormat getInstance(Locale locale)
```
Returns the default number format for the default or given locale.

```
public int getMaximumFractionDigits()
```
```
public void setMaximumFractionDigits(int val)
```
Returns or sets the greatest number of fractional digits allowed in this `NumberFormat`.

```
public int getMaximumIntegerDigits()
```
```
public void setMaximumIntegerDigits(int val)
```
Returns or sets the greatest number of integer digits allowed in this `NumberFormat`.

```
public int getMinimumFractionDigits()
```
```
public void setMinimumFractionDigits(int val)
```
Returns or sets the smallest number of fractional digits allowed in this `NumberFormat`.

```
public int getMinimumIntegerDigits()
public void setMinimumIntegerDigits(int val)
```
   Returns or sets the smallest number of integer digits allowed in this `NumberFormat`.

```
public static final NumberFormat getNumberInstance()
public static NumberFormat getNumberInstance(Locale locale)
```
   Returns the `NumberFormat` for numbers for the default or given locale.

```
public static final NumberFormat getPercentInstance()
public static NumberFormat getPercentInstance(Locale locale)
```
   Returns the `NumberFormat` for percentages for the default or given locale.

```
public int hashCode()
```
   Returns the hash code for `NumberFormat`.

```
public boolean isGroupingUsed()
public void setGroupingUsed(boolean toggle)
```
   Returns or sets the toggle flag for the grouping indicator.

```
public boolean isParseIntegerOnly()
public void setParseIntegerOnly(boolean toggle)
```
   Returns or sets the toggle flag for parsing numbers as integers only.

```
public Number parse(String str) throws ParseException
```
   Parses the given string as a number.

```
public abstract Number parse(String str, ParsePosition pos)
public final Object parseObject(String str, ParsePosition pos)
```
   Parses the string as a long (if possible) or double, starting at position pos. Returns a number or an object.

Object (java.lang)

This is a public class. It is the root of the hierarchy tree for all classes in Java.

constructors

```
public Object()
```
   Creates a new instance of the object class.

methods

```
protected Object clone() throws OutOfMemoryError,
CloneNotSupportedException
```
   Returns an exact copy of the current object.

```
public boolean equals(Object arg)
```
   Returns true if the current object is equal to `arg`.

```
protected void finalize() throws Throwable
```
   The `finalize` method is called as the object is being destroyed.

```
public final Class getClass()
```
   Returns the class of the current object.

```
public int hashCode()
```
   Returns a hash code for the current object.

```
public final void notify() throws IllegalMonitorStateException
public final void notifyAll() throws
IllegalMonitorStateException
```
   Tells a thread that it may resume execution. `notifyAll` tells all paused threads.

```
public String toString()
```
   Returns a string representation of the current object.

```
public final void wait() throws IllegalMonitorStateException,
InterruptedException
public final void wait(long msec) throws
IllegalMonitorStateException, InterruptedException
public final void wait(long msec, int nsec) throws
IllegalMonitorStateException, InterruptedException,
IllegalArgumentException)
```
   Causes a thread to stop executing for `msec` milliseconds and `nsec` nanoseconds. The `wait()` method (without parameters) makes a thread stop until further notice.

Random (java.util)

This is a public class, derived from `Object` and implementing `Serializable`. It produces pseudo-random numbers.

constructors

```
public Random()
public Random(long rnd)
```
   Creates a new instance of a random class using the value of `rnd` as the random number seed. When the default constructor is used, the current time in milliseconds is the seed.

methods

```
protected int next(int b)
```
   Returns the next random number (from the given number of bits).

```
public void nextBytes(byte[] b)
```
   Creates an array of random bytes as defined by `b[]`.

```
public double nextDouble()
public float nextFloat()
```
   Returns a random number between 0.0 and 1.0 in the given primitive type.

```
public int nextInt()
public long nextLong()
```
Returns a random integer value from all possible `int` or `long` values (positive and negative).

```
public double nextGaussian()
```
Returns a Gaussian double random number with a mean value of 0.0 and a standard deviation of 1.0.

```
public void setSeed(long rnd)
```
Sets the seeds for this random number generator to `rnd`.

Stack (java.util)

This is a public class, derived from `Vector`. It represents a last-in-first-out (LIFO) stack.

constructors

```
public Stack()
```
Creates a new, empty stack.

methods

```
public boolean empty()
```
Returns true if this stack is empty.

```
public Object peek() throws EmptyStackException
```
Returns the item on the top of the stack, but does not remove it.

```
public Object pop() throws EmptyStackException
public Object push(Object obj)
```
Returns and removes the item on the top of the stack (pop) or pushes a new item onto the stack (push).

```
public int search(Object obj)
```
Returns the position of item `obj` from the top of the stack, or –1 if the item is not in the stack.

String (java.lang)

This is a public final class, derived from `Object` and implementing `Serializable`. It contains methods for creating and parsing strings. Because the contents of a string cannot be changed, many of the methods return a new string.

constructors

```
public String()
public String(byte[] arg)
public String(byte[] arg, int index, int count)
```

```
public String(byte[] arg, String code) throws
UnsupportedEncodingException
```

```
public String(byte[] arg, int index, int count, String code)
throws UnsupportedEncodingException
```

Creates a new instance of the `String` class from the array `arg`. The parameter `index` tells us which element of `arg` is the first character of the string. The parameter `count` is the number of characters to add to the new string. The `String()` method creates a new string of no characters. The characters are converted using `code` encoding format.

```
public String(char[] chars)
```

```
public String(char[] chars, int index, int count) throws
StringIndexOutOfBoundsException
```

Creates an instance of the `String` class from the array `chars`. The parameter `index` tells us which element of `chars` is the first character of the string. The parameter `count` is the number of characters to add to the new string.

```
public String(String str)
```

```
public String(StringBuffer str)
```

Creates an instance of the `String` class from the parameter `str`.

methods

```
public char charAt(int idx) throws
StringIndexOutOfBoundsException
```

Returns the character at index `idx` in the current object. The first character of the source string is at index 0.

```
public int compareTo(String str)
```

Compares the current object to `str`. If the strings are equal, returns 0 (zero). If the string is less than the argument, returns an `int` less than zero. If the string is greater than the argument, returns an `int` greater than zero.

```
public String concat(String source)
```

Returns the product of concatenating the argument `source` to the end of the current object.

```
public static String copyValueOf(char[] arg)
```

```
public static String copyValueOf(char[] arg, int index, int
count)
```

Returns a new `String` that contains the characters of `arg`, beginning at `index`, and of length `count`.

```
public boolean endsWith(String suff)
```

Returns true if the object ends with the given suffix.

```
public boolean equals(Object arg)
```

```
public boolean equalsIgnoreCase(String arg)
```

Returns true if the object is equal to `arg`. `arg` must not be null, and must be exactly the same as the current object. `equalsIgnoreCase` ignores whether characters are upper- or lowercase.

```
public byte[] getBytes()
```

```
public byte[] getBytes(String enc) throws
UnsupportedEncodingException
```
　　Returns the contents of the object in an array of bytes decoded with enc. If there is no decoding format, the platform default it used.

```
public void getChars(int start, int end, char[] dest, int
destStart)
```
　　Copies the contents of the object, starting at start and ending at end, into the character array dest, starting at destStart.

```
public int hashCode()
```
　　Returns the hash code of the object.

```
public int indexOf(char c)
public int indexOf(char c, int index)
```
　　Returns the index of the first c in the object not less than index (default of 0). Returns a −1 if there is no c.

```
public int indexOf(String str)
public int indexOf(String str, int index)
```
　　Returns the index of the first str in the object not less than index (default of 0). Returns a −1 if there is no str.

```
public String intern()
```
　　Creates a new canonical string with identical content to this string.

```
public int lastIndexOf(char c)
public int lastIndexOf(char c, int index)
```
　　Returns the index of the last c in the object not less than index (default of 0). Returns a −1 if there is no c.

```
public int lastIndexOf(String str)
public int lastIndexOf(String str, int index)
```
　　Returns the index of the last str in the object not less than index (default of 0). Returns a −1 if there is no str.

```
public int length()
```
　　Returns the integer length of the current object.

```
public boolean regionMatches(boolean case, int cindex, String
str, int strindex, int size)
public boolean regionMatches(int cindex, String str, int
strindex, int size)
```
　　Returns true if the subregion of str, starting at index strindex and having length size, is the same as a substring of the current object, starting at index cindex and having the same length. Whether characters are upper- or lower-case is ignored.

```
public String replace(char oldC, char newC)
```
　　Returns a new string with all occurrences of the oldC replaced with the newC.

```
public boolean startsWith(String str)
public boolean startsWith(String str, int index)
```

Returns true if the current object starts with the string `str` at location `index` (default of 0).

```
public String substring(int startindex) throws
StringIndexOutOfBoundsException
```

```
public String substring(int startindex, int lastindex) throws
StringIndexOutOfBoundsException
```

Returns the substring of the current object, starting with `startindex` and ending with `lastindex-1` (or the last index of the string in the case of the first method).

```
public char[] toCharArray()
```

```
public String toString()
```

Returns the current object as an array of characters or a string. Linked to the automatic use of the `toString` method in output routines.

```
public String toLowerCase()
```

```
public String toLowerCase(Locale loc)
```

Returns the current object with each character in lowercase, taking into account variations of the specified locale (`loc`) (for example, if a specific acronym needs to remain uppercase).

```
public String toUpperCase()
```

```
public String toUpperCase(Locale loc)
```

Returns the current object with each character in uppercase, taking into account variations of the specified locale (`loc`).

```
public String trim()
```

Returns the current object without whitespace.

```
public static String valueOf(boolean arg)
```

```
public static String valueOf(char arg)
```

```
public static String valueOf(char[] arg)
```

```
public static String valueOf(char[] arg, int index, int size)
```

```
public static String valueOf(double arg)
```

```
public static String valueOf(float arg)
```

```
public static String valueOf(int arg)
```

```
public static String valueOf(long arg)
```

```
public static String valueOf(Object arg)
```

Returns a string representation of `arg`, with a starting `index` and specified `size`.

StringBuffer (java.lang)

This is a public class, derived from `Object` and implementing `Serializable`. It contains methods for creating, parsing, and modifying string buffers. Unlike a `String`, the content and length of a `StringBuffer` can be changed dynamically.

constructors

`public StringBuffer()`

`public StringBuffer(int size) throws NegativeArraySizeException`
Creates an instance of the `StringBuffer` class that is empty and that has a capacity of `size` characters (16 by default).

`public StringBuffer(String arg)`
Creates an instance of the `StringBuffer` class from the string `arg`.

methods

`public StringBuffer append(boolean arg)`

`public StringBuffer append(char arg)`

`public StringBuffer append(char[] arg)`

`public StringBuffer append(char[] arg, int index, int size)`

`public StringBuffer append(double arg)`

`public StringBuffer append(float arg)`

`public StringBuffer append(int arg)`

`public StringBuffer append(long arg)`

`public StringBuffer append(Object arg)`

`public StringBuffer append(String arg)`
Returns the current object with the `String` parameter `arg` added to the end. A substring of a character array can be added by naming an index and `size`.

`public int capacity()`
Returns the capacity of this `StringBuffer`.

`public char charAt(int idx) throws StringIndexOutOfBoundsException`
Returns the character at the specified index of this `StringBuffer`.

`public void ensureCapacity(int min)`
Sets the smallest capacity of this `StringBuffer` to be no less than `min`. The new capacity set by this method may actually be greater than `min`.

`public void getChars(int start, int end, char[] dest, int destindex) throws StringIndexOutOfBoundsException`
Copies the characters, `start` to `end`, from this `StringBuffer` to `dest`, starting at index `destindex`.

`public StringBuffer insert(int index, boolean arg) throws StringIndexOutOfBoundsException`

`public StringBuffer insert(int index, char arg) throws StringIndexOutOfBoundsException`

`public StringBuffer insert(int index, char[] arg) throws StringIndexOutOfBoundsException`

`public StringBuffer insert(int index, double arg) throws StringIndexOutOfBoundsException`

`public StringBuffer insert(int index, float arg) throws StringIndexOutOfBoundsException`

```
public StringBuffer insert(int index, int arg) throws
StringIndexOutOfBoundsException
public StringBuffer insert(int index, long arg) throws
StringIndexOutOfBoundsException
public StringBuffer insert(int index, Object arg) throws
StringIndexOutOfBoundsException
public StringBuffer insert(int index, String arg) throws
StringIndexOutOfBoundsException
```
Inserts the string representation of parameter `arg` into this `StringBuffer` at `index`. Characters to the right of the index are shifted to the right.

```
public int length()
```
Returns the length of this `StringBuffer`.

```
public StringBuffer reverse()
```
Returns the value of this `StringBuffer` with the order of the characters reversed.

```
public void setCharAt(int idx, char c)
```
Sets the character at the given index to c.

```
public void setLength(int size) throws
StringIndexOutOfBoundsException
```
Truncates this `StringBuffer`, if needed, to the new length of `size`.

```
public String toString()
```
Returns the `String` representation of this `StringBuffer`.

StringTokenizer (java.util)

This is a public class, derived from `Object` and implementing `Enumeration`. It manipulates string values into tokens separated by delimiter characters.

constructors

```
public StringTokenizer(String arg)
public StringTokenizer(String arg, String delims)
public StringTokenizer(String arg, String delims, boolean
tokens)
```
Creates a new instance of a `StringTokenizer` with the string initialized to `arg`. Uses the given delimiters or the defaults (" \t\n\r": a space, tab, newline, and carriage return). If `tokens` is true, the delimiters are treated as words within the string and can be returned as tokens.

methods

```
public int countTokens()
```
Returns the number of tokens in this string.

```
public boolean hasMoreElements()
```

```
public boolean hasMoreTokens()
```
Returns true if there are more tokens to be returned. hasMoreElements() is the same as hasMoreTokens() and completes the implementation of the Enumerated interface.

```
public Object nextElement() throws NoSuchElementException
```

```
public String nextToken() throws NoSuchElementException
```

```
public String nextToken(String delims) throws
NoSuchElementException
```
Returns the next token in the string. nextElement() is the same as nextToken() and completes the implementation of the Enumerated interface. New delimiters can be named in the last method and can stay in effect until changed.

System (java.lang)

This is a public final class, derived from Object. It contains the standard input, output, and error streams, as well as system-related methods.

variables and constructs

```
public static PrintStream err
```

```
public static InputStream in
```

```
public static PrintStream out
```
These are constant values: the standard error output stream (stderr), standard input stream (stdin), and the standard output stream (stdout).

methods

```
public static void arraycopy(Object source, int srcindex, Object
dest, int destindex, int size) throws
ArrayIndexOutOfBoundsException, ArrayStoreException
```
Copies a subarray of size objects from source, starting at srcindex, to dest starting at destindex.

```
public static long currentTimeMillis()
```
Returns the current system in milliseconds from midnight, January 1st, 1970 UTC.

```
public static void exit(int num) throws SecurityException
```
Exits the program with the status code of num.

```
public static void gc()
```
Executes the gc method of the Runtime class, which tries to garbage collect any unused objects, freeing system memory.

```
public static Properties getProperties() throws
SecurityException
```

```
public static void setProperties(Properties newprops) throws
```

```
SecurityException
```
Returns or sets the current system properties.
```
public static String getProperty(String name) throws
SecurityException
public static String getProperty(String name, String default)
throws SecurityException
```
Returns the system property for name, or returns the value default as a default result if no such name exists.
```
public static SecurityManager getSecurityManager()
public static void setSecurityManager(SecurityManager mgr)
throws SecurityException
```
Returns or sets the security manager for the current application. If no security manager has been initialized, the get method returns a null value.
```
public static int identityHashCode(Object arg)
```
Returns the hash code for the object. This will return the default hash code if the object's hashCode method has been overridden.
```
public static void load(String name) throws
UnsatisfiedLinkError, SecurityException
```
Loads name as a dynamic library.
```
public static void loadLibrary(String name) throws
UnsatisfiedLinkError, SecurityException
```
Loads name as a system library.
```
public static void runFinalization()
```
Asks the Java Virtual Machine to execute the finalize method on any outstanding objects.
```
public static void runFinalizersOnExit(boolean toggle)
```
Allows the execution of the finalizer methods for all objects, when toggle is true.
```
public static void setErr(PrintStream strm)
public static void setIn(InputStream strm)
public static void setOut(PrintStream strm)
```
Reassigns the error stream, input stream, or output stream to strm.

Throwable (java.lang)

This is a public class, derived from Object and implementing Serializable. It is the superclass of all of the errors and exceptions thrown.

constructors

```
public Throwable()
public Throwable(String str)
```
Creates a new instance of a throwable object with the given message (str) or none present.

methods

```
public Throwable fillInStackTrace()
```
Fills in the executable stack trace for this throwable object.

```
public String getLocalizedMessage()
```
Returns the locale of this object. Locale-specific messages should override this method; otherwise, the same message that the getMessage method produces will be returned.

```
public String getMessage()
```
Returns the detail message for this throwable.

```
public void printStackTrace()
public void printStackTrace(PrintStream stream)
public void printStackTrace(PrintWriter stream)
```
Prints the stack trace to the standard error stream or to the given stream.

```
public String toString()
```
Returns a string representation of this throwable object.

TreeMap (java.util)

This is a tree-based implementation of the Map interface. This class guarantees that the map will be in ascending key order, sorted according to the natural order for the key's class or by the comparator provided at creation time, depending on what constructor is used.

constructors

```
TreeMap()
```
Constructs a new, empty map, sorted according to the natural order of the keys.

```
TreeMap(Comaparator c)
```
Constructs a new, empty map, sorted according to the given comparator.

```
TreeMap(Map m)
```
Constructs a new map containing the same mappings as the given map, sorted according to the natural order of the keys.

methods

```
public void clear()
```
Removes all mappings from TreeMap.

```
public Comparator comparator()
```
Returns the comparator used to order this map, or null if this map uses the natural order of keys.

```
public boolean containsKey(Object key)
```
Returns true if this map contains a mapping for the given key.

```
public boolean containsValue(Object value)
```
Returns true if this map maps one or more keys to the specified value.

```
public Set entrySet()
```
Returns a set of the mappings contained in this map.

```
public Object firstKey()
```
Returns the first (lowest) key in this sorted map.

```
public Object get(Object key)
```
Returns the value to which this map maps the given key.

```
public Set keySet()
```
Returns a Set view of the keys contained in this map.

```
public Object lastKey()
```
Returns the last (highest) key stored in this sorted map.

```
public Object put(Object key, Object value)
```
Associates the value with the key. If there is already a value associated with that key, the old value is returned.

```
public Object remove(Object key)
```
Removes the mapping for this key from this TreeMap (if present) and returns the value previously associated with that key.

```
public int size()
```
Returns the number of key value mappings in this map.

TreeSet (java.util)

This class implements the set interface backed by a Tree instance. This class guarantees that the sorted set will be in ascending element order, sorted by the natural order of the elements, or by the comparator provided at set creation, depending on which constructor is used.

constructors

```
TreeSet()
```
Constructs a new, empty set, sorted by the elements' natural order.

```
TreeSet(Collection c)
```
Constructs a new set containing the elements in the given collection, sorted by the elements' natural order.

```
TreeSet(Comparator c)
```
Constructs a new, empty set, sorted by the given comparator.

methods

```
public boolean add(Object o)
```
Adds the given element to this set if it is not already there.

```
public boolean addAll(Collection c)
```
Adds all of the elements in the given collection to this set.

```
public void clear()
```
Removes all of the elements from this set.

```
public Comparator comparator()
```
Returns the comparator used to order this sorted set, or returns null if this set uses natural ordering.

```
public boolean contains(Object o)
```
Returns true if this set contains the given element.

```
public boolean isEmpty()
```
Returns true if this set contains no elements.

```
public Iterator iterator()
```
Returns an iterator over the elements in this set.

```
public boolean remove(Object o)
```
Removes the given element from this set, if it is there.

```
public int size()
```
Returns the number of elements in this set.

Index